Survey of the Bible

Survey of the Bible

A Treasury of Bible Information

Fourth Revised Edition

William Hendriksen

A Division of Baker Book House Co
Grand Rapids, Michigan 49516

North American Edition

Published by Baker Books
a division of Baker Publishing Group
P. O. Box 6287, Grand Rapids, MI 49516-6287
United States of America
www.bakerbooks.com

First paperback edition 1995

ISBN 978-0-8010-5415-0

United Kingdom Edition

Published by Evangelical Press
12 Wooler Street, Darlington, Co. Durham, DL1 1RQ
England

Third paperbound edition 1995

Reprinted 2001

ISBN: 0 85234 174 1

Printed in the United States of America

Contents

Contents of Part Three Arranged According to the Order of the English Bible

Old Testament

New Testament

PART FOUR
Bible Chapters and Passages

Photographs

Lists, Charts, Diagrams, and Maps

Preface

The aim of this book is to reach all classes of people who are interested in the Word of God. There are those whose knowledge of Scripture is exceedingly meager. There are others who have a rather detailed knowledge of this or that story, book, or chapter of the Bible. Yet, they do not know the Bible as a whole: they have never made a systematic study of the Holy Book. A study of this nature is very necessary if one is to be able to interpret the Word in the proper manner, for, if it be true that the Bible is its own best interpreter, then surely it must be known in its organic unity first of all.

It is our firm conviction, moreover, that before one is able to give a satisfying interpretation of a difficult Scripture passage, he must first have acquired a more or less comprehensive grasp of the contents of the entire Bible, both Old and New Testaments. One can never interpret the Old Testament without a knowledge of the New, nor the New apart from the Old; for, "the Old is by the New explained: the New is in the Old contained." Or, if you prefer: "The New is in the Old concealed: the Old is by the New revealed." Students of the Bible have always known this. Nevertheless, in recent years the study of the influence of the Aramaic upon the style and grammar characteristics of the Greek New Testament has given additional emphasis to this fact.

We regard it as being a very grave error to study ever so many critical problems touching date, authorship, or composition of a Bible book, and at the same time to neglect the study of the actual contents of that book. One should listen to the voice of God speaking in his Word, rather than to the voice of the radical theologian speaking in some work written with the express purpose of undermining the influence of the sacred writings. We fear that in the past much valuable time may have been wasted in presenting all kinds of counter-arguments to the arguments of the critics. Even if all these counter-arguments should have been valid, they did not as such furnish us with a comprehensive grasp of the contents of Scripture. Why should we permit the critics to determine our method of studying the Bible? Should we not be distinctive even in the choice of a method? Let us listen once more to the voice of God Almighty speaking in His own Word. And let all the earth be silent before him!

As the reader must have realized, the approach and spirit of this *Survey of the Bible* is that of the conservative theologian. This does not mean that it is merely a restatement of all the traditional views. It is nothing of the kind! During recent decades new light has been shed on old problems. The writings of brilliant but thoroughly conservative Old Testament scholars bear testimony to the fact that some of the old ideas as to date, authorship, etc., of certain Bible books are in need of reexamination. Similarly, with respect to the New Testament, not everything that has been maintained in the past by conservative scholarship with respect to the synoptic problem, the language problem, and others, can be repeated in unaltered form. Some revision has become necessary. However, such a revision need never and should never depart by even a hairbreadth from the position of absolute fidelity to Scripture as God's infallible Word, inspired from beginning to end by his Spirit.

It is hardly necessary to state that no attempt whatever has been made to offer a work which can be regarded as being in any sense *complete*. That is the one thing which this work does not desire to be. It is not to be regarded as a work on Bible interpretation or hermeneutics; nor as a Bible history, either Old Testament or New Testament; nor yet as an introduction to the Old Testament or New Testament. It merely endeavors to lay the foundation for these and related Biblical studies. It strives to create an interest. It is what its name implies: a *Survey of the Bible*.

We have left no stone unturned in our attempt to present our material in a manner which, we hope, will be found to be both in harmony with the facts and also easy to digest and to retain in the memory. May this work, on which we have spent many joyful hours and much labor, receive the same kind reception accorded both at home and abroad to *More Than Conquerors*, a commentary on the Book of Revelation. We also use this opportunity to express deep gratitude for the cordial manner in which that work and also the New Testament Commentary are being received. May God be glorified by means of the prayerful study of his wonderful special revelation!

May, 1976 W. Hendriksen

Part One

The Bible

A section of the Isaiah scroll
(Hebrew text) from Cave 1 at Qumran.
Israel Information Office

1 Facts About the Bible

Never have Bible societies been as busy as they are today. Already the Good Book has been translated, in entirety or in part, into about fourteen hundred languages or dialects, and the work is being pushed as never before. Bible study groups and Bible conferences, too, are flourishing everywhere. Men and women, old and young, are taking an active interest in them.

Moreover, questions, are being asked. Questions not only about various incidents or teachings recorded in Scripture and their practical value for our day, but also about the Bible as a whole. We shall try to answer some of these questions in this book. Our answers will never be complete. It is our purpose to touch upon the essentials only. This book is, let it be constantly remembered, a *Bible Survey.* It is not intended to be more than that. Accordingly, in Part I we shall endeavor to answer *very briefly* the following questions which are being asked again and again:

1. What is the real difference between the conservative and the liberal view of the Bible?
2. In what sense is it true that the Bible is inspired?
3. How did the sacred writings look originally, and how did they grow into a Bible?
4. Why do we not include the Apocryphal books in our Bible?
5. Is it true that because long ago the church officially declared these sixty-six books to be the authoritative Word of God we now believe them to be such?
6. When were the Bible books written, and how have they been arranged?
7. How did we get our translated Bible?

8. How should the Bible be studied?
9. How should it be interpreted?

Questions 1-5 will be answered in the present chapter; questions 6 and 7, in chapter 2; question 8 in chapter 3; and question 9 in chapter 4.

What is the real difference between the conservative and liberal views of Scripture?

The conservative takes the position that whenever Scripture gives an answer to any question, that answer is the ultimate touchstone of the truth, the final court of appeal for the reason. This is true whether the teaching of Scripture pertains to the sphere of history or of hamartiology (the doctrine of sin), of science or of soteriology (the doctrine of salvation). The Sermon on the Mount, to be sure, is inspired; but so is the Creation Account. The *entire* Bible is God-breathed. "No prophecy ever came by the will of man: but men spake from God, being moved by the Holy Spirit" (II Peter 1:21). Again, "All scripture is given by inspiration of God, and is profitable for doctrine, for reproof, for correction, for instruction in righteousness" (II Tim. 3:16, King James or Authorized Version, to which we give the preference for this passage). See also: Exod. 20:1; II Sam. 23:2; Isa. 8:20; Mal. 4:4; Matt. 1:22; Luke 24:44; John 1:23; 5:39; 10:34, 35; 14:26; 16:13; 19:36, 37; 20:9; Acts 1:16; 7:38; 13:34; Rom. 1:2; 3:2; 4:23; 9:17; 15:4; I Cor. 2:4-10; 6:16; 9:10; 14:37; Gal. 1:11, 12; 3:8, 16, 22; 4:30; I Thess. 1:5; 2:13; Heb. 1:1, 2; 3:7; 9:8; 10:15; II Peter 3:16; I John 4:6; and Rev. 22:19.

The real issue between faith and unbelief is this: Are these Scriptures the *living oracles* of God or are they not? Is it true or is it not true that men spake from God being moved by the Holy Spirit? Is it correct or is it incorrect to say that *the entire Bible, as originally written,* is the Word of God, and that *all* of its teaching is trustworthy? Faith answers these questions in the affirmative, aiming to impart to us the saving knowledge of God's will; unbelief, in the negative.

Today an attempt is being made to confuse the issue in order to make the position of faith look ridiculous. The question is asked again and again: "Is it not true that in the process of copying Bible manuscripts, translating them, and printing the translations errors have been committed?" But who denies this plain fact? The edition of the King James Bible which was published in 1702 contained a very amusing error. In Psalm 119:161 the psalmist was made to complain: "*Printers* [instead of *Princes*] have persecuted me without a cause." But does anyone seriously maintain that the Word of God has lost its infallible and normative character because a certain copyist, printer, proofreader, or translator erred? Does not everyone immediately realize that when we expose error of this character we are criticizing *the work of men,* not *the Word of God?* Let us not confuse the issue!

In what sense is it true that the Bible is inspired?

The Bible is God-breathed. Its human authors were powerfully guided and directed by the Holy Spirit. As a result what they wrote is not only without error but also of supreme value for man. It is all that God wanted it to be. It constitutes the infallible rule of faith and practice for mankind.

The Spirit, however, did not suppress the personality of the writer but raised it to a higher level of activity (John 14:26). And because the individuality of the human author was not destroyed, we find in Scripture a wide variety of style and language. There is a vast difference between the deeply emotional tenor of Hosea and the vividly descriptive manner of expression which characterizes Nahum; between the exhortations of Haggai and Hebrews, and the argumentations of Malachi and Galatians. Nevertheless, all are equally the Word of God. Inspiration, moreover, should never be considered in separation from those many activities which served to bring the human author upon the scene of history. By causing him to be born at a certain time and place, bestowing upon him specific endowments, equipping him with a definite kind of education, causing him to undergo predetermined experiences, and bringing back to his mind certain facts and their implications, the Spirit prepared his human consciousness. Next, that same Spirit moved him to write. Finally, during the process of writing, that same Primary Author, in a thoroughly organic connection with all his preceding activity, suggested to the mind of the human author that language (the very words!) and that style, which would be the most appropriate vehicle for the interpretation of the divine ideas for people of every rank and position, age and race.[1] Hence, though every word is truly the word of the human author, it is even more truly the Word of God.

How did the Sacred Writings look originally and how did they develop into our Bible?

The original manuscripts (MSS.) of the Bible, the autographs, have all perished. Although this fact can easily be explained, we do well, nevertheless, to see in this an evidence of God's special care or providence. If we, today, were in possession of these original documents, we would almost certainly consider them objects of veneration and worship, just as in the days of Hezekiah the Israelites burned incense to the brazen serpent (II Kings 18:4).

How did a Bible book look as it came forth from the "pen" (i.e., pointed reed, Jer. 8:8) of the author? The laws, prophecies, etc., of the Old Testament were written in ink (Jer. 36:18), on skins prepared for writing and rolled up into a scroll (Ps. 40:7; Jer. 36:14ff.; Ezek. 2:9; Zech. 5:1). They were written in the Hebrew language (Phoenician script which was later changed to Aramaic script), with the exception of Ezra 4:8–6:18; 7:12-26; Jer. 10:11; and Dan. 2:4–7:28, which are in the Aramaic tongue. Only consonants were used. Not until a much later time—probably about seven centuries *after* the birth of Christ—were the vowels written into the text. This was done by the Masorites, Jewish scholars to whom we shall refer again.

The New Testament scriptures were probably written on papyrus rolls, varying in size with the length of the written composition. The papyrus is a tall sedge which grows near the Sea of Galilee and Lake Merom. Formerly it flourished near the Nile. The Egyptians used it in the manufacture of shoes, boats, baskets, etc. It is found in many of our American museums. The pith of the papyrus was cut into thin, flat strips, six or seven inches in length. These would be laid at right angles to the side of a table until there were as many as needed. Then a thick paste or glue would be applied, and other strips would be laid crosswise and pressed. Thus the papyrus sheet was produced. Several sheets attached to one another would form a roll. We owe the preservation of many papyri to the dry climate of Egypt. A papyrus

1. H. Bavinck, *Gereformeerde Dogmatiek*, Kampen, 1918, third ed., vol. I, p. 464. Cf. also J. Orr, *Revelation and Inspiration*, London, 1910, esp. ch. 8.

scrap (7Q) of Mark 6:52, 53 has been assigned a date of approximately A.D. 50 (see pp. 30 and 373.) Another papyrus containing verses from the eighteenth chapter of John probably dates from the first part of the second century A.D..

The autographs did not last forever. Copies had to made, both of the Old Testament and the New Testament writings. And all this work had to be done by hand, for the art of printing had not yet been invented. Moreover, in the course of time, the sacred writings (the originals) began to multiply. Hence, they were collected and arranged in a certain order. This, too, was not done in a day. The various laws of Moses were assembled into "the book of the law" (Josh. 1:7, 8; 23:6; I Kings 2:3; II Kings 14:6; II Chron. 25:4; 34:30, 31; Ezra 7:6; Neh. 8:2, 15; 13:1 ff.). The prophecies, too, were collected (Isa. 34:16; Dan. 9:2). And so were the Psalms; there were collections of the Psalms of David, Psalms of Asaph, Psalms of Korah, etc. In II Maccabees 2:13, 14, we read:

> *Nehemiah . . . founding a library, gathered together the books about the kings and prophets, and the books of David, and letters of kings about sacred gifts [such as Ezra 6:6-12?]. And in like manner Judas also gathered together for us all those writings that had been scattered by reason of the war that befell, and they are with us.*

In the new dispensation the Old Testament scrolls were viewed as a unity. Thus, in II Corinthians 3:14 (KJV) mention is made of "the reading of the Old Testament." Similarly, about A.D. 100 the four Gospels were viewed as a unity; and so were the epistles of Paul. About the middle of the second century it had become clear to the church that these two (Gospels and "Paul") belonged together. About the year 200 the unity of the entire New Testament—in fact, of the entire Bible—was beginning to become apparent. Moreover, when sometime during the second or third century, the *book* began to replace the *scroll,* and what was formerly written on *many* separate scrolls could now be written in *one* far more practicable book, visible expression was given to the unity of Old and New Testament. A few of these very ancient Bibles have been discovered. None of them is in perfect condition: leaves are missing from all of them. Their Old Testament is some form of the Old *Greek* or Septuagint (LXX) translation; see p. 36. Their New Testament is, of course, also in Greek. Codex D, however, contains, in addition, a

Latin translation. These ancient capital-letter MSS. are called *uncials.* In the oldest uncials the words are not separated. As to chapter divisions, in 1228 Stephen Langton divided the Bible into chapters. The division of the New Testament into verses was accomplished by Robert Stephens in 1551. The Masorites had previously divided the Old Testament into verses. While this division has its advantages, it also has its disadvantages. Today the tendency is to give more prominence to paragraph division than to verse division. An excellent example of this new tendency is to be found in The New Testament, Revised Standard Version. The following five uncials are among the most famous:

1. **B**—the Vatican MS., dating from the fourth century A.D.

2. **Aleph** (the first letter of the Hebrew alphabet)—the Sinaitic MS., discovered by C. Tischendorf in the convent of St. Catherine, Mt. Sinai. This uncial also dates from the fourth century.

3. **A**—the Alexandrian MS., fifth century.

4. **C**—the Ephraem MS., fifth century. Ephraem the Syrian, living in the seventh century A.D., covered up the sacred text with his own sermon or treatise. Someone has remarked that this was not the only time when a sermon served the purpose of blotting out the text! Most of the original has, however, been recovered.

5. **D**—the MS. of Beza, fifth or sixth century.

About the ninth century the cursives—MSS. in small, running hand, and with division of words—began to replace the uncials. For a while uncials and cursives existed side by side. Finally, the uncials disappeared.

The Masorites, those Jewish scholars who flourished between the destruction of Jerusalem and the tenth century, but whose activity, in its most comprehensive sense, antedates the period of the Maccabees and extends to the year 1425, exercised great care in copying. They counted the very letters of their copy, comparing everything with the text before them. The detection of a single mistake was often held to be a significant reason for destroying an entire copy and making a new beginning. Scholars, however, in trying to determine the original reading of the Old Testament do not depend solely upon the Masoritic text and notes, but also make use of the following: the Samaritan Pentateuch, the Targums (Aramaic), the Septuagint or old Greek version, the later Greek versions (by Aquila, Theodotion, Symmachus), the Latin Vulgate, and the Syriac Peshitta.

The Old Testament which we read today was the one recognized by our Lord; i.e., it contained the same books. The arrangement of the books was different. See also p. 33. In all probability, for Jesus Chronicles was the last Old Testament "book." It is in this book (II Chron. 24:21), that the murder of Zechariah is mentioned. Now, in Matthew 23:35 Jesus is quoted as saying: ". . . that upon you may come all the righteous blood shed on the earth, from the blood of Abel, the righteous, unto the blood of Zechariah, whom ye slew between the sanctuary and the altar." Notice: "from Abel . . . to Zechariah, son of Barachiah." Why does Jesus phrase it thus? That he does not have in mind a purely chronological order is apparent from the fact that the murder of Uriah, son of Shemaiah, was later than that of Zechariah. See Jeremiah 26:23. The only reasonable explanation is that the Lord was referring to all the righteous blood shed on earth from the murder mentioned in the very first book (Genesis) to the one recorded in the very last book (Chronicles). It is true that in Christ's day the Old Testament was written not in one book but on several scrolls. This, however, does not cancel the fact that the scrolls were so arranged that Genesis was viewed as being first, and Chronicles last.

While we have a uniform Old Testament text, so that, as was noted above, the work of Old Testament textual criticism consists in the comparison of this uniform text with various translations, the case is entirely different with the text of the New Testament. The Greek text of the New Testament is not the same in the many MSS. which have come down to us. We are even able to distinguish manuscript families. Nevertheless, only about a thousandth part of the New Testament presents "substantial variation," i.e., variation which really alters the sense of the passage. It is on this thousandth part that the labors of New Testament textual criticism has been largely expended, with excellent results.[2] God, in his kind providence, has guarded his Word in such a manner that we can say, without fear of successful contradiction, that today we have an Old as well as a New Testament which is *substantially* as it was when it came forth from the pen of the inspired writers. The way of salvation is clearly revealed in every Bible, whether written in Hebrew, Aramaic, and Greek, or in English. On the Old Testament text see also p. 28.

---

2. A. T. Robertson, *Introduction to the Textual Criticism of the New Testament,* New York, 1925, p. 22. More recent is B. M. Metzger, *The Text of the New Testament, Its Transmission, Corruption, and Restoration,* Oxford, 1964.

We have now told you the main points in the story of the manner in which the original sacred writings grew into a Bible. The word *Bible* is derived from the Greek *Biblia,* which means books. But the many "books" have become one book, the best book of all.

Why do we not include the Apocryphal books in our Bible?

The Apocryphal–i.e., hidden; also: of unknown origin, spurious, uncanonical–books consist of the surplus of the Septuagint over the Hebrew Old Testament. The Roman Catholic Church, through the Council of Trent, in the year 1546, declared the following apocryphal books to be canonical: Tobit, Judith, The Wisdom of Solomon, Ecclesiasticus (i.e., The Wisdom of Jesus, the Son of Sirach), Baruch, and I and II Maccabees. The same Council also added The Rest of Esther to the canonical Esther, and incorporated the History of Susanna, The Song of the Three Holy Children, and Bel and The Dragon, with Daniel. We maintain, however, that these books are not to be regarded as inspired Scripture. Observe the following:

1. **They are not found in the original, i.e., Hebrew, Old Testament.** Here, moreover, are the words of Flavius Josephus, the famous Jewish historian, who was a contemporary of the apostle Paul:

> *For it is not the case with us to have vast numbers of books disagreeing and conflicting with one another. We have but* twenty-two, *containing the history of all time, books that are justly believed in. And of these,* five *are the books of Moses, which comprise the laws and the earliest traditions from the creation of mankind down to the time of his (Moses') death. . . . From the death of Moses to the reign of Artaxerxes, king of Persia, the successor of Xerxes, the prophets who succeeded Moses wrote the history of the events that occurred in their own time; in* thirteen *books. The remaining* four *documents comprise hymns to God and practical precepts to men. From the days of Artaxerxes to our own time every event had indeed been recorded. But these recent records have not been deemed worthy of equal credit with those which preceded them, because the exact succession of the prophets ceased. But what faith we have placed in our own writings is evident by our conduct; for*

> *though so great an interval of time (i.e., since they were written) has now passed, not a soul has ventured either to add, or to remove, or to alter a syllable. But it is instinctive in all Jews at once from their very birth to regard them as commands of God and to abide by them, and, if need be, willingly to die for them.*[3]

The twenty-two books which Josephus has in mind are the following:

a. Five of Moses: Genesis, Exodus, Leviticus, Numbers, Deuteronomy.

b. Thirteen Prophets: Joshua, Judges and Ruth (taken as one), Samuel, Kings, Isaiah, Jeremiah and Lamentations (as one), Ezekiel, the twelve Minor Prophets (as one), Daniel, Job, Esther, Ezra and Nehemiah (as one), and Chronicles.

c. Four Hymns to God and practical precepts: Psalms, Proverbs, Song of Solomon, and Ecclesiastes. Josephus clearly did not recognize any Apocryphal book as being on a par with the twenty-two.

2. **They are never quoted by our Lord**; in fact, it is almost certain that they are never quoted in the entire New Testament.

3. **Some of the authors of these Apocryphal books disclaim inspiration.** See the Prologue to The Wisdom of Jesus, the Son of Sirach; also II Macabees 2:23; 15:38.

4. **The fact that the Apocryphal books were read in the churches must be interpreted in the light of the statement of Jerome:**

> *As therefore the Church reads the books of Judith, Tobit, and Maccabees but does not receive them among the canonical Scriptures, so it also reads these two volumes (Wisdom of Solomon, and Wisdom of Jesus, the Son of Sirach) for the edification of the people, but not for authority to prove the doctrines of religion.*[4]

5. **The quality of the material contained in these writings, though varying greatly in worth, ranks far below that of the canonical books.**

---

3. Josephus, *Against Apion*, I, 37-43, pp. 177-181 in the *Loeb Classical Library, Josephus I.*
4. Cf. also art. "Apocrypha," in *Westminster Dictionary of The Bible*, Philadelphia, 1944, p. 33.

Tobit and Judith are full of gross anachronisms. The Wisdom of Solomon contains philosophical vagaries that are worthless.[5]

Accordingly, on this point Protestants are in agreement with the earliest (i.e., Hebrew) view of the Old Testament Canon and with the Belgic Confession, 1561, art. VI, which reads:

> *We distinguish those sacred books from the apocryphal . . . which the Church may read and take instruction from, so far as they agree with the canonical books; but they are far from having such power and efficacy that we may from their testimony confirm any point of faith or of the Christian religion; much less may they be used to detract from the authority of the other, that is, the sacred books.*

Similarly, the Westminster Confession of 1647, article III, declares:

> *The books commonly called Apocrypha, not being of divine inspiration, are no part of the Canon of the Scripture; and therefore are of no authority in the Church of God, nor to be any otherwise approved, or made use of, than other human writings.*

Is it true that we believe these sixty-six books to be the authoritative Word of God, because long ago the church officially declared them to be such?

From the Prologue of The Wisdom of Jesus, the Son of Sirach (also called Ecclesiasticus), which, like I Maccabees, is one of the best of the Apocryphal writings, there are those who conclude that already in the year 290 B.C. the Canon of the Old Testament had become fixed. This was not long after 336 B.C., the approximate date when the last book of the Old Testament had been completed.

As to the books of the *New* Testament, in the year 367 Athanasius prepared a list of twenty-seven books, the identical twenty-seven which constitute our New Testament. The Council of Hippo, 393, and of Carthage, 397, confessed the canonical character of these

5. Worthy of careful study is B. M. Metzger, *An Introduction to the Apocrypha, New York,* 1957.

same twenty-seven books. We have already seen that the Protestant Reformation, on very solid grounds, rejected the Roman Catholic Old Testament list which included the Apocryphal writings, and returned to the original Hebrew Canon. Accordingly, the Belgic Confession, in article IV lists sixty-six books as being canonical. In reality only sixty-five are mentioned, but Lamentations was simply subsumed under Jeremiah. The Westminster Confession, article II, mentions all sixty-six.

This, however, does not mean that the church or some ecclesiastical assembly "decided" or "made" the Canon. What the church actually did was to confess before the world that which had long been the conviction of believers.

It is not because the church upon a certain date, long ago, made an official decision, that these sixty-six books constitute the inspired Bible. On the contrary, it is because God's people had long since accepted these books as being the very Word of God that the church finally made this official declaration before the world. The sixty-six books, by their very contents, immediately attest themselves to the hearts of God's children as being the *living oracles* of God. Hence, believers are filled with deep reverence when they listen to the very words of God contained in these books. Instructive in this connection is II Kings 22 and 23:

> *And Hilkiah the high priest said unto Shaphan the scribe, I have found the book of the law in the house of Jehovah . . . . And Shaphan read it before the king. And it came to pass, when the king had heard the words of the book of the law, that he rent his clothes. And the king commanded Hilkiah the priest . . . saying: Go ye, inquire of Jehovah for me, and for the people, and for all Judah, concerning the words of this book that is found; for great is the wrath of Jehovah that is kindled against us, because our fathers have not hearkened unto the words of this book, to do according to all that which is written concerning us . . . And the king sent, and they gathered unto him all the elders of Judah and of Jerusalem. And the king went up to the house of Jehovah and all the men of Judah, and all the inhabitants of Jerusalem with him, and the priests, and the prophets, and all the people, both small and great: and he read in their ears all the words of the book of the covenant which was found in the house of Jehovah. And the king stood by the pillar, and made*

> *a covenant with Jehovah, to walk after Jehovah, and to keep his commandments, and his testimonies, and his statutes, with all his heart, and all his soul, to confirm the words of this convenant that were written in this book: and all the people stood to the covenant.'*"[6]

The Holy Spirit, who has taken up his abode in the church and imparts to that church faith in the Word, recognizes his own voice speaking in the Word. The official declaration is necessary to guard against all heresy and misunderstanding, and to make a public confession before the world. There have always been those who have disputed certain books of the Bible. In the second century A.D. there were those who denied the canonicity of Proverbs, Ecclesiastes, the Song of Solomon, and Esther. Similarly, there were those who did not immediately accept James, II Peter, II and III John, Jude, Hebrews, and Revelation. And even at a much later date Luther called the Epistle of James "a right strawy epistle." These divergent opinions, however, do not cancel the fact that, in harmony with the most ancient tradition for both Testaments, these sixty-six books, and these only, constitute the Holy Bible.

In recent years what important discoveries have been made?

Scholarship marches on. This is true in every field. In almost any area of knowledge there comes a time when theories once regarded sacrosanct have to be discarded or at least substantially modified. Accordingly, at times changes are needed. At other times the proposed changes are too radical, so that after a period of trial and error the truth dawns upon those who are willing to admit that the older views were not so bad after all. Have we not seen this happen even within the last few years? Think of such areas as teaching children how to read and how to figure, of instructing young mothers how to nurture their little ones. We might as well admit that we learn by experience! The writer will never forget a demonstration of a so-called "new method" of teaching geography. The year was 1943; the

6. See S. E. Anderson, *Our Dependable Bible,* Grand Rapids, 1960; also C. F. H. Henry (ed.), *Revelation and the Bible,* Grand Rapids, 1958.

place a famous educational center in the eastern United States. Ever so many curious people, including the writer, were standing around to see what this new method might be. How delighted was he to discover that his fourth grade teacher, thirty-three years earlier in The Netherlands, had hit upon the "new method" of teaching geography!

Sometimes what is presented as "new" is simply "relearned." Sometimes discoveries are made. When, in 1945 and 1946, what became the first edition of *Bible Survey* was being composed, the now famous Dead Sea Scrolls had not yet been brought to light. At that time many a scholar was still saying, "There's many a slip twixt the cup and the lip," and that, accordingly, since the most ancient copy of a *Hebrew* Old Testament which had been discovered dated from about the tenth century A.D., if any copy of an Old Testament, or of an Old Testament book, made a thousand years earlier, were ever unearthed, we would find it to differ *very substantially* from the one to which we had become accustomed.

So, by the grace of God, with faith in his watchfulness with respect to his written revelation, the following words were written:

> *The most ancient* Hebrew *Old Testament which has been discovered dates from about the tenth century A.D. However, if we had in our possession a first- or second-century MS., we would find it to have substantially the same text as those of much later date.*[7]

Little did the author realize that he was typing this sentence very shortly before the Dead Sea Scrolls were beginning to be discovered. By now "everybody" knows that the scholarly world, after minute examination of a complete Isaiah Scroll, has confirmed that it has "*substantially* the same text" as does the Isaiah to which Bible readers had become accustomed throughout the centuries. The same is true of another Isaiah manuscript, less complete.

By this time the story of the discovery—with variations, so that the exact and full details are still not known—has been told many a time. The most popular version is as follows: While herding sheep among the caves located in the cliffs close to the northwestern corner of the Dead Sea, hence south of Jericho, a young Arab threw a stone

---

7. *Bible Survey,* 1947, p. 17.

into a hole of one of these rocks. As the stone landed, the youth heard the shattering noise of a jar. He ran to the place and discovered several jars. They were sealed and contained leather scrolls.

Some of these scrolls were subsequently taken to the American School of Oriental Research in Jerusalem and were photographed. Among the many discovered at that time and later, the complete *Isaiah Scroll,* the *Habakkuk Commentary* (the text of Habakkuk 1 and 2 plus running commentary), and the *Manual of Discipline* are some of the most famous. Today these, together with many other ancient manuscripts, are housed in the Shrine of the Book, which is part of the Israel Museum, a rather recent and very beautiful addition to the Hebrew University, Jerusalem. Among the scholars who recognized the value of the scrolls and made known their views were Professor Eleazer L. Sukenik, Dr. John C. Trever, and Professor William F. Albright.

Literally hundreds of scrolls or scroll fragments have been discovered. With the exception of Esther they cover every book of the Old Testament, generally only in part, and much besides.

Where and when were these scrolls written? They were evidently produced in the so-called "Monastery," the remains of which were discovered a little to the south of those cliffs. It is called Khirbet Qumran (=Qumran Ruin), often simply Qumran. On the basis of their writings—see especially their *Manual of Discipline*—it is held that the writers (copyists) and those associated with them were a sect of Jews who, no longer satisfied with the Jerusalem priesthood, had decided to live by themselves and under their own rules. They *may have been* Essenes, described by Josephus.[8] But we know too little about conditions prevailing before and in the first century A.D. to identify these Qumran people definitely. What we do know, from their writings, is that they were ascetics.

The scrolls contain references to celibacy, community of possessions, fastings, vigils, sobriety, supererogatory observance of the Law, and strict obedience to superiors. These people held the Scripture in high esteem but often interpreted it in a very narrow sense; for example, as if the Old Testament prophets in their writings had in mind particularly the Qumran community. They placed great emphasis on the study of the law of Moses and on ritual purity, baptisms, etc.

---

8. *The Life* (his autobiography), 7-12; *Jewish War* II.119-161; *Antiquities* XVIII.18-22. See also Pliny the Elder, *Natural History* V.73; Philo, *Fragment of the Apology for the Jews* XI.1-17.

Some of them seem to have accepted marriage and family life; others were probably celibates.

They seem not to have been very mission-minded, some of their statements probably implying that knowledge of spiritual matters is for the purpose of being concealed rather than revealed. They accepted a kind of dualism of light versus darkness. For them this meant that they, as the sons of light, must hate the sons of darkness. This dualism, however, is not one of spirit over against matter but of good over against evil. They had much to say about angels, especially *evil* angels.

However, we hasten to mention that they also here and there stressed the necessity of wholehearted devotion to God and confidence in his promises. On the other hand, what detracts from the value of this emphasis is the additional fact that they seem to have regarded such devotion and such confidence as being possible only for those belonging to their group.

Those who would like to have more information on the Dead Sea Scrolls and the beliefs of the people who wrote them are advised to *begin* their study by reading Millar Burrows' richly illustrated two-volumed work *The Dead Sea Scrolls* and *More Light on the Dead Sea Scrolls* (New York, respectively 1956 and 1958) and to continue by perusing the more recent biblical and archaeological articles on these scrolls. See the ongoing bibliographical references and summaries in *New Testament Abstracts.* A very interesting map of the Qumran "Monastery" complex, showing its bathing pool, cisterns, stable, watchtower, scriptorium, assembly hall, mill, bakery, etc. can be found in *Great People of The Bible and How They Lived.*[9]

On the basis of the kind of script and of coins and other articles found in the general area of this cluster of buildings it is generally held that, with an interruption of about thirty years, this sect occupied the Qumran Monastery from the last part of the second century before Christ until the first Jewish Rebellion against Rome, A.D. 66.

How is it to be explained that the discovery of the Dead Sea Scrolls aroused such interest? One of the many reasons is certainly that when their discovery was first brought to light sensational writers made excessive claims for them. They were immediately advertised as "the cradle of Christianity," the source from which

9. G. E. Wright, ed., The Reader's Digest Association, Pleasantville, N. Y., 1974, pp. 302, 303.

both John the Baptist and Jesus derived their teachings. Extremists created the impression that there was really nothing unique about the Christian religion; it might as well be abandoned!

The facts, however, are the very opposite. Careful writers have pointed out that not a single historic statement of the Christian faith has in any way been disproved by these scrolls. In fact, the careful reading of some of this material shows that as a result of its discovery the uniqueness, truth, and beauty of God's revelation in Old and New Testament stand out more clearly than ever before.

To be sure, the Dead Sea Scrolls have contributed their quota to biblical science. In more than one way they have enriched our knowledge and are continuing to do so. Examples:

a. As mentioned earlier, these scrolls have shown that the text of the Old Testament—the Masoretic text—has come down to us *substantially* intact. This verdict does not cover every little detail, to be sure. In minor points these scrolls sometimes differ from the text with which we are familiar, and may even differ among themselves. There are slight variations in script, word transpositions, etc. At times a word has been omitted, sometimes an entire line, which a later copyist reinserts. There is, in fact, enough variation to lead some to the conclusion that the Old Testament text of that day was not as thoroughly uniform as some had expected it to be. There are those who believe that taking account of this fact may shed light upon certain New Testament quotations from the Old.

However, nothing has happened to change the conclusion already openly expressed by many scholars, namely, that, for example, the prophecies of Isaiah as found in our Bible have come down to us *substantially* intact. This holds also for the other Old Testament books. And this discovery was a great surprise to many critics who had for years been affirming the opposite.

b. The "Teacher of Righteousness" mentioned in the scrolls, cannot by any stretch of the imagination be identified with Jesus Christ. The contrast between the two is so great than any unbiased student will immediately have to admit that no writer of a New Testament book can have derived his teaching concerning the death, resurrection, ascension, and coronation of Jesus Christ from this so-called "Teacher of Righteousness."

c. After the discovery of the Dead Sea Scrolls many have attempted to link John the Baptist with the Qumran movement. Among the resemblances that have been pointed out in some of the many books and articles are these: Both the Baptist and the Qumran community were associated with the desert in the general vicinity of the Dead Sea. Both were austere. Both emphasized the need of repentance and baptism. Both originated in the priesthood (John's father was a priest). Both reacted vigorously against "the establishment," that is, the recognized authority of Pharisees and Sadducees, etc.

There are certain outward resemblances, and it must be admitted that the Baptist may have been acquainted with the Qumran community. Nevertheless, in connection with certain more or less essential items, he was different. He did not try to keep his doctrines a secret but welcomed multitudes. Not only men but also women went to hear him and were converted (Matt. 21:31, 32). His disciples were not a highly organized group, kept under control by strict rules and regulations and by a rigid code of discipline. Most of all, John proclaimed a Messiah who had already arrived. He said, "Look, the Lamb of God, who is taking away the sin of the world." "I on my part baptize you with water with a view to conversion, but he who is coming behind me is mightier than I. . . ."

d. The Dead Sea Scrolls shed light upon conditions prevailing in Bible lands just before and at the time when the New Testament books were written. They illumine the then current beliefs against which the New Testament reacts.

As to *teaching,* the New Testament is entirely distinctive. "Jesus Christ spake unlike any other man, for the simple reason that he was unlike any other man," as E. J. Young has stated in a fine article, "The Teacher of Righteousness and Jesus Christ."[10] But as to *the errors* which the New Testament combats, there is no principial reason why these unjustifiable practices and doctrines, or something resembling them, could not be included in the asceticism practiced by the Qumran community.

For example, in Colossians 2:21 Paul *condemns* those who are constantly saying, "Do not handle, do not taste, do not touch." When we now turn to the *Manual of Discipline,* one of the scrolls, and find these very restrictions, not condemned but *ordered,* we begin to feel more at home in the circumstances prevailing in Bible times. Not as if the Colossian heresy was identical with that of the men of the scrolls. On the contrary, the error combated by Paul was probably far more complex (see *N.T.C., Colossians,* pp. 18-21). But asceticism, and the belief that a person by practicing it could

10. *Westminster Theological Journal,* Vol. XVIII, No. 2, (May 1956), p. 145.

help to save himself, was part of this heresy. And the study of the Dead Sea Scrolls brings such then prevailing beliefs and conditions more vividly before our minds, so that we can almost see the people of that day and hear their conversations.

Closely related to the above was another no less sensational and far more recent discovery, namely, that of a small papyrus scrap found in Qumran Cave No. 7, and deciphered by the Spanish priest Father O'Callighan as being part of Mark 6:52, 53. The scrap belonged to material to which, upon discovery, the date approximately A.D. 50 had been ascribed. This scrap would therefore seem to point back to a very early date for the composition of that Gospel. Is this conclusion warranted?

It is probably too early to be positive about this. Comments made by today's scholars range all the way from "nothing has changed" to "the mathematical probabilities that Dr. O'Callighan is right are astronomical."[11] To those who are deeply interested in this subject I would recommend the reading of William White's articles,[11] and also P. Garnet's article, "O'Callighan's Fragments: Our Earliest New Testament Texts?"[12]

---

11. *Westminster Theological Journal,* No. 35 (Fall 1972), pp. 15-20; also No. 35 (Winter 1973), pp. 221-226.
12. *Evangelical Quarterly,* Vol. XLV, No. 1 (Jan.-March 1973), pp. 6-12.

Eastward view of the Old City
of Jerusalem, the temple area, the Kidron
Valley, and the Mount of Olives.
Israel Information Office

2 More Facts About the Bible

When were the Bible books written, and how have they been arranged? (See also pp. 203-207, 315.)

Here it is necessary to be very careful. We know so little. Nevertheless, without a general idea of the order in which the books follow one another it is impossible to study the Bible in an adequate manner. We shall not try, however, to fix a definite date for each of the sixty-six books. We shall simply group the books with respect to successive periods. The Chronological Table for the Books of the New Testament is found on p. 315. With respect to the Old Testament see below, p. 35.

The arrangement found in our English Bible is not the original but that of the LXX (Septuagint) version. It divides the books into three groups: *Historical:* Genesis to Esther; *Poetical:* Job to Song of Solomon; and *Prophetical:* Isaiah to Malachi. The New Testament presents a somewhat similar arrangement: *Historical:* Matthew to Acts; *Epistolary:* Romans to Jude; and *Prophetical:* Revelation. This division, accordingly, is on the basis of the subject matter or the type of inspired literature. It is a remarkable arrangement and one should be thoroughly familiar with it; see also p. 203.

Nevertheless, the order in which the books are arranged in the Hebrew Old Testament is more nearly chronological. It is moreover, the arrangement to which reference is made in the New Testament in Luke 24:44: "And he said unto them, These are my words which I spake unto you, that all things must needs be fulfilled, which are written in *the law of Moses,* and *the prophets,* and the *psalms,* concerning me." Accordingly, the entire Old Testament was divided into *The Law, The Prophets,* and *The Psalms* or *Writings*. Instead of counting thirty-nine books as we do, the Jews counted twenty-four (according to the Talmud) or twenty-two (according to Josephus). The number twenty-four is obtained by counting the Twelve Minor Prophets as *one* book; Samuel, Kings, and Chronicles each as *one* book (instead of I and II Samuel, etc.); and Ezra and Nehemiah as *one* book. Further, when Jeremiah and Lamentations are taken as one book, and also Judges and Ruth as one, the total is reduced to twenty-two. The following list, giving the twenty-four books in their original arrangement, should be commited to memory:

THE BOOKS OF THE OLD TESTATMENT, AS ARRANGED IN THE HEBREW

I The Law
- Genesis
- Exodus
- Leviticus
- Numbers
- Deuteronomy

II The Prophets
- A. *The Earlier Prophets*
  - Joshua
  - Judges
  - Samuel
  - Kings
- B. *The Later Propehts*
  - Isaiah
  - Jeremiah
  - Ezekiel
  - Minor Prophets (counted as one)
    - Hosea
    - Joel
    - Amos
    - Obadiah
    - Jonah
    - Micah
    - Nahum
    - Habakkuk
    - Zephaniah
    - Haggai
    - Zechariah
    - Malachi

III. The Writings
- A. *Psalms to Esther:*
  - Psalms
  - Proverbs
  - Job
  - Song of Solomon
  - Ruth
  - Lamentations
  - Ecclesiastes
  - Esther
- B. *Historical Books*
  - Daniel
  - Ezra-Nehemiah; but see also pp. 310-311
  - Chronicles

(Hebrew Bibles, however, have since 1448 adopted the division: I Samuel, II Samuel; also I Kings, II Kings; I Chronicles, II Chronicles; and Ezra and Nehemiah as two books.)

The dates of the Old Testament books, as given below, are rather uncertain. With respect to the prophetical writings it should be borne in mind that while some uttered Jehovah's oracles over a lengthy span of time, others carried on their prophetic labors for only a little while within a given period. The list below is intended merely as a general indication—easy to memorize—of the periods to which the sacred writers belong. The *groups*, not necessarily the *books* included in a given group, follow one another chronologically. This list should be compared with the charts on pp. 69-72.

For some books even the relative dates are in dispute among conservative scholars; e.g., Jonah, Obadiah, Joel, Job, Song of Solomon, and Ecclesiastes. Others were "in the making" over a long period of time; e.g., the Pentateuch, Kings, Chronicles, Psalms, and Proverbs. Perhaps, the following arrangement is an approach to the truth:

THE BOOKS OF THE OLD TESTAMENT ARRANGED IN PROBABLE CHRONOLOGICAL ORDER

I. 1450-1000 B. C.
- Genesis
- Exodus
- Leviticus
- Numbers
- Deuteronomy
- Joshua
- Judges
- Ruth

II. 1000-786
- I and II Samuel
- Song of Solomon?

III. 786-836
- Amos
- Jonah (time of; see p. 234)
- Hosea

IV. 736-686
- Hosea (continues)
- Isaiah (his prophetic activity begins shortly before and ends shortly after this period).
- Micah
- Job?

V. 686-636
- Proverbs (date when the book was brought to completion?)
- Nahum

VI. 636-586
- Zephaniah
- Habakkuk
- Jeremiah
- Daniel, but see pp. 307-308
- Ezekiel
- Obadiah (in the year of Jerusalem's Fall or very shortly thereafter?)

VII. 586-536

Lamentations
Daniel (continues)
Ezekiel (continues)
I and II Kings (date when the book was brought to completion?)

VIII. About 520

Haggai
Zechariah

IX. About a century later; probably before 420

Joel?
Malachi

X. 420-336

Psalms (date when the book was brought to completion?)
Ecclesiastes? see p. 297
Esther
Ezra
Nehemiah
I and II Chronicles (date when these books were brought to completion).

How did we get our translated Bible?

The work of Bible translation began at a very early time. The Jews who returned from the Babylonian exile no longer spoke Hebrew but Aramaic. Hence, the Hebrew passage read in the synagogue services had to be translated into Aramaic. These oral targums or translations were later reduced to writing. When, after the conquests of Alexander the Great, Greek was becoming a world language, the Hebrew scriptures were translated into that tongue. The work of translating began in the days of Ptolemy Philadelphus who became king of Egypt in 285 B.C. Josephus tells us a very interesting story, not entirely trustworthy, of the seventy-two Jewish translators, six from each tribe, who made the journey from Jerusalem to Alexandria, received a most hearty welcome, performed their important task on a quiet island in the harbor of Alexandria and finished the translation of the Law in seventy-two days! It would seem probable that the translation of the entire Old Testament was finished by the year 150 B.C. The quality of this Old Greek version is not equal for every book. This LXX rendering is usually quoted (with or without minor changes) in the New Testament. The Ethiopian eunuch was reading the LXX version of Isaiah 53 when Philip met him and interpreted the chapter for him. During the second century A.D., Tatian, writing in Syriac, produced a Harmony of the Four Gospels (Diatessaron), which has disappeared, except in translations. However, two very early manuscripts of the separate Gospels in Syriac have been discovered. There is also a later Peshitta (i.e., *simple*) Syriac version of the Bible. By the end of the second century A.D. a Latin translation was in circulation in Africa; a little later, another Latin version appeared in Italy. The Vulgate (also Latin) translation was made by Jerome, who carried on his task in the place of the Saviour's birth. He settled there in the year 387. It was revised several times, and is held in high honor by the Roman Catholic church. Yet, Jerome himself received slight praise for his work. The Roman Catholic Douay version is a translation, with certain modifications, of the Vulgate.

Soon after Jerome had completed his task, missionaries began to carry the gospel into the regions of Great Britain. Many of the eager listeners were unable to read, and of those who had acquired the art very few had access to a Latin Bible. Soon certain portions of the Bible were translated into the vernacular; e.g., the Gospel of John, translated by Beda (died 735). Nevertheless, from the beginning of the evangelization of England in the last decade of the sixth century to almost the last decade of the fourteenth century there was not a complete English Bible. The man who first translated the entire Bible into English was Wycliffe. Religious conditions in his days were, indeed, very bad. Bishops and priests were worldly. Popes cared more for material wealth than for the spiritual welfare of their people. Believers were kept in ignorance. But Wycliffe's pen was never idle. For the Bible he did three things: First, he boldly proclaimed that everyone should read it. Said he, "Christen men and women, old and young, shulden study fast in the New Testament, and no simple man of wit shulde be aferde unmeasurably to study in the text of Holy Writ." Secondly, he translated it from Latin into English. For this accomplishment he was called by his *religious* enemies "that pestilent wretch of damnable memory, yes, the forerunner and disciple of antichrist." Thirdly, he organized a band of voluntary workers—called Lollards—to preach the cardinal truths of the Bible and to place it in the hands of the common people. The editions of the Wycliffe Bible appeared between the years 1382 and 1388. They not only helped to mold the English language but exerted a powerful influence for good upon the nation. Nevertheless, the Bible which Wycliffe gave to his people was not a translation from the original. It was a translation of a translation. Besides, it should be remembered that the art of printing had not yet been invented. What was needed was an easily distributable (i.e., printed) English Bible translated directly from the original. This, too, God was about to provide.

One hundred years after Wycliffe's death Tyndale was born. The fifteenth century was filled with events of far-reaching importance. In the middle of that century the art of printing from movable type was invented. In the year 1453 the Turks captured Constantinople. Hundreds of Greek scholars were driven westward. Hence, the study of Scriptures in the original languages was stimulated in Western Europe. Men began to demand a Bible translated directly from the original. To supply this need Tyndale began his great work of translating the New Testament. He went to Wittenburg to see Luther, and from there to Cologne, to put into print his completed translation of the New Testament. The authorities, however, discovered his "crime." But Tyndale saved the printed sheets and sailed to Worms. Later, he went to Antwerp, revised his New Testament, and began his work on the Old. At last he was betrayed into the hands of his enemies. On October 6, 1536, he was strangled and burned as a heretic. His last words were: "Lord, open the king of England's eyes."

This prayer was heard. Of the many Bibles which followed we wish to call the attention of the reader to The Great Bible—sometimes erroneously called Cranmer's Bible, because he wrote the preface—which appeared in seven editions between the years 1539 and 1541. Its pages measured 16½ by 11 inches. King Henry ordered that every church in the realm be provided with a copy. Of this Bible no less than 20,000 copies were printed during a period of three years. Especially significant is the title page. It pictures God Almighty in the act of pronouncing his blessing upon King Henry VIII. That king—who was not exactly a pious individual—is here called a man after God's own heart, ready to perform all the wishes of the Lord. He is pictured in the act of handing one copy of the Bible to Archbishop Cranmer, who leads a group of clergy, and another one to Cromwell, who is followed by the nobles. Cranmer, again, hands the Bible to a priest; the priest, in turn, preaches from it to the people. He has chosen as his text: "I exhort, therefore, first of all, that supplications, prayers, intercessions, thanksgivings, be made for all men; *for kings and all that are in high place . . .* " (I Tim. 2:1). At the bottom of the beautiful page one beholds the motley throng shouting, "Long live the king! God save the king." And in order to remind people what would happen if they did not shout in this manner, there is a picture of a prison tower on the very title page of this Bible. The faces of its inmates do not look very cheerful![1]

The King James or Authorized Version, which appeared in the year 1611, was prepared by the best Hebrew and Greek scholars of the day. There is, however, not much difference between Tyndale's version of the New Testament and the King James. Although this translation has many excellent features and has justly endeared itself to the hearts and lives of the English-speaking people, in course of time the need for more modern versions began to assert itself. So the English Revised Version appeared in 1885, the American Revised (Standard edition) in 1901. However, since language is constantly changing, and discovery and biblical science are continually advancing, even these revisions no longer satisfy. Result: many new translations. Some of them, however, are so "free" that they hardly deserve the name *translations.* These can best be described as *paraphrases.* A really "good" translation is one that not only sounds well in English (German, French, etc.) but also truly reflects the original.

The following summary of important dates in early Bible translation may aid the memory; notice the 36s and 86s:

I. Dates B. C.

336 The last O. T. book completed (this is the date as given by Dr. G. Ch. Aalders)

286 Ptolemy Philadelphus accedes to the throne of Egypt. During his reign the Septuagint is begun.

II. Dates A. D.

386 Jerome to Bethlehem, the Vulgate.

736 The Venerable Beda dies, having finished translating the Gospel of John into English vernacular.

1386 (a thousand years after the Vulgate) Wycliffe's Bible.

1536 Tyndale is put to death. His New Testament was translated directly from Greek. It is reproduced, to a considerable extent, in the Authorized or King James Version of the Bible, which appeared in the year 1611. Other versions appearing about this time (i. e., about 1536 or shortly thereafter) were the Coverdale and the Great Bible.

1886 The English Revised Version, which was the basis

1. H. R. Willoughby, *The First Authorized Bible and the Cranmer Preface.*

for the American Revised Version published in the year 1901.

The given table is not exact. It is, however, easy to memorize. Once learned, it is a small matter to remember that Ptolemy Philadelphus, during whose reign the LXX was begun, acceded to the throne of Egypt in 285; that Jerome went to Bethlehem in 386; that Beda died in 735; and that the real date of the English Revised Version was 1885. For the rest, who will wish to say that these 86s and 36s are not really important? And who will deny that also those dates are turning points in history?

Concerted efforts are being put forth to reach "the ends of the earth" with the gospel. The task is enormous. In many cases the language of a tribe has not even been reduced to writing, and exact or meaningful equivalents for words used in the original are lacking.

Among popular *modern* English translations are the Revised Standard Version (R.S.V.), the New English Bible (N.E.B.), New American Standard (N.A.S.), and New International Version (N.I.V.). And do not ignore the Berkeley Version, and the Jerusalem Bible (sponsored by Roman Catholics).

The Peak of Moses (Mount Sinai)
as viewed from the Rock Cave area.
Charles F. Pfeiffer

3 How the Bible Should Be Studied: Themes, Outlines, and Other Helps

How can we become rather thoroughly acquainted with the contents of the Bible? First of all, by reading the *Bible* itself. Read not a small portion but a book at a time; say, Genesis in its entirety. What next? Read it again! At least three times! Get into the spirit of the book! See the Christ revealed in it!

Furthermore, consult books such as those listed in the *Beginner's List of Bible Helps* on the next page.

More, however, is necessary. When any event of Bible history is mentioned—whether it occurred in the Old or in the New Dispensation—one should be able *immediately* to assign to it an approximate date. This "immediate date-consciousness" or historical perspective is absolutely essential to the mastery of the meaning of Scripture. Nevertheless, little if anything has been done to help the student in acquiring this ability. Charts of dates for *reference*, although very valuable in themselves, are almost useless for this purpose. It is for that reason that we have spent considerable time and effort in devising memorizable chronological charts. See pp. 69-75. The dates given in these charts should be thoroughly mastered. They should become part of you, so that when anyone mentions an event of Bible history, you can at once assign to that event its proper place in history.

We come now to what is, perhaps, *most* necessary. We refer to *themes and outlines.* Few people are able to commit to memory entire books of the Bible. Themes and outlines, properly prepared, can be mastered by the average student. One should become as thoroughly familiar with them as with the multiplication table. When anyone mentions Galatians, the student of the Bible should be able, without the least hesitation, to give theme and outline. If you

BEGINNER'S LIST OF BIBLE HELPS

Interpretation

Berkhof, L., *Principles of Biblical Interpretation,* Grand Rapids, 1950.

Archaeology and Geography

Free, J. P., *Archaeology and Bible History,* Wheaton, 1952.

Turner, G. A., *Historical Geography of the Holy Land,* Grand Rapids, 1973.

Unger, M. F., Archaeology and the New Testament, Grand Rapids, 1962.

Introduction

Berkhof, L., *New Testament Introduction,* Grand Rapids, 1915.

Metzger, B. M., *The New Testament, Its Background, Growth and Content,* New York-Nashville, 1965.

Raven, J. H., *Old Testament Introduction,* New York, 1910.

Dictionaries & Encyclopedias

Davis, J. D., revised by H. S. Gehman, *The Westminister Dictionary of the Bible,* Philadelphia, 1944.

Orr, J., (gen. ed.), *The International Standard Bible Encylopaedia,* rev. ed., Grand Rapids, 1943.

Concordances:

Various editions of the Bible have helpful concordances; see also the more comprehensive works by (respectively) J. Strong and R. Young.

Commentaries

On the Entire Bible

Calvin, J., *Calvin's Commentaries,* tr. into English, ed. 1948 ff., Grand Rapids.

Lange, J. P., (ed. and part author) *Commentary on the Holy Scriptures* Grand Rapids reprint (no date).

Nicoll, W. R., (ed.), *The Expositor's Bible.*

On the New Testament

Erdman, C. R., *Exposition of the New Testament* (in 17 small volumes).

Hendriksen, W., *New Testament Commentary,* Grand Rapids, various dates; not completed as yet.

Stonehouse, N. B. (ed.) and Bruce, F. F. (ed. and co-author), *The New International Commentary on the New Testament,* Grand Rapids, various dates.

develop this ability, you will begin to see the precious passages of Holy Writ in the light of their contexts, and you will not misapply them.

First, the theme! When we devise a theme, we must see to it that it is in harmony with the intent of the author who wrote the book. Thus, the theme of the book of Joshua is not *The Conquest and Division of the Holy Land* but *The Lord Establishes Israel in the Promised Land.* Similarly, the theme of Judges is *The Lord Proves Israel in the Days of the Judges* (see Judg. 2:22). Often a theme is given in or suggested by the book. Either the idea is there or the very word. Thus, the idea of Ruth's *wise choice* is indicated in 1:16, 17. The very phrase *"full reward"* is found in 2:12. Hence, the theme which we have chosen is *Ruth's Wise Choice and Full Reward.* Similarly, Nehemiah stresses *The Lord's Goodness to His People* (2:8). By including the very word *goodness* in the theme, we immediately introduce the reader to the very flavor of the book and to the spirit of its author. Habakkuk's striking statement, "*The righteous shall live by his faith,*" makes an excellent theme. The Book of Acts also suggests its own theme and even its own division. See p. 402. Colossians clearly stresses *Christ's pre-eminence* (1:18). I Peter dwells on *the living hope* (1:3). The author of the Epistle to the Hebrews wishes to have his message viewed as *a word of exhortation* (13:22). The Book of Revelation mentions its theme in 17:14. Most of the books have definite themes. A little study easily reveals what these are.

This, however, is not true with respect to *every* Bible book. What do you suggest as the theme of Philippians? I have tried several—such as, *Christlikeness, Christmindedness, Joy in Christ,* etc.—but not a single one satisfies. The contents of the epistle cannot be properly viewed as the development of a central, material theme. To his beloved church at Philippi the great apostle is writing a letter, and he writes about several matters. To be sure, the letter is well organized. It is not a jumble. It has, however, no central theme. See p. 357. The same holds with respect to II Corinthians; and, in a sense, also with respect to I Corinthians and I Thessalonians. The captions which we have placed above these letters can hardly be considered central, material themes.

Having selected the theme or the caption, whatever the case may be, the outline is next in order. Now, such an outline, if it is worth while, must have the following characteristics:

1. It must be indicative of the material contents of the book. Before me lies an outline which informs me that the first division of

Haggai comprises a prophecy delivered on the first day of the sixth month. It says *that,* and nothing else. It also tells me that the second division comprises a prophecy delivered on the twenty-first day of the seventh month. Now, this is all true, but it tells me next to nothing about the Book of Haggai. The Book of Job presents another classic example: the easiest way to rid oneself of the task of delving into the book and of presenting its real contents is to make an outline of its artistic structure—*that,* and nothing else. But if one really desires to master the Book of Job, he must become acquainted not only with its artistic structure—this requires a formal outline—but also with its material contents—this requires a material outline. See both, pp. 286-288.

2. **If possible, it must be taken from the book itself.** Thus, the author of the Book of Joshua gives us an outline at the beginning of the sacred narrative. See p. 222. We have something similar in the Epistle of James, p. 318. The divisions of Ezekiel, Galatians, and Revelation are clearly marked. With respect to Revelation, the outline which we give is definitely suggested by the book itself: lampstands, seals, trumpets, bowls, etc., constitute distinct sections of the book, whether we like it or not! This is John's own grouping. Moreover, the author of the Apocalypse is constantly speaking in terms of *seven.* That number occurs fifty-four times. What is even more striking is the fact that he again and again arranges his sevens in groups of three and four or of four and three. Hence, our outline (p. 441), far from being artificial, is exactly in harmony with the genius of the book.

3. **It should reveal a unity of thought if such a unity is discernible.** Take, as an example, the Book of Daniel. The author is clearly telling us one, connected story. He himself gives us the "links" between the various parts of that story. We learn from the first chapter that as a reward for his faithfulness Daniel received an "understanding in all visions and dreams." Hence, it does not surprise us that in chapter 2 he is represented as interpreting a dream. Again, when, as a result of this interpretation, honors are bestowed on *him* not only but also on his three friends (2:49), it does not cause surprise that, through the envy of his enemies, these three friends are cast into the fiery furnace (chapter 3). Moreover, the sentence pronounced on Belshazzar in chapter 5 results from the fact that the king had disregarded the lesson which his "father's" humiliation, recorded in chapter 4, should have taught him. That this connection is definitely present to the mind of the author is clear from 5:22: "And you, his son, O

Belshazzar, have not humbled your heart, though you knew all this." See our entire outline on the book of Daniel, p. 309.

Similarly, the unity of Deuteronomy is so evident that its central contents can be summarized in one sentence, p. 218. See also the outline of Esther, p. 304.

If we look for organic unity, it will also be much easier to retain the outline in one's memory. This brings us to the last point:

4. **It should be memorizable.** This, to be sure, is not our point of departure. It does not rank highest in the list of characteristics of a good outline. Nevertheless, after we have taken care of 1, 2, and 3, it will be well to arrange or rearrange the wording of the summary so that it can be easily mastered. A lengthy analysis, unaccompanied by a summary or summary outline will be of little use. A person looks at such a lengthy analysis, which amounts to a loosely-knit table of contents, and probably admires the man who went through the trouble of making it. How hopeless a task to try to commit to memory sixty-six analyses of that character! As we see it, there should be a not too lengthy outline for each Bible book. We suggest that you make your own outline, if it be deemed necessary, for those books which consist of only one chapter: Obadiah, Philemon, II John, III John, and Jude. We have given the themes of these books and have tried to include in these themes the very words used in the books themselves. Study especially Obadiah. How many words of the theme are derived from the prophecy itself? See p. 265.

Sometimes memory helps may be used. Mnemonical devices are not to be despised. They certainly cannot do any damage if the outline is true to the actual contents of the book. If one wishes to ignore them, he can do so. We believe, however, that they can be of actual value in helping the mind to acquire a factual knowledge of the Bible. We have read and studied books of human anatomy and on logic which have them. Why, then, should the theologian despise them? Also, it should be remembered that Orientals, famous for their retentive memories, used many of them, and that the Bible itself has them, e.g., alphabetical arrangements of a psalm (119) and instances of play upon words (Micah 1:10-16), in Hebrew, of course.

Street scene in Hebron, a familiar town
in the Genesis accounts of the Patriarchs.
It also served as King David's first capital.
Levant Photo Service

4 How the Bible Should Be Interpreted: Essential Steps in Exegesis

A minister has chosen a text for a sermon. What does he have to do next? First of all, he must discover the exact meaning of the text. Secondly, he seeks the main thought, the central theme and its divisions. Thirdly, on the basis of the work already accomplished, he now writes his sermon. In writing it he bears in mind the needs of his congregation. In this chapter we shall say nothing about the second and third steps which enter into the task of producing a sermon. We limit ourselves entirely to the first of these: discovering the meaning of the text. This scholarly investigation is called *interpretation* or *exegesis*. Our chapter is merely suggestive. It is not comprehensive in any sense. That would be impossible in a Bible survey. What, then, does a minister do when he endeavors to discover the meaning of his text? What means does he employ?

1. **If the particular Bible book in which the text occurs happens to be small, he reads the book in its entirety.** He does this in order to catch the spirit of the author. Of course, if the book is very large, he reads the section—perhaps, several chapters—in which his text occurs. Whenever he discovers anything which might have a bearing upon the meaning of his passage, he makes a note of it.

2. **In order to become even better acquainted with the book, he now turns to a volume that is an introduction to the Bible** (or to this *Survey of the Bible*), so that he may gain additional information with respect to the theme of the Bible book from which his text is taken, its outline, its original readers, the conditions which prevailed when it was written, etc. He makes a note of all this and of whatever additional information he may gather. He consults a chronological chart—but, perhaps, this is no longer necessary: he may have one ready-at-hand in his own mind—for he desires to interpret his text in

the light of the historical setting. If the passage be taken from a historical section of Scripture, the minister consults the best textbooks on Bible history and Bible archaeology.

3. **He now reads the chapter in which his text occurs.** If he can, he reads it first in the original; i.e., in Hebrew, Aramaic, or Greek. He does this not once but at least twice. As at every step, he writes down his discoveries. Having already read the chapter in the original and in English in the version with which he is most familiar (see partial list on p. 40), he now turns to other translations, whether English, or foreign, such as Latin, French, German, Dutch, Swedish, Spanish, or some other tongue. This is very valuable if it be done with discretion. Let the reader study I Corinthians 13 in as many different versions as he is able to understand.

4. **If necessary—this depends somewhat upon the choice of text—he now turns to a good Bible Atlas** in order to become thoroughly acquainted with the lay of the land. The minister who has consulted a map can preach a much more interesting sermon about Genesis 12:1-9, Jonah 1:1-3, or Acts 2:5-13 than the one who has not done this.

5. **Next, he turns his attention to the immediate context of the passage which he has selected.** Nothing is more necessary. Thus, a minister who is going to preach on Luke 18:8b, studies very carefully the entire preceding context: 17:20–18:8a. The succeeding context is also important. Thus, Matthew 26:31-35 cannot be correctly interpreted apart from verse 40 and from verses 69-75. In reality, it cannot be adequately explained without a careful study of at least all the rest of the chapter. Let us give another example. The person who reads Nahum 2:4 may think that the passage is a prediction of the invention of the automobile. If he will now read the passage in the light of the entire context, he will soon discover that the meaning is wholly different. Yet, audiences have even been told that Joel predicts modern bombing planes when he speaks about "chariots leaping from the mountain tops" (2:4). Diligent study of the context is the indispensable prerequisite for proper interpretation.

6. **Having studied the book, the chapter, the historical and geographical background, and the immediate context, the minister turns to his text itself,** which is already beginning to have more meaning than at the beginning of the investigation. What does he do first? He determines the correct reading! He desires to be certain that he is preaching the Word of God itself. Being a minister, he has, of course, studied the rules of internal and external textual criticism and he is

able to interpret the various symbols used in this type of work. And what a vast difference one letter can make. Shall we read: "Glory to God in the highest, And on earth peace among men in whom he is well pleased," or shall we read: "Glory to God in the highest, on earth peace, goodwill to men?" In the original the difference in the reading is exactly *one Greek letter!* Hence, the minister takes very seriously his task of discovering the correct reading.

7. **Having found the correct reading, the interpreter reads and translates his text.** Of course, he has done this before in a very general way, but he now rivets all his attention upon the correct rendering. But is this really necessary? We might answer that question by pointing to such a passage as Genesis 27:39. Whether that passage is to be construed as a real blessing in the sense in which we generally understand that term, or as being, in reality, a curse, depends to a large extent upon the interpretation of a Hebrew prefix. The text of the American Standard Version has: "Behold, *of* the fatness of the earth shall be thy dwelling, And *of* the dew of heaven from above." The margin, however has: "Behold *away from* the fatness of the earth shall be thy dwelling, And *away from* the dew of heaven from above."

This second translation is in harmony with the immediately following context: "And by thy sword shalt thou live." It is also true to the actual facts of history. It is *not* in conflict with Hebrews 12:17, interpreted correctly. Let this suffice to indicate the importance of proper translation.

8. **The arrangement of the sentence, the order in which the words follow each other, now requires the minister's attention.** In a Hebrew transitive sentence the regular order is: predicate, subject, object; as in Genesis 1:1: "In the beginning created God the heavens and the earth." In the intransitive sentence the order of Genesis 1:2 is normal: subject, predicate, just as in English: "And the earth was waste and void." In a Greek sentence the normal word order is: subject, predicate. The verb is followed by the object. If this order is changed, we know that it was the intention of the author to place special emphasis on a certain word, and we should follow his example. This principle can be applied to John 3:16, in which passage we find that in the first clause the verb is placed before the noun for emphasis: "For *so loved* God the world. . . ." The emphasis is clearly on the greatness of *love* divine. In the second clause the *object* is placed first: "that *his Son, the only-begotten,* he gave. . . . " All the stress is on the infinite greatness of the sacrifice. We are

reminded of Genesis 22:2: "Take now thy son, thine only son, whom thou lovest, even Isaac, . . . and offer him for a burnt-offering!" The last clause of John 3:16, "that whosoever. . . ," by way of contrast, rolls on in regular word order. This arrangement of clauses is very impressive.

9. Next comes word study. This requires the use of such books as a concordance, a lexicon, a Bible encyclopedia. The exact flavor of a word must be determined by taking notice of the synonyms, antonyms, and other words with which it is used. The derivation of a word is important. What is the etymology of the word "boldness" in Hebrews 4:16? The current use is even more important. In spite of arguments to the contrary which we have read and studied, we still believe that the two different Greek words rendered "love" in John 21:15-17 do not have exactly the same meaning. Love of devotion is not the same as love of emotion. The meaning of the story hinges somewhat on the correct interpretation of these two words.

10. Grammar, too, must receive its due share of attention. There are sermons in prepositions (e.g., Gal. 3:13). Again, every *question* is not alike. The disciples did not ask: "Is it I, Lord?" (Matt. 26:22). What they asked was: "Surely, not I Lord?" Tense, mood, and voice are also of great importance in determining the precise meaning. If one merely reads the translation, he might arrive at the idea that perfectionism finds support in I John 3:9: ". . . he cannot sin because he is begotten of God." However, the author uses the present infinitive; hence, the meaning is: ". . . he cannot go on sinning," or ". . . he cannot live in sin." It is one thing to commit an act of sin. We all do that. It is quite a different matter to practice sin continually, to live in it and rejoice in it as does the devil (see 3:8), who from the beginning has been constantly sinning and is doing it today. In combating error, how necessary a thorough knowledge of grammar becomes. Moreover, not only of *Greek* grammar, but also of *Hebrew* and *Aramaic!* Without knowledge of these the minister will be handicapped in his exegesis.

11. The interpreter is aware of the fact that not every word can be given a literal meaning. There are figures of speech, and the Bible employs them constantly; e.g., the simile (Ps. 19:5), metaphor (Luke 13:32), brachylogy (Rom. 11:18), zeugma (I Cor. 3:2), pregnant expression (Ps. 74:7b), ellipsis (Exod. 32:32), euphemism (Acts 7:60), litotes (Ps. 51:17), epizeuxia (Luke 10:41), hyperbole (II Chron. 28:4), irony (Job 12:2), sarcasm (I Kings 18:27), and many others. Try to imagine what would happen if the minister interpreted literally Job 12:2, which describes the sorely afflicted saint as saying to his friends: "No doubt but ye are the people, And wisdom shall die with you." Did Job *actually* mean that? Symbolic language, too, abounds. Our Lord was constantly struggling with people who misconstrued his figurative speech. The Jews thought that Jesus was speaking about the literal temple (John 2:19); Nicodemus wondered whether the Master was referring to physical rebirth (3:3, 4); the woman was of the opinion that she would need a bucket in order to draw the *water* (4:10, 11); and so one could easily continue. The minister, in order to be able to interpret his text, must be thoroughly familiar with this field; for, figures of speech and symbols lurk in the most unexpected corners.

12. **Another question which the minister asks himself as he approaches his text is this: Does it contain a parallelism, or perhaps a word which is explained elsewhere by means of parallelism,** i.e., by the repetition of a thought in such a manner that a word or a phrase in the second line answers to one in the first? Thus, the second line in Psalm 25:14 explains the first: "The friendship of Jehovah is with them that fear him; And he will show them his covenant."

The expert is thoroughly acquainted with the various types of parallelism—such as synonymous, antithetic, synthetic, and chiastic—and he makes use of this handy tool again and again. A concordance, moreover, is ever lying on his desk when he prepares his exegesis.

13. **Not only parallelisms but also parallel passages, whether word parallels or thought parallels, and parallel accounts enter into the task of interpreting the meaning of a text.** Say, e.g., that the minister has chosen as his text Revelation 6:2: "And I saw, and behold, a white horse, and he that sat thereon had a bow; and there was given to him a crown; and he came forth conquering and to conquer." Now, this passage does not identify the Rider. Who is he? The answer is not difficult to find. The context helps, but the parallel passages settle the matter once for all. In Revelation 19:11 the Rider upon the white horse is the Word of God, Faithful and True. His name is King of kings and Lord of lords. In hunting for parallel passages we must always begin with words of similar import in the *same* book. Hence, our closest and most meaningful parallel is Revelation 19:11. However, passages in other books also have their value. We refer in this connection to Psalm 45:3-5 and Zechariah 1:8 ff. The Rider is evidently the Christ, who is, indeed, the Word of God, Lord of lords and King of kings.

Another volume which is on the minister's desk whenever he

preaches from the Gospels is a good harmony, in order that the parallel accounts may shed their light upon the story chosen as the text.

Now, in explaining a text in the light of parallel passages the minister is fully aware of one fundamental rule, namely, that he should not try to explain an easy passage on the basis of whatever may be his own explanation of a more difficult one. Do not begin with the Book of Revelation until you have made a rather thorough study of the Old Testament, in which it is rooted, and, in general, of the simple, didactic portions of Scripture!

14. If the minister's text happens to be a prophecy, he is careful to observe the principles of interpretation which apply to that type of literature. Let us state just a few. There are many others:

a. The interpreter must always *begin* his exegesis by asking the question: "What did this prophecy mean for the people who lived at the time in which it was uttered?" Of course, this does not exhaust the meaning of the prophecy, but it is a necessary beginning.

b. Old Testament prophecies that recur in the New Testament, or that are similar to those to which reference is made in the New Testament, should be interpreted in the light of the newer revelation. Thus Amos 9:11, in the light of Acts 15:16; Hosea 2:23, in the light of Romans 9:24-26.

c. In the interpretation both of the prophecies themselves and of their expected fulfillment one should never lose sight of the *conditional* character, whether expressed or unexpressed, of many of them. See Jeremiah 18:7-10.

15. If the text is a parable, diligent care must be exercised that the various elements of the parable, even when a figurative meaning must be assigned to them (Matt. 13:24-30, 36-43), are interpreted in harmony with the one main thrust of the illustrative story. Usually, either the introductory words or the moral stated at the close of the parable furnish the key to its interpretation. See Luke 15:1, 2, 7, 10; 18:1. The wise interpreter will make full use of these keys which Scripture itself supplies. Thus, in interpreting the parables of Luke 15, he is quick to understand that the main purpose of these stories is to indicate how greatly the Father rejoices in the penitent return of those who have gone astray. What a lesson for scribes and Pharisees—and for all of us!

16. The interpreter endeavors to do full justice to the place which Christ occupies in the organism of Holy Writ, and will not rest satisfied until he has shown the relation of his selected passage to the central revelation of the Triune God in Christ. See pp. 83-84, 93 on this point. And so we could continue. There are many other principles of interpretation which the minister understands and applies. Besides, having finished his task, according to the methods indicated, he compares his own results with those of others; i. e., he makes a wise use of the best commentaries. From some of these—sometimes even from those which are characterized by lack of doctrinal soundness—he derives valuable philological information; others are consulted for their exegetical excellence; still others for their practical, devotional, and homiletical emphasis. If only all are used with discretion, much value can be derived from them. Above all, the interpreter recognizes the importance of prayer, a devout spirit, a consecrated life. God himself is his teacher.

The question remains: Is the believer who has not enjoyed a theological training able to interpret the Bible? Our answer is: "Yes, to a considerable extent." He, too, is able to grasp the general sense of Scripture and the thrust of most of its chapters. He reads the Word of God with much profit for his own soul. It is written in clear and understandable language. It has a message for all men. The way of salvation, revealed in Scripture, is presented in such a lucid manner that those who reject it will be without an excuse. All this, however, does not mean that anyone without specialized training is able to interpret difficult passages of Scripture. Even in the interpretation of the simplest passage, all other things being equal, the person conversant with the original languages and an expert in such sciences as hermeneutics, textual criticism, exegesis, and isagogics has an advantage over others. But the untrained Bible student can acquire a little of the skill of the expert. He is able to employ some of the methods described in this chapter: 1, 2, 4, 5, 13, 14, 15, 16, and to some extent a few of the others. If he is a man gifted with a logical mind, endowed with a spirit of true humility so that he is willing to learn from others; above all, if his heart is filled with genuine love for the Lord whose glories are revealed in his Word, he can accomplish much. Then, too, as stated on p. 44, he can make use of such helps as a concordance, a Bible encyclopedia (e.g., the *International Standard Bible Encylopedia*) Sunday school lesson explanations, good popular commentaries, works on Bible history and Bible archeology, etc. Much edification can be derived from a commentary on the entire Bible such as that by Jamieson, Fausset, Brown, from C. R. Erdman's

Exposition of the New Testament, or *Barnes' Notes on the Old and New Testaments.* Permit me also to call attention to my own *New Testament Commentary.* A list of the completed volumes may be obtained from the publisher of this volume. Most of all, *the Bible itself* should be read and reread. *It is its own best interpreter!*

Part Two

The Bible Story

The Sumerian king list, in cuneiform, gives the earliest tradition of rulers who reigned before the Flood. The list also includes later rules whose reigns reached to historical times. ***Ashmolean Museum***

Streamlined Dates 5

Bible Chronology Simplified

It is impossible to obtain a clear view of Bible history apart from what we like to call "*immediate date-consciousness.*" Ideally, the dates to be stored away in the memory should have three characteristics:

1. *They should be* **accurate** *or as nearly accurate as possible.*

2. *They should be* **important**. Dates which are to be committed to memory should refer to actual turning points in history. Other dates should be reserved for reference. To require of the student that he memorize a long list of dates of every character, important and unimportant, is unpedagogical. Not only must the dates which are to be learned be important, but all the most important dates must be included in the list.

3. *They should be* **memorizable**. Dates are prone to pass through the mind as through a sieve. A student prepares for an examination in history. He crams and crams. When the examination is over, the dates have been forgotten. They do not "stick," because the fundamental psychological laws of association have been ignored to a very considerable extent. It is our conviction that first a list of dates should be prepared without any regard to memorizability. Then, when the list is ready, an effort should be made to assist the memory, if it can be done!

Now, it must be admitted that a series of dates which will combine the three characteristics mentioned is not easy to prepare. It is easier to make a list of dates that are merely *accurate*. The list will, in all probability, fail in two respects: the dates included will bear no relation to one another as figures: they cannot be retained in the memory; secondly, *un*important as well as important dates are included in the list. Again, it is rather easy to combine 1 and 2 by eliminating from the list all the unimportant dates. This gives us a better list, but it still fails in one important respect: it cannot be retained in the memory: the dates do not hang together by means of some mnemonic device. *"Immediate date-consciousness"* will not be developed in this way. Again, one could combine 1 and 3—accurate and memorizable—but such a list might exclude many important dates. An artificial list of that nature would be hurtful, not helpful. Or, combine 2 and 3—important and memorizable—but many of the dates in such a list might be far from accurate. This, too, will never do. An ideal list of dates for Bible history—and the same holds for history in general—must combine all three features. We have tried to construct such a list. It has not been easy, but we believe that it will be helpful. The charts, once committed to memory, will not readily be forgotten. Date-consciousness has been the aim. Let us look first at chart I, p. 69.

With the help of Assyrian inscriptions, astronomy, and a few Biblical data it has been established that Solomon began to reign about the year 972 B.C. It was in the fourth year of his reign, 969, that he began to build the Temple (I Kings 6:1). The same passage tells us that this event occurred 480 years—twelve *forties*!—after the Exodus. This gives us the year 1449 (or thereabout; for, 480 *looks like a round figure*) as the year of the Exodus.

Beginning again with the year 972 we obtain the dates 972-932 for the reign of Solomon, *forty years,* (I Kings 11:42).

Figuring backward from the year 972, it becomes clear that David reigned during the period 1012-972, also *forty* years (II Sam. 5:4). Similarly, that Saul (or Samuel and Saul) ruled from 1052-1012 (Acts 13:21). These dates—probably round figures—are as *accurate* as the furnished information allows them to be. They are *important.* They are memorizable (three *forties*).

The period 1449-1052—the Exodus to the beginning of the reign of Saul—may be divided as follows: (1) From the Exodus to the death of Joshua; (2) From the death of Joshua to the beginning of the reign of Saul. This is the period of the judges.

It is impossible to determine the exact length of either of these periods. If, as seems probable, Joshua was not less than *forty* years of age at the time of the Exodus, then the maximum extent of the period *The Exodus to the Death of Joshua* is seventy years, for Joshua died at the age of one hundred-ten (Josh. 24:29). The minimum would be about fifty-two years, for the period includes the wilderness journey of forty years (another round figure, Acts 13:18; Deut. 2:7), the seven years of conquest (implied in Josh. 14:6-10), and at least the "many days" of Joshua 23:1 (which can hardly be less than five years). When we accept a figure mid-way between fifty-two and seventy, we cannot be far from the truth. We shall, accordingly, assign sixty-one years to the period *From the Exodus to the Death of Joshua,* making the dates 1449-1388. Having already established that Saul became king about the year 1052, we obtain the dates 1388-1052 for the Period of the Judges. This means that the judges ruled for about 336 years, a figure which, in the light of what is found on pp. 39-40 and 70 will be very easy to remember. A noted authority on the Book of Judges, C. J. Goslinga, reaches exactly this same figure—336 years—for the period under discussion. If we add the number of years assigned to each judge we get a much higher figure; but certain passages seem to indicate that some of the judges were contemporaneous (Judg. 10:7; 13:1).

Starting again with the figure 1449 or thereabout (but not *many* years later) as the date of the Exodus, it becomes clear that "Israel" (i.e., Jacob) settled in (or "descended into") Egypt about the year 1879, for the period of sojourn in that land is given as 430 years (Exod. 12:40; cf. Gen. 15:13). (In a Bible survey we do not have the space to discuss the dispute concerning this figure. Neither is this the place to discuss the problem with respect to Gal. 3:17 or Acts 13:19).

Jacob was then one hundred-thirty years of age (Gen. 47:9). Isaac was sixty years old when Jacob was born (Gen. 25:26). Twenty-five years intervened between the call of Abraham and the birth of Isaac (Gen. 12:4; 21:5). This brings us to the year 2094 or thereabout as the date of Abraham's call, a date rejected by some thoroughly conservative authors, but upon grounds which we do not deem valid.

We shall not even try to establish the length of the period *From the Flood to Abraham's Call* or of the period *From the Dawn of History to the Flood.* If every conservative scholar could assure himself that the genealogies given in chapters 5 and 11 of Genesis are to be interpreted as similar genealogies written today would certainly be interpreted, there would be no argument. By adding the figures given in Genesis 11 (and 12:4) we obtain 367 years for the period *The Flood to Abraham's Call.* The date of the Flood, by this calculation, is found to be 2461 (2094 + 367). By applying the same method to Genesis 5 (and 7:11) we would reach the conclusion that the creation of Adam occurred 1656 years before the Flood; i.e., that it took place about the year 4117 B.C. But it has been repeatedly affirmed that what we know concerning the history of Babylonia and of Egypt makes 367 years between the Flood and Abraham too short a period. Also, it is emphasized that ancient genealogies are hard to interpret: generations are often skipped. Compare Ezra 7:3 with I Chronicles 6:3-15; also Matthew 1:8—"Joram begot Uzziah"—with II Kings 8:25; 12:2; 14:2; and 15:1: Joram, Ahazia, Joash, Amazia, Uzziah. Finally, compare Matthew 1:13-16 with Luke 3:23-27. Most conservative scholars reach the conclusion that it is not possible on the basis of the Biblical record to establish a date for the Flood and for the creation of Adam, although H. C. Leupold reaches the opposite conclusion.[1] In a survey the problem can merely be *mentioned.*

The second and third charts should be studied together. Let us take the second chart, p. 70. No one will wish to affirm that the dates *86-36*, repeated several times in the history of Israel and Judah, are not truly indicative of *turning points* in Old Testament History. Notice these significant events:

932 The Disruption of the Kingdom.

886 Omri begins to reign. Through intermarriage the royal house of Israel merges with that of Judah.

836 In Israel the House of Omri ends in 842. In Judah, the change comes in 836, with the death of Athaliah.

786 The Glamor Age begins in Israel with accession of Jeroboam II; and in Judah, with accession of Uzziah (as co-regent?).

736 Uzziah dies: end of the Glamor Age.
722/21: Fall of Samaria.

686 Considered by many to be the date which separates the reign of pious Hezekiah from that of wicked Manasseh, but see pp. 77, 78.

636 The reign of wickedness ends with the accession of Josiah.

586 Fall of Jerusalem. Beginning of Babylonian Exile.

536 Fall of Babylon. Return of the Remnant.

To be sure, the exact date may not always have been 86 but sometimes within the period 88-84. Similarly, the date given as 36 may represent an event which occurred anytime within the period

---

1. H. C. Leupold, *Exposition of Genesis*, p. 237.

38-34. Thus interpreted, our list of dates is closer to the truth than any attempt to pin down a date to an exact year, say, 87 or 85, 37 or 35. Moreover, for those who are deeply interested in this subject we have added a chronological note giving *tentative* dates of individual reigns. See pp. 78-80; also the chart on p. 81. Observe especially the figures printed in italics on pp. 78-80 and compare them with the dates given in our chart on p. 66. We hardly need to emphasize that our dates on p. 66, in addition to being *correct,* when interpreted, as we desire to have them interpreted, and *important,* are also *memorizable.* Once learned, the scheme 86-36, 86-36, repeated several times, is not easily forgotten. Observe moreover, that the letter *I* of the word Intertribal Warfare is the *ninth* letter of the alphabet. Hence, the period which that word represents begins in the year *nine* hundred thirty-two. Similarly, the *H* of the House of Omri is the eighth letter. Hence, this period begins in the year *eight* hundred eighty-six, and so on.

We turn next to the third chart, found on p. 71. Also for this period, 536-5 B.C., we have devised a date scheme which *cannot be readily forgotten.* And, again, the dates are *very, very important.* Just remember that the number *536* consists of *500* and *36.* Now, *500* = 333 plus 167. Also, *500* = 300 plus 200.

As to the remaining *36* (for our total number is *536*), reversing the digits gives us *63*. And that is about all we really need. We have now learned most of the significant dates during this period: 536, 333, 300, 200, 167, and 63. Here, again, the calculation approaches *accuracy*. The only date about which there can be any controversy would be 300. Medo-Persian rule over Judah may be said to have ended in the year 333/332; for, it was then that Alexander the Great, having won the battles of Granicus and Issus, and having finally taken Tyre, visited Jerusalem. Alexander's death in the year 323 inaugurated a period of confusion: 323-300. The empire was divided among his generals. It was not, however, until the year 301-300 (i.e., after the Battle of Ipsus in Phrygia) that Egypt's Ptolemy Soter *definitely* gained the mastery over Judea. About a century later, in the year "200" = 198, Judea was annexed to Syria. In December of 168, in obedience to an order of Antiochus Epiphanes, an idolatrous altar was dedicated and heathen sacrifices were offered in the Temple at Jerusalem. This gave rise to the rebellion under the Maccabees, 167. In the year 63 Pompey entered Jerusalem. Roman rule, already felt for some time, was now definitely established. It would seem, therefore, that no one, unless he wishes to do violence to history, can quarrel with the appropriateness of the date scheme: 536, 333, 300, 200, 167, 63. Other dates, such as 312, when Seleucus Nicator founded the kingdom of the Seleucidae; and 142, when the Jews achieved political emancipation, are of no lesser importance. Jewish documents were dated in accordance with them. See, e.g., I Maccabees 1:10. Hence, any date scheme which did not include these items would be faulty.

The second and third charts are combined in chart IV, given on p. 72. This scheme, too, is logical and forms the basis for our discussion.

Chart V, p. 73, summarizes the earthly ministry of our Lord. Tradition and the Gospels themselves furnish us with natural and easily memorizable dates. Since the middle of the fourth century the birth of Christ has been commemorated on the twenty-fifth of December. Before that time Christmas had been celebrated on various dates, such as January 6, March 28, April 19, etc. No one knows on what day or in what month Christ was born. *December* for the month of Christ's birth, and *December* or *January* (Jan. 6 or 10, according to the Basilideans) as the month of his baptism and first public appearance thirty years later, may be as good a guess as any. It has been said that Jesus could not have been born in the month of December because this would be in conflict with Luke 2:8, December being unsuitable for the pasturing of flocks; but others consider this objection to be without value and state that in a climate like Palestine's sheep can be kept out all winter.[2] Some even point out that the December date is implied in Luke 1:5.[3] According to the most natural interpretation of John 4:35 another December month is indicated in that passage; another in John 10:22, 23 (the Feast of the Dedication, winter). When, in addition to these December indications, we bear in mind that the Passovers, to which constant reference is made, fell in or about the month of April, we get a very logical and very easy scheme. Once you see it, you cannot readily forget it. And who will claim that these dates are not very significant? Every period (except 1 and 7) is either a *December to April* or an *April to December* period. The Great Galilean Ministry lasted from December to April, *sixteen* months later. All the dates are as *accurate* as possible; they are all very *important*; they are *memorizable*. Again we have an easy sevenfold division.

---

2. R. C. H. Lenski, *Interpretation of Luke's Gospel*, p. 82. See also W. Hendriksen, *N. T. C., Matthew*, p. 182.
3. A. Fahling, *The Life of Christ*, pp. 60, 732.

So much for the critical *months* of our Lord's sojourn on earth. But what about the *years?* Are we able to establish the year when he was born, the year when he began his public ministry, and the year when he was crucified? We believe this can be done, if we allow a margin of possible error of about a year. First of all, it must be pointed out that our present reckoning of time is based on the calculations of Dionysius Exiguus, a Roman abbot of the sixth century A.D. He made the date of Christ's birth to correspond with the year 754 from the founding of Rome. But in this he erred; for, we know from astronomical computation that King Herod died before the Passover of the year 750 A.U.C. (*ab urbe condita,* from the founding of the city [i.e., Rome, in 753 B.C.]) And our Lord was born even before Herod died (Matt. 2:1); therefore, probably in the year 749 A.U.C. or even earlier. Hence, when we speak of the year A.D. 1976, this may really have to be A.D. 1981. But it is probably too late to change the calendar. Because of the error that was made in the sixth century we have to use the clumsy expression that "Christ was born five years (or more) before the Birth of Christ." This means, of course, that he was born five or more years before the date of his birth as fixed by Dionysius Exiguus.

What information do the Gospels furnish with respect to the year of Christ's birth, of the beginning of his public ministry, and of his death and resurrection? Observe the following:

1. As already indicated, according to Matthew 2:1 Jesus was born before the death of King Herod. The probable date is, therefore, 5 B.C. or even earlier, but not several years earlier (see Matthew 2:16).

2. John 2:20 states that when Jesus attended the first Passover and cleansed the Temple, that structure had been in building for a period of forty-six years. According to Josephus the work was begun about 19 B.C. This brings us to the spring of A.D. 27, as the year of the first Passover. If A.D. 27 be correct, then the baptism and first public appearance occurred a few months earlier, i.e., December-January (Dec. of A.D. 26 or Jan. of A.D. 27).

3. Luke 3:23 tells us that when Jesus began to teach he was about thirty years of age. If, as we have just indicated, his first public appearance occurred about December of the year A.D. 26, or a trifle later, then the date *December of the year 5 B.C.* would carry us back thirty years. The year 5 B.C. is, therefore, probably the year of Christ's birth. This is in harmony with 1 above.

4. From Luke 1:26, 36 it may be inferred that John the Baptist was born a little less than six months before the birth of Christ. If he,

too, made his first public appearance at the age of thirty, then (see under 2 above) this event must be dated about the summer of the year A.D. 26. This was, moreover, the "fifteenth" year of the reign of Tiberius (Luke 3:1). See p. 400.

It is for this reason that the year of Christ's birth and also the year of his first public appearance seem to be rather definitely fixed. We cannot allow a wider margin of error than, at the very most, a year. Our Lord, then, was born about December of the year 5 B.C. (or possibly, but not probably 6 B.C.). Those who make it much earlier—7, 8, or 9 B.C.—fail increasingly to do justice to the fact that then Luke would not have been able to say that when Jesus began to teach he was about thirty years of age. The word "about" is given too much latitude. Besides, there is Matthew 2:16! A man like Herod would allow himself a wide safety margin. Some have accepted the theory that the three conjunctions of Jupiter and Saturn in May, September, and December of the year 7 B.C. are indicated by the "star" of the Wise Men, but in view of Matthew 2:9 this is improbable.

The date of Christ's crucifixion is fixed by the fact that whatever the feast of the Jews mentioned in John 5:1 may have been, four Passovers are clearly implied; i.e., the Passover of 6:4 cannot have been the one which occurred one year after the Passover mentioned in 2:13. Three Passovers are definitely mentioned: John 2:13, 6:4, and 19:14. Accordingly, Christ's earthly ministry, from baptism to resurrection, lasted a little longer than three years; i.e., from December of the year A.D. 26 (or January of A.D. 27) to April of the year A.D. 30. This is followed by the seven weeks: Passover to Pentecost.

Chart VI covers the period A.D. 30-96: from Pentecost to Patmos. This includes the life of Paul from his conversion in A.D. 33/34 to his death in A.D. 67.

But is this figure of A.D. 33/34 for the apostle's conversion correct? This depends somewhat upon the year of the accession of Festus (Acts 24:27). This date is, however, in dispute. If it be A.D. 60, then the dates of Paul's chronology are as given in our chart. Let the reader examine the following passages in the order given: Acts 24:27; 28:30; now again 24:27; 20:31, 3; 18:11; 15:36; Galatians 2:1, 18 (cf. Acts 15; we believe that Galatians 2:1 and Acts 15 refer to the same visit to Jerusalem, and that the period of "fourteen years" of Galatians 2:1 means, as the context clearly indicates, fourteen years after the visit to Jerusalem described in Galatians 1:18-20, *not* fourteen years after Paul's conversion (Galatians 1:15, 16, 18). It is however, possible that the accession of Festus occurred a few years earlier than A.D. 60; say, in A.D. 58. In that case the dates in our chart would all have to be pushed back. However, though we grant the *possibility* that our chart is off by one or two years, we do not regard this as probable. Certainly the dates should not be pushed back even farther; for this would lead to a conflict with other facts or probabilities. One of these is that Gallio, before whom Paul was accused on his second missionary journey (Acts 18:12-17) was governor in Corinth during the period 51-53. Hence our date for this journey must include the years 51-53. Also, if we bear in mind that Felix was appointed governor in the year A.D. 52, our chronology, which dates the defense of Paul before Felix in the year 57/58, does greater justice to the words of the apostle recorded in Acts 24:10 than an earlier dating would do. Says Paul, in the passage referred to, "Forasmuch as I know that thou hast been of *many years* a judge to this nation, I cheerfully make my defense."

We are on safest grounds if we divide the period 33/34-50 into two subdivisions. This is Paul's own division as given in Galatians 1:18–2:1. We read: "Then *after three years* I went up to Jerusalem to visit Cephas, and tarried with him fifteen days . . . . Then *after the space of fourteen years* I went up again to Jerusalem with Barnabas, taking Titus also with me." For the period 50-67 we follow the data furnished by Luke in the Book of Acts in the passages already given. The sevenfold division is *natural*. The dates are *as nearly accurate* as it is possible for them to be. They are all *very important*. And the entire scheme is so *easy to commit to memory* that once seen it can hardly be forgotten. Observe the resemblance between the figures:

33-37	37-50	50-53
53-57	57-60	60-63
63-67		

The chart given on p. 74 should be compared with the one on p. 315. Instead of fixing a definite date for the writing of each of Paul's epistles and for the other New Testament books, we have divided them into groups, assigning each group to a period. We did the same for the books of the Old Testament (see pp. 35-36). We believe that this is a more *accurate* way of stating the facts. One cannot be nearly as certain that Paul wrote Philippians in the year 60 or, let us say, in the year 63, as he can be in assigning the epistle to the general period of the first Roman imprisonment. We believe, therefore, that this scheme not only "memorizes" easily but is even more accurate than the usual method of assigning a specific date to each book. Moreover, we have allowed a margin of error of one or two years.

Chart VII shows how the dates of the imperial reigns can be

retained in the memory indefinitely. Once you know the names of the Roman emperors, all you have to do is begin with the number 14; then add 13, 14, 13, 14, 13, 15. It's very, very simple.

In the year 27 B.C. (14+13!) Augustus was formally invested with imperial powers. He ruled until A.D. 14. Then we get:

A.D. 14 plus 13 = 27, Tiberius. But see also p. 415.
27, plus 14 = 41, Caligula.
41, plus 13 = 54, Claudius.
54, plus 14 = 68, Nero.
68, plus 13 = 81, Period of Confusion, Vespasian, Titus.
81, plus 15 = 96, Domitian.

Change the 27 to 37, and all your dates are correct. Without the ever ready knowledge of important dates—a kind of "*immediate date consciousness*"—and of important *places,* history means nothing. The seven chronological charts that follow can be memorized easily, providing a chronological framework for biblical history.

I
CHRONOLOGICAL CHART
FOR
THE PERIOD
EXTENDING FROM THE DAWN OF HISTORY
TO THE DIVISION OF THE KINGDOM

1.	?–? B. C.	**From the Dawn of History to the Flood.**
2.	? –2094	**From the Flood to the Call of Abraham**
3.	2094–1879	**From the Call of Abraham to the Descent into Egypt, (a period of 215 years)**
4.	1879–1449	**From the Descent into Egypt to the Exodus, (a period of twice 215 years)**
5.	1449–1388	**From the Exodus to the Death of Joshua**
6.	1388–1052	**From the Death of Joshua to the Accession** of Saul or of Samuel, (a period of 336 years). **The Period of the Judges.**
7.	1052– 932	From the Accession of Saul or of Samuel to the Division of the Kingdom, (a period of 120 years):
		a. 1052–1012 The Reign of Saul (or: judgeship of Samuel and reign of Saul), 40 years.
		b. 1012– 972 **The Reign of David, 40 years**
		c. 972– 932 **The Reign of Solomon, 40 years**

NOTE: The dates are based on "round figure" data; hence, most of them may be approximate, not exact.

II
CHRONOLOGICAL CHART
FOR
THE PERIOD
EXTENDING FROM INTERTRIBAL WARFARE
TO THE RETURN FROM BABYLONIAN CAPTIVITY

This chart should be compared with the notes on the chronology of the Kingdoms of Judah and Israel found on pp. 76-81. The divergence in dates is very trivial.

1. From Intertribal Warfare to the Fall of Samaria	**932–886**	**I**	**ntertribal Warfare.**
	886–836	**H**	**ouse of Omri.**
	836–786	**H**	**azael's Oppression.**
	786–736	**G**	**lamor Period.**
	736–686	**G**	**rowth of Assyria.** **Samaria Falls in 722.**
2. From the Fall of Samaria to the Fall of Jerusalem	**686–636**	**F**	**oreign Domination.**
	636–586	**F**	**all of Judah.** **Jerusalem Falls in 586.**
3. Babylonian Exile	**586–536**	**E**	**xile, Babylonian.**

NOTE: 886 means sometime between the beginning of 888 and the end of 884 B.C. Similarly, 836 means some time between the beginning of 838 and the end of 834 B.C., and so also for the other dates.

III
CHRONOLOGICAL CHART FOR THE PERIOD EXTENDING FROM THE RETURN TO IMMANUEL'S BIRTH

Remember: **536=500+ 36**
500=333+167
500=300+200
36, digits reversed,=63

4. Medo-Persian Rule		536–333	**Medo-Persian Rule.**
5. Greco - Macedonian and Resulting Rule	a.	333–300	**Alexander (died 323) and his immediate successors. Kingdom of the Seleucidae founded in 312.**
	b.	300–200	**Egyptian Rule.**
6. Resulting Rule (continued)	c.	200–167	**Syrian Rule.**
	d.	167– 63	**Maccabean Rule. Political emancipation for the Jews 142.**
7. Roman Rule, from Pompey's Entrance into Jerusalem to Immanuel's Birth		63– 5 B. C.	**Roman Rule, from Pompey's Entrance into Jerusalem to Immanuel's Birth.**

NOTE: 200 means approximately 200.

IV
CHRONOLOGICAL CHART FOR THE PERIOD EXTENDING FROM INTERTRIBAL WARFARE TO IMMANUEL'S BIRTH (A COMBINATION OF CHARTS I AND II)

	1.	**932–722**	**From Intertribal Warfare to the Fall of Samaria.**
	2.	**722–586**	**From the Fall of Samaria to the Fall of Jerusalem.**
	3.	**586–536**	**Babylonian Exile.**
	4.	**536–333**	**Medo-Persian Rule.**
Greco-Macedonian and Resulting Rule	**5.**	**333–200**	**Alexander and his immediate successors; Egyptian Rule.**
	6.	**200– 63**	**Syrian Rule; Maccabean Rule.**
	7.	**63– 5 B.C.**	**Roman Rule, from Pompey's Entrance into Jerusalem to Immanuel's Birth.**

V
CHRONOLOGICAL CHART FOR THE PERIOD EXTENDING FROM THE MANGER TO THE MOUNT

This chart should be compared with the summary outline of the Synoptics found on pp. 383-385 and the chronological references to the Gospel of John on p. 427.

1. **December, 5 B.C.—December, A.D. 26: Preparation**
2. **December, 26—April, 27: Inauguration**
3. **April, 27—December, 27: Early Judean Ministry**
4. **December, 27—April, 29—Great Galilean Ministry**
5. **April, 29—December, 29: Retirement Ministry and Later Judean Ministry**
6. **December, 29—April, 30: Perean Ministry**
7. **April-May, 30: Passion, Resurrection, and Ascension**

VI

CHRONOLOGICAL CHART FOR THE PERIOD FROM PENTECOST TO PATMOS

1. 30–44 The Extension of the Church in and from Jerusalem
   - 30–33/34 In Jerusalem
   - 33/34–44 From Jerusalem into all Judea, Samaria, and the Surrounding Regions
2. 44–67 The Extension of the Church from Antioch, mainly through the Missionary Labors of Paul

Summary of Paul's Labors from His Conversion to His Martyrdom. Cf. pp. 417, 418.

33/34–37 From his conversion to his visit to Jerusalem to become acquainted with Cephas, Gal. 1:18.	37–50 a. 37–44 Paul at Tarsus and Antioch. His trip to Jerusalem to administer relief, Acts 11:29, 30. b. 44–50 Extension of the church from Antioch. First Miss. J. & Jer. Conference.	50/51–53/54 Second Missionary Journey Galatians I and II Thessalonians
53/54–57/58 Third Missionary Journey I and II Corinthians; Romans	57/58–60 Paul in Jerusalem and Cesarea	60–63 Voyage to Rome Arrival First Roman Imprisonment Colossians; Philemon Ephesians; Philippians
63–67 Release Second Imprisonment Martyrdom I Timothy; Titus; II Timothy	For the probable dates of all N. T. books see p. 315	

3. 67–96 The Close of the Apostolic Age: the Epistle to the Hebrews; Gospel of John; I, II, III John; Revelation

VII
CHRONOLOGICAL CHART OF THE IMPERIAL REIGNS

1.	**— A.D.14**	**Augustus**	**Add 13=**
2.	**— 27**	**Tiberius**	**Add 14=**
3.	**— 41**	**Caligula**	**Add 13=**
4.	**— 54**	**Claudius**	**Add 14=**
5.	**— 68**	**Nero**	**Add 13=**
6.	**— 81**	**Confusion, 68–69; Vespasian, 69–79; Titus, 79–81**	**Add 15=**
7.	**— A.D.96**	**Domitian**	

NOW CHANGE 27 TO 37

Notes on the Chronology of the Kingdoms of Judah and Israel

The following facts should be borne in mind:

1. The so-called long term or old chronology, found in the older Bible commentaries, encyclopedias, and certain editions of the King James Version of the Bible is unsatisfactory. It fails to figure sufficiently with the probability that there were several coregencies. Thus, Amaziah may have assumed the duties of his father Jehoash when the later became "very sick" (II Chron. 24:25). II Kings 14:22 seems to indicate that Uzziah, in turn, reigned during his father's lifetime. And, again, Uzziah's son Jotham became the actual ruler when his father was afflicted with leprosy, (II Kings 15:5; I Chron. 5:17). We must also bear in mind that at least in the Kingdom of the Ten Tribes the year when a new king was crowned is counted twice, being included in the number of years assigned to the reigns of both the retiring and the new king (see I Kings 15:25, 33; 16:8, 15, 16, 23, 29).

2. It is impossible, on the basis of our present knowledge, to present a chronology which solves every problem. However, one should not be too ready to assume a copyist's error. It is true that even conservative scholars grant the possibility of such errors of transmission, especially with respect to *numbers.* (An instance in which such an error is admitted by many is II Chron. 28:1; cf. 29:1; then 27:1, 8; II Kings 16:2; 18:2.) This admission on their part is not in conflict with the most unqualified belief in an inspired and infallible original. See p. 15. Nevertheless, in our own study of biblical chronology we have discovered several instances in which it was not at all necessary to assume even a copyist's error. When the figure given in the text does not seem to harmonize with other data, it is possible that we are not interpreting the text as we should. So, e.g., it is possible that in one passage the years of the reign of a certain king are figured from the time when he began to rule in his own right, while in another the point of departure is the beginning of his coregency. Or, the years may be reckoned from the time when the king succeeded in casting off his vassalage. Can this be the explanation of II Kings 15:8, 13, and 17? An interesting case is that of Pekah. II Kings 15:27 tells us that he "began to reign over Israel in Samaria" in the fifty-second (or death-) year of King Uzziah of Judah (cf. 15:2). This was about the year 736/35. But the passage

also informs us that Pekah reigned twenty years! But how was it possible for him to reign twenty years and for his successor to reign nine years (17:1)—together, twenty-nine years—if Samaria fell in the year 722? Many are, therefore, inclined to assume a copyist's error. But this is not absolutely necessary. On the basis of II Kings 15:25 it is at least *possible* that Pekah began to rule over the territory east of Jordan toward the close of Jeroboam's long reign. As long as we do not have more definite information it is best to reserve our judgment with respect to such questions. Assuming a copyist's error when there are not sufficient indications which unmistakably point in that direction is unscholarly.

The date of Hezekiah's reign presents another difficulty. According to one view, II Kings 18:13 refers to Sennacherib's invasion in the year 701 B.C., the "fourteenth" year of King Hezekiah. We are told, moreover, that "in those days" Hezekiah was sick unto death, and that in answer to his prayer "fifteen years" were added to his life (20:1, 6). Hence, it would seem that, in all, this king reigned twenty-nine years—fourteen plus fifteen—which is exactly what 18:2 tells us. According to this reasoning his reign began in 715/14, for 701 was the fourteenth year of his administration. It must have ended about the year 687/86, making twenty-nine years in all. But 18:1, 9, 10 clearly indicate that, in some sense, this king assumed control in the year 728/27; for we are told that he began to reign "in the third year of Hoshea," and that Samaria, which was taken in the year 722/21, fell in the sixth year of his reign. According to this information, if Hezekiah's reign lasted until about 687/86, he ruled for a period of at least forty years. And this, again, would seem to be in conflict with 18:2 ("he reigned twenty-nine years."). Among the many solutions to this problem there are especially two which deserve attention. One fixes Hezekiah's reign during the period 728/27-699/98. The proponents of this theory interpret II Kings 18:13 as referring to an invasion of Judah which occurred about the year 714 (Hezekiah's fourteenth year), while verse 17 is said to introduce a new paragraph, describing the great invasion of the year 701. The expression, "in those days" (20:1), is interpreted as referring back to the earlier invasion of 714. Accordingly, fifteen years having been added to the king's life, he must have died about the year 699.[4]

The opponents of this theory argue that the student of the Bible

---

4. Thus E. Mack, art. "Chronology," in *I. S. B. E.*

who lights upon the words, "In *those days* was Hezekiah sick" (II Kings 20:1), will find it difficult to persuade himself that the term "those days" refers *not* to the invasion about which he has just been reading but to an earlier one. Accordingly, they divide the reign of Hezekiah into minority rule (728/27-715/14) and a majority rule of twenty-nine years (715/14-687/86.)

Both theories encounter a difficulty in the duration of the reign of Manasseh. The first, in adding the figures assigned to each reign, lacks a sufficient number of years between the death of Hezekiah—supposedly 699—and the fall of Jerusalem in 586. An interregnum is assumed, or else some years are simply added to the already very long reign of Manasseh. One author has: "Manasseh 699-641 (55)."

Scripture does, indeed, inform us that Manasseh ruled for a period of fifty-five years; but 699-641 indicates a reign of *fifty-eight* or *fifty-nine years!*

The difficulty encountered by the second theory is of the opposite character: if Hezekiah died about the year 687/86, the one hundred-year interval between that date and the Fall of Jerusalem is not entirely long enough to include the reigns of all the kings who followed. The problem has not been solved. Was there a coregency somewhere?

As long as we have no certainty, a question mark will have to follow the dates assigned to the reigns of Hezekiah and Manasseh.

We shall now give a list of tentative dates. See also the charts on pp. 70, 72, and 81.

KINGS OF JUDAH

I Kings 14:21	Rehoboam	932-915
I Kings 15:1, 2	Abijah	915-913
I Kings 15:9, 10	Asa	913-873
and II Chron. 16:12	(a brief coregency: Asa-Jehoshaphat)	
I Kings 22:41, 42	Jehoshaphat	873-849
and II Kings 1:17	(a brief coregency: Jehoshaphat-Jehoram)	
II Kings 8:16, 17	Jehoram	849-842
II Kings 8:25, 26	Ahaziah	842-842
II Kings 11:3	Athaliah	842-836
II Kings 12:1	Jehoash	Total reign: 836-798/97
and		
II Chron. 24:25		Amaziah coregent: 804-798/97?

II Kings 14:1, 2 . . . . Amaziah . . . . See preceding line.
. . . . . . Total reign:804-775?
. . . sole ruler: 798/97-787/86
Uzziah coregent . . . . 787/86-775?
II Kings 14:21-22 . . . . . . Uzziah . . . . .See preceding line
and . . . . .Total reign: 787/86-736?
. . . . sole ruler: 775-749?
II Kings 15:1, 2, 23, 27 . . . . .Jotham coregent; Uzziah a leper:
. . . . 749-736/35?
II Kings 15:32, 33 . . . . . Jotham . . . . .See preceding line
. . . . Total reign: 749-734?
. . . . .sole ruler: 735-734
II Kings 16:2 . . . . Ahaz . . . . 734-728/27?
II Kings 18:1, 2, 10, 13 . . Hezekiah . . .Total reign: 728/27-687?
II Kings 20:1, 6 . . . . Minority rule: 728-715?
. . Majority rule: 715-687(the 29th yr.)?
II Kings 21:1 . . . . Manasseh . . . . 687-639?
II Kings 21:19 . . . . Amon 639-638
II Kings 22:1 . . . . Josiah 638-608
II Kings 22:31 . . . . Jehoahaz 608-608
II Kings 23:36 . . . . Jehoiakim 608-597
II Kings 24:8 . . . . Jehoiachin 597-597
II Kings 24:18 . . . . Zedekiah 597-586

KINGS OF ISRAEL

I Kings 14:20 . . . . Jeroboam 932-911
I Kings 15:25 . . . . Nadab 911-910
I Kings 15:33 . . . . Baasha 910-887
I Kings 16:8 . . . . Elah 887-886
I Kings 16:15 . . . . Zimri 886-886
I Kings 16:21, 23 . . . . Tibni and Omri 886-882
Omri alone 882-875
I Kings 16:29 . . . . Ahab 875-854
I Kings 22:51 . . . . Ahaziah 854-853
II Kings 3:1 . . . . Joram 853-842
(In a sense Joram must have begun to reign before 853.)
II Kings 10:36 . . . . Jehu . . . . . . Total reign: 842-815/14
. . . . .Sole ruler: 842-816
Joahaz coregent 816-815/14

II Kings 13:1	Joahaz	See preceding line
		Total reign: 816-800/799
		Sole ruler: 815/14-800/799
II Kings 13:10	Joash	800/799-785/84
II Kings 14:23	Jeroboam II	785/84-745
II Kings 15:25		749: Pekah begins rule over Gilead?
II Kings 15:8	Zechariah	745-745
II Kings 15:13	Shallum	745-745
II Kings 15:17	Menahem	745-736
Kings 15:23	Pekahiah	736-735
II Kings 15:27	Pekah	736/735-730 See under 749.
II Kings 15:30	Hoshea	730-722

By combining these two lists of dates we arrive at the following chart:

CHRONOLOGICAL CHART OF THE HISTORY OF THE DIVIDED KINGDOM

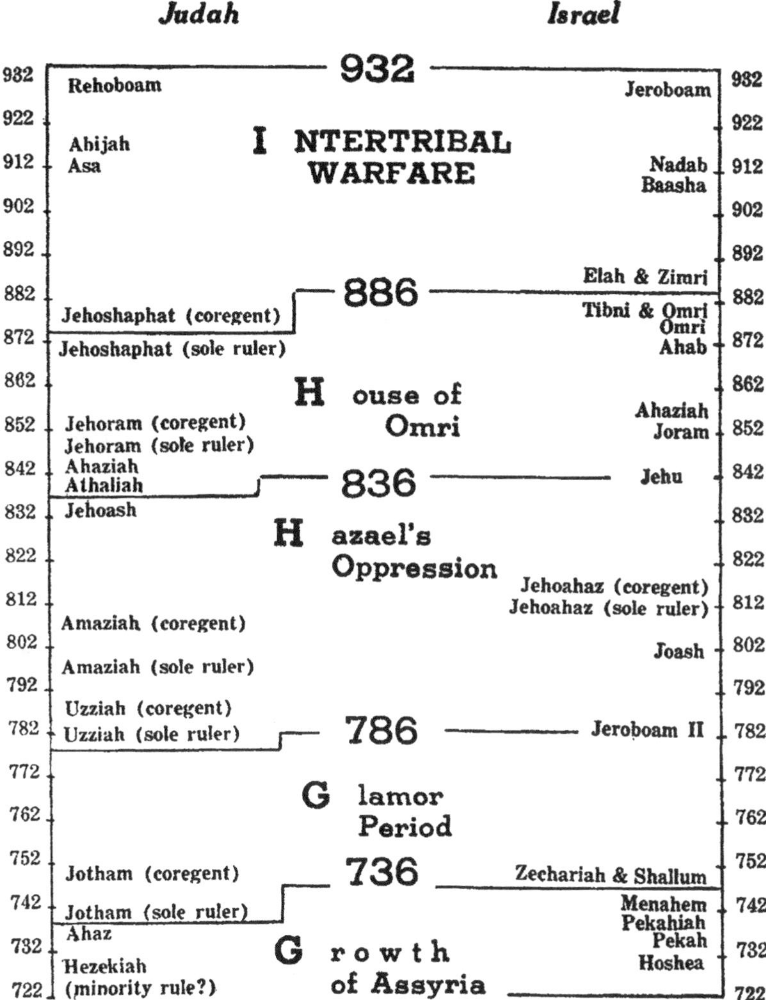

This Assyrian record depicts boats transporting logs, carrying some on board and towing some. The logs are the famed cedars of Lebanon.
The Louvre

From the Dawn of History to the Division of the Kingdom 6

1. From the Dawn of History to the Flood

Scripture: Gen. 1-5

There is *one,* central theme which, like a golden thread, runs through all the stories of the Old Testament. That theme is *The Coming Christ.* As long as one does not see this, the Old Testament remains a *closed* book. As soon as this idea is grasped, the scriptures are *opened.* This is clear from Luke 24:32. Our Lord, risen from the grave, had been speaking to the two disciples who were on their way to the village of Emmaus. At their urging he had entered the house with them, had reclined at table, had taken bread and blessed it, and, having broken it, had given it to them. When, suddenly, they recognized him, he had vanished! It was then that they said to each other, "Was not our heart burning within us, while he spake to us in the way, *while he opened to us the scriptures?*" And how had Christ *opened* the Scriptures? The answer is given in 24:27: *"And beginning from Moses and from all the prophets, he had interpreted to them in all the scriptures the things concerning himself."* Once they saw the Christ as the theme of the entire Old Testament, its scriptures had become an "*open book*" to them.

Many years later Paul is addressing the Jews in Rome. He is dwelling on the theme which makes of the many Old Testament stories *one,* glorious story. He is "persuading them concerning Jesus, both from the law of Moses and from the prophets, from morning till evening" (Acts 28:23). Read also the following passages: Luke 24:44; John 5:39, 46; Acts 3:18, 24; 7:52; 10:43; 13:29; 26:22, 23; and I Peter 1:10.

This is the only *proper* way of telling the Old Testament story. Our Lord himself and his apostles have given us the example. Accordingly, in this and in the following chapter we shall not attempt to discuss all the events which occurred during the Old Dispensation, but we shall simply allow the main trends to pass in rapid review as a connected account of the Coming Christ. We shall endeavor to show how the way for his coming was prepared.

The story of the Coming Christ begins in Genesis 1. In the first verse we read: "In the beginning God created the heavens and the earth." Like a granite rock, this majestic sentence stands before us at the very dawn of history. It is the refutation of materialism which insists on the eternity of matter as the one and only substance. It is the overthrow of pantheism with its teaching that everything is God, and that God is everything. It gives the lie to polytheism: the verb "created" is in the *singular,* though the noun "God" is in the plural, which facts are in beautiful harmony with the later revelation concerning the triune God.

"And the earth was waste and void; and darkness was upon the face of the deep: and the Spirit of God moved upon the face of the waters" (Gen. 1:2).

The earth, then, was lying, as it were, in a vast ocean, as a sponge in water. It was embedded in a huge watery mass (cf. also Ps. 104:6-9). Milton caught the idea:

The earth was formed, but, in the womb as yet
Of waters, embryon immature, involved,
Appeared not. Over all the face of earth
Main Ocean flowed.

Upon the face of the waters hovered the life-imparting Spirit. The Christian religion is, indeed, a reasonable religion; all else is unreasonable. The Bible ascribes the origination of all *living* creatures to the *living* God, the *life-giving* Spirit.[1] The word *God* is used thirty-two times in Genesis 1. It is *God* who does all things. It is *he* who creates, speaks, sees, divides, calls, makes, sets, and blesses. When the earth is *without content* it is he who fills it with grass, herbs, trees, and animals. When it is *without definite form* it is he who imparts to it a definite and visible form by means of a threefold separation process: dividing the light from the darkness; the waters above from the waters below; the seas from the dry land.

Fully in line with the later revelation concerning Father, Son, and Holy Spirit is the statement of Genesis 1:26: "And God said, "Let *us*

---

1. Cf. L. S. Keyser, *The Philosophy of Christianity*, p. 31

make man in *our* image, after *our* likeness." (See also Gen. 9:6; Ps. 8:4 ff.;I Cor. 11:7; Eph. 4:24; Col. 3:10; James 3:9). How the Christ stands revealed in this majestic statement! How the way is paved for his coming! As a result of the fact that man was created as God's image, Christ was able to take upon himself the human nature. Are we becoming too bold when we assert that the all-knowing Triune God created man as his image *with a view to the Incarnation?*[2] Again, whereas man was created as God's image, God "*so* loved the world that his Son, the only-begotten, he gave, that whosoever believes in him should not perish but have everlasting life" (John 3:16; see the original).

Christ is even more clearly revealed in the next two chapters, Genesis 2 and 3. The fall *actually* took place as here recorded. This is the only logical view for anyone who accepts the infallibility of Scripture. This representation by no means excludes the fact that, in the plan of God, the various objects mentioned were intended to symbolize spiritual realities. Thus, there is an echo of the "Garden of Eden" in Revelation 2:7; of the "tree of life" in Proverbs 3:18; 11:30; 13:12; 15:4; Revelation 2:7; 22:2; 14:19; and of the "river" of Paradise in Revelation 22:1. But a later symbolical use presupposes an earlier literal use of the term. Or, shall we say that the Jews were never in a real, visible desert, and never lived in a real, earthly Jerusalem, because these terms (*desert, Jerusalem*) are later on used in a symbolical sense?

Having placed man in the Garden, Jehovah came to him with this probationary command: "Of every tree of the garden you may freely eat; but of the tree of knowledge of good and evil, you shall not eat: for in the day you eat of it, you shall surely die" (Gen. 2:16, 17). To obey in the face of the implied sinful alternative, to obey simply because *God said so* would have been an act of the highest ethical value. Such thoroughly voluntary, loving obedience would, by God's gracious decree, have raised man to a much higher spiritual level than he had hitherto attained. It would have changed the one who was "able not to sin" into one who was "not able to sin." Observe that God did not encourage man to disobey. On the contrary, he definitely forewarned him: " . . . for in the day you eat of it, you shall surely die." Hence, when man fell, and in his fall involved the race, it was he—not God—who was guilty.

Genesis 3 records the beginning of sin, but also the beginning of

2. Cf. J. Orr, *God's Image in Man*, p. 270 ff.

salvation from sin. Most gloriously and directly is the coming Christ revealed in Genesis 3:14, 15: "And Jehovah said unto the serpent, Because you have done this . . . I will put enmity between you and the woman, and between your seed and her seed; he shall bruise your head, and you shall bruise his heel." The figure of the promised Redeemer is in the very foreground here. Over against Satan viewed as an individual—"*you* shall bruise his heel"—stands the one, definite person; namely, the coming Redeemer, "the Seed of the woman." All later revelation is the story of the conflict between these two. See also Revelation 12:1-6. It is ever the dragon—i.e., the devil—who tries to frustrate the redemptive plan of God. Again and again it seems as if Satan might succeed in this sinister purpose; but again and again he fails utterly.[3]

Sons are born to Adam and Eve: Cain and Abel. The former becomes a farmer; the latter, a shepherd. Both bring an offering to the Lord: Cain, some produce of the soil; Abel, a firstling of his flock. God accepts the offering of Abel, but rejects that of Cain (Gen. 4:1-5). Why? Because Abel offered "by faith," and Cain did not (Heb. 11:4). Abel was a man of faith in God and in his glorious, redemptive promise. Hence, we do not merely read that Jehovah accepted Abel's *offering,* but "Jehovah had respect unto *Abel and to his offering*." But how did Cain know that Jehovah had not accepted him and his offering? And how did Abel discover that the Lord had taken favorable notice of him and his offering? We do not know, for the Bible is silent on this point. Divine acceptance is at times indicated by fire falling from heaven and consuming the sacrifice (Lev. 9:24; Judg. 6:21; I Kings 18:38; I Chron. 21:26; II Chron. 7:1), but we do not know whether something similar happened then.

Though divinely admonished, Cain hardened his heart and murdered his brother (Gen. 4:8). Gross wickedness, moreover, characterized his descendants. In Gen. 4:19-24 we read:

> *And Lamech took unto him two wives; the name of the one was Adah, and the name of the other Zillah . . . . And Lamech said unto his wives:*
>
> *"Adah and Zillah, hear my voice;*
> *You wives of Lamech, hearken to my speech:*
> *For I have slain a man for wounding me,*
> *And a young man for bruising me:*
> *If Cain shall be avenged sevenfold,*
> *Truly Lamech seventy and sevenfold."*

---

3. W. Hendriksen, *More Than Conquerors,* pp. 162-170.

This spirit of unmitigated selfishness and boastful aggressiveness was fast becoming the dominant one. It would have resulted in total destruction, had not God intervened. The boundary between God's people—the children of Seth, the son who had replaced Abel (Gen. 4:25–5:4) and the posterity of Cain had been almost obliterated: "the sons of God" married "the daughters of men." It looked as if the evil one had triumphed, for, with the total self-destruction of the race there would have remained no people to be redeemed; there would have arrived no Seed of the Woman to redeem them.

2. From the Flood to the Call of Abraham

Date: ?-2094 B.C.
Scripture: Gen. 6-11

So God sent the Flood! From the mass of mankind which had corrupted itself he separated Noah and his family in order that the kingdom of God might be established in the line of his descendants; and in order that, a remnant of humanity having been thus preserved, the future Seed might be able to assume the human nature. The mass of mankind was about to perish in its sins.

Deluge stories are found among many primitive peoples. The most reasonable explanation seems to be that these multiform accounts point back to a common origin.

Geology, too, has made its contribution to the literature on the subject. If the theory of Flood geologists be correct, sudden disaster must have overtaken the animal kingdom of the long ago. Furthermore, it is suggested that at that time, i.e., before the Flood, a warm and equable climate prevailed over every region of the globe. There was sufficient moisture for a very luxuriant vegetation. Such a vegetation was necessary to support the huge animals which in immense numbers roamed over the earth. Fossil reptiles are found in the earth's strata as far north and south as these strata have been investigated. In Siberia are found the mammoth elephants, tropical animals as is indicated by the fine hair which covers their bodies, the absence of sweat glands, and the food found in their mouths and stomachs. The condition of the fossils seems to indicate that they were overwhelmed by sudden catastrophy. It was not a case of the food supply giving out gradually, for the animals found in Siberia are in the prime of condition. The fossil fish also show that disaster must have overtaken them suddenly, for they are found with their fins extended and in a curved position. All these things, according to the theory of the Flood geologist, point back to the worldwide deluge.[4] The condition of the world before the Flood causes some to believe that the axis of the earth was not tipped away from the perpendicular during that predeluvian time. The Biblical record informs us that after the flood the seasons would follow one another in regular succession. And the seasons are caused by the inclined axis of the earth. It is further claimed that the shock which produced a sudden change of axis from 0 degrees inclination to 23½ degrees inclination would set loose violent disturbances on earth; in fact, the very disturbances described in the Genesis Flood account.

From a plausible theory let us now turn to the infallible record. Scripture stresses the fact that it was God himself who brought about the Flood (Gen. 6:13; 7:4) as a means both of destruction (7:23) and of salvation (I Peter 3:18-22; II Peter 2:5). Not only was there a forty-day cloudburst, but the fountains of the Great Deep were also opened. When the Flood had subsided, the family of Noah left the ark. How everything had changed! Before the Flood, giants were no exceptions, and men reached a very advanced age. This was different now. Before the Flood vegetable food was given to man (Gen. 1:29), but after the Flood, also the meat of animals (Gen. 9:3). Moreover, God blessed Noah and made his rainbow covenant with all flesh that was upon the earth.

Very striking is the foreglimpse of the coming Redeemer which is contained in Noah's prophecy concerning his sons. He said:

Cursed be Canaan

. . . .

God enlarge Japheth.

Between these two lines we read: *"Blessed be Jehovah, the God of Shem!"* It was in the line of Adam-Seth-Noah and now Shem that the Messiah was to be born.

From the mountain range of Ararat the descendants of Noah traveled in a southeasterly direction until they arrived in Shinar, the region between the lower Tigris and Euphrates. Why was it wrong for Noah's descendants to design a city and a tower whose top might "reach to heaven?" (a) Their purpose was self-glorification (Gen. 11:4). (b) Their action was contrary to God's explicit command (Gen. 11:4; cf. 9:1). Accordingly, God confounded their language. This shows us that the great language families arose suddenly. Yet, within each (e.g., the Indo-European) there are several tongues which

---

4. See also G. McCready Price, *The Phantom of Organic Evolution*, p. 48 ff.

resemble one another and point back to a common origin. Is not this somewhat similar to what is found in the realm of plants and animals? Within the larger classifications, all kinds of common-origin variants arise during the course of the centuries.

The history of mankind during the period from Noah to Abraham is one of increasing wickedness. We learn from Joshua 24:2 (see also Gen. 31:29-31) that among the immediate ancestors of Abraham there were those who served other gods. Besides, a branch of the descendants of Ham, which originally inhabited the same general region as the descendants of Shem (Gen. 10:6-10; cf. 11:28), in all probability had been dragging the race downward religiously and morally. Conditions were fast becoming as they had been before the Flood. Again it seemed as if the "serpent" had triumphed. But the promise of the Coming Seed (Gen. 3:15) must stand. Hence, another separation was about to occur.

3. From the Call of Abraham to the Descent into Egypt

Date: 2094-1879 B.C.
Scripture: Gen. 12 (11:27, to be exact)–36

This time it was Abraham who received the divine summons to separate himself. He is known as "the father of all them that believe" (Rom. 4:11). His life is an illustration of the manner in which men, in all ages, are saved (Rom. 4:3). God's *covenant* with him (Gen. 17) is still in force. Scripture clearly teaches that it was never abrogated (Gal. 3:17). It applies to all believers: "And if ye are Christ's, then are ye Abraham's seed, heirs according to promise" (Gal. 3:29). *Confidence* in God, come what may, and resulting *obedience* to God's command, characterizes Abraham's life. His faith is constantly being put to the test. By God's grace he triumphs again and again. When God appears to him in Ur of the Chaldees (Acts 7:3; cf. Gen. 11:28-32) he is told to leave country and kindred. Fully trusting that God will make all things well, he obeys. When Jehovah appears the second time, in Haran of Mesopotamia (Gen. 12:1), the test is even more severe: he must leave his father's house. Again he trusts and obeys. "By faith Abraham, when he was called, obeyed to go out into a place which he was to receive for an inheritance; and he went out, not knowing whither he went" (Heb. 11:8). It is at this time that he receives that wonderful promise: "In thee shall all the families of the earth be blessed." Here we clearly see that when God separated Abraham from the rest of humanity, he did not forget the race. On the contrary, he chose *one* family in order that in the Seed which would come forth from it *all* the families of the earth might be blessed. God's particularism had a universalistic purpose. At Shechem, in the land of Canaan, Jehovah appears again, with the promise: "To your *seed* will I give *this land.*" This paradoxical promise constituted another test of faith, for Sarai was barren (Gen. 11:30), and "the Canaanite [who was not at all willing to yield his soil to a stranger] was then in the land" (Gen. 12:6). After the unhappy incident in Egypt (Gen. 12:10-20), in which the weaker side of Abraham's character becomes manifest, Jehovah appears to him at Bethel, after he had separated himself from Lot (Gen. 13). He is promised "all the land" which he sees, and a seed "as the dust of the earth." The Book of Exodus shows us that the promise of an *abundant posterity* was realized. The Book of Joshua proves that also *the land* became the possession of Abraham's descendants. But Abraham himself during his lifetime did not see the fulfillment of these promises. He lived *by faith.* Be sure to read the entire passage: Hebrews 11:8-12. Beautiful also is Hebrews 11:13: "These all died in faith, not having received the promises, but having seen them and greeted them from afar, and having confessed that they were strangers and pilgrims on the earth."

The greatest test of all came when God said to Abraham: "Take now *your son, your only son,* whom you love, even Isaac, and go to the land of Moriah; and offer him there for a burnt offering upon one of the mountains which I will designate to you" (Gen. 22:1, 2). Compare this with John 3:16: "So loved God the world that *his Son, the only-begotten,* he gave. . . ." Abraham's willingness to render even this supreme sacrifice, miraculously prevented from literal execution, receives the glorious reward: "And in your seed shall all the nations of the earth be blessed; because you have obeyed my voice" (Gen. 22:18).

Abraham's active obedience points forward to the *active* obedience of the Seed.

In Isaac, Abraham's son, of miraculous birth the *passive* obedience of our Lord is foreshadowed. Very instructive is the story of the betrothal of Isaac and Rebeccah (Gen. 24); also the passage, so characteristic of Isaac: "And he digged again the wells of water, which they had digged in the days of Abraham his father . . . and he called their names after the names by which his father had called them" (Gen. 26:18).

The story then turns to the sons of Isaac: Jacob and Esau. In Jacob the line of the promise is continued. We see him first at his home in Beersheba. Then, having deceived his brother (Gen. 27), he flees to Haran (Gen. 28). After many years he returns to Canaan, having been blessed with a large family of children (Gen. 29–31). Finally, at the invitation of his beloved son Joseph, whom he had given up as dead, he goes down into Egypt (Gen. 46).

Perhaps the two most striking and revealing events of all those connected with Jacob are *The Vision at Bethel,* which occurred on his flight to Haran (Gen. 28:10-22) and his *Wrestling with the Angel* (Gen. 32:22-32) on the return. In both of these happenings the Coming Christ is clearly revealed; which is evident when one compares Genesis 28:12 with John 1:51; also Genesis 32:28 with Hosea 12:3, 4.

4. From the Descent into Egypt to the Exodus

Date: 1879-1449 B.C.
Scripture: Gen. 37-50

The son who caused his father to go down into Egypt was Joseph. His story will live forever. In *Act I* of this real drama he is a good but pampered boy, his father's darling, a telltale hated by his brothers. They sell him to a band of Ishmaelites. He becomes a slave; then, prisoner in far away Egypt. *Act II*: He is sanctified through suffering, becomes genuinely interested in the sorrows of two fellow prisoners and interprets their dreams. One of the two, Pharaoh's butler, restored to honor, tells the king about Joseph, the dream-interpreter. *Act III*: Joseph, having interpreted Pharaoh's dreams, has become prime minister of Egypt. His very affliction has brought him there. And now the home life of long ago seems to have been transplanted to Egypt: his brothers and his father are with him again. but no, *transplanted* is not the word; the home circle has been trans*formed* gloriously: the aged father has dropped his former favoritism; the brothers, their envy; and Joseph, his self-centeredness. Joseph's life is a sermon. Its text is II Corinthians 4:17; or perhaps better, Genesis 50:20. And the sermon has three points! Read Genesis 37-50.

For a while all is well in Goshen. Israel is dwelling in the best part of Egypt. The Shepherd Kings (Hyksos), Asiatic intruders, treat their pastoral brethren with great kindness. But when the nationalistic spirit of Egypt reasserts itself and the never-to-be-forgotten Eighteenth Dynasty begins to exercise its tremendous power, the Hyksos are driven from the country. Consequently, for Israel matters take a turn for the worse. A "new"–not just "another"–king rules over Egypt, one who "knew not Joseph" (Exod. 1:8).

There were probably many pharaohs who afflicted Israel during the sixteenth and the first half of the fifteenth centuries B.C. The list may include: Amosis I, Amenhotep I, Thothmes I, Thothmes II, especially the great, cruel, and able Thothmes III (during whose reign the frontiers of Egypt's empire reached their greatest expansion, extending from the Libyan desert to the Tigris and the Euphrates), and finally, Amenhotep II.

It was in this time of great affliction that Jehovah raised up Moses for the deliverance of his people. Pharaoh's refusal to let Israel go brought upon Egypt the Ten Plagues (Exod. 7-12). These plagues, miracles in the fullest sense of the term, closely followed the order of nature and probably lasted from the rise of the Nile in June until the following April. They proved Jehovah's sovereign power over the gods of the Egyptians. The Nile (whose waters were turned into blood) was considered a god. The frogs (which came swarming into kitchens and bedrooms) received divine honors. The cattle (afflicted by later plagues) were the objects of worship. The sun (darkened during the ninth plague) was by the Egyptians identified with deity. And the crown prince (slain during the last plague, Exod. 12:29) was believed to be in very close touch with heaven. Over all these gods Jehovah triumphed!

Who was this pharaoh of the Exodus, whose firstborn son was slain, and when did he reign? If those are correct who, on the basis of recent archaeological discoveries in the *Jericho* region, accept a date in the neighborhood of 1400 B.C. for the fall of that ancient city, Israel must have left Egypt sometime during the decade 1450-1440. (At this point it is in order to remind the reader of the fact that the date of the Exodus given in our Chronological Table, 1449 B.C., is based on what is probably "round figure calculation," i.e., on the *twelve forties* which, according to I Kings 6, elapsed between the Exodus and the building of Solomon's temple. The *exact* year cannot be determined with certainty. Garstang, the archaeologist, regards 1447 as the probable date.) It is evident, therefore, that both the Bible and archaeology seem to point to Amenhotep II as the Pharaoh of the Exodus.[5] It is a remarkable fact that the death of his firstborn son is implied, though not definitely stated, in Egyptian records.

---

5. F. Kenyon, *The Bible and Archaeology*, p. 189. J. P. Free favors "1440 B. C. or a little earlier" as the date of the Exodus, *Archaeology and Bible History*,

In the story of Israel's oppression one clearly discerns "the great red dragon" of Revelation 12, trying to destroy the Coming Christ. But no Pharaoh would ever be able to wipe out God's promise. When Jacob was about to be gathered to his fathers—long before the oppression—he had pronounced blessings upon his sons (Gen. 48:49). One of these prophecies, the greatest of them all, was as follows:

The scepter shall not depart from Judah
Nor the ruler's staff from between his feet,
Until Shiloh come;
And to him shall the obedience of the peoples be.

Adam-Seth-Noah-Shem-Abraham-Isaac-Jacob-Judah ... that was the line!

5. From the Exodus to the Death of Joshua

Date: 1449-1388 B.C.
Scripture: Exod.; Num.; Josh.

It has become evident that the Old Testament points forward to the coming of the Christ and definitely prepares the way for his arrival. There are, as it were, four lines which, running through the Old Testament, converge at Bethlehem: the *historical, typological, psychological,* and *prophetical.*

By the *historical* preparation we mean that again and again the forces of evil direct their attack against the people of God, endeavoring to render impossible the fulfilment of God's promise with respect to the Coming Christ (Gen. 3:15, etc.); and that whenever the need is highest, help is nighest: man's extremity is God's opportunity. Thus, when man falls (Gen. 3:6), and involves himself and the race in ruin, the Mother Promise (Gen. 3:15) resounds through the glens of Eden. Again, when "the wickedness of man is great in the earth, and every imagination of the thoughts of his heart is only evil continually" (Gen. 6:5), God sends the Flood and makes a new beginning with the family of Noah. When his posterity turns away from the only Living God to serve other gods (Josh. 24:2), Abraham is made the heir of the promise. And when Israel, out of whom the Christ is to come forth as to the flesh, is about to perish in Egypt, God brings it out "by a mighty hand and by an outstretched arm" (Deut. 5:15).

---

p. 88. Among those who reject the Bible there are many who are either silent about this new archaeological evidence or regard it as being of slight significance.

Having observed the Passover and consecrated their firstborn to Jehovah, Israel departs from Egypt (Exod. 12-14). When the people are pursued by Pharaoh and face the Red Sea, "Jehovah causes the sea to go back by a strong east wind all the night, and makes the sea dry land, and the waters are divided" (Exod. 14:21). The Egyptian host perishes in the sea, but Israel marches on toward Sinai!

Jehovah, in his great mercy, also feeds his people with *manna,* and he gives them a goodly supply of *water* from the *smitten rock* (Exod. 16:17). Here we have the *typological* preparation, for these things are types of Christ. In the light of the New Testament—and that is the only correct method of reading the Old Testament—this cannot be denied. That the water from the smitten rock is a type of the Saviour is clear from such passages as John 7:37: "If any man thirst, let him come unto me and drink," and I Cor. 10:4: ". . . . and the rock was Christ." The manna, too, was a type (John 6:32, 35). And so also was the Passover lamb (John 1:29); the pillar of fire (Exod. 13:21; John 8:12); the tabernacle, its various pieces of furniture, the entire sacrificial ritual (see the Epistle to the Hebrews); and finally, the serpent lifted up (Num. 21:8; cf. John 3:14). In fact, the desert journey, from the bondage of Egypt, to the Rest of Canaan, under the leadership of Moses and Joshua, is a type of our salvation from sin and our entrance into heavenly Rest through the work of Christ (Heb. 4).

The *psychological* preparation points to the fact that during the entire Old Dispensation one truth is brought home with increasing clarity: in his own strength man can never achieve true happiness or salvation. The bringing about of this conviction was one of the chief objectives of the giving of the Law at Sinai (Gal. 3:24). If man is ever to be saved, Another will have to save him. That Other One is the Christ.

This brings us, finally, to the *prophetical* preparation. Also by means of direct prophecies the coming of Christ, his work, suffering, and consequent glory had been announced. We have already taken note of Genesis 3:15; 9:26; 22:18; 28:10-14; 49:10. To this we would now add Deuteronomy 18:15-19: ". . . I will raise them up a prophet from among their brethren. . . ."

It was Christ himself—alive according to the Spirit even during the Old Dispensation, though not yet incarnate—who prepared the way for his own incarnation. In fact, that glorious event was most beautifully foreshadowed toward the close of the period which we are now discussing. He appeared to Joshua in the form of The Prince of *Jehovah's Hosts* (Josh. 5:13-6:5). After all, it was he himself who led his people to Canaan, and Joshua was his *servant* (Josh. 24:29).

We now give an outline of the story from Sinai to Joshua's Death. It should be compared with the outlines of Exodus, p. 213, Numbers, p. 217, and Joshua, pp. 222-223.

I. Israel is consecrated at Sinai (Exod. 20-40). Preparations for leaving Sinai (Num. 1-9).

II. The people journey from Sinai to the Plains of Moab. This is a story of repeated sin and resulting failure, until Jehovah, in his grace, causes the serpent to be lifted up. (Num. 10-21).
   A. From Sinai to Kadesh (Num. 10-14).
   B. From Kadesh to Kadesh again (Num. 15-19).
   C. From Kadesh to the Plains of Moab (Num. 20, 21), including the Lifting up of the Serpent, and the Conquest of E. Palestine).

III. They are given the victory over the Midianites in the Plains of Moab (Num. 22-36).

IV. Jehovah causes them to *enter* W. Palestine—the crossing of the Jordan (Josh. 1-5).

V. He causes them to *conquer* W. Palestine (Josh. 6-12).
   A. Central Campaign (Josh. 6:8)
   B. Southern Campaign (Josh. 9, 10).
   C. Northern Campaign (Josh. 11, 12).

VI. He causes them to *inherit* W. Palestine (Josh. 13-22).

VII. Joshua, in his farewell address, emphasizes Israel's resulting obligation to serve and love Jehovah; Joshua's death (Josh. 23, 24).

6. From the Death of Joshua to the Accession of Saul

Date: 1388-1052 B.C.
Scripture: Judg.; I Sam. 1-7

For the length of this period see p. 61.

This is the Period of the Judges: Othniel, Ehud, Shamgar, Deborah and Barak, Gideon, Tola, Jair, Jephtha, Ibzan, Elon, Abdon, Samson, Eli, and Samuel. The judgeships of all except the last two are discussed in the Book of Judges. For the story of Eli and Samuel we must turn to I Samuel.

The "judges" were deliverers and temporary rulers. Their authority was in no sense hereditary: they were not *kings*. Moreover, their sway was not nationwide. Deborah and Barak exercised authority over Ephraim, Manasseh, Benjamin, Naphthali, Zebulon, and Issachar; Gideon, over Manasseh, Naphthali, Zebulon, Asher, and subsequently also over Ephraim; Jephtha, over Gad and Mansseh. And even Samuel, though, in a sense, a judge over all Israel from Dan even to Beer-sheba—his spiritual and political influence was nationwide—(I Sam. 3:20)—actually "ruled" over a very small territory: Benjamin and the adjacent region of Ephraim (I Sam. 7:15-17).

If this is borne in mind it will also become evident that these judges did not all follow one another chronologically; see p. 61. Some "judged" simultaneously, one over this region; the other over that district or combination of tribes.

The Period of the Judges is a period of probation. Israel rejoiced in the fulfilment of God's promises; it had received both an abundant posterity and a country to dwell in. Jehovah, moreover, had given his law to Israel and all the necessary regulations for the religious and civil affairs of the nation. He had also assigned a specific task: the expulsion of the Canaanites, whose measure of iniquity was full. To this task the Lord had added the promise, "I will be with you." He had established in Israel the purest theocracy, and had placed the symbol of his presence, the ark, at Shiloh. Hence, Israel was given the opportunity to show its gratitude to God and its willingness to meet its covenant obligations. In this task Israel failed again and again. Hence, the story here recorded is a constant cycle: Relapse, Retribution, Repentance, Rescue.

Israel's relapse into sin is always followed by oppression, whether from the side of Mesopotamia or Moab or Philistia or Northern Palestine or Media or Ammon or a combination, e.g., Philistia and Ammon, each foe attacking the region nearest to it. By means of its repeated spiritual failure Israel was gradually made conscious of the need of outside deliverance. The pious began to look forward to the fulfilment of God's wonderful promise (Gen. 3:15, etc.).

By far the greatest of all the judges was Samuel. Given in answer to prayer, he was himself a man of prayer. A nation assembled to hear him pray. In I Samuel 7:5 we read, "Gather all Israel to Mizpah, and I will pray for you to Jehovah." And when the people in their ingratitude and sinful impatience rejected him and asked for a king, "like all the nations" (I Sam. 8:4, 5), then this truly great man did not take revenge but, having denounced the sin, answered, "Far be it from me that I should sin against Jehovah in ceasing to pray for you; but I will instruct you in the good and right way" (I Sam. 12:23). He anointed Saul; afterward, David. Significant is I Sam. 25:1: "And Samuel died; and all Israel gathered themselves together, and lamented him."

Is it possible not to see in Samuel a type of the Christ? The comparison is true from many aspects. Observe the parallel:

With respect to Samuel we read, "And the child Samuel grew on, and increased in favor both with Jehovah, and also with men" (I Sam. 2:26).

With reference to Christ we read, "And the child grew, and waxed strong, filled with wisdom; and the grace of God was upon him . . . And Jesus advanced in wisdom and stature, and in favor with God and men" (Luke 2:40, 52).

When Samuel functions as a "seer," or prophet; when, in addition, he offers sacrifice and prays for the people; and when beside all this he "judges" Israel, do we not see in him a clear type of Christ, the Prophet, Priest, and King?

7. From the Accession of Saul to the Division of the Kingdom

Date: 1052-932 B.C.
Scripture: I Sam. 8-31; II Sam.; I Kings 1-11

Saul and David were Israel's first two kings. Their lives run parallel to a certain extent. In both we see early success followed by grievous sins. But at this point the similarity ends. In the case of Saul sin leads to embitterment and to the persecution of God's anointed. In the case of David sin is followed by genuine sorrow; hence, pardon, though the consequences of having gone astray do not remain absent. See the outline of I and II Samuel on pp. 224-225.

Saul's "glory"–if it may be called by that name–is that of a meteor flashing for a moment; then, streaking through the sky to its doom. David's glory is that of the sun "as a bridegroom coming out of his chamber."

Saul's Early Success. His victory over the Ammonites (I Sam. 11) was, in a sense, the payment of an old debt. Saul's own tribe, Benjamin, owed its self-perpetuation, to some extent, to the virgins of Jabesh-gilead (Judg. 21). Saul's great victory, his remarkable success, strengthened the bond between himself and his people, who were now all the more ready to ratify the choice of their new leader (I Sam. 11:14).

His Grievous Sins. When Saul "took over," the country was in the hands of the Philistines (I Sam. 9:16; cf. 13:6). In the migration about the year 1200 B.C. they had left their island, Crete, and crossed the sea to S. W. Asia Minor, and had traveled east, then south to their "present" territory along the east coast of the Mediterranean, just west of Israel (consult a map). To be sure, even before this time there were Philistines in *Palestine* (named after them), but the great migration left Crete about the year 1200. Israel was suffering grievously under the yoke of these "uncircumcised." In this emergency it was Saul's noble son Jonathan who brought deliverance. It was he who not only destroyed the Philistine garrison (I Sam. 13:3) but also, by means of a most daring strategy, a deed of faith (I Sam. 14:6), broke through the three-pronged iron ring (I Sam. 13:17, 18) and re-established contact between Benjamin and the northern tribes. Saul himself, acting in unbelief and arrogance, had refused to wait for Samuel's arrival; and, like a typical Oriental monarch who regards himself to be the highest priest, had offered sacrifice (I Sam. 13:9). (It is natural to suppose that Samuel's coming had been delayed by the encirclement of which we spoke).

At another occasion, when Jehovah commanded Saul to destroy the Amalekites, so that their punishment might stand out as a Divine retribution for their sins and not as a mere plunder-reprisal (I Sam. 15:1-3), Saul disobeyed, thereby fully earning the divine rejection (I Sam. 15:7-9).

His Lack of Genuine Sorrow. "I have sinned," was Saul's reply to Samuel's reproof, but this sorrow was not genuine (I Sam. 15:30). His one great ambition now was to slay Jehovah's newly anointed one; namely, David. In this endeavor he failed. Then, at the end of his life, when he was forced once more to turn his attention to the Philistines for the most decisive battle of all, he was defeated. He falls upon his sword and dies. His decapitated body is fastened to the wall of Bethshan. The same lot befell his sons (I Sam. 31). The inhabitants of Jabesh-gilead, recalling Saul's kindness to them, recovered the bodies.

Saul's life points forward to Christ, by way of contrast. This becomes particularly striking when one compares I Samuel 8:10-18 with John 10:28 and Galatians 2:20. With respect to Saul we read,

". . . he will *take* your sons . . . and he will *take* your daughters . . . and he will *take* your fields . . . and he will *take* the tenth of your seed . . . and he will *take* your menservants, and your maid-servants . . . and he will *take* the tenth of your flocks . . . And you shall cry out in that day because of your king whom you have chosen you for yourselves, but for Jehovah will not answer you in that day." On the other hand, Christ said, "And I *give* to them eternal life; and they shall never perish; and no one shall snatch them out of my hand." Paul calls him "the Son of God, who loved me, and *gave* himself up for me."

The failure of Saul's reign, following hard upon Israel's failure during the Period of the Judges, underscored the necessity of the coming Deliverer.

The prelude to David's reign is interwoven with the life of King Saul and is recorded in I Samuel. First, there was the David-Goliath contest. The challenge to a duel or single combat, recorded in I Samuel 17, will not surprise us in a Philistine, a man whose people hailed from Crete. In the early history of Greece and Crete such a method of determining the will of the gods was not unusual. Consult Homer's *Iliad.* When David had triumphed over the swaggering bully, the women sang: "Saul has slain his thousands, And David his *ten thousands*" (I Sam. 18:7).

This is the key verse of all that follows in I Samuel. The verse is repeated in I Samuel 22:11 and 29:5. The Philistines never forgot it. Neither did Saul. Filled with envy, he tried to kill David. First David remained near his headquarters at Gibeah, while Saul attempted to destroy him by his own hand (I Sam. 18:11) or by the hand of the Philistines (18:17) or of Jonathan—who, however, was most unwilling—(19:1), or of Saul's servants (19:1, 11). Later David fled to the region of the south, wandering from west to east and back again. Perhaps, the most beautiful passage in this entire story is that which records the self-forgetfulness of Jonathan, the crown-prince (I Sam. 23:16-18). Upon Saul's tragic death, David became king.

David's Early Success. As a result of the battle of Gilboa the Philistine yoke was again heavy upon Israel (I Sam. 31:7). David's little kingdom was confined to the south. His capital was Hebron. Meanwhile, Saul's son Ish-bosheth (really, Esh-baal) ruled over Gilead in his capital, Mahanaim (II Sam. 2:8-11). When Ish-bosheth's general, Abner, became vexed over an insult and tranferred his master's kingdom to David, and Saul's son was murdered, David became king over all Israel (II Sam. 5:4, 5). He made Jerusalem his religious and political capital, having captured the stronghold from the Jebusites (II Sam. 5:6-10).

The conquest of Jebus suggests an important date in the story of the formation of the books of the Old Testament. It is clear that the first seven (probably eight) books came into existence before the fortress was taken; for, when *Joshua* and *Judges* were brought to completion, it was still held by the Jebusites, as is clear from Joshua 15:63 and Judges 1:21. Now, in these books there are many clear references to the *Pentateuch.* Hence, when we assign the date 1450-1000 B.C. to Genesis-Judges (and probably Ruth), we cannot be far from the truth. See, for these books, pp. 212-224, 296.

It is clear, therefore, that David had access to these sacred writings. He was guided by the teaching contained in this glorious heritage. It showed him how to conduct his government to the glory of God. It instilled in his heart a deep reverence for Jehovah, for his law and the symbol of his presence, the ark of the covenant.

David *finally* succeeded in bringing the ark to "Zion." He made preparations for the building of the Temple, a project which was to be carried out by his great son Solomon (II Sam. 6:7). Having defeated the Jebusites, he also gained a decisive victory over the Philistines. He took out of their hands "the bridle of the mother city" (II Sam. 8:1).

His Grievous Sins. It was while David's general, Joab, carried on the war against the Ammonites, and was engaged in the siege of Rabbah, that the king committed adultery with Bathsheba and caused her husband to perish in battle (II Sam. 11). In order to obtain a true estimate of the despicable character of his double sin, one should study carefully verses 8-10 and 13. These "minor" details, so important for the proper understanding of the story, are often ignored.

If anyone desires to make a list of the recorded instances of questionable or, at times, downright wicked behavior on the part of David, let him consult the following passages: I Samuel 25:43; II Samuel 5:13; 8:2; 11; 12:31(let us hope that the milder of the two possible interpretations is correct); 21:9 (cf. I Sam. 24:21, 22; I Kings 2:5-9). The record of David's life ends with the word *blood* in I Kings 2:9, 10.

But there is another side to the story. Therefore, see also the following passages: I Samuel 17:45-47; 24:6; 26:6-12; II Samuel 1:23; 7:18-29; 9; 12:13 (and Ps. 51); 18:5, 33; 23:5.

His Genuine Sorrow. Saul's religion was "outward." It consisted of external sacrifices, not inner obedience. His "sorrow" also was an outward sorrow. *David's* religion is that of the heart. His sorrow is genuine. He is, after all, the man after God's heart. Nevertheless, though pardoned, the results of his sin begin to manifest themselves: his own failings reappear in his children.

When, by means of a touching parable, Nathan the prophet had pictured the king's sin under the guise of someone else's imagined crime, David had said: "He shall restore the lamb *fourfold*." One author points out that David, from whose house the sword does not depart, loses *four* sons: the child of Bathsheba (II Sam. 12:18), Amnon (13:29), the rebellious son Absalom (18:15), and Adonijah (I Kings 2:25).

For a true estimate of David's character one should read II Samuel 23, especially verse 5. And then, those beautiful psalms in which the Holy Spirit has poured a meaning which even the psalmist himself did not fully fathom. They point forward to the Christ, e.g., 8, 16, 22, 31, etc.

And now Solomon! A certain poet has said:

Rising, Shining, and Declining
Is the theme of every day.

When we divide the reign of Solomon in accordance with these three words, we do justice to the record of Scripture, and one is not apt to forget what he has learned.

Rising. It was a strong realm which Solomon inherited. And he made it stronger still. Moreover, he received from Jehovah an understanding heart, and riches and honor besides. He centralized his government and gave to it a strong organization.

Shining. He made a covenant with Hiram, king of Tyre, and with the building material thus obtained, erected a splendid temple for Jehovah and dedicated it. This was the crowning work of his reign. In this temple the Lord himself manifested his presence, so that it became a type of the Incarnation.

Declining. But, though warned, (I Kings 9:6-9), Solomon allowed his many foreign wives (11:1) to lead him astray. Southeast of Jerusalem, on the Mount of Offence—the exact peak is unknown—the king built shrines in honor of heathen deities. He did it for business reasons and in order to please his foreign wives. And they "turned away his heart after other gods." His soul was no longer "completely" consecrated to Jehovah. On the basis of Nehemiah 13:26, and also for other reasons, we believe that God in his grace, cured him of these grievous sins.

When the Queen of Sheba beheld the glory of Solomon's kingdom and administration, her amazement knew no bounds: ". . . there was no more spirit in her" (I Kings 10:5). Nevertheless, the glory of his kingdom was only a dim adumbration of the glory which was to come, that of the Kingdom of Christ.

Moreover (as we shall see in the next chapter) at Solomon's death, the nation is disrupted. The United Kingdom becomes the Divided Kingdoms.

The Assyrian king, Ashurbanipal, depicted on a palace relief. The king is amusing himself hunting lions.
British Museum

7 From Intertribal Warfare to Immanuel's Birth

1. From Intertribal Warfare to the Fall of Samaria

Date: 932-722 B.C.
Scripture: I Kings 12—II Kings 17

a. 932-886: Intertribal Warfare

After Solomon's death Israel's representatives, gathered at Shechem, gave utterance to the grievances of the heavily burdened nation, in the following request, addressed to the crown-prince, Rehoboam:

> *Your father made our yoke grievous: now therefore lighten the grievous service of your father, and his heavy yoke upon us, lighter, and we will serve you* (I Kings 12: 1-5).

The king's answer is related in these words:

> *And the king answered the people roughly, and forsook the counsel of the old men which they had given him, and spoke to them after the counsel of the young men, saying, My father made your yoke heavy, but I will add to your yoke: my father chastised you with whips, but I will chastise you with scorpions,* (12:13, 14).

The result should have been foreseen by the new king:

> *And when all Israel saw that the king hearkened not to them, the people answered the king, saying, What portion*

> *have we in David? neither have we inheritance in the son of Jesse: to your tents, O Israel: now look to your own house, David"* (12:16).

Ahijah's prophecy had been fulfilled: Jeroboam, the Ephraemite, spokesman of the disgruntled majority, now begins to rule over ten tribes; Rehoboam, over the remaining two tribes of Judah and Benjamin.

This disruption was not born in a moment. It was the climax of a series of events which extended over a long period. Read Judges 5:14-18; II Samuel 2:1-4; 19:41-44; 20:1, 2. Rehoboam's absurd answer was the "breath which kindled the dead coal of wars." Did not the representatives of the contending tribes realize that there is strength in union? Did they not consider the fact that they were dividing themselves in order that the *great* nations–Assyria, Egypt, Babylonia–might rule over them? Did they not ponder the prospect that the *smaller* bordering nations which had been brought into bondage by David would rise in rebellion as soon as they knew that the balance of power had been disturbed?

How deplorable, this disruption! Gone was the political unity, the strongly centralized government, which David had labored so strenuously to bring into being. Gone, too, the religious consolidation–*one* temple for *all* the tribes–which Solomon had added. The throne had lost its luster. The glory had departed!

That is one way of looking at it. While fully maintaining the true element in this appraisal we must not forget the *divine* point of view as stated in I Kings 11:12, 13; 12:15, 24b, and especially in 11:36. We read:

> I . . . *will rend . . . ; it was a thing brought about by* Jehovah . . . *this thing is of* me . . . *that David my servant may have a* lamp[posterity, cf. I Kings 15:4] *always before me in Jerusalem.*

It was God himself who tore asunder . . . in order that he might save. The nation was "broken down" that grace might "break through." We have here another instance of that series of *separations* by means of which Jehovah chooses for himself a certain minority in order that he may use it for the realization of his Messianic program. Solomon's spirit of compromise with respect to many foreign gods was beginning to exert its sinister influence upon the people. Therefore, a separation had again become necessary, just as in the case of Abraham and for the same reason. This separation was to be followed, in course of time, by the Assyrian and the Babylonian captivities. Then Judah will serve one God, and will make propaganda for its monotheistic worship among the Gentiles. For many of the latter the road to salvation will lead from polytheism by way of monotheism to Christianity.

The war between the two kingdoms, the ten tribes over against the two, amounted at times to border skirmishes; at other times, to open conflict (I Kings 14:30; 15:6). In Judah Rehoboam was prevented from carrying out his designs against Israel. He was warned by a prophet: "You shall not go up, nor fight against your brothers" (I Kings 12:24). Besides, he suffered shameful defeat at the hands of Egypt and its allies (II Chron. 12). Abijah, however, waged war against Jeroboam and took away some of his cities (II Chron. 13). On the other hand, Baasha of Israel attacked Asa of Judah (II Chron. 16). In both of these wars between Israel and Judah the latter was in league with Syria. This military alliance was contrary to the will of Jehovah (II Chron. 16), whose prophet rebuked Asa, and reminded him of his victory over the Ethiopians at a time when he had placed his full reliance upon God.

Worse even than the political estrangement between Judah and Israel was the religious alienation. The story is told in the following words:

> *And Jeroboam said in his heart, Now will the kingdom return to the house of David: if this people go up to offer sacrifices in the house of Jehovah at Jerusalem, then will the heart of this people turn again to their lord, even unto Rehoboam king of Judah. Whereupon the king took counsel, and made two calves of gold . . . and he set the one in Bethel, and the other put he in Dan* (I Kings 12:25 ff.).

b. 886-836: House of Omri

Soon after the establishment of the House of Omri, in the year 886, a new period commences for both kingdoms. Asa's son Jehoshaphat makes peace with Omri's son Ahab (I Kings 22:44). The political and military constellation changes. No longer is Judah in league with Syria in opposition to Israel, but Judah and Israel have become allies. Again and again their kings fight side by side, especially against Syria. See I Kings 22 (Jehoshaphat and Ahab against

Syria), II Kings 3 (Jehoshaphat and Joram against Moab), II Kings 8:25-29 (Ahaziah and Joram against Syria).

The two royal houses of Judah and Israel not only form an alliance; they *merge* through intermarriage: Jehoshaphat's son Jehoram is married to the monstrously wicked Athaliah, daughter of spoiled Ahab and idolatrous Jezebel. This Jezebel was a child of Ethbaal, king of Sidon, a former priest of Astarte (I Kings 16:31). She swayed her husband at will. She was not only an ardent worshiper of Baal but also an intolerant opponent of all other religions. She put to death many prophets of Jehovah (I Kings 18:4-13) and brought upon herself and her family a terrible curse (21:23). She was the evil genius of her weak husband Ahab, and also of her children. She tried to bring about a religious revolution, changing a nation of *nominal* worshipers of Jehovah (under the symbolism of a calf) into one of all-out idolaters. In the kingdom of *Israel* two of her *sons,* Ahaziah and Joram, successively occupied the throne. Both were wicked (I Kings 22:51-53; II Kings 1); yet, there was a difference: compare I Kings 22:52 with II Kings 3:2. Over the kingdom of *Judah* Jezebel's *daughter* Athaliah wielded the scepter; first as queen-consort, Jehoram being the king; then, as queen-mother, her son, Ahaziah occupying the throne for only one year; and finally, as queen-dowager, supreme ruler of the nation.

These were the days of the prophets Elijah and Elisha. Their stories, recorded in I Kings 17–II Kings 13, will live forever. The former predicted the drought as a divine judgment upon Ahab and Jezebel and their wicked followers: "As Jehovah, the God of Israel liveth, before whom I stand, there shall not be dew nor rain these years, but according to my word" (I Kings 17:1). The story of the contest on Mount Carmel, (I Kings 18) is too well known to require repetition. Among the many miracles performed by Elijah's successor, Elisha, those of the increase of the widow's oil, the raising of the Shunamite's son, and the healing of Naaman's leprosy (II Kings 4), are perhaps the most familiar.

For Israel the end of the dynasty of Omri came in the year 842, when Jehu, an army-captain, killed Joram with an arrow sent with great force from his bow. Ahaziah, king of Judah, was also smitten. And Jezebel, by Jehu's order, was hurled from a window to her death. In their destruction a divine curse was fulfilled (I Kings 21:17-26, cf. also 22:37, 38; II Kings 9:21-37).

For Judah, however, the real change occurred six years later; i.e., about the year 836. From 842-836 wicked Athaliah ruled supreme. In order that she might have absolute power she conceived in her heart to destroy all the seed of David. The coming of the Mediator in human form was threatened. The "dragon" of Revelation 12 was standing in front of "the woman." His wrath was kindled against her "child." It seemed that this time he would be fully successful: "Now when Athaliah the mother of Ahaziah saw that her son was dead, she arose and destroyed all the seed royal." Destroyed *all the seed royal*! Of course, if *all* the seed royal is destroyed, then the Christ cannot be born as the legal son of David, the heir of his royal splendor. Then God's plan is frustrated. Then the promise has failed. Athaliah destroyed *all* the seed royal. That is, she *thought* she did! Read the next line (II Kings 11:1, 2 ff): "But Jehosheba took Jehoash, the son of Ahaziah, and stole him away from among the king's sons that were slain, even him and his nurse, and put them in a bed-chamber; and they hid him from Athaliah, so that he was not slain."

How wonderful are God's ways! How marvelous his providence! By and by we see Jehoash again. And upon his head there is a crown. We hear people shouting, "Long live the king!" The promise is saved. Christ will be born of David's line, according to prophecy, (II Sam. 7:12, 13). Therefore, we read in Matthew 1:8: "And Joram [i.e., Jehoram of Judah] begat Uzziah." Yes, by way of Ahaziah. *Jehoash*, and Amaziah!

c. 836-786: Hazael's Oppression

On the day when Jehoash was made king, Athaliah was slain. For Judah a new era began with the destruction of the worship of Baal and the repair of Jehovah's temple (II Kings 12:1-16). However, all was not well with Judah and Israel during this period. In both kingdoms the majority did not worship Jehovah *from the heart*. Therefore, Jehovah raised up an oppressor in order to punish the people (I Kings 19:17; II Chron. 24:24) His name was Hazael, king of Syria, a most bitter enemy of both Israel and Judah. When his program of destruction had been revealed to Elisha, the latter had wept. In II Kings 8:12-13 we read:

> . . . *And the man of God wept. And Hazael said, Why does my lord weep? And he answered, Because I know the evil you will do to the children of Israel: their strongholds you will set on fire, and their young men wilt thou slay with the*

sword, and you will dash to pieces their little ones, and rip up their women with child. And Hazael said, But what is your servant who is but a dog, that he should do this great thing? And Elisha answered, Jehovah has shown me that you shall be king over Syria.

Hazael was a scourge for both Judah and Israel. First, for Judah (II Kings 12:17, 18; II Chron. 24:23, 24), whose king Jehoash deserved this punishment, for his worship of Jehovah was outward and formal: "he did that which was right in the eyes of Jehovah *all his days wherein Jehoiada the priest instructed him*" (II Kings 12:2); afterward it was this same Jehoash, who, when rebuked because of his departure from Jehovah, "remembered not the kindness which Jehoiada . . . had done to him, but slew his son [Zechariah]" (II Chron. 24:22; Matt. 23:35). See pp. 19, 164.

Secondly, also for Israel: Jehu of Israel was not any better than Jehoash of Judah. Though outwardly the deeds of this ferocious ex-captain were good—he destroyed Baal-worship in Israel (II Kings 10:25-30—yet, the *motive* was far from pure, as is clearly stated in verse 31. And Jehu's son Jehoahaz walked in the ways of his father. Hence, we are not surprised to read:

"And the anger of Jehovah was kindled against Israel, and he delivered them into the hand of Hazael, king of Syria, and into the hand of Benhadad, the son of Hazael continually" (II Kings 13:3; cf. 14:26). And even though affairs began to take a turn for the better in the days of Jehu's grandson Joash, yet the change did not become a *decisive* one until the days of Jeroboam II. See II Kings 13:14-19, especially verse 19b.

The period which we are studying ends very dismally: we see Amaziah, the son of Jehoash of Judah, at war with Joash of Israel. The latter, who had made an earnest attempt to avoid this strife among brethren, was victorious (II Chron. 25).

During these melancholy days God-fearing people must have turned again and again to the living oracles of Jehovah. In I and II Samuel, which had been added to the list of written books (see p. 224), they could read the admonitions of Samuel. They could see in the life of King Saul the results of departure from the law of Jehovah. They were able to assure themselves, by reading (or hearing) the story of David, that God rewards the man with a truly contrite heart. The tender love of Jehovah for his people was also revealed to them in the beautiful marriage symbolism of the Song of Songs (see pp. 296, 297-299).

d. 786-736: Glamor Period

In Judah this is the period of Uzziah, though during the latter part of his life he was king only in name, while his son Jotham was the actually ruling monarch. In Israel Jeroboam II began to rule in 786 and held sway during almost this entire period.

Uzziah succeeded in throwing off Judah's vassalage to Israel, and became very strong. He defeated the Philistines to the west as well as the Ammonites to the east, and greatly strengthened his army and the defenses of Jerusalem (II Chron. 26:1-15).

Jeroboam's military success was even greater. He greatly extended the boundaries of his realm, and not only held his own over against Syria but captured Damascus (II Kings 14:28). Did he fail to realize the meaning of a buffer state; i.e., that by too effectively weakening *Syria* he was simply paving the way for an invasion of Israel by *Assyria*? Assyria and Syria! These two were keeping each other busy so that the countries to the south were in no *immediate* danger of attack, and were well along on the *long* road that would lead to ultimate ruin. All that was needed was a really strong and energetic Assyria which would destroy the buffer state. And Jeroboam, in his blindness, is hastening the day!

At present, all is wonderful–*from the outside!* Great victories are being won by Israel–hastening Israel's doom! Judah "has rejected the law of Jehovah, and has not kept his statutes" (Amos 2:4). And Israel? Amos and Hosea tell us all about it (see pp. 229-238). Very religious is Israel. The people busy themselves with the art of inventing musical instruments *just like David.* They use these instruments to sing their . . . "idle songs," the glamor-age equivalent of modern jazz; while they relax on couches inlaid with ivory and covered with tapestries from the looms of Damascus (Amos 6:4-6). Religious? Yes, indeed! They bring offerings galore, and tithes every three days, because this pleases . . . *them*! Sacrifices in abundance . . . at the wrong place, from the wrong motive (Amos 4:4, 5). Meanwhile, the poor are not neglected. No, they are exploited and oppressed, while the rich eat dainties out of season and drink wine by the bowlful (Amos 4:1; 5:11, 12; 6:4; 8:4-6). Priests are in evidence everywhere . . . especially in the company of robbers (Hos. 6:9). The sabbath, too, is being kept, and so are the religious feast days—*outwardly*. While these days are being *observed*, the people are saying in their hearts:

> *When will the new moon be gone, that we may sell grain? and the sabbath, that we may set forth wheat, making the ephah small, and the shekel great, and dealing falsely with balances of deceit; that we may buy the poor for silver, and the needy for a pair of shoes, and sell the refuse of the wheat* (Amos 8:5, 6)*?*

A certain author characterizes this age as "the last burst of glory before total extinction." We disagree. Take it from any aspect: political, economic, social, and you will have to admit that this was not the *glory age*. It was the *glamor* age, during which Israel was like a beautiful polished piece of furniture, but inside the termites were at work! *The period may be said to end with Uzziah's death in 736* (cf. Isa. 6:1).

e. 736-722: Growth of Assyria; Fall of Samaria

The process of inner decay may fell a tree. A violent storm may accomplish the same result. When the two forces cooperate—the one from within, the other from without—the tree is doomed. So it was with Israel during the period 736-722—inner decay, as we have seen, and from without the storm, the growing power of Assyria capturing and annexing nation upon nation. We have called the period 736-686 *The Growth of Assyria*. To the next period, 686-636, we have assigned the title *Foreign Domination* (both political and religious). See p. 70. The "Foreign" means "Assyrian" in this case. Hence, the entire century, 736-636, is definitely the *Assyrian century*. The new Assyrian empire was established about the year 745 and lasted until 612 (in a sense, a few years longer). After 636 its decline was very rapid. The Assyrian kings who ruled during the period were the following:

Tiglath-pileser, 745-727; i.e., from the beginning of the reign of Menahem in Israel until about the beginning of the reign of Hezekiah in Judah.

Shalmaneser, 727-722; i.e., until the year of the fall of Samaria.

Sargon, 722-705; i.e., until *a century before* the battle of Carchemis and the beginning of the Babylonian world empire under Nebuchadnezzar (in the year 605).

Sennacherib, 705-681; i.e., until after the close of Hezekiah's reign.

Esar-haddon 680-668; i.e., during the early years of the reign of Manasseh.
Ashurbanipal, 668-626; i.e., during the remainder of the reign of Manasseh, the reign of Amon, and the early part of the reign of Josiah.

In Israel, Jeroboam's son Zechariah represented the "fourth generation" after Jehu. When after a reign of only six months he was killed by Shallum, the prophecy of II Kings 10:30 was fulfilled: "And Jehovah said unto Jehu, Because you have done well in executing that which is right in my eyes, and have done to the house of Ahab according to all that was in my heart, your sons in the fourth generation shall sit on the throne of Israel." Of the six kings who followed Jeroboam II upon the throne of Israel only one was succeeded by his son; namely, Menahem, who paid tribute to Tiglath-pileser.

Pekah, the man who assassinated Menahem's son Pekahiah, launched an anti-Assyrian campaign. In this he was assisted by Rezin of Syria. When Jotham's son Ahaz, of Judah, refused to cooperate, he was attacked by these two conspirators. Their threat was to destroy the seed of David and establish a king of their own choice, "even the son of Tabeel." These were the days of Isaiah and Micah. See pp. 241-246. What would become of the promise of Gen. 3:15; and especially that of II Sam. 7:12, 13, if this plan succeeded? Would Immanuel ever be born, as the son and legal heir of David? Everything was at stake. Isaiah is sent to Ahaz to admonish him to place his trust in Jehovah, and to ask for a sign of God's protection. When he refuses, feigning a pious excuse, he receives the answer: "Therefore the Lord himself will give you a sign: behold a virgin shall conceive, and bear a son, and shall call his name Immanuel." Isaiah 7:14 is shown by Matthew 1:22, 23, to refer to the virgin-birth of Christ. Compare also Isaiah 8:8; 9:6; and the entire 11th chapter; also see *N.T.C., Matthew*, pp. 133-144.

Ahaz, however, fails to heed Jehovah's admonition, and calls in the help of Assyria. The latter arrives, overturns Damascus in 732; annexes part of the kingdom of Israel in 730, taking the people into captivity (II Kings 15:29); and does not at all object, to put it mildly, when Pekah is murdered by Hoshea. When the latter, after first paying tribute to Assyria, transfers his allegiance to Egypt, Samaria is surrounded by the armies of Shalmaneser and after a long siege is taken by Sargon. The remaining people of Israel, with the exception of the very poor are driven forth from their country (II Kings

17:3-6) and carried away to "Assyria . . . Halah, and the Habor, the river of Gozan, and the cities of the Medes," where they could join their brothers who, eight years earlier, had been deported from the east of the Jordan and from the northern districts of Israel's territory (I Chron. 5:26). Meanwhile, foreigners (II Kings 17:24) are brought to Samaria and the surrounding towns. These intermarried with the Israelites who had been left behind. To this mixed population the name Samaritans was given. Read II Kings 17:34-41.

2. From the Fall of Samaria to the Fall of Jerusalem

Date: 722-586 B.C.
Scripture: II Kings 18-25

a. 722-686: **Fall of Samaria to the Death of Hezekiah** (see pp. 77-78).

No longer were there any buffer states between Assyria and Judah, for both Syria and Israel had been annexed by the great conquering world empire. Moreover, when in 705 Sargon was succeeded by Sennacherib, this very change caused the subjugated nations to the west of Assyria (proper) to rise in rebellion. Hence, we are not surprised to read in II Kings 18:13 that shortly before the year 700 "Sennacherib, king of Assyria, came up against all the fortified cities of Judah, and took them." According to an Assyrian inscription, a large multitude of people was deported at this time. If, as is probable, these Judean exiles were brought to the same general region—northern Media and northern Mesopotamia—to which also the ten tribes had been deported, the conclusion would seem to be warranted that the twelve tribes became amalgamated into *one* community.[1]

Sennacherib also sent an army to besiege Jerusalem. The great reformer-king, Hezekiah, in this hour of sore crisis, placed his reliance upon Jehovah. Jerusalem's case seemed hopeless, but Isaiah was sent by Jehovah to assure the king of a wonderful deliverance. This deliverance is described in Isaiah 37:36 ff.:

> *And the angel of Jehovah went forth, and smote in the camp of the Assyrians a hundred and fourscore and five*

1. We recommend the excellent book by A. Pieters, *The Ten Tribes in History and Prophecy.*

thousand; and when men arose early in the morning, behold, these were all dead bodies.

About this time the Chaldeans were beginning to challenge the power of Assyria, and were trying to obtain allies. They sent a delegation to Hezekiah. When the latter yielded to his pride and showed these men the contents of his armory, etc., Isaiah announced that all these things and also the remaining people of Judah would be carried away to this very Babylon which was now seeking confederates (Isa. 39). With the death of Hezekiah (in 686?) this period ends.

b. 686-636: Foreign Domination

The glorious reformation instituted by the devout king Hezekiah (II Chron. 29-31)[2] did not have a lasting effect. During the long reign of Hezekiah's son Manasseh images were set up all over the land, even in the very Temple of Jehovah (II Chron. 33:7). Those who refused to follow his wicked example were put to death. Jeremiah 15:4 contains this startling verdict: "And I will cause them to be tossed to and fro among all the kingdoms of the earth because of Manasseh, the son of Hezekiah, king of Judah, for that which he did in Jerusalem."[3] During the reign of this wicked king Assyria reached the zenith of its power. Both politically and religiously Judah was being dominated by this foreign empire. To the believing remnant of a nation thus enslaved the prophet Nahum announced the fall of Nineveh and the coming of a glorious era. See pp. 249-250.

c. 636-586: Fall of Judah

Though Manasseh repented in his old age, this conversion came too late to undo the evil which had been committed. His son Amon was a wicked king. His servants assassinated him, and the people placed his God-fearing son Josiah on the throne, (II Chron. 33:21-25). Accordingly, here begins a new era, a little before 636 B.C. These were the days of Zephaniah, the prophet. See pp. 251-252. While workmen were restoring the temple, "the book of the law of Jehovah by the hand of Moses," was found. See pp. 23-24. According to many, this was probably the book (scroll) of Deuteronomy; compare Deuteronomy 28 with II Kings 22: 13, 17, 19. That

---

2. W. M. Smith has written an interesting booklet on this reformation, *The Glorious Revival under King Hezekiah.*
3. Read the stirring sermon by C. G. Chappell, "A Good Man's Hell," in *Sermons on Biblical Characters.*

this book could not have been *written* during the reign of Josiah and then falsely represented as if it were a very old document which had just been found is clear to anyone who takes the time to read it. The contents do not fit the historical situation of Josiah's age. Read Deuteronomy 20; also 25:17ff. Many other references could be cited.

Josiah attempted to draw to Jerusalem and its environs all who loved Jehovah's law, whether they were living in Judah or in the territory of the former kingdom of Israel. In the battle of Megiddo the king received a mortal wound (II Chron. 35:20-37). His son Jehoahaz, the people's choice, was quickly removed by Pharaoh Necho, and replaced by the deposed king's brother, Jehoiakim. In the battle of Carchemish, 605, (see II Chron. 35:20, Jer. 46:2) Nebuchadnezzar of Babylon defeated Pharaoh Necho, and the seventy years of Babylonian dominion began (Jer. 25:1, 12; Dan. 9:1, 2).[4] It was at this time, or shortly afterward, that among others, Daniel and his friends were carried away to Babylon (Dan. 1:1). Habakkuk prophesied during the reign of the wicked Jehoiakim. See pp. 252-254. And so did Jeremiah, whose prophetic labors extended over a period of at least forty years, about 626-586.[5] It was this prophet's duty to predict the destruction of Judah by Babylon, as a divine punishment. But Jehoiakim, sitting in his winter palace and listening to the reading of Jeremiah's prophecies, burned the scroll on which they were recorded. It was rewritten, but a terrible curse upon Jehoiakim was added (Jer. 36). This curse was fulfilled when the king, placing his reliance upon Egypt, made an attempt to shake off the Babylonian yoke. After a reign of only three months (of the year 597) Jehoiachin, the young son of Jehoiakim, was deported to Babylon. A goodly number of nobles, priests, craftsmen, etc., were also carried away. In their company was the prophet Ezekiel (I Kings 24:14-16; Ezek. 33:21). On Jeremiah see pp. 257-264.

Zedekiah, a third son of Josiah, was Judah's last king. Disregarding the warnings of the prophets Jeremiah and Ezekiel, and placing his trust in Egypt, he rebelled against the king of Babylon. As a result, the Chaldean army came and destroyed Jerusalem, including Solomon's beautiful temple. Zedekiah's tragic end is vividly described in II Kings 25:4-7:

---

4. Dr. G. Ch. Aalders, in several of his writings, points out that the "seventy years" of which Jeremiah speaks (25:11, 12; 29:10) refer not to the length of the Babylonian captivity but to the length of the Babylonian sovereignty.
5. One of the finest books on Jeremiah is F. Werfel's *Hearken unto the Voice.*

And the king went by the way of the Arabah. But the army of the Chaldeans pursued after the king, and overtook him in the plains of Jericho; and all his army was scattered from him. Then they took the king, and carried him up unto the king of Babylon to Riblah; and they gave judgment upon him. And they slew the sons of Zedekiah before his eyes, and put out the eyes of Zedekiah, and bound him in fetters, and carried him to Babylon.

The people, except the poorest, were carried away to Babylon (II Kings 25:11). The deepest reason for the Babylonian captivity is given in II Chronicles 36:14 ff.:

Moreover, all the chiefs of the priests, and the people, trespassed very greatly after all the abominations of the nations; and they polluted the house of Jehovah which he had hallowed in Jerusalem. And Jehovah, the God of their fathers, sent to them by his messengers, rising up early and sending, because he had compassion on his people, and on his dwelling-place: but they mocked the messengers of God, and despised his words, and scoffed at his prophets, until the wrath of Jehovah arose against his people, till there was no remedy.

Jehovah did not take delight in the calamity of his people. When the Edomites, blood-relatives of the men of Judah, rejoiced in Jerusalem's fall, the prophet Obadiah was commissioned to announce Edom's doom. See pp. 264-265.

3. Babylonian Exile

Date: 586-536 B.C.
Scripture: II Kings 25;
II Chron. 36

In speaking about the Exile, it is well that we distinguish first of all between the Assyrian and the Babylonian. With respect to the former we should differentiate between (1) the deportation in the days of Pekah (II Kings 15:29); (2) of Hoshea (II Kings 17:3-6); and (3) of Hezekiah (II Kings 18:13; cf. Assyrian inscription). The first and the second concern the kingdom of the Ten Tribes; the third concerns Judah. With reference to the Babylonian Exile we distinguish between (1) the deportation which took place during the reign of Jehoiakim (Dan. 1:1); (2) the one which occurred at the close of the brief reign of Jehoiachin (II Kings 24:14-16); (3) another, at the close of Zedekiah's reign (II Kings 25:11); and (4) the one which is dated five years later (Jer. 52:30), i.e., about the year 581.

The total period of Babylonian exile—beginning with the deportations of 605 and 597 and ending in 536—may be divided as follows:[6]

First, there were **years of false hopefulness.** The early exiles were confident that conditions would soon change and that they would return to their land. Was not Jehovah's temple in Jerusalem still standing? Jeremiah sends a letter to these deluded individuals and tells them not to trust their false prophets, but to build houses and plant gardens, i.e., to plan for a long stay in the country of their exile. Read Jeremiah 29. Compare also Ezekiel 17:11-24.

Secondly, there were **years of hopelessness.** When in the year 586 Jerusalem fell and the temple was destroyed, when it seemed as if Jehovah had forsaken his people, and when many years after the fall of Jerusalem the restoration to honor of the prisoner Jehoiachin failed to result in total deliverance and return, dejection bordering on despair entered the hearts of the people. They said:

How shall we sing Jehovah's song
In a foreign land?
If I forget you, O Jerusalem,
Let my right hand forget her skill.
Let my tongue cleave to the roof of my mouth,
If I remember you not;
If I prefer not Jerusalem
Above my chief joy (Psalm 137:4-6).

Ezekiel is God's chosen vessel to comfort the exiles. See pp. 265-268. Daniel intercedes for them constantly and champions their cause. See pp. 307-309. Isaiah's prophecies, chapters 40-66, had been written with the express purpose of imparting consolation to all those exiles who remained faithful to the worship of Jehovah.

Thirdly, there arrived a **season of revived hopefulness** for those who availed themselves of the opportunity to return to their country, and also for those who, in spirit, accompanied them but were unable to do so literally (because of age or office), e.g., Daniel.

---

6. Cf. art. "Captivity" in *I.S.B.E.* and articles "Captivity" and "Dispersion" in *Westminster Dictionary of the Bible.*

For others the time of *indifference and amalgamation* had arrived. Babylonia to the south, Media and Mesopotamia to the north had become "home" to them. They intermarried with the people of the land and adopted their religion (Ezek. 20:31, 32).

The Babylonian Exile and the later Dispersion of the Jews among many nations must be viewed from a threefold aspect:

First, it was a *punishment for their sins* (II Chron. 36:14-17).

Secondly, it was a *means of sanctification for the remnant* (Ezek. 36:22-31). In this connection observe the deeply spiritual tone of Lamentations, e.g., 1:8, 18; 3:40, 41; 5:19-21. See pp. 300-301.

Thirdly, it was a *blessing for the nations in the midst of whom the remnant dwelt* (Mic. 5:7). Believers made propaganda for their worship of the one, true God (monotheism) and they proclaimed the Messianic Hope everywhere. See also pp. 133, 189, 191-192.

4. Medo-Persian Rule

Date: 536-333 B.C.
Scripture: Ezra; Neh.

Shortly before 536, under Cyrus, Babylon fell, and the Persian Empire replaced the Babylonian. The new ruler allowed the Hebrew exiles to return to their own land. Read his decree in Ezra 1. Of the kings who followed him the most important from the point of view of Bible History are the following:

(1) Darius, 521-486 (Note this date, another significant *86*!). During the reign of this king the temple was rebuilt.

(2) and *(3) Xerxes,* who succeeded him. This is the Ahasuerus of the Book of Esther. Successful against Egypt, he attempted an invasion of Greece, but was repulsed with heavy loss. It is easy to remember that he reigned about twenty years, and that his son *Artaxerxes,* who succeeded him, held sway for about forty years.

Artaxerxes allowed Ezra to lead a number of Jews back to Jerusalem. It was this King who sanctioned the rebuilding of the walls under Nehemiah.

Let us return now to Cyrus.

When Cyrus issued his decree, only a remnant returned, 42,360, besides their men-servants and their maid-servants, of whom there were 7,337, and . . . 200 singing men and singing women" (Ezra 2:64).

Most of those who returned belonged to the tribe of Judah. But inasmuch as, especially in the north (see p. 113), the twelve tribes were in all likelihood dwelling together in the same general region, and whereas the edict concerned all the exiles, whether living in the north or in the south, we are not surprised to find among those who returned men who do not belong to Judah or Benjamin (I Chron. 9:23). Israel and Judah have, as it were, become united. That among those who returned there were also some whose ancestors had been carried away in the *Assyrian* deportations, i.e., long before the Babylonian deportation of 586, seems to be implied in Ezra 2:59. When during the reign of Darius (see p. 119) the temple was rebuilt and dedicated, a sin-offering was brought "... *for all Israel,* twelve he-goats, according to the number of the tribes of Israel" (Ezra 6:17). This is also the New Testament view. It looks upon Israel as a reunited people, consisting of twelve tribes (Matt. 19:28; Acts 26:7; James 1:1; Rev. 7:1-8; 21:12). Moreover, in connection with the story of the birth of John the Baptist and of Christ we read not only about Joseph (also Mary, see p. 137) of the tribe of *Judah* (Matt. 1:20), but also about Anna, a prophetess, of the tribe of *Asher* (Luke 2:36). Over all the tribes rules the One Shepherd, according to prophecy! (Ezek. 37:15-28).

The returned Jews built the altar of burnt offering and laid the foundation of the temple (Ezra 3:1-10). Jealous Samaritans and their allies interrupted the work (Ezra 4). Discouragement gained the upper hand. But in the second year of Darius, about 520, Haggai urged the rebuilding of the temple. Zechariah joined him in this exhortation and predicted the future glory of Zion; also the coming, suffering, and exaltation of the Branch. See pp. 271-276.

The *typological* and the *prophetical* lines of preparation for the coming of the Christ unite at this juncture. Joshua, the high-priest, one of the leaders of the Return—the other leader was Zerubbabel—typified the coming Priest-King (Zech. 6:9-11). In this connection a glorious prophecy was recorded:

> *Thus speaks Jehovath of hosts, saying, Behold the man whose name is the Branch: and he shall grow up out of his place; and he shall build the temple of Jehovah; and he shall bear the glory, and shall sit and rule upon his throne; and he shall be a priest upon his throne; and the counsel of peace shall be between them both* (Zechariah 6:12, 13).

Study also the glorious Messianic prophecies in Zechariah 3:8, 9; 9:9; 11:12; 12:10; 13:7; Haggai 2:6-9. See pp. 273, 454.

The *historical* line, too, is clear; for, guiding the hand of Cyrus with his wise policy toward subject peoples, permitting them to return to countries of their birth, we see God's firm decree, according to which the Messiah was to be born in Bethlehem of Judah (Mic. 5:2). This explains the necessity of the Return. Zerubbabel—the name means *Seed of Babylon*—the descendant of Jehoiachin, must return in order that in the line of his generations and on holy soil both Joseph and Mary may be born. See pp. 135-137.

Under Xerxes, who began to reign in the year 486, we again see the clear evidences of this historical preparation; for, the Jewish people living in the entire empire were saved from the decree which would have destroyed both them and their Hope. See p. 304.

And now the *psychological* line. After the rebuilding of the temple about the year 516—about five hundred years before the beginning of Herod's temple (see p. 272 and p. 65)—Judea experienced a long period of spiritual and moral deterioration. The Jews began to modify their exclusiveness toward the mixed population which surrounded them. They even married foreign wives and grew lax with respect to the law of Jehovah. It was Ezra the scribe who started the reform movement. About the year 458, during the reign of Artaxerxes, this "ready scribe in the law of Moses" (Ezra 7:6) led a company of Jews to Jerusalem. Arriving there (Ezra 7, 8), he persuaded the people to separate themselves from their foreign wives (Ezra 9, 10). The work begun by Ezra was continued by Nehemiah, the king's cupbearer, who in 444 obtained leave to proceed to Jerusalem with full authority to rebuild its walls and to govern the Jews (Neh. 1-7). The task was performed amid much opposition, but the wall was finished and dedicated (Neh. 12).

About this time Ezra reappears upon the scene. In connection with the Feast of Tabernacles he reads to the people "the book of the law of Moses, which Jehovah had commanded Israel." The service is very impressive. There is a public confession of sin. The people covenant to keep the law (Neh. 9, 10). See pp. 310-312.

Ezra the scribe, is remembered by later generations because he was instrumental in promoting the attitude of deep and proper reverence for God's law. He was the forerunner of those men who in the New Testament are called "scribes," and "lawyers," and "teachers of the law." They saw to it that the sacred text was preserved. They interpreted it. They taught it throughout the land. It is, therefore, probable that the institution of the *synagogue* can be traced to them. As long as they adhered to the inner, spiritual meaning of the law, all was well. But when they began to attach greater significance to their own fallible deductions, and superimposed a series of manmade ordinances upon the law, "making void the law of God by their tradition" (Matt. 15:6), they ceased to be a blessing. They "loaded men with burdens grievous to be borne" (Luke 11:46). The people began to groan under this heavy load. See pp. 152-153. Thus, psychologically the way was being prepared for the coming of Him who would one day address the burdened multitudes in these words of grace: "Come unto me, all who are weary and burdened, and I will give you rest" (Matt. 11:28).

Thus, most strikingly, the *typological, prophetical, historical,* and *psychological* lines blend during this period, and they all point to Christ!

After twelve years, in the year 432, Nehemiah returned to the court of King Artaxerxes. During his absence the Jews reverted to their evil ways. Moreover, the tide of hope began to ebb. It seemed to many that Jehovah's promises of exaltation would never reach fulfilment. In their discouragement some were beginning to ask the question: "Does Jehovah still love us?" It is probable that Malachi and perhaps also Joel carried on their prophetic labors during this interval. If so, then to the picture of other woes we must add a plague of locusts (Joel 1, 2; Mal. 3:11). These prophets assured the faithful remnant that Jehovah's love for those who truly trust him remains unchanged (Joel 3:16; Mal. 1:1; 3:6). The fault was not with Jehovah but with those in Israel who had departed from his ways and had permitted his love to go unrequited. See pp. 276-278.

Predictions of the coming Messianic era with its effusion of the Spirit abound in these prophecies.

Malachi rebuked the people for their sins with respect to mixed marriages and the withholding of the tithe (Mal. 2:11; 3:8). Nehemiah, upon his return to Jerusalem, instituted reforms with respect to these same matters (Neh. 13), and also with respect to Sabbath-breaking.

Not only the common people sinned, but so did the priests. In fact, *they* had set the example. A grandson of the highpriest had married the daughter of Sanballat, the Horonite (Neh. 13:28). Nehemiah, therefore, chased him from his presence. In all probability it was this same excommunicated priest, Manasseh, who thereupon founded the Samaritan temple. See pp. 126, 147.

With the addition of the Psalms, Ecclesiastes(?), Esther, Ezra, Nehemiah, and I and II Chronicles, which were brought to completion during this period, the Old Testament was now finished. See pp. 281-283, 296-297, 310-311.

Accordingly, we now leave the scene of *sacred* history, which will be taken up again on p. 131.

5. Greco-Macedonian and Resulting Rule
Date: 333-200 B.C.

---

a. Alexander and His Immediate Successors (333-300)

Very suddenly the he-goat of Daniel 8 appears upon the scene. He comes from the west and advances over the face of the earth with such terrific speed that he does not even touch it. Between his eyes there is a conspicuous horn. When the goat (Greece under Alexander the Great, v. 21) sees the two-horned ram (the Medo-Persian Empire), he dashes at him with tremendous fury and smashes him. The goat completely crushes the ram's two horns and tramples upon the former champion. The ram is "down and out," without even the faintest hope of rescue. That was the symbolic prophecy. And so it actually happened. Alexander the Great, with incredible speed, crushed the proud but unwieldy Persian hordes at the battles of strategically situated Granicus and Issus. Locating them on a map will be helpful in understanding their importance.

Tyre was next in order. Ezekiel had predicted: "And they shall lay your stones and your timber and your dust in the midst of waters" (26:12). This prophecy was literally fulfilled when the ruins of ancient Tyre were used in order to make a mole or causeway through the sea to the new island-city. Then came Palestine. When Alexander approached Jerusalem, a solemn procession could be seen streaming forth from the city's gates in order to welcome the conqueror. Jaddua, the highpriest, was the leader. He was dressed in his official robes and was attended by the priests and Levites in white garments. A large multitude of citizens followed. It is said that as a result of the cordial welcome extended to Alexander he treated the Jews in a friendly manner and granted them many privileges.

Greek conquest and colonization constituted mighty factors in the preparation of the world for the reception of the Gospel. Greek language and culture began to spread throughout the civilized world so that in the days of Christ and of the apostles it was possible, by employing this one tongue, to preach the Good Tidings to people of widely different race and origin. Nevertheless, the dissemination of the Greek language was not an unmixed blessing. Greek vices were welcomed along with the language. In Judea worldly-minded individuals adopted Greek names, games, habits, customs, etc. Over against this worldly tendency the pious in the land began to attach ever-increasing significance to the law of Jehovah, as interpreted by the scribes. See pp. 121-122.

Alexander's powerful empire was short-lived. Daniel 8:8 (cf. also 7:6) has given us the prophetic picture in these words:

> *And the he-goat magnified himself exceedingly: and when he was strong, the great horn was broken; and instead of it there came four notable horns toward the four winds of the heaven.*

When Alexander died in the year 323, there was no one able to rule over his farflung domain. After more than twenty years of strife and warfare the empire was divided into four regions, each with its own ruler: Lysimachus received Thrace; Cassander, Macedonia; Ptolemy Soter, Egypt; and Seleucus, Syria. Whereas Judea was located between Egypt to the south and Syria to the northeast, its soil became once more the battlefield of nations. About the year 300 Egypt achieved the victory, which, however, was not of an enduring character.

b. Egyptian rule (300-200)

During the greater part of this century the Jews enjoyed a considerable measure of peace and prosperity. This period, too, was of importance in the preparation of the world for Christ and his Gospel; for, it was while Ptolemy Philadelphus was king that the Old Testament was translated into Greek so that men of every tribe and nation could read and study the glorious tidings of salvation through the coming Messiah. See p. 36.

6. Resulting Rule (cont'd); Syrian Rule and Maccabean Rule

Date: 200-63 B.C.

About the year 200 (to be exact, 198), Palestine became subject to Syria. The ruling nation, in trouble with Rome and forced to pay a heavy penalty for its unsuccessful attempt to meddle in the affairs of the city on the Tiber, imposed a burdensome tribute upon the Jews. When about the year 175 Antiochus Epiphanes became king, conditions became even worse. The new ruler farmed out the high-priesthood to the highest bidder and employed it as a collection agency for the government. Menelaus succeeded in outbidding Jason to the extent of three hundred talents and gained the highpriesthood! Later, while Antiochus was leading an expedition into Egypt, Jason tried to regain the lost prize. The Jews, moreover, rejoiced when a false rumor of the death of the king gained currency. Returned, Antiochus massacred thousands of Jews and sold others into slavery. After another attempt to take Alexandria, Antiochus was thwarted by the Romans at the very moment when he regarded the final victory to be within his grasp. He decided to vent his wrath upon the Jews. He waited for the sabbath; then fell upon the defenseless city, killing people right and left. Moreover, he determined to wipe out the Jewish religion root and branch. He ordered the cessation of the regular, divinely ordained evening and morning offering in the temple. This continual burnt offering, according to the prediction of the Book of Daniel, was omitted 2,300 times: "And he said unto me: evening, morning, two thousand three hundred; then shall the sanctuary be restored," (Dan. 8:14).

This period indicated by 2,300 offerings comprises 1,150 days, i.e., a little more than three years; from October of the year 168 to December of the year 165. Not only did he order the regular offering to cease, but he also entered the Holy of Holies and thoroughly desecrated the temple. At his command a hog was offered on an altar which had been erected over the altar of burnt offering in the court. (Exactly three years elapsed between this defilement and the rededication in December of 165). Antiochus, moreover, prohibited the continuation of sabbath observance and of the administration of the rite of circumcision. He put to death all those who were found to have concealed a copy of the law of Jehovah.

In this time of sore affliction and distress the saints cried to Jehovah for help. This prayer was heard. The revolution arrived.

b. Maccabean Rule (167-63)

At Modein, not far from Jerusalem, there lived an aged priest, Mattathias. When the commissioner of Antiochus requested that he take the lead in offering a pagan sacrifice, he not only refused to do this but slew both the commissioner and an apostate Jew who was about to comply with the request. This was the beginning of the revolt. After the death of Mattathias, his son Judas, a humble child of God and a military genius, achieved victories which constitute a classic in the science of strategy. He was always battling greatly superior forces. As a result of his triumphs the temple at Jerusalem, which by the wicked Antiochus had been consecrated to Zeus, was cleansed and rededicated to Jehovah. The Jews had regained religious freedom. After the death of Judas, his brother Jonathan ruled for a while. In his attempt to outwit the Syrians he was himself outwitted and executed.

Under the next son of Mattathias, Simon, a very wise administrator, a truly glorious period was ushered in. Read about it in I Maccabees 14. One cannot help but wonder whether perhaps some of the prophecies of weal for Israel (cf. Mic. 4:4) attained their initial fulfilment during his prosperous reign. In the year 142 the Jews gained *political* independence. A grateful people decreed that "Simon should be their leader and highpriest forever, until there should arise a faithful prophet. . . ." In the year 135 Simon was treacherously slain by his own son-in-law.

The Maccabean rulers who followed had imbibed the Hellenistic spirit. They placed greater emphasis upon secular affairs than upon the spiritual. From this date one can expect to find Greek personal names replacing Hebrew names. Simon's son John Hyrcanus was the first of these worldly-minded rulers. Though he was the highpriest as well as the civil ruler, he was a first-class warrior. *To the north* he conquered Samaria and destroyed the Samaritan temple built on Mt. Gerizim. *To the south* he brought Edom into subjection. When the Pharisees of his day demanded that he relinquish his highpriestly office and content himself with the civil administration of the country, he turned against them and joined the party of the Sadducees.

Who were these Pharisees and Sadducees?[7] The Pharisees were the people who desired to live in harmony with the system of legalism which the scribes had superimposed upon the law of God. See pp. 124, 152-153. They *separated* themselves from worldly people; hence they were called *Pharisees; i.e.,* Separatists. They abstained from politics and placed great stress on religious purity. They believed that their own strict adherance to the law would bring about the coming of the Messiah and would result in their own entrance into the kingdom of heaven. They accepted the immortality of the soul and the resurrection of the body; they believed in the existence of angels. The *Sadducees* were the liberals of their day. They refused to acknowledge the binding character of scribal pre-

7. A. T. Robertson in his popularly written but scholarly book, *The Pharisees and Jesus,* gives a list of important works on this subject.

cepts and interpretations. They were secularistic and materialistic in their entire attitude. They denied the existence of angels and the doctrine of a future bodily resurrection. In brief, they constituted the worldly party and busied themselves with the affairs of this present age.

If Hyrcanus may be termed a bad ruler, his son Alexander Janneus (*Jonathan*) was even worse. His hands reeked with blood. He extended his realm *to the east* and *to the west.* Once, when he was functioning in his highpriestly capacity at the Feast of Tabernacles, the people pelted him with citrons. At another time when he asked the Pharisees what he could do to please them, they answered that he could kill himself! As a result of this Pharisaic opposition he took bitter vengeance upon them, crucifying eight hundred of them, while before their very eyes he massacred their wives and children. One happening which occurred during his reign must not remain unmentioned, for it had far-reaching consequences. Over the country of Edom, conquered by his father, he appointed a governor whose son, Antipater, was going to play an important role in the history of the Jews. See p. 128.

Alexandra, Alexander's widow, who assumed leadership after the death of her husband, sided with the Pharisees. Hence, there was a reversal of political policy during her reign.

After her death, her sons Hyrcanus II and Aristobulus contended for the throne. Some of the people sided with Hyrcanus II who was the *elder*; some, with Aristobulus, who was the *stronger* of the two. There was also a third class consisting of those who were thoroughly tired of these degenerate rulers and longed for the abolition of the monarchy and the establishment of a form of government in which the priests should rule the country in accordance with the law of Jehovah. The three parties appealed to Rome. Hence, we have now reached a new era in the history of the Jews.

7. Roman Rule, from Pompey's Entrance into Jerusalem to Immanuel's Birth

Date: 63-5 B.C.

When Aristobulus became impatient with Rome's delay in reaching a decision, he decided to take matters into his own hands. The result was Pompey's invasion of Judea and the capture of Jerusalem in the year 63 B.C.

It is well at this point to present a brief review of the history of Rome from about the year 60 to the reign of Augustus:

First Triumvirate, 60: Crassus, Pompey, Julius. They "went down" in that order: first Crassus, then Pompey, finally Julius (in 44).

Second Triumvirate, 43: Lepidus, Antony, Octavius (the grand-nephew and adopted son of Julius). Octavius is better known by his later title: Emperor Augustus. By winning the battle of Actium he became supreme ruler, but it was not until the year 27 that he was formally invested with imperial power. It was he who was reigning when Jesus was born (Luke 2:1).

When Hyrcanus II and Aristobulus were contending for mastery, the forementioned Antipater took full advantage of the situation. Both Antipater and his son Herod (known later as Herod the Great) were characterized by slyness. They would court the favor of whoever happened to be "on top" in Rome. As soon as the government changed hands they would immediately change their allegiance and shower their compliments and presents upon the man whom "until yesterday" they had opposed. And so it happened that when the Jews were unable to settle their own affairs, Antipater, the hated Idumean, was made procurator of Judea. His son Herod, became governor of Galilee; later, "king of the Jews."

This is the Herod of Matt. 2 and Luke 1, and mentioned nowhere else in the New Testament. For a much more detailed description of the man see *N.T.C., Matthew,* pp. 149-193.

Very cleverly Herod betrothed himself to Mariamne I, who was the granddaughter of both Hyrcanus and Aristobulus, hoping thus to secure the loyalty of the Jews of both parties.

Herod ruled from 37-4 B.C. He had a passion for building; witness Samaria, which he rebuilt and called Sebaste, and Caesarea with its famous harbor and its temple in honor of Caesar. About the year 19 B.C. he began to rebuild the temple at Jerusalem.

The name of Herod is associated in the minds of most people with wanton cruelty. This appraisal is correct in every way. Words fail to describe his well-nigh insane jealousy, unrestrained egoism, and dark suspicion. In his opinion somebody was always plotting to deprive him of power. It had taken a long time before he was fully established as "king of the Jews." Hence, let no one attempt to deprive him of this distinction! It is in this light that one should view Herod's consternation when very shortly before his death wise men came from the east, saying: "Where is he that is born *king of the Jews*?" See Matthew 2.

In his lust for power and the fear that he might lose it he put to death Marianme's brother Aristobulus, her grandfather, her mother, herself, and her two sons. He tried to kill "the newborn King" proclaimed by the wise men. On the part of Satan this was an attempt to frustrate the plan of God with respect to the redemption of his elect. The best commentary is Revelation 12:4: ". . . the dragon stood in front of the woman who was about to give birth, that the moment she gave birth to the child he might devour it."

But Herod did not have his way. Neither did Satan. We read, "And she gave birth to a son, a male child, who is to rule all the nations with a rod of iron: and her child was caught up to God, and to his throne" (v. 5).

We hear the angels singing: "Glory to God in the highest, And on earth peace among men in whom he is well pleased."

GROUND PLAN OF THE TEMPLE IN THE DAYS OF JESUS

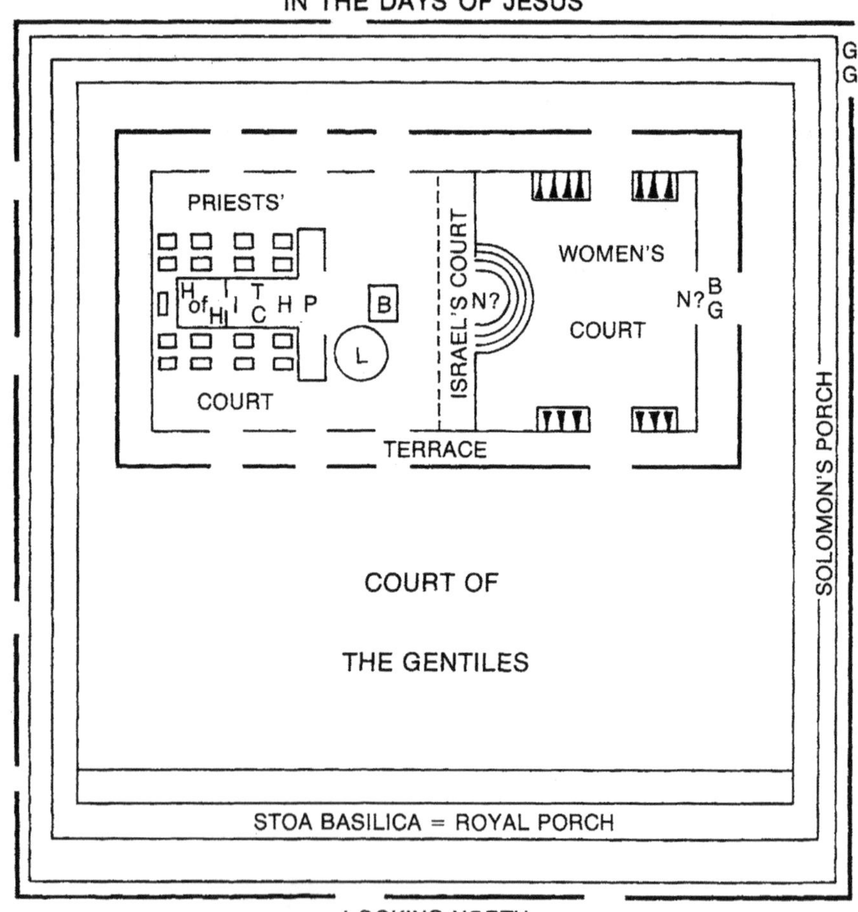

LOOKING NORTH

H = Holy Place with Table of Showbread, Incense Altar, and Candelabrum
H of H = Holy of Holies
B = Burntoffering Altar
L = Laver (Washbasin)

P = Porch
N? = Nicanor's Gate (location disputed)
B G = Beautiful Gate
G G = Golden Gate

8
From the Manger to the Mount

1. The Preparation

Date: December, 5 B.C.–December, 26 A.D.
Scripture: Matt. 1, 2; Luke 1, 2; 3:23-38; John 1:1-14

a. Introduction: The Fulness of the Time

Is the church right in declaring that the Jesus of history is the Christ, the Son of God?

"No," said the so-called liberal critics, "the human Jesus of the Gospels, who gradually, if at all, attained to Messianic consciousness, stands in striking contrast to the Divine Christ of Paul's epistles. Therefore, the Christ of the epistles is not the Jesus of history. We must go back to the Gospels; particularly, to Mark. *The church,* in accepting Paul's (and John's) Christ, *was wrong.*"

"No," say some of the later critics, "for, though the Gospels—including even Mark—do, indeed, picture a superhuman, a Divine Christ, and though we have to admit that the men of the liberal school of criticism were wrong; nevertheless, these Gospels are not to be viewed as the records of actual history but as the products of the faith of the early church. Accordingly, *they cannot be regarded as being entirely trustworthy.*"

"No," say also other critics, "for, though the Gospels may be regarded as giving us, on the whole, a true account with respect to a Jesus who imagined that he was very shortly and very suddenly to become the Christ, it did not actually happen. In other words, *Jesus himself erred.* He labored under a delusion."

Most Gospel criticism, accordingly, can be summed up under these three headings: (1) The church was wrong. (2) The Gospels are not to be trusted. (3) Jesus erred.[1]

Take it any way you wish. The final result is the same: the Jesus of history is not really the Christ, the Son of God.

It is, therefore, all important that at the very beginning of our brief survey of New Testament history, we declare that we believe and are convinced that the Jesus of history is the Christ, the Son of God. This faith cannot be the result but must be the presupposition of historical inquiry. Nevertheless, the study of history does not shake this persuasion, but confirms it!

It was, moreover, the *purpose* of the Gospel writers to proclaim Jesus as the promised Messiah. A *Life of Jesus* they do not offer. They show us that the Son of God came into this world *in order to die* as a ransom for sin.

Nevertheless, it cannot be denied that there is a certain broad outline of events which can easily be traced through all the Gospels. See pp. 383, 384.

It is of great advantage to the student to master a brief summary of *Old* and *Intertestamentary* history—such as given on pp. 59-129—before he takes up the study of the *New* Testament. If he has not done this, it will take him a long time to become orientated. Among the many items mentioned in the New Testament which have already been explained or at least introduced—are the following:

Herod, the king. See pp. 128-129.

Caesar Augustus. See pp. 68, 75, 128.

The synagogue (its origin). See pp. 121-122.

The scribes. See pp. 121-122, 126-127.

The Pharisees. See pp. 126-127.

The Sadducees. See p. 127.

The Samaritans and their temple (which had been destroyed). See pp. 114, 122, 126.

The Temple at Jerusalem. See pp. 65, 101, 117-118, 120-121, 128.

That the Jews were expecting the coming of the Messiah is clear from such passages as Matthew 11:1-3; Luke 2:25, 26, 38; 3:15; John 1:19-28, 41. See also p. 126. That a somewhat vague expectation existed among Samaritans and heathen—no doubt derived from

---

1. Read also W. Hendriksen, *N. T. C., Matthew,* pp. 54-76.

the Jews—is clear from John 4:25, 29, 42; Matthew 2:1, and from several other sources.[2]

A great king was going to arrive; one who, according to popular opinion, would throw off the yoke of the oppressor and restore the throne of David. Was he going to be, in the fullest sense of the term, the Son of God, the One in whom all the fulness of the godhead would dwell bodily? Was he going to bring *spiritual* salvation to his people, and was this going to be his *chief* task? On questions such as these the prophetic voice had been clear. See especially Isaiah 9:6 and chapters 42, 53; Zechariah 12:10; 13:1. The Jews, however, had failed to grasp the full meaning of these Scriptures. They rather emphasized—and misinterpreted—passages like II Samuel 7:12, 13; Daniel 7:13, 14. (Cf. also "Book of Enoch") But, of course, not all people thought alike. Without a doubt the Messianic expectation of a Simeon and an Anna was far more spiritual than that of the majority of the Jews. See Luke 2:25, 38. At any rate, there was an abundance of material upon which the Messianic expectation could be based; e.g., in addition to the passages already cited, there were these: Genesis 3:15; 49:10; Deuteronomy 18:15-18; Psalm 2:8; 16; 22; 40; 45; 48; 69; 89; 95; 102; 109; 110; 118; Micah 5; Zechariah 6; 9; Malachi 3; to mention only a few. Nevertheless, the people did not expect a Messiah who would be *crucified* and by means of the cross would secure redemption from sin for his elect. Yet, the idea is in harmony with Isaiah 53. Besides, had not every bloody sacrifice pointed in this direction?

Jesus was born in "the fulness of time" (Gal. 4:4). Not only was his coming *expected,* as we have seen; but it was also *needed.* The Greeks, whose philosophy had exhausted the possibilities of the sin-darkened human mind, were in need of *wisdom.* The Jews, groaning under the yoke of the law, as interpreted by tradition (see pp. 121-124) and not finding peace for their souls, were in need of *righteousness.* The Romans, who had to admit that the morals of those whom they called barbarians were on a higher plane than their own; among whom the women married in order to be divorced, and were divorced in order to be married; and who as spectators of the

---

2. On the subject of Messianic Expectations see A. Edersheim, *The Life and Times of Jesus, The Messiah,* Vol. I, p. 168 ff.; P. J. Gloag, *The Messianic Prophecies*; A. Pieters, *Psalms in Human Experience,* p. 38 ff.; A. Fahling, *The Life of Christ,* p. 27; W. Hendriksen, *N. T. C., Matthew,* pp. 153, 154.
3. Cf. A. Pieters, *Psalms in Human Experience,* p. 42.

gladiatorial combats had descended to a level even lower than that of the beasts; were in need of *sanctification. All* needed *redemption* (and, of course, all were also in need of wisdom, righteousness, and sanctification; but with varying degrees of emphasis, as Scripture itself indicates (I Cor. 1:20-25). It was *then* that Jesus Christ entered the darkness of this world, the One "who was made unto us *wisdom* from God, and *righteouensss,* and *sanctification,* and *redemption*" (I Cor. 1:30).

It was "the fulness of the time," in one additional sense: the world had been *prepared* for Christ's coming. Hence, not only was there a yearning *expectation,* and a universal *need*; there was also a glorious *opportunity*. The Jews, who had established synagogues everywhere, religious meetingplaces which were attended not only by people of their own nationality but also by select Gentiles, had provided a point of contact between the Christian missionary and the Gentile world. The Greek language provided a medium of communication. See p. 124. Moreover, the sacred writings of the Jews—the Old Testament—had been translated into the universal Greek language. Here was another point of contact. See Acts 8:26 ff. Finally the Romans had established peace and had provided roads, two indispensable requirements for the rapid spread of the Gospel.[4] Truly, it was the fulness of the times!

b. The Word Becomes Flesh

The Christmas story precedes the manger! It must be understood in the light of John's Prologue. See p. 424. Christ, the Word (Greek: *Logos*)—the very expression of the mind of God—existed from eternity with God, rejoicing in the presence of his Father. It was the Word who created all things. But though his name was inscribed on every creature and none could live apart from him, his handiwork rejected him. Nevertheless, he did not reject those whom he had brought forth. On the contrary, day after day, year upon year, century upon century "the light was shining in the darkness," beckoning men unto salvation, earnestly pleading with them, through the voice of the prophets. "But the darkness apprehended it not . . . The world knew him not . . . His own—by virtue of creation and preservation—received him not." Very significant and very tragic is

4. T. G. Tucker, *Life in the Roman World of Nero and St. Paul,* pp. 6-29. See also art. "Roman Empire and Christianity (by S. Angus) in I. S. B. N., and the bibliography that accompanies it. In *The Westminster Historical Atlas,* see esp. Plate XIII and pp. 77-82.

ıat word *not . . . not . . . not* in John 1:5, 10, 11. What happened ıen? The mystery of his love was *fully* revealed. Instead of com-letely rejecting the world, the Logos then "became flesh, and dwelt mong us, and we beheld his glory, glory as of the only-begotten rom the Father, full of grace and truth" (John 1:14).

c. The Two Genealogies (Matt. 1:1-17; Luke 3:23-38)

Jesus alone was born because he *chose* to be born. He was born *in rder to die* for sinners.

Matthew and Luke have given us the genealogy of Jesus. From the nany generations between Abraham and Jesus the first evangelist elects three fourteens. See p. 61. Did he do this in order to represent Christ as the seventh seven, the fulness? It is clear from Matthew's ccount that *Jehovah had been faithful to his promise*: neither luring the glorious reign of David, who stands at the close of the first ourteen, nor during the shameful period of the captivity, at the end of the second fourteen, did he forget his plighted word! Again, both genealogies clearly indicate that the blood of many nations coursed hrough the arteries of Jesus. He took upon himself the *human*—not nerely the Jewish—nature. He was, indeed, the Savior "of the world" John 4:42). Finally, we cannot read these genealogies without being eminded of human *sin*; e.g., "Judah begat Perez and Zerah of Tamar!" Read the story of Judah's shame in Genesis 38. "Salmon begat Boaz of Rahab," a harlot! (see Josh. 2:1). And David begat Solomon of her that had been the wife of Uriah" (see p. 100). Moreover, among the kings of Judah mentioned here we find Ahaz not to speak of Manasseh, who was converted very late in life)!

Although the view according to which both Matthew and Luke give us the genealogy of Joseph has always had many and strong advocates, we do not regard it as probable. The arguments against it presented by A. T. Robertson, still hold.[5] As we see it, therefore, Matthew gives the descent of Joseph; Luke, the descent of Mary.

The diagram on page 136 represents one of the many possible variations of this view. The particular form in which the theory appears in the diagram has its difficulties. But so has every variation of either theory. Hence, though we regard the *theory*—Matthew: Genealogy of Joseph; Luke: Genealogy of Mary—as having the weight of probability on its side, we are not ready to adopt any particular *form* of that theory.

---

5. A. T. Robertson, *A Harmony of the Gospels*, p. 259 ff.

There are, however, some representations which we definitely reject. Thus, we cannot agree with those scholars who believe that

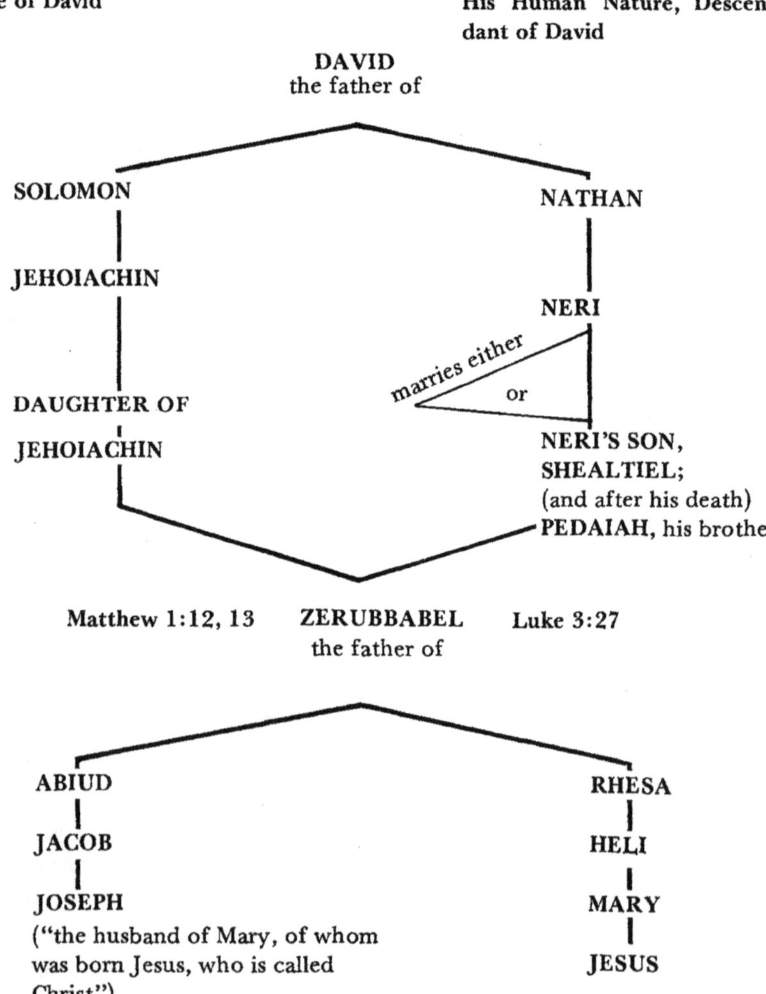

Jehoiachin was Zerubbabel's great-great-grandfather (line of descent: Jehoiachin–Assir–Assir's daughter, wife of Neri–Shealtiel and Pedaiah–Zerubbabel). There just was not enough time between 597 and 536! And in 536 Zerubbabel is not a baby but a leader!

Neither do we agree with the view of those who hold that the line of Solomon became extinct in Jehoiachin (on the basis of what we regard as a faulty interpretation of II Kings 24:8, 12; Jeremiah 22:30; 36:30; and I Chronicles 3:17); and that then the succession passed over to the collateral line which sprang from Nathan. But though we cling to the view that Jehoiachin was "childless" only in the sense that he had no son *who sat upon the throne of David,* and though we believe that according to the clear teaching of I Chronicles 3:17 (cf. Matt. 1:12) Jehoiachin had natural offspring; nevertheless, we admit that what is stressed by Matthew is not physical descent but legal title. It is, however, probable that in Matthew physical descent and legal title are combined in the genealogy. At any rate, it is the clear teaching of Scripture that Joseph was of the house and family of David, (Luke 1:27; 2:4, 5; Matt. 1:20). It is equally clear that Mary was of Davidic lineage; for, in spite of what Zahn and others have said to the contrary, basing their views upon what we believe to be an erroneous explanation of Luke 1:5, 36,[6] Jesus, who, according to his human nature was Mary's son, is plainly declared to have been the son ("seed") of David, the fruit of his loins. Study II Samuel 7:12, 13; Acts 2:30; Romans 1:3; II Timothy 2:8; Revelation 5:5. In a sense, Luke 1:32 can be added to this list.

d. The Annunciations.

The beautiful story of the Incarnation begins with an account of the annunciation of the birth of the forerunner, John. Zechariah was executing the priest's office, and "his lot was to enter into the sanctuary of the Lord and burn incense."[7] The angel Gabriel appeared to him and brought him the wonderful news that his wife Elisabeth was going to bear a son, whose task it would be to make ready for the Lord a people prepared for him. The angel told Zechariah that this son was to be called "John." This is significant: The child whose name was "Jehovah is [or: has been] *gracious*" was going to be a preacher of *sin and judgment*! Nevertheless, this name was very appropriate, not only because it was expressive of the

6. R. C. H. Lenski's sharp criticism of Zahn's position (*Interpretation of Luke,* p. 49) is entirely correct.

7. A. Fahling, *The Life of Christ,* pp. 60, 732.

kindness of Jehovah in blessing the aged couple with a child, but also because Israel could attain to grace and pardon only through the consciousness of sin and impending judgment. When Zechariah expressed doubt with respect to the word of the angel, he was punished with dumbness. This punishment, however, was only temporary; for when John was born, Zechariah, in a wonderful hymn, praised Jehovah for his covenant faithfulness (Luke 1:57-80, especially vss. 72, 73).

Six months after the annunciation of John's birth, Gabriel is sent to Nazareth in Galilee to announce to Mary the coming of the Savior. The words of the angel are (in part):

> *Fear not, Mary; for you have found favor with God. And behold, you shall conceive in your womb, and bring forth a son, and shall call his name Jesus. He shall be great and shall be called the Son of the Most High: and the Lord God shall give him the throne of his father David: and he shall reign over the house of Jacob forever: of his kingdom there shall be no end . . . The Holy Spirit shall come upon you, and the power of the Most High shall overshadow you: wherefore also the one who is to be born shall be called holy, the Son of God. And behold, Elisabeth your relative has conceived a son in her old age; and this is the sixth month with her who was called barren. . ."* (Luke 1:30-37).

Mary's faith deserves admiration. Three well-nigh incredible facts had been revealed to her: (1) that *she* would be the mother of the Savior; (2) that this Savior, i.e., his human nature, was going to enter her womb without the agency of a human father; and (3) that Elisabeth had conceived in her old age. Nevertheless, she did not express doubt, as Zechariah had done, but believed. It does not surprise us, therefore, that when she visited Elisabeth (Luke 1:39-45) she was greeted with the words, "Blessed is she that *believed*."

Not only Mary's faith, however, but also her humble *obedience* is remarkable. Though conception at this particular time would arouse suspicion, she was willing to be the instrument through which the Eternal Word would "become flesh." In reply to the angel's message, she said: "Behold, the handmaid of the Lord; be it unto me according to your word." After Mary had visited Elisabeth, she returned to her home in Nazareth.

Joseph, too, received an announcement of the Savior's birth:

> *Joseph, son of David, do not hesitate to take Mary, your wife, into your home, for what was conceived in her is of the Holy Spirit. She will give birth to a son, and you shall call his name Jesus, for he will save his people from their sins.* (Matt. 1:20, 21).

Especially striking is the fact, which often escapes observation, that the Virgin Birth is definitely *emphasized* in all these nativity stories. It is either stated or implied in the following passages: Matthew 1:16, 18, 21-23, 25; Luke 1:34, 35; 2:50; 3:23. Being the Son of the Divine Father and of a human mother, Jesus is both God and man; hence, the Mediator, able to save.[8]

e. The Birth of Jesus and His Life at Nazareth

In order that the Savior might be born in Bethlehem, according to Micah's prophecy (5:2), God made use of an event of world politics. A decree went forth from Emperor Augustus that everyone in the empire should be registered. This was probably the beginning of a periodic census which was going to take place every fourteen years. Its earliest occurrence had been decreed for the year 8 B.C., when Quirinius was for the first time governor of Syria. See p. 400. But due to the opposition of the Jews to any census—they had not yet forgotten the events recorded in II Samuel 24—and especially to one that had been ordered by *Rome,* and probably also for other reasons, this registration in his realm was postponed a few years. At last, in the year 5 B.C. it took place. In Herod's kingdom the census was taken in accordance with family origins. Hence, Joseph and Mary went to Bethlehem to be enrolled. Here the Savior was born. We read:

> *And she gave birth to her firstborn son; and she wrapped him in swaddling cloths, and laid him in a manger, because there was no room for them in the inn.* (Luke 2:7).

In the fields of Ephratah the birth of the Savior was announced to shepherds "keeping watch by night over their flock." First one angel conveyed to them the "tidings of great joy." Then from the land

8. This point is elaborated fully in J. G. Machen, *The Virgin Birth of Christ.* See also J. Orr, same title, and Hendriksen, *N.T.C., Matthew,* pp. 133-144.

where everyone sings and no one has ever been heard to weep there descended a multitude of the heavenly hosts, praising God and saying (as they surrounded the shepherds):

> *Glory to God in the highest,*
> *And on earth peace to men with whom he is well please.* (Luke 2:14).

A sign had been given to the shepherds: a babe wrapped in swaddling cloths, and lying in a manger. They *believed, obeyed, saw, proclaimed*! Read Luke 2:15-20.

On the eighth day Jesus was circumcised, according to the law (Gen. 17:12; Lev. 12:3), for he was born "under the law." This act of circumcision indicated that upon him rested the sin of *the world*—for he himself had no sin; hence it is in this very connection that we read that "his name was called Jesus" i.e., Savior from sin (literally, Jehovah is salvation, Luke 2:21).

On the fortieth day the Redeemer was Himself redeemed! Strange as it may sound, the statement is true. Of course, he was not redeemed in the sense in which he redeems his people, for he was sinless; but, being the first-born—and not of the tribe of Levi—he had to be exempted from temple-service by the payment of five shekels of silver—about $3.00 (Num. 3; 18:16). The underlying idea of the ancient redemption ritual was this: in God's holy sight not only the Egyptians but also the Israelites have forfeited their lives (Exod. 13). Now, *in the place of* actual death God is willing to accept from the tribe of Levi life-long service in the tabernacle or temple, and from the first-born of the other tribes the five shekels, as a symbolic offering, a confession, as it were. Jesus, too, was under the sentence of death, not because of any personal sin or guilt but because upon him rested the sin of the world. On this same visit to the temple Mary brought the prescribed purification offering; in her case, the offering of the poor: a pair of turtledoves or two young pigeons (Luke 2:22-24; cf. Lev. 12). At this occasion Simeon and Anna rendered homage to the Christ. The former, holding the child in his arms, saw in him Jehovah's salvation, "a light for revelation to the Gentiles, and for glory to thy people, Israel."

When Joseph and Mary, with their child, had returned to Bethlehem, they were visited by wise men from the East (Matt. 2:1-12). From the lips of the Jews of the dispersion these men may have heard about the Messianic expectations. In their own country they had seen a miracle-star, which by them had been associated with the birth of the king of the Jews. They had traveled to Jerusalem. From Jerusalem to Bethlehem they had been guided by the prophecy of Micah (5:1, 2) and by the same low-hanging heavenly body, which "went before them"–proceeding, therefore, from north to south!– "till it came and stood over [the house, see next verse] where the young child was." The wise men, offering their gifts to the child, were the forerunners of the elect from *all the nations,* which would be gathered into the church.

Matt. 2:8, 16 describe a Herod who is both crafty and cruel, just as Josephus pictures him [9] See also p. 128. When the wise men failed to return, this murderer added another gross crime to the lengthy list of he enormities. "He slew all the male children that were in Bethlehem and in all its borders, from two years old and under. . . ." However, the child and his parents were safe in Egypt. After Herod's death the family left Egypt and, by divine direction, settled in Nazareth (Matt. 2:19-23).

When Jesus was twelve years old, he accompanied his father and mother to Jerusalem to attend a Passover feast. When the parents were on their way back to Nazareth, they noticed that Jesus was not in the company of those who were returning to Galilee. They found him in the temple, "sitting in the midst of the teachers, both listening to them and asking them questions." Turning to his surprised parents he asked: "How is it that you were searching for me? Didn't you know that I had to be in my Father's house?" This answer clearly indicates that those critics are wrong who say that Jesus' consciousness of a very extraordinary relation to the Father did not arise until much later.

Having returned to Nazareth Jesus spent many years of quiet preparation for the task laid upon him by the Father. Moreover, he "advanced in wisdom and stature, and in favor with God and men." See p. 97.

2. The Inauguration

Date: December, 26–April, 27
Scripture: Matt. 3:1–4:11; Mark 1:1-13
Luke 3:1-22; 4:1-13; John 1:15–2:12

---

a. Brief Summary

During this brief period four great events occurred. For each one, Scripture furnishes a key passage. Moreover, there is a very close relation between the four texts. They are as follows:

9. Josephus, *Antiquities*, Book XV.

(1) When Jesus had been baptized, a voice spoke from heaven: "*Thou art my beloved Son,* with thee I am well pleased " (Mark 1:11).

(2) When Jesus was tempted, Satan based his evil suggestion upon the words which had just been spoken from heaven. Whereas the Father had called Jesus "my beloved Son," the devil addressed the Savior in these words: "*Since you are God's Son,* throw yourself down . . . " (Matt. 4:6).

(3) Again, by his voluntary submission to the rite of baptism and also by his equally voluntary obedience to the Father while he was being tempted, thereby fulfilling the law which the first Adam had transgressed, Jesus clearly indicated that *he had taken upon himself and was taking away* "the sin of the world." Therefore, the third significant passage was uttered immediately after baptism and temptation. It was then that John the Baptist exclaimed, "Behold, the Lamb of God, *who is taking away the sin of the world* (John 1:29).

(4) It was in this connection that Jesus made his first disciples. But did they accept the testimony of John with reference to him, a testimony which was confirmed by his own first sign (changing water into wine)? In other words, did they recognize in him the Son of God, the Lamb of God? That on their part there was, at least, a beginning of real faith in him—a faith which, to be sure, did not yet comprehend the *manner* in which he would take away the sin of the world—is clear from the fourth passage, which describes their relation to the Christ immediately after the miracle at Cana: "This beginning of his signs did Jesus in Cana of Galilee, and manifested his glory, *and his disciples believed in him*" (John 2:11).

Accordingly, once these four passages are understood, the proper relation of the events and their spiritual significance will have been grasped.

Let us now take up, in order, the four main events: Christ's baptism, temptation, first disciples, first miracle.

b. The Baptism

Probably during the last days of December of the year 26 or in the beginning of January of 27 Jesus left Nazareth in order that he might voluntarily take upon himself the great task assigned to him by the Father. He went to Bethany beyond the Jordan, probably located at a ford of the river, not far from the Sea of Galilee. Here John was baptizing. That great preacher of repentance, beginning in the vicinity of the Dead Sea, had gradually ascended the Jordan Valley until he had reached this Bethany, probably located about twenty miles from Nazareth. The burden of his message had been the same everywhere: "Be converted, for the kingdom of heaven is at hand." Being not only a prophet but a man in whom prophecy was fulfilled (Isa. 40:3-5; Mal. 3:1; 4:5), even the immediate herald of the Christ, and performing his task with genuine humility (Luke 3:16; John 3:29, 30), he was truly great, so great, in fact, that Jesus once testified: "Among those born of women there has not arisen anyone greater than John the Baptist" (Matt. 11:11). Yet he never belonged to the *inner circle* of Christ's disciples, and he did not partake of the *privileges* of those who associated with their Master from day to day and saw him not only in his suffering and death but also in the glory of his resurrection. Hence, it does not surprise us that we also read: " . . . yet he who is least in the kingdom of heaven is greater than he."

Now when Jesus was baptized by John, God *the Father* was so pleased with the fact that *the Son* had taken upon himself the sin of the world that (as we have seen) he spoke from heaven, saying: "Thou art my beloved Son, with thee I am well pleased" (Mark 1:11). And *the Holy Spirit* "descended in a bodily form, as a dove, upon him" (Luke 3:22), thoroughly qualifying him unto the performance of his great task.

c. The Temptation

From the Jordan Valley Jesus was led to the heights of the wilderness, to be tempted. Though the temptations came solely from without and not also from within, as in the case of sinful men (James 1:14), they were, nevertheless, real, just as real as those which occur to other men (Heb. 4:15). Moreover, Jesus was hungry, having fasted forty days and forty nights. If, then, he be the Son of God, let him provide for his own sustenance. Why should he trust any longer in the Father? Let him change stones into bread. Jesus, in his answer—which is an appeal to the Word (Deut. 8:3)—shows that life depends not on bread as such but on the sustaining power of God. He is God's own Son; hence, the Father will provide for him and will sustain him. "Prove that you trust him," answers Satan, as it were, "by casting yourself down from the pinnacle of the temple!" The devil then quotes—rather, purposely misquotes—Scripture, to prove that no harm will befall Jesus. (Be sure to compare Satan's misquotation, Matthew 4:6, with the original in Psalm 91:11, 12). With an appeal to Deuteronomy 6:16, Jesus parries this assault. Finally, the greatest temptation of them all: Satan is willing to relinquish his dominion, his powerful influence, over all the kingdoms of the world. The Messiah will not need to suffer at all: no crown of thorns, no cross, no death, no burial, none of it! All that is necessary is that "you fall down and worship me." The answer flies back like an arrow: "It is written, you shall worship the Lord your God, and him only shall you serve" (Deut. 6:13–*again* Deuteronomy!).

By *NOT* falling into the devil's traps, neither now nor afterward, by *NOT* yielding to his allurements, Jesus actually obtained those very things which Satan had promised him (but could never have given): bodily sustenance (his God upheld him!), the ministry of the angels (Matt. 4:11), and the kingdoms of the world and their glory (Phil. 2:5-11).

By means of this great victory over Satan we see Jesus as: a. our sympathetic Highpriest, who "can be touched with the feeling of our infirmities" (Heb. 4:14), whereas he, too, was tempted; b. the second Adam (note the connection between Luke 3:38 and 4:1),–who succeeded where the first Adam failed (I Cor. 15:45), and who by means of his obedience achieved salvation for us; and c. the Conqueror, who bound Beelzebub, and was going to destroy his kingdom (Matt. 12:22-29; cf. Rev. 20:1-3).

d. The First Disciples

The greatness of the Baptist is evident from the fact that he rejoiced when his disciples left him in order to follow Jesus. Two pairs of brothers were the first to do this after our Lord's return from the temptation experiences; namely, Andrew and Peter, and without a reasonable doubt, James and John (John 1:35-42). Besides these four, two other men came to Jesus at this time: Philip and Nathaniel, (vss. 43-51). Note the exalted titles given to the Master by these early disciples: "the Messiah," "him of whom Moses in the law and the prophets wrote," "the Son of God, the king of Israel." Thus, at the very beginning of the Lord's public appearance the Christology is already very high. The *earliest* witnesses proclaimed his greatness, and they did so *immediately*. Hence, it need not surprise us that the Gospel According to John, in which these facts are recorded, has been attacked with such persistence by rationalists of every hue and color.[10]

---

10. See John Chapman, *John the Presbyter and the Fourth Gospel*; J. Drummond, *An Inquiry into the Character and Authorship of the Fourth Gospel*; B. W. Bacon, *The Fourth Gospel in Research and Debate*; W. Sanday, *Criticism of the Fourth Gospel.*

e. The First Sign

With his disciples Jesus attended a wedding at Cana in Galilee (John 2:1-11). When the wine failed, he performed his first miracle by changing water into wine. He thereby revealed his glory. The disciples believed in him. The Son of Man, limitless in sympathy, the Friend of marriage and of the family, stood revealed before them as being also the Son of God, infinite in power and love, able to save.

Having spent a few days at Capernaum, Jesus went up to Jerusalem to attend the Passover (2:12, 13).

3. The Early Judean Ministry

Date: April-December, 27
Scripture: John 2:13–4:42

---

a. Brief Summary

As in the preceding period, four events require our attention:

(1) Reformation. The urgent necessity of a reformation was symbolized by the cleansing of the temple.

(2) Regeneration. The indispensability of personal regeneration was emphasized in the conversation with Nicodemus.

(3) "Recessional." The Baptist's glorious recessional was heard when a few of his disciples, moved with envy, assailed the work of Jesus in the country districts of Judea.

(4) Recognition. The recognition of Jesus as the Savior of the world occurred after the Lord had held a conversation with the "woman of Samaria."

The Light was shining into the darkness. Moreover, the circle of illumination was becoming wider and wider. Whereas in the preceding period the *immediate disciples* of the Christ saw his glory and believed in him, in this Early Judean Ministry the Light began to penetrate the mental, moral, and spiritual darkness which reigned in the minds and hearts of *the people of Jerusalem,* (1) and (2) above; *of Judea* outside the capital, (3) above; and finally, *of Samaria,* (4) above. Thus, the spiritually illumined area gradually increased. Let us now briefly review the four events:

b. Reformation

When the true Passover Lamb entered the temple, in order that he might take part in the activities of the Feast of Passover, he was shocked deeply as he saw that the court of the Gentiles resembled a stockyard or a market place. The sacrificial animals filled the outer enclosure with their bleating and lowing. Here stood the little tables of the moneychangers and there were the wicker crates containing doves. Of course, the privileged venders filled the moneychests of Annas and his family! Jesus, having made a scourge of cords, drove out not only the sheep and the oxen but, according to the best interpretation of the original, also the traffickers themselves.[11] By this act he not only punished sacrilege and exposed greed, but also assailed the spirit of narrow exclusivism: the place originally intended as a court of prayer for *all the nations* had been converted into a *Jewish* market! Cf. (in connection with a similar cleansing toward the close of Christ's earthly ministry) Mark 11:17. May we not observe in this event the initial fulfilment of the prophecy of Malachi 3:1ff.?

c. Regeneration

In this well-known story we see three things:

(a) Penetrating insight. With reference to Jesus we read: "He knew all men . . . and did not need to have anyone bear testimony concerning man; for he himself knew what was in man." Hence, he went straight to the heart of the matter and said to Nicodemus: "Except one is born anew, he cannot see the kingdom of God." This birth from above is, accordingly, the

(b) Prerequisite for entering (and even for *seeing*) the kingdom. Now, with respect to this act of regeneration man is necessarily passive. He cannot save himself. Accordingly, Jesus also revealed to Nicodemus the Divine

(c) Provision for the sinner's salvation. See especially verse 16: "For *so* loved God the world that his son, the only-begotten, he gave that whosoever believes in him should not perish but have everlasting life" (as we prefer to translate the original).

Having stressed the fact that Israel needs not only outward reformation but also—even more so—inner regeneration, Jesus departed from Jerusalem, and, by means of his disciples, carried on a ministry of baptism in the country districts of Judea.

d. Recessional

First, we note a seeming—not real—*rivalry* between John and Jesus: there was the same call to conversion; the same reason given

11. Though one may not agree with all the arguments, it is hard to disagree with R. C. H. Lenski's conclusion on p. 199, *Interpretation of John's Gospel.* See also W. Hendriksen, *N.T.C., John,* Vol. I, pp. 122, 123.

("for the kingdom of heaven is at hand," cf. Matt. 3:2 with 4:17); and the same symbolic act: baptism. This brought about evident *resentment* on the part of some of John's disciples. However, the Baptist now "sings" his glorious *recessional;* i.e., he takes himself out of the picture. Having brought the bride to the bridegroom, he, being the friend of the latter, rejoiced. Said John: "He must increase, but I must decrease" (John 3:30). Soon afterward Jesus went back to Galilee. The reason for this return is given in John 4:1-4 (cf. Matt. 4:12). He passed through Samaria, and sat down "by the well" of Sychar. It was here that a conversation took place between Jesus and a woman of Samaria who had come to the well to draw water.

e. Recognition[12]

The contrast between the third and the fourth chapters of John's Gospel is striking. In the former chapter Jesus was described as dealing with a *man* (Nicodemus); here, in chapter 4, with a *woman*; there, with a *Jew*; here, with a *Samaritan*; there, with a person of *high moral standing*; here, with an individual of *low repute.* Nevertheless, the Lord proved himself able to save both.

In the process of winning the soul of this woman Jesus appeals to her *sympathy*: "Give me a drink," to her *inquisitive spirit*: "If you knew . . . ," and to her *conscience*: "Go, call your husband." Truly the great Soul-winner is at work, calling a soul out of the darkness into the light.

And what is the woman doing? One would almost be justified in saying: she is trying her utmost NOT to be saved. When Jesus reminds her of her sinful past, the talkative one suddenly becomes close-mouthed. She utters only the terse remark: "I have no husband." She refuses to be unmasked. But Jesus answers: "You were right when you said, 'I have no husband': for you have had five husbands; and the one whom you now have is not your husband. . . ." How adroitly she thereupon attempts to change the subject. She seizes upon the fact that by means of his last remark Jesus has revealed himself as a prophet; therefore, he will be anxious to answer a question touching his main field of interest: religion; e.g., whether one should worship God on Gerizim or at Jerusalem See pp. 122, 126. But her question, intended as a shrewd device to cover up her guilt, actually serves to reveal the inmost depths of her heart. Jesus

12. This section should be compared with that on Paul's Missionary Methods, pp. 190-196 of this book.

tells her that what God demands is not this or that particular place of worship but *sincerity* (John 4:24, a worship in spirit *and truth*), which happened to be in direct contrast with her attempt at camouflage. Thus, again the "Word of God" proves to be "sharper than any two-edged sword, piercing even to the dividing of soul and spirit, of both joints and marrow, and quick to discern the thoughts and intents of the heart" (Heb. 4:12). There follows a last, desperate attempt to sidetrack the real issue. Says she: "I know that Messiah is coming. When he is come, he will declare unto us all things." Like a shot comes the answer: "I that speak to you am he." Thus, in one dramatic moment, Christ's discourse, which had been exerting its silent though potent influence upon her subconscious self, reaches its climax. But did the Lord's self-revelation as the Messiah lead to her salvation? We do not doubt that she was saved and that many others, too, were converted during Christ's stay in Samaria. See verses 35, 36, 39-42. They recognized Jesus as being the Savior of . . . *the world*!

Thereupon the Lord departed from Samaria and began his lengthy ministry in Galilee.

4. The Great Galilean Ministry

Date: December, 27–April, 29

Scripture: Matt. 4:12–15:20; Mark 1:14–7:23;
Luke 4:14–9:17; John 4:43–6:71

---

a. Brief Summary

When, in the year 4 B.C., Herod the Great died (see pp. 65, 128), his kingdom had been divided among his sons in the following manner:

Archelaus had become king of Judea and Samaria, ruling over these regions from 4 B.C.-A.D. 6. When he was deposed, his territory was placed under procurators, who succeeded each other. One of them was Pontius Pilate, the "governor" who ordered Christ's crucifixion.

Philip had been made ruler of the N.E. region (Iturea, Trachonitis, etc.). The years of his reign were 4 B.C.-A.D. 33.

Herod Antipas had been made tetrarch of Galilee and Perea, in which capacity he continued from 4 B.C.-A.D. 39. This ruler was a full brother of Archelaus.

Hence, during the Great Galilean Ministry Jesus labored in the domain of Herod Antipas. This is the "Herod" of the Gospels (except Matt. 2 and Luke 1). He had married a daughter of Aretas, king of the Arabs, but afterwards in Rome had rejected her in favor of Herodias, the wife of his half-brother Herod Philip. (Note: this "Herod Philip" must not be confused with the "Philip" who ruled over the N.E. region and was also a half-brother of Herod Antipas. Let it be remembered that Herod the Great had, in all, ten wives).

About the time when Jesus began his Great Galilean Ministry, John the Baptist, having reproved Herod Antipas for living in sin with the wife of his half-brother, was committed to prison (Mark 1:14; Luke 3:19, 20). Accordingly, the herald had performed his task. All the attention was now concentrated on the One whom he had introduced as the Lamb of God.

The Great Galilean Ministry began when at Cana Jesus imparted healing to the nobleman's son of Capernaum. The Lord fulfilled the prophecy found in Isaiah 9:1: " . . . in the former time he brought into contempt the land of Zebulun and the land of Naphtali; but in the latter time has he made it glorious, by the way of the sea, beyond the Jordan, Galilee of the nations."

This ministry may be summarized as follows: Jesus amazed the multitudes by his teaching and his miracles and aroused their enthusiasm. As a result, the religious leaders of the Jews were filled with jealousy. Their antagonism became especially evident when the Lord healed certain persons on the Sabbath, in conflict with a corrupt "traditional" interpretation of the law. Hence, in the Sermon on the Mount, Christ set forth the true, spiritual meaning of the commandments, and over against the accusations of the Pharisees exhibited himself as the Fulfiller of the law. The hostility of the leaders increased, but so, on the whole, did the enthusiasm of the common people. The former accused him of being in league with Beelzebub; the latter wanted to take him by force and make him king. However, when Jesus not only refused to become an earthly king but also clearly taught the multitude that salvation was possible only by believing in him—eating his flesh and drinking his blood—there was a large-scale desertion.

Accordingly, we can distribute this material under the following headings:

G reat Enthusiasm. Luke 5:26: "And amazement took hold on all, and they glorified God."

A ntagonism of the leaders. John 5:18: "For this cause, therefore, the Jews sought the more to kill him, because he not only broke the sabbath, but also called God his own Father, making himself equal with God" (cf. Mark 2:27, 28; Luke 6:6-11).

L aw Interpretation (Sermon on the Mount) and organization. Matthew 5:43 ff: "You have heard that it was said, You shall love your neighbor and hate your enemy: but I say to you, Love your enemies and pray for those that persecute you. . . ." Luke 6:13: " . . . and he chose from them twelve, whom he also named apostles. . . ."

I ncreasing Antagonism versus Increasing Enthusiasm. Mark 3:22: "And the scribes who came down from Jerusalem said, He has Beelzebub." John 6:15: "Jesus, therefore, perceiving that they were about to come and take him by force, to make him a king, withdrew again into the hill by himself."

L arge-scale Desertion. John 6:53-66: "Jesus, therefore, said to them, Unless you eat the flesh of the Son of man, and drink his blood, you have no life in yourselves . . . Upon this many of his disciples drew back, and were no longer walking with him."

Let us now take up these five points in their order:

b. Great Enthusiasm

Jesus made Capernaum his "headquarters." It was here that he performed many of his greatest miracles; such as, healing a demoniac, restoring Peter's mother-in-law who "lay sick with a fever," and, a little later, bestowing forgiveness of sin and physical healing upon a paralytic who had been lowered through the roof of the house in which Jesus was speaking.

Again and again we read in the Gospels that Jesus cast out demons. Now, in demon possession we are confronted with a phenomenon which is not easily explained.[13] It is *not* true that the Gospels unscientifically ascribe all human ailments to demon-possession. Note how carefully the evangelists distinguish between this and other afflictions (Matt. 4:24). Neither is it correct to say that this strange phenomenon is the equivalent of what we would call mental disease. Nor, again, is it to be identified with multiple personality or dissociation. In the latter the "control" would seem to have its center of operation in the individual's subconsciousness; it does not have independent existence outside of the individual; and it is neither always operative nor always evil. In demon possession, however, the "control" is an independent, foreign personality which is always evil and always operative. This foreign personality has

13. A few splendid articles on demon possession appeared in *The Banner*, Sept. 2, 1932; March 31, April 7, 14, 1933, by H. Schultze and J. D. Mulder. Also J. D. Mulder, *Psychiatry*, p. 154.

entered and has gained the mastery over the individual. When the demon is cast out, he may choose another person or even an animal as his next place of residence (Mark 5:13). Now, it ought not to surprise us that the chief of the demons (Satan), alarmed by Christ's appearance and redemptive work, became very aggressive, "because he knows that he has but a short time left" (Rev. 12:12). By means of the Master's victory over Satan in the desert of temptation the process of binding the strong one (Matt. 12:29) had been initiated. See p. 144. It would reach its climax in Christ's death, his resurrection, and the pouring out of the Holy Spirit. Whereas (in a relative sense) all nations had been under the thraldom of Satan (Acts 14:16), soon the gospel would go forth far and wide, and the power of the devil would be seriously curtailed. Already the Lord by means of his teaching and the casting out of demons was beginning to dispel Galilee's darkness, in fulfilment of Isaiah's prophecy (Isa. 9:1). The Gospel Age had arrived (Matt. 24:14; cf. Rev. 11:3; 20:2, 3).

When Jesus cast out the demons, he "suffered them not to speak, because they knew him" (Mark 1:34). Similarly, we read in Mark 3:11, 12: "And the unclean spirits, whensoever they beheld him, fell down before him and cried, saying, Thou art the Son of God. *And he charged them much that they should not make him known.*" Our Lord not only gave this charge to demons but also to men (Mark 7:36; 8:30; 9:9). On this subject of our Lord's self-concealment much has been written.[14] It should be borne in mind, however, that the concealment was by no means complete. From the very beginning the disciples recognized in Jesus the Christ (John 1:41, 45, 49). See p. 144. He himself had said to the Samaritan woman: "I, the One who is talking to you, am he" (John 4:26). Moreover, at Nazareth—see p. 155—he clearly proclaimed himself to be the Messiah (Luke 4:16-21). And still later, during the Ministry of the Retirement—see p. 157—in answer to Peter's assertion, "Thou art the Christ, the Son of the living God," he said: "Blessed are you, Simon Bar Jonah: for it is not flesh and blood but my Father who is in heaven who has revealed this to you."

We conclude, therefore, that the self-concealment was, in reality, a *gradually increasing self-disclosure.* Even the disciples failed to take account of the fact that the Messiah had to *suffer.* Little by little the secret was disclosed to them (John 16:12). Had Jesus immediately revealed himself to the multitudes as the Messiah, he would have aroused false hopes of political upheaval (cf. John 6:15). In all

14. Well known is the excellent work by G. Vos, *The Self-disclosure of Jesus.*

likelihood this would have brought his career to a premature close: the Roman government would have intervened. Another reason for the fact that Jesus did not desire to reveal himself at once in all his glory is recorded in Matthew 12:16 ff., which teaches that it would not have been proper for him to do so during the period of his *humiliation.*

The evangelists place great emphasis on the fact that especially during this first stage of the Galilean Ministry the multitudes were *amazed* both by his teaching and miracles (Mark 1:27, 32-34, 35). From every quarter the people gathered around the new Prophet. They brought their sick and demon-possessed. They left again, filled with contagious enthusiasm.

c. Antagonism of the leaders

The common people heard Jesus gladly, but this very popularity filled the Pharisees with envy (cf. Matt. 27:18). See what was said about Pharisees and Sadducees, pp. 126-127. They were angry because of the "success" of the new leader, because of the manner in which he interpreted the Law, and because of the fact that he "called God his own Father, making himself equal with God."

The scribes had superimposed their own elaborate set of rules upon the Old Testament sabbath commandment. Some of these rules were as follows: "Every one who makes a journey, or attends to his cattle, and he who kindles a fire, or rides upon any beast, or sails upon a ship on the sea upon a sabbath day, shall die." Again, "If any one has sprained his hand or foot on the sabbath, he may not pour cold water on it." Women were not allowed to look in a mirror on the sabbath because they might see a gray hair and be tempted to pull it out. One was allowed to *swallow* vinegar on the sabbath, as a remedy for sorethroat, but not use it as a gargle. That would be *working*! The climax of this nonsense was, perhaps, the rule that an egg laid on the sabbath could be eaten, provided one *intended* to kill the [naughty] hen!

Accordingly, it does not surprise us that when Jesus on the sabbath healed the man at the Pool of Bethesda in Jerusalem, there arose a storm of angry protest. Jesus had not only restored this man to health but had even told him to carry his pallet on the sabbath. Hence, as the Pharisees saw it, he was guilty of a double transgression of the sabbath commandment. So thoroughly in love with their sabbath tradition were these religious leaders of the Jews that they considered the transgression of the sabbath tradition to be of far greater significance than the welfare of the individual. If any one had asked them to furnish proof for their contention that carrying a pallet on the sabbath was wrong, they would have referred to Exodus 20:10, Jeremiah 17:19-27, and Nehemiah 13:15. Of course, it was another case *of "burying the Law of God under the mountain of their tradition."* These men were no longer able to see straight. They had no *Open* Bible!

In their blind rage some of the Jerusalem Pharisees followed Jesus as he returned to Galilee. It would seem that about this time the Master and his disciples were going on the sabbath through the grainfield, and the disciples began to pluck and to rub the ears of grain. As the Pharisees saw it, this was *reaping and threshing*! In this connection Jesus asserted his lordship over the sabbath, as the Son of man. A little later in a Galilean synagogue the Lord on the sabbath healed the man with the withered hand. The Pharisees departed from the synagogue in a towering rage.

Yet, the real point at issue was not the sabbath question as such, but the underlying contrast between Christ's deeply spiritual interpretation of the Law and the hairsplitting "traditional" interpretation offered by the scribes and accepted by the Pharisees. Hence, in the Sermon on the Mount, which immediately followed these sabbath controversies, Jesus placed his own interpretation of the Law over against that of the religious leaders of the Jews.

d. Law-interpretation (Sermon on the Mount) and organization

Notice the wonderful contrast indicated in Luke 6:11, 12, "But *they* were filled with *madness* . . . *he* went out into the mountain *to pray*." Consider that the Sermon on the Mount was preached the day after Christ spent a whole night in prayer. The prayer was followed by the choosing of the twelve disciples (Luke 6:13). (How appropriate that after the appointment of the apostles as preachers of the gospel of the Kingdom, Christ in this sermon teaches them this gospel). The choosing of the Twelve was followed by the healing of many sick (cf. Matt. 4:23, 24; Luke 6:18, 19). Then came the sermon. How fitting that Christ, having shown himself to be the Great Physician for the body, by means of this discourse, revealed himself as being also the Great Physician for the soul! (cf. Heb. 7:25). The Sermon has a definite theme and divisions.[15] The theme is *The Gospel of the Kingdom.* First, Jesus discusses *The Citizens of the Kingdom.* Under this heading he describes their character and

15. W. Hendriksen, *The Sermon on the Mount*; also *N.T.C., Matthew*, pp. 254-383.

blessedness, and their relation to the world. Secondly, *The Righteousness of the Kingdom.* Jesus points out that this righteousness is in full accord with the moral law of the Old Testament; that it is *not* in conformity with the current and traditional Jewish interpretation and application of the Law; that, with respect to God, the essence of this righteousness is: "Love God above all"; and that, with respect to man, its meaning may be summed up in the command: "Love your neighbor as yourself." The third part of the Sermon is an *Exhortation to Enter the Kingdom.* (A little later Jesus was going to tell the Galilean multitudes that entrance is possible only through living faith in himself. See p. 155.)

e. Increasing Antagonism versus Increasing Enthusiasm

When Jesus had finished "these words"—i.e., the Sermon on the Mount—"the multitudes were astonished at his teaching." Wherever he went, great crowds followed him, eager to listen to his discourses, even more desirous to see his miracles. To them all he revealed his wonderful power and his tender sympathy: to the centurion, by healing his servant; to the widow at Nain, by raising her son; to John the Baptist, by showing him clearly that he himself, even Jesus of Nazareth, was the Christ, in whom Old Testament prophecy reached its fulfilment; and to the sinful woman who (while Jesus sat at meat in the house of Simon the Pharisee) anointed him, by forgiving her sins.

But the opposition also increased in boldness. Although Simon criticized Jesus *"within himself,"* other Pharisees *openly* accused him of being in league with Beelzebub. Their envy was aroused when they observed that "all the multitudes were amazed." having just witnessed the healing of a demon-possessed man, who was blind and dumb, and were saying: "Can this be the son of David?" Retiring to the seashore, Jesus began to teach the multitudes in parables. He instructed them regarding the manner in which the kingdom of heaven is received (The Four Kinds of Soil); its growth and development, both outward and inward (The Mustard Seed, The Leaven); its preciousness (The Treasure Hid in the Field; The Pearl of Great Price); and its present mixed character and future consummation (The Tares; The Dragnet). See Matt. 13. By means of these parables Jesus *concealed* the truth from those who had hardened their hearts against it, and *revealed* it more fully to those who were eager to learn it.[16] When, after stilling a tempest, Jesus crossed over to the land of

16. See W. M. Taylor, *The Parables of Our Savior,* Introduction.

the Gadarenes and cured a demoniac but caused the demons to enter into a herd of swine which "rushed down the steep and perished in the sea," the people of that region "began to beseech him to depart from their borders." Having returned to Capernaum, a great multitude thronged him as he healed the woman who touched the hem of his garment. And when a little later he raised the daughter of Jairus, those who witnessed this great miracle "were amazed straightway with great amazement." But when in the synagogue of Nazareth he showed how Isaiah 61 had attained its glorious fulfilment in his own ministry, he was rejected. He sent forth the Twelve as kingdom ambassadors and gave them a definite mandate (Matt. 10). When Herod Antipas, who had beheaded John the Baptist, heard about the miracles which the Lord and his disciples were performing, he was so impressed by them that his guilty fears were thoroughly aroused. It was then that Jesus sought temporary retirement with the Twelve, but the multitudes followed him to a desert place on the northeast shore of the Sea of Galilee. Here, looking upon the people with compassion, he miraculously fed them. Their enthusiasm now reached its climax, for they wished to take him by force and make him king. This very fact indicates that they failed completely to understand the spiritual character of his mission.

f. Large-scale Desertion

The time had now arrived for Jesus to reveal himself more clearly to the multitudes, namely, as the Bread of Life who had come down from heaven. He told them that only by eating his flesh and drinking his blood was salvation possible. He, moreover, rebuked the multitudes and the scribes for their externalism. When the people discovered that Jesus was not the kind of Messiah for whom they had been waiting, they deserted him in large numbers. Turning to his disciples, he asked them: "Would you also go away?" Simon Peter answered him, "Lord, to whom shall we go? thou hast the words of eternal life. And we have believed and know that thou art the Holy One of God." Thus the Great Galilean Ministry came to a close.

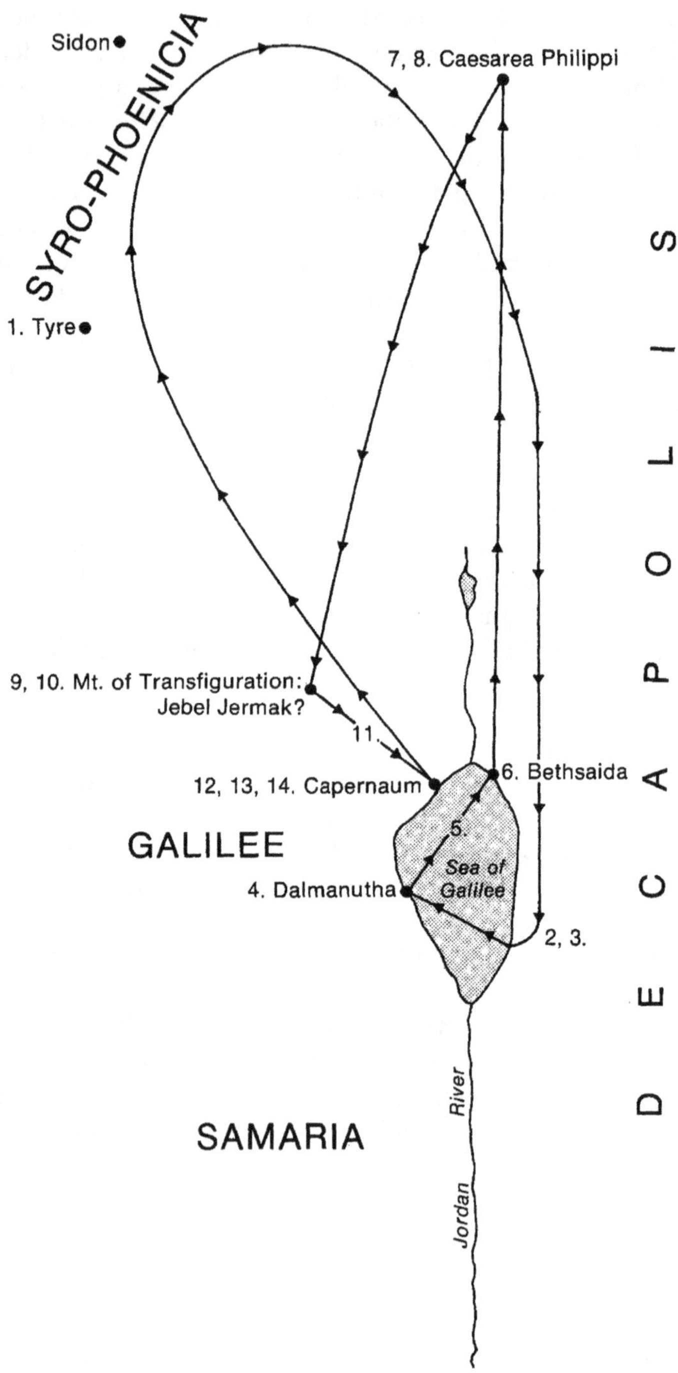
THE RETIREMENT MINISTRY
Begin at Capernaum and follow the arrows
Sidon
SYRO-PHOENICIA
7, 8. Caesarea Philippi
1. Tyre
D E C A P O L I S
9, 10. Mt. of Transfiguration:
Jebel Jermak?
11.
12, 13, 14. Capernaum
6. Bethsaida
GALILEE
5.
Sea of Galilee
4. Dalmanutha
2, 3.
SAMARIA
Jordan River

9
From the Manger to the Mount (continued)

5. The Retirement Ministry and Later Judean Ministry

Date: April-December, 29
Scripture: Matt. 15:21–18:35; Mark 7:24–9:50; Luke 9:18-50; John 7:1–10:39

a. **Retirement Ministry**: April-October

During this ministry Jesus withdrew himself from the Capernaum multitudes. He instructed his disciples with respect to the significance of his coming suffering. He departed from Galilee and went to Phoenicia, where he healed the daughter of the Syrophoenician woman. Had not Simeon predicted that the child which he had taken up in his arms would be "a light for revelation to the *Gentiles,* as well as for glory to thy people Israel?" Next, Jesus sought seclusion in Decapolis, southeast of the Sea of Galilee. Here he healed a deaf stammerer and, by his divine power, fed a great multitude. He then crossed the Sea of Galilee to Dalmanutha, and having rebuked the Pharisees who approached him with unbelieving requests for a sign, again crossed the sea, and at Bethsaida healed a blind man who saw "men as trees walking." Finally, Jesus went with his disciples to the regions of Caesarea Philippi. It was here that Peter made his great confession: "Thou art the Christ, the Son of the living God." It is true, of course, that by the disciples Jesus had been recognized as the Messiah from the very beginning. See pp. 144, 151. But the confession of Peter *at this particular moment* was, nevertheless, very significant because it occurred after the Lord had shattered the hopes of the multitudes that he would be the kind of Messiah for whom *they* had been yearning. And now, in spite of the fact that the

Galilean multitudes had, to a large extent, deserted Jesus, Peter *still* confesses him to be the Christ.

Jesus said to Peter: "Blessed are you, Simon Bar-Jonah: for it is not flesh and blood but my Father who is in heaven who has revealed this to you. And I say to you, you are Peter, and upon this rock I will build my church; and the gates of Hades shall not prevail against it. I will give you the keys of the kingdom of heaven; and whatever you shall bind on earth shall be bound in heaven, and whatever you shall loose on earth shall be loosed in heaven." That this authority to govern the church was not given solely to Peter is evident from two considerations:

(1) Peter had spoken representatively; for Jesus had asked: "But who do you [pl.] say that I am?"

(2) The same authority is given to the other apostles (Matt. 18:18, 19). See also *N.T.C., Matthew,* pp. 645-652.

It is not reasonably open to doubt that Jesus in these words established the foundation of ecclesiastical law. It is Christ who, through the divinely instituted offices (first, the extraordinary offices; later, the ordinary offices) governs his church. It is he himself who has given to this divinely created institution authority over the life and doctrine of its members.[1] In this connection the following passages should also be carefully studied: Matthew 10:20, 40; 28:18; John 20:23; Acts 1:20; I Corinthians 5:3, 4; II Corinthians 5:4; 10:8; Revelation 1:18; 3:7. Of course, this authority should be exercised in the spirit of love, in the name of Christ, unto edification. See especially Ephesians 4:12. According to the clear teaching of Scripture the church is, accordingly, a Christocracy. It is governed by Christ and in accordance with his teachings.

Matthew 16:17-19 has been misinterpreted and otherwise abused in various ways. According to the Roman Catholic Church it establishes the primacy of Peter. And, on the other hand, there are those who have tried to argue that by all the rules of historical criticism it must be cast aside. Neither opinion has any basis in historical fact or in literary evidence.

After Peter's acknowledgment of Jesus as the Messiah, the Lord began to teach the disciples the meaning of his Messianic office. He

---

1. This question of "authority" and "office" has ever been a burning issue. See E. De Witt Burton, *American Journal of Theology,* 1912, p. 579; A. Harnack, *The Constitution and Law of the Church,* p. 5; F. J. A. Hort, *The Christian Ecclesia,* p. 84; C. von Weizsacker, *The Apostolic Age of the Christian Church,* vol. 2, p. 292; art. "Apostle," *I.S.B.E.*

instructed them with respect to the cross on which he would suffer and die as a ransom for many: its necessity and glory; also, the fact that its blessings are limited to those who manifest a childlike spirit. This teaching was, indeed, very necessary, for even the disciples had expected nothing of the kind. Peter even began to rebuke the Master, but was himself rebuked in these words: "Get out of my sight, Satan; you are a stumbling block to me: for you are looking at things, not from God's point of view but from men's."

Six days later our Lord took Peter and James and John with him upon a high mountain. He was "transfigured" before them: "his face shone as the sun, and his garments became white as the light." With him appeared Moses and Elijah. The Lord again, as often before, gave evidence of his voluntary sacrifice, to which the law (as represented by Moses) and prophecy (as represented by Elijah) had pointed.

From this glorious mountaintop experience Jesus descended to the valley of human agony and *manifold* unbelief. "There came to him a man, kneeling to him and saying, 'Lord, have mercy on my son: for he is an epileptic, and suffers grievously; for often he falls into the fire, and often into the water. And I brought him to thy disciples but they could not cure him.' And Jesus answered and said, 'O faithless and perverse generation, how long shall I be with you? how long shall I bear with you? bring him to me.' And Jesus rebuked him; and the demon went out of him: and the boy was cured from that hour."

Having returned to Capernaum, Jesus gave his disciples a lesson in humility, self-sacrifice, service, and love, the very characteristics which would be exemplified in his own atoning death on the cross. The Lord then left Capernaum for the last time. He went on his way toward Jerusalem.

b. Later Judean Ministry: October-December

It is impossible to point out the exact order of the movements of the Lord during this Ministry and the next. Jesus, leaving Galilee, "stedfastly set his face to go to Jerusalem" (Luke 9:51). In journeying through Samaria he was rejected by the Samaritans but refused to take vengeance upon them. He arrived in Bethany (just east of Jerusalem) and reminded Martha of her needless care, while Mary had chosen the good part. Probably during this ministry—or a little later—he uttered some of his most beautiful story-parables: The Good Samaritan, The Embarrassed Host, The Rich Fool, The Barren Fig Tree, etc.

In Jerusalem he was present at the Feast of Tabernacles and the

Feast of the Dedication. See p. 126. Though he had been rejected in Judea (John 5:18), Galilee (John 6:66), the land of the Gadarenes (Matt. 8:34), and Samaria (Luke 9:53), he nevertheless made his tender appeal to sinners: "If any man thirst, let him come to me and drink." In connection with the affair of the woman taken in adultery, on whom he had mercy, and the man born blind, whom he healed and lovingly admonished, he called himself the Light of the world (John 8:12; 9:5). He said, moreover, "He who follows me shall not walk in the darkness, but shall have the light of life" (John 8:12). The healing of the blind man on the sabbath had aroused the ire of the Pharisees. Replying to their charge Jesus pointed out the difference between robbers who break into the sheepfold, and himself, the Good Shepherd, who was about to lay down his life for the sheep. He said, in tender appeal, "My sheep hear my voice, and I know them, and they follow me; and I give to them everlasting life; and they shall never perish, and no one shall snatch them out of my hand."

But the teachings of Christ created such opposition that he left the city. He went to Bethabara, where he had been baptized, and there he prepared for his tour in Perea. He had already sent out the Seventy to proclaim his coming.

6. Perean Ministry

Date: December, 29—April, 30
Scripture: Matt. 19:1—20:34; Mark 10;
Luke 9:51—19:27; John 10:40—12:11

When we assign the title *Perean Ministry* to this period, we do not mean to imply that Jesus remained in the Trans-Jordanic region during these entire four months. He may have made more than one trip to Judea. One journey was for the purpose of bearing testimony concerning himself by means of a great sign, a most notable miracle. We refer, of course, to the fact that the Lord went to Bethany and raised from the dead Lazarus, the brother of Martha and Mary. The corpse had been in the grave four days! This sign filled the religious leaders of the Jews with such envy that they decided to carry out their plan of long standing to put Jesus to death. But as the hour had not yet come for Jesus to die, he withdrew to the village of Ephraim, north of Jerusalem. We next find Jesus in Perea where he went through cities and villages teaching and performing a few miracles. The parables recorded by Luke, some probably uttered during this ministry, will live forever. They are sublime both in content and form. They are human interest stories and describe the riches of God's grace to poor, lost sinners and the generous character of the invitation extended to them. The following titles may be assigned to them: The Slighted Invitation, The Father's Welcome to Sinners Who Repent (here we refer to the trilogy: Lost Sheep, Lost Coin, Lost—"Prodigal"—Son), The Steward Who Had Foresight, The Rich Man and Lazarus, The Widow Who Persevered, The Pharisee and The Publican, The Pounds. Christ's teaching concerning divorce and "little children" also was imparted during this ministry.

The Lord "took to him the Twelve," and continued his instruction with respect to his coming suffering. He pointed out that the blessings of the cross are distributed according to God's sovereign will. He enlarged on the subject of the self-sacrificing motive and the substitutionary character of his death. He said: "For the Son of man also came not to be served but to serve, and to give his life a ransom in the place of many."

The words *"in the place of many"* clearly indicate that Jesus had Isaiah 53 in mind. There we read: "By the knowledge of himself shall my righteous servant justify *many*; and he shall bear their iniquities . . . he bare the sin of *many*. . . ." Anyone who reads Isaiah 53 and then turns to the words of Jesus can no longer doubt that it was Jesus himself who not only predicted his death *but definitely interpreted its meaning.* His passion was a ransom. It was a voluntary, vicarious, and limited atonement.[2] No one has a right to say that Scripture has left us without an interpretation of Christ's death. In fact, no one has even a right to say that Paul was the first one who attached a definite meaning to the Lord's death. Jesus himself—as is clear from *all* the Gospels—interpreted his coming cross!

Recrossing the Jordan for the last time, the Lord entered and passed through Jericho. He healed two blind men and converted the publican, Zaccheus. To him the Lord revealed the purpose of his earthly mission in the striking sentence: "For the Son of man came to seek and to save that which was lost."

At last, six days before the Passover, Jesus arrived at the village of Bethany where a supper was prepared for him in the house of Simon, the leper, and he was anointed by Mary, the sister of Martha and

---

2. See L. Berkhof, *Vicarious Atonement Through Christ*; also A. A. Hodge, *The Atonement*.

Lazarus. The Lord interpreted her deed as having been performed "against the day of my burying."

7. Passion, Resurrection, Ascension

Date: April-May, 30

Scripture: Matt. 21:28; Mark 11-16; Luke 19:28–24:53; John 12:12–21:25; Acts 1

Sunday

On the day after the supper at Bethany—i.e., on Sunday—Jesus entered Jerusalem riding on an ass's colt. The multitudes were filled with wild enthusiasm. Certainly, one who was able to raise from the dead a man who had been in the tomb four days would also be able to deliver the Jews from the galling yoke of the Romans! Hence, the people strewed palm branches in the way, and loudly cried: "Hosanna, to the Son of David." But when our Lord noticed that the masses misinterpreted his mission and saw in him the fulfilment of their carnal expectations, he poured out his grief in bitter tears, saying: "If you, even you, had only known on this day the things that pertain to [your] peace! But now they are hidden from your eyes. For the days shall come upon you when your enemies shall cast up an embankment against you, and encircle you, and hem you in on every side. They shall dash you to the ground, you and the children within you. And they shall not leave in you one stone upon another, because you did not recognize the time of your visitation" (Luke 19:42-44; cf. vs. 37; see also Mark 11:10).

It was, indeed, a strange sight: a weeping king amid a shouting multitude! The people must have been deeply disappointed—cf. their disappointment in Galilee, p. 155—when it became clear to them that Jesus was *not* the king of their dreams. Nevertheless there was no excuse for their ignorance. Had they studied the Scriptures with a prayerful heart, they would have seen in this triumphal entry the manifestation of a Messiah who was "just, having salvation, lowly," ready to pour forth upon Jerusalem "the spirit of grace and supplication," and about to "open a fountain for sin and for uncleanness" by means of the shedding of his own blood. But they did not understand the meaning of the prophecies of Zechariah which the Lord was fulfilling (Zech. 9:9), or about to fulfill (Zech. 12:10, 13:1).

In the evening Jesus returned to Bethany with his disciples (Mark 11:11).

Monday

Returning to Jerusalem the next morning, Jesus saw a fig tree in full foliage, just as if it were loaded down heavily with the earlier fruit. But when he came to it "he found nothing on it but leaves." So the Lord cursed it, saying: "Never again let there be fruit from you!" The barren fig tree was a fit emblem of Israel. See Isaiah 5; Luke 13:6-9. Jesus himself would interpret the figure the next day (Tuesday) when he said: "Therefore I say to you, the kingdom of God shall be taken away from you, and shall be given to a nation *bringing forth its fruit*" (Matt. 21:43). In fact, the disciples did not even have to wait until the next day to witness Christ's explanation: the pretentious fig tree had its counterpart in the temple, where a lively business was being transacted so that sacrifices might be made, while at the same time its priests were plotting to put to death the One apart from whom these offerings had no meaning whatever. The Lord cleansed the temple as he had done once before. See pp. 145-146.

Tuesday

On the next day the representatives of the Sanhedrin formally challenged the right of Jesus to cleanse the temple. The Lord, in reply, demanded that they first answer his question: "The baptism of John, was it from heaven or from men?" They did not dare to answer the question either way: to denounce John as an imposter would have brought them into conflict with the people; on the other hand, to accept the ministry of John as having been divinely ordained would have implied an admission of the authority of Jesus whom John had extolled. When, therefore, they answered: "We do not know," Jesus by means of the Parables of The Wicked Tillers ("Husbandmen") and The Marriage of The King's Son predicted the woes which would come upon those who had rejected him. See especially Matthew 21:43, already cited. It is a remarkable fact that at least five times, during this week of his suffering and atoning death he who was himself a Jew predicted Israel's doom; he who loved the Jews so much that he wept over Jerusalem definitely declared that: "Jerusalem shall be trodden down of the Gentiles until the times of the Gentiles be fulfilled." See Luke 19:43, 44; 21:24; Matthew 21:43; 23:37; Mark 13:1, 2; and Luke 23:27-31. And, in fact, Scripture does not contain a single prediction concerning a national restoration of the Jews which is still future. There is no special promise for the Jews as a people. There is but *one* Gospel, *one* way of salvation for all. Accordingly, our message to the Jews and to every one else must be: "Believe on the Lord Jesus, and you shall be saved, you and your house" (Acts 16:31).

The Lord, in his infinite mercy, has promised that throughout the ages, until he comes again, such Christ-centered missionary activity shall be blessed, also when it is carried on among the Jews: *the remnant,* in every age, shall be saved. For a fuller explanation, see the author's booklet, *Israel in Prophecy.*

On this same day by answering the questions of his adversaries—Is it lawful to give tribute to Caesar? Is there a resurrection? Which is the great commandment?—and by asking them a question—What do you think of the Christ?—Jesus thoroughly confuted them. Our Lord was teaching in the court of the temple. Publicly he denounced the religious leaders for their hypocrisy, uttering a sevenfold woe upon them. He declared that the accumulated guilt of "all the righteous blood shed on earth, from the blood of Abel the righteous to the blood of Zechariah, son of Barachiah," rested upon them. See pp. 19, 110. He said: "They bind heavy burdens and grievous to be borne, and lay them on men's shoulders; but they themselves are unwilling to move them with so much as a finger." See pp. 121-122.

The religious leaders were more determined than ever to put Jesus to death. Nevertheless, there was a ray of light shining into the darkness: some Greeks desired to see the Lord, forerunners of the vast throngs from the Gentile world which would accept him on and after Pentecost.

When Jesus had departed from the temple and had ascended the Mount of Olives, on the way to Bethany, he taught his disciples about the coming destruction of Jerusalem and the end of the world.

In order to obtain the right approach to this so-called Eschatological Discourse, recorded in Matthew 24, 25, Mark 13, and Luke 21, it is important to bear in mind that, according to the Gospel of Matthew, the disciples, having heard Christ's prediction of the destruction of the beautiful temple, asked him this question: "Tell us, when shall *these things be?* and what shall be the sign of thy coming, and of *the end of the world*?" (Matt. 24:3).

It is clear that these men erroneously assumed that the destruction of Jerusalem and of its temple would coincide with the end of the world. It is for this very reason that Jesus in his answer *must needs* discuss both these matters. He taught his disciples that the wars and rumors of wars which would result in Jerusalem's destruction would *not* spell the end of the world. Said he: "And you shall hear of wars and rumors of wars, but watch out; do not be disturbed . . . the end is not yet."

As we see it, this wonderful discourse of our Lord can be divided as follows:

1. Mark 13:1-7; Matthew 24:1-6; Luke 21:5-9: *Relation between Jerusalem's Fall and the End of the World:* Imminent political upheavals and the coming of false Christs must not terrify the disciples: they do not indicate the second coming and the end of the world.

2. Mark 13:8-13; Matthew 24:7-13; Luke 21:10-24a: *Jerusalem's Fall:* Signs in the political, physical, and religious realm shall precede and accompany the Fall of Jerusalem. The signs (1) and (2) actually occurred, just as Jesus had predicted.

3. Mark 13:10; Matthew 24:14; Luke 21:24b: *The Present Age:* The Gospel of the kingdom shall be preached to the whole world. Jerusalem shall be trampled down by the Gentiles until the times of the Gentiles are fulfilled (i.e., until the very end).

4. Mark 13:14-23; Matthew 24:15-28: *The Great Tribulation at the Close of the Present Age, as Prefigured by the Destruction of Jerusalem:* Great tribulation, false Christs, false prophets shall manifest themselves at the time of Jerusalem's fall and again in connection with the end of the world. For the elect's sake, the season of intense persecution and of "the abomination of desolation" (Dan. 9:27; 12:11) shall be *shortened.*

5. Mark 13:24-27; Matthew 24:29-31; Luke 21:25-28: *The Second Coming and the Signs that Shall Accompany It:* Signs in sun, moon, and stars; the roaring of the sea and its billows; the distress of nations shall immediately precede the Second Coming. The Son of man will come for the redemption of his elect.

6. Mark 13:28-37; Matthew 24:32–25:46; Luke 21:29-36: *Exhortation unto Watchfulness.* Jesus urged upon his disciples that they should always be ready. This exhortation unto watchfulness was illustrated by a number of parables, such as, The Fig Tree, The Five Wise and Five Foolish Virgins, The Talents.

It is instructive to observe that this same broad outline of the course of history is also clearly indicated in the Book of Revelation. There, too, items 3, 4, and 5 occur in that same order, that is, the lengthy period during which the "two witnesses" prophesy and "Satan is bound" is followed by the very brief season ("shortened for the elect's sake") during which men look upon the dead bodies of the witnesses and Satan is loosed out of his prison; and this, in turn, is followed by the public rapture of the witnesses at the second coming upon the great white throne. *Gospel Age, Tribulation, Second Coming:* that is the order which is found everywhere in Scripture. See the author's *More Than Conquerors, a Commentary on the Book of Revelation.*

Wednesday

It is probable that on or even before Wednesday the "chief priests and scribes" mapped out the details of their plan to kill Jesus, and Judas received the thirty pieces of silver, blood money for which he agreed to betray Jesus into the hands of his enemies. About this same time the Lord made the definite prediction that during the Passover Feast he would be handed over to be crucified.

Thursday

That Jesus ate the Passover at the regular time is not open to reasonable doubt.[3] Notice especially these two passages:

Luke 22:7: "And the day of unleavened bread came, on which the passover *must* be sacrificed."

Mark 14:12: "And on the first day of unleavened bread, *when it was the custom to sacrifice the passover,* his disciples say to him, Where wilt thou that we go and make ready that thou mayest eat the passover?" In the original the imperfect of customary practice is used. Verkuyl translates: "when the Passover Lamb was annually sacrificed."[4]

It is clear, therefore, that Jesus and his disciples celebrated Passover at the *proper* and *customary* time; i.e., on Thursday night, the "night to be much observed unto Jehovah" (Exod. 12:42; Num. 28:16). It is true that John 13:1, 29, and 28:18 place us before a difficulty. Nevertheless, we should not try to "solve" that difficulty by denying the clear teaching of the Synoptics (Matthew, Mark, Luke). A possible solution, accepted by many, is that which, on the basis of Numbers 28:16, 17, assumes that John, in the given references, refers to the entire Feast of Unleavened Bread. This Feast lasted seven days and was preceded by the eating of the lamb.[5]

Jesus and his disciples were gathered in an upper room in order

3. See W. Hendriksen, *N.T.C., John,* Vol. II, pp. 400-404.
4. G. Verkuyl, *Berkeley Version of The New Testament,* p. 122.
5. For an even better solution see W. Hendriksen, *N.T.C., John,* Vol. II, pp. 400-404.

that they might eat the passover. When the disciples began to quarrel about the question "who should be the greatest," the Lord gave a striking example of humility by washing their feet. Then he startled the company by stating: "I solemnly assure you that one of you shall betray me."

This called forth three questions:

(1) The question of wholesome self-distrust, asked by all the disciples with the exception of Judas: "Surely, not I, Lord?" (as the original has it, Matt. 26:22).

(2) The question of quiet confidence: "Lord, who is it?" (John 13:25). That was John's question.

(3) The question of loathsome hypocrisy, which filled the heart of Judas as he said: "Surely, not I, *Rabbi*?" (Matt. 26:25).

Jesus not only pointed out the traitor but also predicted that all the disciples would forsake him. Peter boasted: "Even if I must die with thee, yet will I not deny thee." Moreover, we read: "Likewise also said all the disciples." *All*, accordingly, gave clear evidence of the fact that they did not know their own hearts.

This was also the night in which Jesus instituted the Lord's Supper. By saying, "This is the blood of the covenant which is shed for many for remission of sins," he plainly referred to his death on the cross as a sacrifice for sin. See also p. 161.

Sorrow had filled the troubled hearts of the disciples because Jesus had spoken of his departure and death, had told them that one of their own number would betray him, had predicted that all would be offended in him, and by means of the feet washing had revealed the sinful pride of his disciples. It is in this light that we can understand the opening words of the wonderful Upper Room discourses which immediately followed:

"Let not your heart be troubled."[6]

First, the Lord mentioned several reasons why the disciples should not feel sad. These reasons are to be found in John 14, to which we have given the title, *A Word of Comfort*. Next, he laid down three fundamental principles for their conduct:

(1) Abide in me.
(2) Love one another.
(3) Also bear witness.

This material is found in John 15, *A Word of Admonition*.

---

6. See W. Hendriksen, *N.T.C., John*, Vol. II, pp. 260-374 for a detailed explanation of John 14-17.

In chapter 16 Jesus predicts the coming and work of the Comforter, the Spirit of truth. He adds this encouraging word: "In the world you have tribulation: but be of good cheer; I have overcome the world." Accordingly, this chapter contains *A Word of Prediction.*

Then Jesus, about to depart, concentrated all his love in a most glorious prayer: for himself, for his disciples, for the church at large (ch. 17).

It must have been well into the night (cf. John 13:30) when Jesus and his little company, having sung a hymn, left the Upper Room and went to the garden of Gethsemane, just east of Jerusalem, on the slopes of the Mt. of Olives.

Friday

In Gethsemane Jesus, "having been heard for his godly fear, though he was the Son, yet learned obedience by the things which he suffered" (Heb. 5:7-10).

Of course, in that perfect heart of Christ there never was even an inkling of disobedience or rebellion. Nevertheless, in the expression of perfect surrender there was this glorious progress:

First prayer: "O my Father, if it be possible, let this cup pass away from me: nevertheless, not as I will, but as thou wilt." Notice that in the first part of this sentence the *main* clause is: "Let this cup pass away from me."

Second and third prayer: "O, my Father, if this cannot pass except I drink it, thy will be done." Here the main clause is: "Thy will be done."

The agony which Jesus began to experience was such that "his sweat became as it were great drops of blood falling upon the ground." Was this because he could no longer feel the closeness of his Father, and did this very desertion give him a preview, as it were, of the most bitter suffering on the cross?

Soon the traitor came with the temple guard. Very vividly the Gospels describe the "Onslaught of the Treacherous" (Judas), the "Defeat of the Defenders" (the disciples, who left him and fled, just as Jesus had predicted), and the "Triumph of the Captive" (he offered himself willingly; otherwise, they could not have captured him).

Jesus was led to the house of Annas, the father-in-law of Caiaphas, the highpriest. It was here that Peter denied the Lord. Before Caiaphas the Lord declared that he was the Christ, the Son of God. He was pronounced worthy of death, a blasphemer, was spit upon and mocked.

Some hours later—very early in the morning—the preliminary sentence was confirmed by the Sanhedrin gathered in formal meeting. It is hardly necessary to point out that just about everything with respect to the trial of Jesus was illegal: the fact that his judge also acted as his accuser; that the city was scoured for witnesses; that the trial took place at night and was confirmed officially only a few hours later; that the sentence was carried out on the day on which it had been pronounced, etc., etc., etc.

Inasmuch as the Sanhedrin did not possess the power to execute a death sentence, Jesus was brought before Pilate, the Roman procurator. This man tried by every possible means to rid himself of Jesus. He did not want to pass sentence. Hence he tried: a. to return the prisoner to the Sanhedrin—"Judge him according to your law," b. to let Herod judge him, c. to persuade the people to take him off his hands—by permitting them to choose between Jesus and Barabbas, and d. to meet the Sanhedrin halfway by scourging Jesus and then releasing him. But all these efforts were in vain. In thorough exasperation he cried out, "What then shall I do with Jesus, who is called the Christ?" The clamor of the crowd became louder and louder: "Crucify him, crucify him."

The knockout blow was dealt Pilate when "the Jews cried out saying: 'If you release this man, you are not Caesar's friend!' " Now, the procurator knew that Tiberius was very suspicious. He reasoned that if the rumor should ever reach the emperor that he, Pilate, had sided with an insurrectionist, deposition and banishment would be the result. So, Pilate finally delivered Jesus over to be crucified. "I found no fault in this man," he had said again and again. Herod, too, had found no fault in him. Nevertheless, he was sentenced to die a most accursed death. The solution of this problem is found in Isaiah 53:5: "He was wounded *for our transgressions*."

Jesus, having been tormented in the soldiers' quarters, was compelled to carry his own cross. When his strength failed, a certain Simon of Cyrene was pressed into service. Jerusalem's aristocratic ladies, who shed tears when they saw that a man so young was being led to such a cruel death, were rebuked by the Savior in these words: "Daughters of Jerusalem, weep not for me, but weep for yourselves and for your children . . . For if they do these things in the green tree, what shall be done in the dry?"

At last the procession reached Golgotha, the place of the skull. It was here that the Lord was crucified, and together with him two thieves. Truly, "he was numbered with the transgressors" (Isa. 53:12).

From nine o'clock in the morning until three o'clock in the afternoon Jesus suffered the agonies of hell upon the cross.

The Seven Words of the Cross:

a. *From 9 o'clock until noon:*

(1) "Father, forgive them: for they do not know what they are doing" (Luke 23:34).

(2) "I solemnly declare to you, To-day you shall be with me in Paradise" (Luke 23:43).

(3)"Woman, look, your son! . . . Look, your mother!" (John 19:27).

b. *The three hours of darkness: from noon until 3 o'clock; no words reported.*

c. *About 3 o'clock:*

(4) "My God, my God, why hast thou forsaken me?" (Mark 15:34).

(5) "I am thirsty" (John 19:28).

(6) "It is finished" (John 19:30).

(7) "Father, into thy hands I commend my spirit" (Luke 23:46).

Just as we speak about the Seven Words of the Cross we may also refer to the Six or Seven—it depends upon how you count them—Miracles of Golgotha.

The Miracles of Golgotha

(1) The Miraculous Darkness, from noon until 3 o'clock (Luke 23:44, 45).

(2) The *Loud* Voice of the dying Lord (Luke 23:46).

(3) The Rending of the Veil (Matt. 27:51).

(4) The Earthquake (Matt. 27:51).

(5) The Opened Graves (Matt. 27:52).

(6) The Resurrection of Saints (Matt. 27:52, 53). (Some count (5) and (6) as one miracle.)

(7) The Undisturbed Gravecloths (John 20:6).

These miracles—as well as the Seven Words—are significant because they set forth the *meaning* of Christ's death on the cross. Thus, the miraculous darkness indicates, as we see it, that the Father's wrath rested upon the One who was made sin for us. The loud voice with which Jesus uttered the seventh word, yielding his spirit to the Father, clearly shows that his death was voluntary. The rending of the veil loudly proclaims the freedom of access to the heavenly Holy of holies, etc. See also on the meaning of the cross, pp. 161, 167.

After Jesus had died, one of the soldiers pierced his side. From the body blood and water issued forth. This, too, was in fulfilment of prophecy (Exod. 12:46; Num. 9:12; Ps. 34:20; see also Exod. 34:24; Deut. 21:22, 23; Zech. 12:10).

Late in the afternoon Joseph of Arimathea removed the body of Jesus from the cross and laid it in a new tomb. This was not at all what the enemies of the Lord had intended. Here, too, prophecy was fulfilled: "And they made his grave with the wicked." Nevertheless, he was "with a rich man in his death, because he had done no violence, neither was any deceit in his mouth." Nicodemus had brought a mixture of myrrh and aloes, *about a hundred pound weight.*

"And the women, who had come with him out of Galilee, followed, and beheld the tomb, and how his body was laid. And they went home and prepared spices and perfumes."

Saturday

Somewhere we read these lines:

> Matthew has nothing to relate
> Of that one day of dreadful gloom.
> Luke had no further word to state.
> The stone had sealed the Master's tomb.

But that is hardly correct. Matthew 27:62-66 tells us what happened on "the day after the Preparation," that is, on Saturday. The story which this evangelist tells is very closely connected with the resurrection narrative found in chapter 28. The material could be divided as follows:

What Happened to the Guard when Jesus Died and Rose Again

(1) *The guard posted.* "Pilate said to them, Take a guard: go, make it as sure as you can." This happened on Saturday morning (Matt. 27:65).

Sunday and Afterward

(2) *The guard scattered.* "And for fear of him the watchers quaked, and became as dead men." This occurred very early on Sunday morning (Matt. 28:4).

(3) *The guard bribed.* "And when they were assembled with the elders . . . they gave much money to the soldiers, instructing them, "Say, his disciples came by night, and stole him away while we slept." This happened a little later on the same Sunday morning (Matt. 28:12, 13).

On Sunday morning, while it was still dark—both in nature and in their hearts—some women who were friends of Jesus sorrowfully trudged their way to the tomb. They intended to anoint the body! At early dawn—both in Nature and in their hearts?—they, having reached the tomb, received the glorious message of the two angels: "Why do you seek the living among the dead? He is not here but is risen: remember how he spoke to you when he was yet in Galilee, saying that the Son of man must be delivered up into the hands of sinful men, and be crucified, and the third day rise again." A little later, perhaps at full dawn—not only in nature but also in their hearts!—Jesus met them and told them to tell the disciples that they depart to Galilee where they would see him. The resurrection itself was not witnessed by human eyes. The accompanying phenomena in the realm of nature had filled the hearts of the guards with consternation so that they had fled.

One of the women who had started out that morning in order to anoint the Lord's body had brought the report to Peter and John. Accordingly, these two disciples ran to the tomb, found it empty, and believed that Jesus was really risen. To Mary Magdalene who, after Peter and John's departure, stood weeping at the tomb, Jesus revealed himself, changing her gloom into gladness.

Not only did the Lord appear to women. To the disciple who had denied him three times, Simon Peter, he also manifested himself. Moreover, on Sunday afternoon he "drew near and went with" two disciples, Cleopas and his companion, who were on their way to the village of Emmaus. "He interpreted to them in all the scriptures the things concerning himself." See p. 83. In the breaking of the bread they suddenly recognized him, and he vanished out of their sight. When it was evening Jesus "came and stood in the midst" of the astonished ten disciples, Thomas being absent. A week later the Lord again revealed himself to the same company, all the eleven being present. He caused the doubts of Thomas to melt away. A while later the Lord manifested himself at the Sea of Galilee to seven disciples, one of them being John, the author of the Fourth Gospel. At this time Peter heard from the lips of his Master three heart-searching questions and received the glorious threefold pastoral mandate: "Feed my lambs . . . tend my sheep . . . feed my sheep." Afterward, on a mountain in Galilee, Jesus appeared to more than five hundred brethren. Here he

(1) Made a Great Claim: "All authority has been given to me in heaven and on earth."

(2) Gave the Great Commission: "Go therefore, and make disciples of all the nations, baptizing them into the name of the Father and of the Son and of the Holy Spirit: teaching them to observe all things whatever I commanded you."

(3) Proclaimed the Great Presence: "And lo, I am with you always, even to the end of the world."

The apostles returned to Jerusalem. It was, in all likelihood, in Jerusalem that Jesus appeared to James, his own brother (I Cor. 15:7). We do not know just how often the Lord manifested himself to the disciples. We read: "he gave commandment to the apostles, whom he had chosen: to whom he also showed himself alive after his passion by many proofs, appearing to them by the space of forty days, and speaking the things concerning the kingdom of God" (Acts 1:2-4).

Finally, forty days after the resurrection, Jesus went with his disciples to the Mount of Olives (Acts 1:12). "And he lifted up his hands and blessed them. And it came to pass while he blessed them, he parted from them and was carried up into heaven (Luke 24:50, 51). The Book of Acts describes the event in these words:

> *As they were looking, he was taken up; and a cloud received him out of their sight. And while they were looking intently into the sky, as he was going, suddenly two men dressed in white stood by them They said, Men of Galilee, why do you stand here looking into the sky? This Jesus, who was received up from you into heaven, shall come back in the same way you saw him going into heaven* (Acts 1:9-11).

The isle of Patmos,
the site of John's exile.
Religious News Service

10
From Pentecost to Patmos

1. The Extension of the Church in and from Jerusalem

Date: 30-33/34
Scripture: Most of Acts 1-12

a. 30-33/34. *In Jerusalem,* Acts 1-7.

The disciples had not at all expected that Jesus would arise from the grave. That thought seems to have been farthest removed from their minds. Jesus was *dead*; he was *gone.* The cross had blasted the hope of the little company. On Sunday morning no one had made preparations to meet the *risen* Lord. Instead the women were trudging sorrowfully through the streets of Jerusalem on their way to the grave, *in order that they might anoint a corpse*! For further evidence of the fact that the disciples did not *expect* Christ's resurrection see Mark 16:11, 13, 14; Luke 24:10, 11, 20, 21. Never was there a more dejected, disappointed, thoroughly crushed group of men and women. Their own experience is perhaps best described in those well-known lines:

> *Now he is dead, far hence he lies*
> *In that lorn Syrian town;*
> *And on his grave with shining eyes*
> *The Syrian stars look down.*

When the master died, the disciples, too, died; i.e., their hopes, aspirations, deepest affections and fondest anticipations were buried with the Lord.

The resurrection of Jesus changed all this. Says Peter:

> *Blessed be the God and Father of our Lord Jesus Christ, who according to his great mercy* has begotten us again to a living hope by the resurrection of Jesus Christ from the dead.

The sudden transformation of the disciples from a group of thoroughly dejected individuals to a company of witnesses filled with exuberant joy and unshakable conviction can only be explained by the fact of the resurrection. That fact changed everything. The Lord risen, ascended to heaven, seated at the right hand of God, became the jubilant theme of every sermon. See Acts 2:31-36; 3:15; 4:10-12, 33; 7:56; 10:40; 13:32; etc. And the resurrection and ascension, in turn, clarified the meaning of the cross. Moreover, the exalted Lord added to this mighty fact of the resurrection the outpouring of the Holy Spirit in order that he might dwell in the hearts of the disciples and impart courage, strength, and spiritual insight to them.

After the ascension of Jesus the apostles returned to Jerusalem, where they waited for the coming of the Comforter. The number of believers increased to about 120. Judas had gone "to his own place," having committed suicide. The assembled disciples chose Matthias to take his place (Acts 1). The idea of some that this was a mistake must be rejected without hesitation. The action was taken after earnest prayer for guidance. Moreover, there is not a hint anywhere in Scripture that the Lord disapproved of it.

At the Feast of Pentecost, ten days after Christ's ascension, the Holy Spirit descended upon the disciples while they were all together in one place. We read:

> *And suddenly there came from heaven a sound as of the rushing of a mighty wind, and it filled all the house where they were sitting. And there appeared to them tongues parting asunder like as of fire; and it sat upon each of them. And they were all filled with the Holy Spirit, and began to speak with other tongues, as the Spirit gave them utterance* (Acts 2).

At the preaching of Peter, explaining the meaning of this great event, three thousand persons were converted. They had gathered from almost every part of the Roman Empire. Acts 2:9-11 should be studied with the aid of a Bible map. Hence, the foundation for the spread of Christianity was laid on this day. The church had not only been established; it had become *international*. Moreover, it had become "of age." The coming of the Holy Spirit meant new joy, new power, new courage, new knowledge (words spoken long ago by Jesus became clear now).

The genuine character of the preaching of the apostles was established by wonders and signs. One of these is narrated in detail: the cure of the lame beggar (Acts 3:1–4:31). This miracle gave Peter the opportunity to proclaim the message of salvation to a large multitude. To the angry Sadducees he preached the Christ in these memorable words:

> *And in none other is there salvation: for neither is there any other name under heaven, that is given among men, whereby we must be saved* (Acts 4:12).

Admonished not to speak or teach in the name of Jesus, Peter and John answered, "We cannot but speak the things which we saw and heard" (Acts 4:20).

Witness bearing and voluntary sharing were a few of the results of the outpouring of the Holy Spirit (4:32–5:11). We read:

> *And they were all filled with the Holy Spirit, and spoke the word of God with boldness. And the multitude of those who believed were of one heart and one soul: and not one of them said that any of the things he possessed was his own; but they had all things in common. And with great power the apostles gave their witness of the resurrection of the Lord Jesus: and great grace was upon them all* (Acts 4:32-33).

In the case of Ananias and Sapphira we see a perversion of this grace of voluntary sharing. Their deceit was punished with death.

The winning of souls, the rapid growth of the church, was another manifestation of the Spirit's presence and power. This resulted in persecution, which, by causing the disciples to be scattered in all directions, brought about the further extension of the church (5:12–7:60):

> *And believers were the more added to the Lord, multitudes both of men and women. . . . But the highpriest rose up, and all those who were with him (members of the party*

of the Sadducees), and put them in the public jail. But during the night the angel of the Lord opened the prison doors, and brought them out, and said, Go and stand and speak in the temple to the people all the words of this Life (Acts 5:14, 17-20).

When they were arrested again, Peter and the apostles said, "We must obey God rather than men." The members of the Sanhedrin were filled with wrath. But Gamaliel, a leading Pharisee, one of the most famous of Jewish teachers, advocated a cautious policy:

Leave these men alone. Let them go: for if this counsel or this work is of men, it will be overthrown: but if it is of God, you will not be able to stop these men; lest you be found even to be fighting against God (Acts 5:38).

When the Greek-speaking Jews complained that their widows were neglected in the daily distributions, seven men were chosen to attend to this matter. One of the seven was Stephen, "a man full of faith and of the Holy Spirit . . . full of grace and power." He not only "performed great wonders and signs among the people," but also preached the gospel in synagogues attended by certain Greek-speaking Jews in Jerusalem. Opposition arose and Stephen was arrested. He was accused of speaking blasphemous words against Moses and God. Valiant was his defense, in which he pointed out that Jesus was the fulfilment of prophecy and that his enemies were the murderers of the Messiah. The defense ended with this daring climax:

You stiffnecked and uncircumcised in heart and ears! You always resist the Holy Spirit: as your fathers did, so do you. Which of the prophets did not your fathers persecute? and they killed those who predicted the coming of the Righteous One; whom you have now betrayed and murdered; you who received the law as it was ordained by angels, but have not kept it (Acts 7:51-53).

The result was that "when they heard these things, they were cut to the heart, and they gnashed their teeth against him." As Stephen was being stoned to death, he prayed, "Lord Jesus, receive my spirit. . . . Lord, lay not this sin to their charge."

The men who stoned Stephen laid their garments at the feet of a young man who was going to become the greatest Christian missionary of all time: Paul.

b. 33/34-44. *From Jerusalem, into All Judea, Samaria, and the Surrounding Regions,* Acts 8; 9:31–12:25.

Up to this time most of the missionary work had been carried on within the city of Jerusalem. But in connection with Stephen's death a great change took place: the membership of the Jerusalem church was dispersed among the towns and villages of Judea and Samaria:

> . . . *And there arose on that day a great persecution against the church which was in Jerusalem; and they were all scattered abroad throughout the regions of Judea and Samaria, except the apostles* (Acts 8:1).

Among the scattered ones was Philip the Evangelist, who, like Stephen, was one of the seven men who had been appointed to care for the distribution to the needy. This man preached the gospel to the people of Samaria. The Lord greatly blessed his missionary labors. The follow-up work was done by the apostles Peter and John. Philip, meanwhile, was told by an angel of the Lord to go "toward the south to the way that goes down from Jerusalem to Gaza." Here he preached Christ to an Ethiopian treasurer who was reading Isaiah 53 as he was seated in his chariot. The eunuch believed and was baptized. Then, "the Spirit of the Lord caught away Philip; and the eunuch saw him no more, for he went on his way rejoicing. But Philip was found at Azotus: and passing through he preached the Gospel to all the cities, till he came to Caesarea." See p. 197.

About this time there occurred an event which was to have the treatest possible significance for the future of Christianity. We refer, of course, to the conversion of Paul. See p. 183.

During the "rest" which the churches enjoyed after Saul's conversion, Peter carried on missionary activity in the cities of the Coastal Plain: Lydda, Joppa, Caesarea. At Lydda he restored to health Aeneas, a paralytic. At Joppa he raised Dorcas from the dead. It was at this same place that he fell into a trance and saw a great sheet "wherein were all manner of four-footed beasts and creeping things of the earth and birds of heaven."

A voice said: "Rise, Peter, kill and eat. . . . Do not call anything impure that God has cleansed." The meaning was clearly this: that Peter must not refuse to enter the home of a Gentile in order to proclaim the gospel to him and his house. Immediately after Peter had seen the sheet and heard the words bidding him to kill and eat, messengers from Cornelius, a Gentile God-fearer (one who worshiped the God of the Jews), arrived and asked him to accompany them to the house of Cornelius in Caesarea. Under Peter's ministry Cornelius and the members of his household accepted Christ, received the Holy Spirit, and were baptized. This reception of Gentiles into the church, without compelling them to submit to the Jewish ceremonial law, marked the beginning of a new era. When Peter explained to the brethren in Jerusalem what had happened, "they held their peace, and glorified God, saying, "Then to the Gentiles also has God granted repentance unto life" (Acts 9:31–11:18).

Soon others followed the example of Peter and began to preach the gospel not only to Jews but also to Gentiles. In large numbers the latter accepted the Lord. This was true especially in the city of Antioch, the capital of the Roman province of Syria. It was here that those outside the church began to look upon the community of Christ-followers as in need of a distinct designation; hence, "The disciples were called *Christians* first in Antioch."

In Jerusalem another persecution was raging. Herod Agrippa I, grandson of Herod the Great, "killed James, the brother of John, with the sword." Desiring to please the Jews he also seized Peter. As a result of God's glorious answer to the prayer of the church—a prayer which was, indeed, *earnest* (12:5), but by no means *perfect* (12:15)—Peter was delivered from prison. Soon afterward Herod died of a horrible sickness (Acts 11:19–12:25).

2. The Extension of the Church from Antioch, Mainly Through the Labors of Paul

Date: 33/34-67 (Date of Paul's Labors from His Conversion to His Martyrdom)
Scripture: Acts 9:1-30; 11:19-30; 13:1–28:31

---

a. 33/34-37. *From Paul's Conversion to His Visit to Jerusalem Recorded in Galatians 1:18: "Then after three years I went up to Jerusalem to visit Cephas."* Acts 9:1-30.

From the imprisonment and release of Peter, about the year 44–cf. Acts 12:3 with verse 23–we must now go back ten years to the event that was to shake the world: the conversion of Paul in the year 33/34.

The Book of Acts does not give us a life of Paul. It records the main facts in order that we may see *The Triumph of the Gospel, The Work of Jesus Christ in the Extension of the Church.* This fact requires emphasis in order that we may gain some conception of the herculean character of the labors of this great apostle. We must ever study what is recorded in the Book of Acts in the light of what Paul himself tells us when on his Third Missionary Journey he writes II Corinthians. Here are his own words, II Corinthians 11:23-28:

In labors more abundantly,
In prisons more abundantly,
In stripes above measure,
In deaths oft.
Of the Jews five times received
I forty lashes minus one.
Once was I beaten with rods,
Once was I stoned,
Thrice I suffered shipwreck,
A night and a day have
I been in the deep;
In journeyings often,
In perils of rivers,
In perils of robbers,
In perils from my countrymen,
In perils from the Gentiles,
In perils in the city,
In perils in the wilderness,
In perils in the sea;
In perils among false brothers,
In labor and toil,
In watchings often,
In hunger and thirst,
In fastings often,
In cold and nakedness.
Besides everything else
There is that which presses upon
me daily,
Anxiety for all the churches.

In this list one notices various items which are not even mentioned in the Book of Acts; e. g., "In prisons more abundantly."

But this was written before the apostle's imprisonment in Jerusalem, Caesarea, and Rome. To be sure, Acts records Paul's imprisonment in Philippi (Acts 16); but where do we find a record of *all* the other times when the apostle was jailed? (cf. Rom. 16:7).

Again, take the statement: "Of the Jews five times received I forty lashes minus one." Acts is silent on this point.

Then: "Thrice was I beaten with rods."

One of these beatings is recorded in Acts 16:23, 37. When did the other two occur? "Thrice I suffered shipwreck, A night and a day have I been in the deep." When Paul wrote these words he did not yet know that he was going to endure one more shipwreck, the fourth, recorded in Acts 27. The other three are not even mentioned in Acts.

Even when we take the story as recorded in Acts we stand amazed at the amount of suffering which this hero of faith endured for the sake of the gospel. But when we add to the record of Acts what Paul himself tells us in II Corinthians 11, words fail to express our admiration for this great gift of God to the church.

The all-consuming motive which forced him on and on regardless of suffering, hardship, and opposition is implied—though not fully stated in passages such as the following:

> *For the love of Christ constrains us . . .* (II Cor. 5:14).
>
> *I have been crucified with Christ; and it is no longer I that live, but Christ lives in me: and the life which I now live in the flesh I live in faith, the faith which is in the Son of God, who loved me, and gave himself up for me* (Gal. 2:20).

Observe, however, that in both passages Paul is not speaking of his love for Christ but of Christ's love for him. Nevertheless, it is clear from statements such as these that Paul loved Christ in return. His faith in Christ was constantly "*working* through love," enabling him to remove mountains: to perform tasks which otherwise would have been impossible of achievement.

Saul, whose Roman name was Paul, was born at Tarsus, a center of Greek culture, a university city located in Cilicia, near the northeastern corner of the Mediterranean Sea. He was a Roman citizen by birth. He received his early training in Jerusalem under that most distinguished doctor of the Law, Gamaliel, grandson of the famous Hillel. We have already mentioned the fact that the witnesses who stoned Stephen laid their garments at the feet of Paul (Acts 7:58). Immediately after Stephen's death Paul took a leading part in the persecution of Christians. He put his whole soul into this task. He "breathed threatening and slaughter against the disciples of the Lord" (Acts 9:1). Not satisfied with waging the persecution in Jerusalem, he even asked of the high priest letters to the synagogues in Damascus that he might bring bound to Jerusalem "any that were of the Way, whether men or women" (Acts 9:2). In all this he was thoroughly sincere. Here are his own words: "I was indeed convinced that I ought to do many things contrary to the name of Jesus of Nazareth" (Acts 26:9).

To be sure, Paul had a conscience, but it was a *misguided* conscience. The words, "It is hard for you to kick against the goad" (Acts 26:14), do not at all mean that Paul doubted whether he was doing the right thing when he persecuted believers. On the contrary, the expression indicates the folly of resisting the purpose of God. This is clear from the entire context (Acts 26:16-18).

It was the hour of noon and the sun was shining in all its strength. Paul was approaching Damascus to destroy the Christian community in that city. Suddenly a light from heaven, brighter than the sun, shone around him. "And he fell upon the earth, and heard a voice saying to him, Saul, Saul, why do you persecute me? And he said, Who art thou, Lord?" The voice answered: "I am Jesus whom you are persecuting; but rise and enter into the city, and you will be told what you must do" (Acts 9:4, 5).

The men who accompanied Paul saw the light but could not distinguish the Person. They heard the voice or sound, but could not understand the words. Paul, on the other hand, saw the Lord and heard his words. Arriving in Damascus, he received his sight through the ministry of Ananias, who also baptized him. He began his evangelistic work in Damascus:

> *And at once in the synagogues he proclaimed Jesus, that he is the Son of God. And all who heard him were amazed and asked, "Is not he the man who in Jerusalem raised havoc among those who call on this name? And has he not come here for the purpose of bringing them bound before the chief priests?" But Saul increased the more in strength, and con-*

founded the Jews who dwelt in Damascus, proving that this is the Christ (Acts 9:20-22).

Paul spent some time in Arabia, but Scripture does not tell us what he did there. When he returned to Damascus, his preaching aroused such opposition that he had to flee for his life, for the Jews were plotting to kill him. They had the cooperation of the civil authorities. Paul's report is as follows:

In Damascus the governor under Aretas the king guarded the city of the Damascenes in order to take me: and through a window was I let down in a basket by the wall, and escaped his hands (II Cor. 11:32, 33).

Fully three years after his conversion Paul arrived in Jerusalem (Gal. 1:18). He tried to join the disciples but they were all afraid of him, for they did not believe that he was really a disciple. But Barnabas, a big-hearted Levite of Cyprus who had been converted earlier (Acts 4:36, 37), removed their apprehension and introduced Paul to Peter and to James, the Lord's brother. "To visit Cephas [Peter]" had been Paul's purpose when he started out from Damascus (Gal. 1:18). While in Jerusalem, the former persecutor preached fearlessly to the Greek-speaking Jews (Acts 9:28, 29). They immediately plotted to kill him. Hence, the brothers decided to send Paul away. In a vision the Lord himself confirmed this decision.

Paul had spent only fifteen days with Peter, as he himself states in Galatians 1:18. This is in complete harmony with the account which we find in Acts 22:17-21:

And it happened that, when I had returned to Jerusalem and was praying in the temple, I fell into a trance, and saw him [the Lord] saying to me, Make haste *and* quickly *get out of Jerusalem; because they will not accept your testimony concerning me. . . . Depart: for I will send you far away to the Gentiles.*

Accordingly, the apostle left Jerusalem before he had seen the rest of the apostles and before he had become known by sight to the churches in Judea. Nevertheless, believers everywhere had heard the good news: "The man who once persecuted us is now preaching the faith he formerly tried to destroy." They glorified God (Gal. 1:23).

Paul's friends brought him to Caesarea and sent him off to Tarsus.

b. 37-50. *From Tarsus to the Jerusalem Conference. The "Fourteen Years" mentioned in Galatians 2:1: "Then after the space of fourteen years I went up again to Jerusalem. . . ."* Acts 11:19-30; 13:1–15:35.

(1) 37-44. *Paul at Tarsus and Antioch. His trip to Jerusalem to Administer Relief.* Acts 11:19-30.

It is probable that the apostle labored in Tarsus and the surrounding territory for about six years, founding the churches of Cilicia which are mentioned in Acts 15:41. When Barnabas, who had been sent to Antioch in Syria, saw the progress of the gospel in that great city—see p. 180—and the need of an additional worker, he went to Tarsus to seek Paul and brought him to Antioch. Together they labored here for a year. The church grew rapidly and became the starting point for Paul's mission to the pagan world.

About this time a great famine occurred "over all the world," just as had been predicted by the prophet Agabus. Luke tells us that this famine took place in the days of Claudius (Acts 11:28). He was emperor during the years 41-54 (p. 75). At Antioch contributions for the relief of the Christians in Judea were made. By the hands of Barnabas and Paul these were sent to Jerusalem. This trip probably occurred about the year 44, shortly before the death of Herod Agrippa I (Acts 12:1). The two men, having accomplished their mission, returned to Antioch.

(2) 44-50. *First Missionary Journey and Jerusalem Conference.* Acts 13:1–15:35.

The extension of the church from Antioch by means of three great missionary journeys begins at this time. The Holy Spirit directed the church to set apart Barnabas and Paul for the work to which God had called them. So, "when they had fasted and prayed and laid their hands on them, they sent them away" (Acts 13:1-3). We do not know how long a time this first missionary journey occupied. All we can say is that it must be assigned, in general, to the period 44-50. The two men took along John Mark as their assistant. *The reader should consult a good Bible map in connection with these missionary journeys. Otherwise, the story from this point on will have little meaning.*

The party sailed to the island of Cyprus. The decision to preach the gospel in this region was indeed very proper; not only because Barnabas had come from Cyprus (Acts 4:36), but especially because the church of Antioch had been founded by the disciples of this island (and of Cyrene) and was, therefore, spiritually indebted to it (Acts 11:20). The missionaries proclaimed the word of God in the synagogues of Salamis. Then they crossed the island until they reached Paphos. Here they rebuked the sorcerer Bar-Jesus and were instrumental in the conversion of the proconsul Sergius Paulus. Sailing north the missionaries arrived in Perga of Pamphilia, where John Mark deserted them. Leaving the unhealthful lowlands, Paul—a sick man? (see Gal. 4:13)—and Barnabas journeyed to higher altitudes and reached Pisidian Antioch. Here the rulers of the synagogue said to them: "Brothers, if you have any word of exhortation for the people, let us hear it."

Beautiful and stirring was Paul's address in which he proclaimed Jesus as the fulfilment of the Old Testament. It ended with a grand climax:

> *And though they were unable to charge him with anything deserving death, yet they asked Pilate to have him executed. And when they had fulfilled all things that were written of him, they took him down from the tree, and laid him in a tomb. But God raised him from the dead: and he was seen for many days by them who came up with him from Galilee to Jerusalem, and who are now his witnesses to the people. And we bring you good tidings of the promise made to the fathers, that God has fulfilled the same to our children in that he raised up Jesus; as also it is written in the second psalm, Thou art my Son, this day have I begotten thee. . . . Be it known to you therefore, brothers, that through this man is proclaimed to you remission of sins: and by him every one who believes is justified from all things from which you could not be justified through the law of Moses. Take care therefore, lest that come upon you which was spoken by the prophets:*
>
> *"Behold, you despisers, and wonder and perish;*
> *For, I work a work in your days,*

> *A work which you shall in no wise believe, if one declare it to you"* (Acts 13:13-41).

The speech made a deep impression, especially upon the devout proselytes. The next sabbath almost the whole city gathered together to hear the word of God. This aroused the jealousy of the Jews, who began to contradict Paul and to ridicule his message. The missionaries, therefore, separated themselves from the Jews and turned to the Gentiles, appealing to Scripture (Isa. 49:6) in justification of their course. "As many as were ordained to eternal life believed." Afterward Paul and Barnabas were expelled from the city as a result of the opposition of its leading men and women.

They arrived in Iconium, where "a great multitude both of Jews and Greeks believed." But opposition again arose, and they journeyed to Lystra. It is probable that at this place Timothy was converted (Acts 16:1; II Tim. 1:2; 3:11). As a result of the miraculous cure of a lame man the people were about to offer sacrifice to the missionaries. Considering them to be gods, they called Barnabas, Zeus and Paul, Hermes. With great difficulty the two restrained the multitudes from offering sacrifice. But Jews came from Antioch and Iconium. They slandered Paul and Barnabas. As a result, Paul was stoned almost to death. He was dragged out of the city. When he revived, he departed with Barnabas to Derbe where they spoke the word. As any map will indicate, it would have been the "natural" thing to travel from Derbe by way of Tarsus to Antioch in Syria, the place from which they had started, thus completing the circle. When the missionaries had reached Derbe, they were not very far from "home." Besides, it should not be forgotten that Paul had been nearly killed at Lystra; hence, he was in need of a rest. Nevertheless, so great was the enthusiasm of these great men and their love for the Lord that, instead of doing the "natural" thing, they retraced their steps, traveling from Derbe back to Lystra, Iconium, and Antioch

> *confirming the souls of the disciples, exhorting them to continue in the faith, and that through many tribulations we must enter into the kingdom of God. And when they had appointed for them elders in every church, and had prayed with fasting, they committed them to the Lord, in whom they had come to believe* (Acts 14:21-23).

After speaking the word in Perga, the missionaries finally returned to the place from which they had started: Antioch in Syria.

Their safe arrival and report brought great joy to the church at Antioch. But this rejoicing was short-lived, for Judaizers came from Jerusalem, saying that unless Gentile converts submitted to the rite of circumcision they could not be saved. As a result, a council or conference was held in Jerusalem. Here the issue was squarely faced. James, the brother of the Lord, Peter, John, and "all the multitude" of believers agreed with Paul and Barnabas that submission to the ceremonial law was not necessary. Peter based his conviction on his experience at the house of Cornelius (see p. 180). Paul and Barnabas made clear to the people that God's approval upon their course of action in proclaiming the gospel to the Gentiles had been made abundantly evident by signs and wonders. James based his reasoning upon the prophecy of Amos 9:11, 12. The result was that the brothers at Jerusalem gave to Paul and Barnabas the right hand of fellowship, in order that these two missionaries might go to the Gentiles and the other apostles to the Jews (Gal. 2:6-10; cf. Acts 15:1-35).

The church at Jerusalem also decided to send a letter to the Gentile Christians to the intent that they should consider themselves free from the ceremonial stipulations of the Mosaic Law. The letter also directed them to refrain from certain Gentile habits which, to say the least, were very abhorrent to Jewish sentiment.

The man who "made the motion" to send this wonderful charter of Christian liberty was James, the Lord's brother (Acts 15:19, 20), the same individual who also wrote the well-known epistle associated with his name. It is therefore highly improbable that in this epistle we would be able to find ideas which militate against the principle of salvation by grace. It is believed that this treatise on the nature of genuine faith—i.e., faith which expresses itself in works of love—was written sometime during the period 37-50. See pp. 315-320. If this idea be correct, then this may have been the first New Testament book.

At the Council of Jerusalem the Judaists, who insisted that the Gentiles in order to be saved must keep the whole ceremonial law, had received a severe blow. They immediately plotted revenge. Their plan seems to have been to follow the missionaries in their track in order to counteract the gospel of free grace, the doctrine of justification by faith in Christ's redeeming love. When the letter of the Jerusalem Council was read in the churches of Antioch, Syria,

Cilicia (Acts 15:23-30), and Galatia (16:4), there was great rejoicing among the brothers. The churches were strengthened in the faith and increased in numbers daily. But, as we shall see in the next section, the Judaists hounded the trail of the messengers of good tidings. On his Second Missionary Journey Paul would find it necessary to take vigorous action against them See p. 193.

c. 50/51-53/54. *Second Missionary Journey.* Acts 15:36–18:22.

The triumph of the gospel during the period of Paul's three missionary journeys was truly amazing. How shall we account for it?

First, there were certain external factors which favored Paul and his message, such as

(1) a world government

(2) world peace

(3) a world language (Greek)

(4) famous Roman roads linking the various parts of the world

(5) world skepticism with respect to pagan deities

(6) the Dispersion of the Jews and of their monotheistic religion among the nations of the world

(7) the translation of the Old Testament into the world language.

Nevertheless, there were also formidable obstacles. Journeying up and down the Roman Empire in order to blaze a trail for the gospel was a task beset with great dangers. See p. 181. Moreover, the enemies were many and relentless. Think of the Jews and the Judaists. Therefore, although we do not wish to detract in the least from the significance of the aforementioned favorable circumstances, *more* than this was needed if the gospel were to triumph. *More* was also divinely provided.

For, in the second place, we must bear in mind that God, in his wonderful providence, prepared not only external conditions which favored the spread of Christianity, but also *the man* who was going to make use of these conditions. Paul had been "separated from his mother's womb" in order to proclaim the gospel to the Gentiles (Gal. 1:15-17). He was "God's chosen vessel." He was "a *Hebrew* of the Hebrews," a *Roman* citizen by birth, and thoroughly versed in the "wisdom" of the *Greeks*. He had experienced a wonderful conversion which had left an indelible impression upon his soul and acted as a motivating force during the remainder of his life. He was filled to overflowing with love for his Lord to whom he owed everything and who had been so very gracious to one who considered himself to be "less than the least of all saints" (Eph. 3:8). He was a man of deep conviction, a man of prayer, a man with a message, a man "in Christ." Such men make excellent missionaries.

Thirdly, this man had a plan (Acts 16:6, 7; 18:21; I Cor. 16:5-8).[1] He did not do his work in a haphazard, come-what-may fashion. He had certain objectives and he tried to realize them. What is even more worthy of note is the fact that he constantly subjected his own plan to the "Spirit of Jesus." Hence, the record of Paul's travels and discourses is the record of what *Jesus* continued to do and teach (cf. Acts 1:1) through his servant Paul.

This point becomes very clear when we study the Second Missionary Journey. Paul thought it best not to take with him John Mark, the man who had withdrawn from the missionaries when they reached Perga. So, the apostle takes Silas, and together they revisit the churches of Syria and Cilicia. From there they journey through the Roman province of Galatia, strengthening the churches which had been established during the First Missionary Journey. See pp. 185-187, 323-326. At Lystra Timothy becomes their associate. As they travel onward, their plans are changed by the intervention of the Holy Spirit. We read:

> *And they went through the region of Phrygia and Galatia, having been forbidden of the Holy Spirit to speak the word in Asia; and when they were come over against Mysia, they tried to go into Bithynia, but the Spirit of Jesus did not allow them to do this* (Acts 16:6, 7).

Finally the three men reached Troas, the site of ancient Troy, the scene of Homer's *Iliad*. Here the vision of the "man of Macedonia" summoned the missionaries from Asia to Europe. Here also they were joined by Luke (Acts 16:10). Setting sail from Troas the company arrived at Philippi. This place is described by Luke in the following words: "Philippi . . . a city of Macedonia, *the first of the district*, a [Roman] colony" (Acts 16:12).

The First Element in Paul's Missionary Strategy

Paul in obedience to the direction of the Spirit, performed most of his labor in the great urban centers such as Pisidian Antioch, Philippi,

1. See, e.g., C. W. Quimby, *Paul for Everyone*; also L. Berkhof, *Paul, the Missionary*.

Corinth, Ephesus, Rome. He would often bypass the smaller towns, in the firm belief that from the larger centers the message would fan outward, as it actually did. Moreover, he generally selected those cities where the gospel had not yet been proclaimed by others (Rom. 15:20).

In Philippi a church was founded which Paul afterward called his "joy and crown" (Phil. 4:1). Here Lydia was converted, and she and her household were baptized. The masters of a girl who had a spirit of divination became angry when Paul expelled the demon. They reasoned that "the hope of their gain" was gone. As a result, Paul and Silas were imprisoned and beaten with rods. About midnight God sent an earthquake which opened the prison doors. The jailer was converted and "he was baptized, together with all his, immediately" (Acts 16:33). Luke remained at Philippi, but the others went to Thessalonica, "where there was a *synagogue* of the Jews" (Acts 17:1). This introduces

The Second Element in Paul's Missionary Strategy

Paul regarded the synagogue as the connecting link between his message and the men whom he tried to reach. Reasons: In the synagogue the Old Testament prophecies, which pointed forward to the coming and work of the Messiah were read and believed. Also, here he was able to reach not only Jews but also Gentile proselytes who had been converted to the worship of the one God (monotheism).

Accordingly, whenever Paul, speaking in the synagogue, would begin his discourse, he would have an immediate point of contact with his hearers. He could say: "It is written in the prophets . . . and these words were fulfilled in Jesus."

The Third Element in Paul's Missionary Strategy

Paul based his reasoning upon Scripture, to which he constantly referred, and he regarded the Christ to be the very heart and center of Old Testament prophecy.

Both of these elements—the second and the third—are so well illustrated in the work of the apostle at Thessalonica that we shall quote Luke's account:

> *Now when they had passed through Amphipolis and Apollonia, they came to Thessalonica,* where was a synagogue of the Jews: *and Paul,* as his custom was, *went in, and* for three

> sabbath days reasoned with them from the scriptures, opening and alleging that it behooved the Christ to suffer, and to rise again from the dead; and that this Jesus, whom, said he, I proclaim unto you, is the Christ. *And some of them were persuaded and consorted with Paul and Silas;* and of the devout Greeks a great multitude, and of the chief women not a few (Acts 17:1-4).

A persecution, instigated by the Jews, caused Paul to depart from Thessalonica. He went to Berea where they "received the word with all readiness of mind, examining the Scriptures daily, to see whether these things were so" (Acts 17:11).

While Silas and Timothy stayed behind in Berea, Paul sailed to Athens. It is not entirely clear when and where they rejoined the apostle. A probable view is that Timothy left Berea and found Paul while the latter was still in Athens; that Paul, anxious about the affairs of the church at Thessalonica, sent him back to that congregation in order to establish and comfort it (I Thess. 3:1, 2); and that both Silas and Timothy rejoined the apostle at Corinth (Acts 18:5; I Thess. 3:6).

At Athens Paul preached not only in the synagogue but also on Mars' Hill (Acts 17:22-31). However, when we study the apostle's address to the "men of Athens" (Acts 17) and compare it with his discourse to the synagogue at Pisidian Antioch (Acts 13), we notice a vast difference. In both cases there is a wise adaptation to the needs of the audience. In Antioch, speaking in the synagogue and addressing people who were versed in Scripture, Paul made several references to Old Testament history. See p. 186. In Athens, directing his message to Epicurean and Stoic philosophers and those who were with them, he quoted Epimenedes and Aratus. He began his discourse in a manner which must have aroused immediate attention:

> *You men of Athens, in all things I perceive that you are very religious. For as I passed along, and observed the objects of your worship, I found also an altar with this inscription,* To An Unknown God. *What therefore you worship in ignorance, this I proclaim to you"* (Acts 17:22, 23).

Needless to say, in both addresses—Antioch and Athens—Paul proclaimed the risen Christ. The *approach*, however, was adapted to the needs of the respective audiences.

Accordingly, we see here:

The Fourth Element in Paul's Missionary Strategy

Paul always adapted his messages to the needs of his hearers. By doing this he obtained their immediate attention and held it. This made his preaching very effective. He was able to say: "I am become all things to all men, that I may by all possible means save some" (I Cor. 9:22).

From Athens, the literary center of the civilized world, Paul went to Corinth, that most wicked commercial and political metropolis of Greece, a synonym for licentiousness. Here he made the acquaintance of Aquila and Priscilla, driven from Rome by the edict of Emperor Claudius (who ruled from 41-54; see p. 75), and stayed with them because he was of the same trade, a tentmaker. He first preached in the synagogue, but afterward in the house of a Gentile who lived next to the synagogue. It seems probable that while Paul was alone at Corinth–i.e., before Silas and Timothy had returned from Macedonia–he received some very disquieting news from the churches of Galatia. He heard that the Judaizers had been at work and had succeeded all too well in their attempt to destroy the edifice which he had reared with so much patience and suffering. Accordingly, the apostle wrote his Epistle to the Galatians. See pp. 323-328.

Soon Silas and Timothy returned with, on the whole, good tidings from the church at Thessalonica. Paul, accordingly, sent a letter to that congregation. It was soon followed by another. See pp. 328-331. The arrival of the two men and the information which they conveyed greatly encouraged the apostle in his preaching (Acts 18:5). He spent at least eighteen months at Corinth and established a numerically flourishing church at this place. When the Jews accused him before the Roman proconsul Gallio, their charges were dismissed and they themselves were driven from the tribunal. Finally Paul left Corinth. By way of Ephesus, where he made only a brief stop, he went to Palestine and returned again to Antioch in Syria.

Paul's brief stop at Ephesus was significant in one respect. He left Aquila and Priscilla there. In the apostle's absence they were a great blessing to the church, and proved their worth especially by expounding the word of God more accurately to that eloquent Alexandrian, Apollos, who, being well versed in the Scriptures, had come to Ephesus and was speaking boldly in the synagogue. Paul himself, moreover, had made a promise to the church: "I will return to you if God will" (Acts 18:21).

The great missionary was always "returning," another stratagem of Paul:

The Fifth Element in Paul's Missionary Strategy

For the confirmation of the churches Paul returned to them again and again, appointed men to carry on the work in his absence, and by means of his epistles greatly strengthened the churches. He was a firm believer in follow-up work. Cf. p. 179.

d. 53/54–57/58. *Third Missionary Journey.* Acts 18:32–21:16.

Paul kept his promise. "Having passed through the upper country," he came to Ephesus.[2] This city, the metropolis of Proconsular Asia, was located a mile from the Aegean Sea and had a splendid harbor, in which the ships of all lands could be seen. Rising above the harbor stood the enormously rich temple of Artemis, which was also a place of refuge and an art museum. It housed the image of the goddess, which was believed to have fallen from heaven. The "temple-keeper" of the great Artemis was filled with wizards and their "Ephesian Letters," i.e., slips of paper on which were written magical symbols or sentences. Such "letters" were worn as charms. Pilgrims who flocked to the temple from every quarter would take home small models of the sanctuary and its goddess. Silversmiths, accordingly, carried on a lucrative business, and so did "the workmen of like occupation" (Acts 19:25). The city was also famous as a pleasure center. The report of its theater and race course was spread far and wide.

In Ephesus Apollos had labored—see p. 193—that famous Christian orator who before he received more adequate instruction from Aquila and Priscilla "knew only the baptism of John" (Acts 18:25). It was also here that Paul found some disciples who admitted that they had been baptized "into John's baptism" Accordingly, they were now baptized "into the name of the Lord Jesus" (Acts 19:1-8).

For three months the apostle preached in the synagogue. Then, when opposition arose, he "continued for the space of two years" in the school of Tyrannus. His ministry was marked by widespread success not only in the metropolis itself but also in the surrounding territory, so that "all who lived in Asia heard the word of the Lord, both Jews and Greeks." It is probable that most of the "seven churches that are in Asia" (Rev. 1:4) were founded during this period. Moreover, inasmuch as Ephesus was full of superstition, the Lord, in his wise providence, enabled Paul to perform many miracles of healing and to cast out many demons. Jewish tricksters who tried

---

2. On Ephesus, see W. M. Ramsay, *The Letters to the Seven Churches.*

to imitate the apostle were discomfited (Acts 19:11-20). Moreover, ever so many humbugs—i.e., "those who practiced magical arts"—were converted. They put their books on a pile and "burned them in the sight of all" (vss. 19, 20). In fact, so great was the triumph of the gospel in this whole region that its metropolis, Ephesus, may justly be called the third capital of Christianity, Jerusalem having been the first and Syrian Antioch, the second. The result of this phenomenal success was fierce opposition: the silversmiths organized a riot against Paul, for the sale of their little silver shrines was dropping off fast (Acts 19:23-41). But the apostle was already thinking of other fields of labor. About this time he received news from the congregation at Corinth which had been established on the Second Journey—see p. 193; so he wrote I Corinthians. See p. 333. Titus was sent to Corinth and according to the original plan was to meet Paul at Troas. For some reason, however, the apostle did not find Titus in Troas but in Macedonia. Having received information from Titus about conditions in Corinth, Paul sent another letter to that church: II Corinthians. See p. 338.

While still at Ephesus Paul's thoughts were turned to the city on the Tiber. We read:

> *Now after these things were ended, Paul purposed in the spirit, when he had passed through Macedonia and Achaia, to go to Jerusalem saying, After I have been there,* I must also see Rome (Act 19:21).

We must not imagine that the great missionary did nothing but preaching and teaching while he was on this journey. He was also gathering funds for the needy in Jerusalem. This was a matter of deep concern to him, not only because by this means the poor in Judea would be benefited but also—and perhaps even *more* so—because those who hesitated to admit the correctness of the Charter of Liberty as drawn up by the Jerusalem Conference—see p. 188—would begin to think more kindly of their brothers, the converts from the Gentile world. Thus, by helping one another in time of need, the churches throughout the Roman Empire would be bound more closely together. This brings us to

The Sixth Element in Paul's Missionary Strategy

Paul did everything in his power to promote the feeling of unity among all the churches. He encouraged them to help one another in their need, imparted information to one church with respect to

conditions in others, and stressed the unity of all "in Christ." Said he: "There is one body, and one Spirit, just as you were called in one hope of your calling; one Lord, one faith, one baptism, one God and Father of all, who is over all, and through all, and in all" (Eph. 4:4 5).

The six elements in Paul's missionary strategy—or if you prefer the six missionary methods—which we have mentioned should be studied carefully. How many of them are applicable today, and to what extent are they applicable?

From Macedonia Paul went to Corinth where he spent the three winter months. While here he wrote Romans. See p. 341. He was about to set sail directly for Syria when a plot was discovered which caused him to change his plans. He, therefore, reversed his course and proceeded toward Jerusalem by way of Macedonia. At Philippi Luke joined him. After "the days of unleavened bread" they crossed the Aegean and arrived in Troas. A religious service was held here "on the first day of the week." It is clear from the account that this had become the *custom*. It seems that believers had gradually begun to see that this day—the very day on which Jesus had risen, hope had been revived, death had been conquered, and the grave vanquished—should be set apart for praise and worship. Hence, on the evening of the day on which Christ arose they had gathered for prayer and meditation, and Jesus had come into their midst, saying, "Peace be to you" (John 20:19). The same thing had happened the next Sunday evening (John 20:26). Paul, too, had admonished the Corinthians to contribute to the cause of benevolence on that day (I Cor. 16:2). Moreover, the glorious visions of the Book of Revelation were going to be shown to John on "the Lord's Day" (Rev. 1:10). To be sure, as far as we can learn from the record, the disciples had never been *ordered* to break with the custom of worshiping on Saturday and to substitute for it Sunday worship. They had started to do so of their own accord. They needed no prodding. But the significant fact is that the Lord himself had shown in every possible manner that their spontaneous action had his full approval. Not only that, but it also becomes abundantly evident from the Word that the Lord's disapproval rested upon the attempt of the Judaists to cling to the Old Testament shadows, including the Old Testament Sabbath (Gal. 4:10, 11; Col. 2:16, 17). The notion that a fourth-century pope changed the day is just that, a mere notion; for, in the first place there was no real pope during the fourth century; and, secondly Emperor Constantine the Great did *not* introduce Sunday worship but legalized the civil observance of that day, by which alone the religious observance could be properly secured. He prohibited manual labor in the cities on that day; also, all juridical transactions, and a little later also military exercises.

Returning now to Troas, it was on a Sunday evening that Paul "prolonged his speech until midnight" (Acts 20:7). A young man, Eutychus, sitting in a window and being borne down with deep sleep, "fell down from the third story and was taken up dead." Paul raised him from the dead, imparting "not a little" comfort to the brothers.

When Paul (and his companion) came to Miletus on the coast of Asia Minor, he sent for the elders of the Ephesian church, and when they came he bade them farewell in a touching address (Acts 20:17-38).

After a brief stop at Tyre, the missionaries arrived at Caesarea and were entertained at the home of Philip the Evangelist. See pp. 187-188. Here Agabus, a prophet from Jerusalem, predicted Paul's imminent imprisonment in Jerusalem. Accordingly, the apostle's friends tried to persuade him not to go up to Jerusalem. The section closes beautifully:

> *Then Paul answered, What are you doing, weeping and breaking my heart? for I am ready not only to be bound but even to die at Jerusalem for the name of the Lord Jesus. And since he refused to yield to our appeal, we ceased, saying, The will of the Lord be done . . . And after these days we took up our baggage and went up to Jerusalem* (Acts 21:12-15).

e. 57/58-60. *Paul in Jerusalem and Caesarea.* Acts 21:17–26:32.

At Jerusalem the missionaries were warmly received by James, the Lord's brother, and by the church (Acts 21:15-26). In order to satisfy the Jewish Christians Paul consented to join four Nazarites in the temple and to pay their expenses. In agreeing to do this the apostle was not inconsistent; for, while he always insisted that no Gentile should keep the ceremonial law and also that no Jew was under any obligation to observe it, he never found fault with Jews who wanted to observe it of their own accord, as long as they did not do so in the expectation that this would in any way help them to be saved. But certain non-Christian Jews from Asia saw Paul in the temple and falsely accused him of having defiled the holy place by bringing Greeks into it (Acts 21:27-40). A riot started, in which the apostle would have been killed had he not been rescued by the Roman chief captain, who was surprised when he learned that Paul could speak *Greek*, (Acts 21:37) and even more surprised when a little later he was informed that this *Jew* was a *Roman* citizen (Acts 22:27). On the steps of the castle Paul was permitted to address the Jewish mob. The people listened until the apostle mentioned his mission to the Gentiles. Then they shouted: "Away with such a fellow from the earth; for it is not fit that he should live" (Acts 22:22). The next day having been brought before the Sanhedrin, Paul cried out: "Brothers, I am a Pharisee, a son of Pharisees: touching the hope and resurrection of the dead I am called in question" (Acts 23:6).

This started a dissension between Pharisees and Sadducees. See pp. 126-127. The chief captain, fearing that Paul would be torn in pieces between the two parties, brought him into the castle. The same night Paul received a comforting vision (Acts 23:11). A plot of the Jews to kill him was frustrated by his nephew. The chief captain sent Paul, under strong guard, to Caesarea, where Felix the procurator had his residence. Hearings before Felix accomplished nothing, and Paul was left in prison in Caesarea until Festus succeeded Felix (Acts 24). Then, in order that he might not be taken to Jerusalem for trial, Paul made use of his right as a Roman citizen and appealed to Caesar (Acts 25:11). Accordingly, after a hearing before Herod Agrippa II—the son of Herod Agrippa I (see p. 180)—Paul was sent to Rome as a prisoner (Acts 26).

f. 60-63. *Voyage to Rome. Arrival. First Roman Imprisonment.* Acts 27, 28.

Luke's account of the voyage to Rome in Acts 27 is so vivid that it should be read very carefully (and, if possible, in the original). After a very perilous journey of many days the ship was wrecked on the island of Malta:

> *The foreship struck and remained immovable, but the stern began to break up due to the violence of the waves. The soldiers planned to kill the prisoners, lest any of them should swim away and escape. But the centurion, desiring to save Paul, kept them from carrying out their plan. He ordered those who could swim to jump overboard first, and get to land. The rest were to get there on planks or on various things from the ship. And so it happened that they all reached land safely* (Acts 27:41-44).

The shipwrecked company was kindly received. Paul healed many sick people on the island. After three months the prisoners were put aboard another ship which took them to Puteoli. Here Paul found friends, and after a week's stay with them he finally departed and arrived in Rome. Here the apostle was held in military confinement, chained to a soldier (Acts 28:16, 20; Phil. 1:7, 13), but permitted to lodge "in his own rented house" (Acts 28:30).

In Rome Paul proclaimed the gospel to the Jews. Some believed, but when others disbelieved he turned to the Gentiles, saying: "Let it be known to you Jews, therefore, that this salvation of God is sent to the Gentiles; they will also listen."

The Book of Acts closes with these words: "And he remained two years in his own rented house, and welcomed all who came to him, preaching the kingdom of God, and teaching the things concerning the Lord Jesus Christ with all frankness, unhindered."

During this first imprisonment Paul wrote Colossians, Philemon, Ephesians, and Philippians. See pp. 347-358.

g. 63-67. *Release. Second Imprisonment. Martyrdom.*

The Book of Acts is silent on this last period of Paul's life. We refer, therefore, to the information which can be derived from the Pastoral Epistles. See pp. 405-408. It is probable that the following New Testament books were written during this period: I and II Peter, Matthew, Mark(?), Luke, Acts, I Timothy, Titus, II Timothy, and Jude. See pp. 361-412.

3. The Close of the Apostolic Age

Date: 67-96

Scripture tells us little about this period. See, however, pp. 67, 75, 415-421, and 422. It *predicts* the destruction of Jerusalem—see p. 165—which occured in the year 70 after a terrible struggle. We also know that during the time which elapsed between the death of Paul and the Vision of Patmos the last of the New Testament books were written. They are: the Epistle to the Hebrews; the Gospel of John; and I, II, and III John. Last of all, about the year 96, the Book of Revelation appeared. See pp. 435-442. This brings us to the close of Sacred History. See p. 442, which forms a fitting conclusion not only for Part III, Bible Books, but also for Part II, The Bible Story.

Part Three

Bible Books

The Jordan River,
close to its source near Dan (Banias).
Trans World Airlines

Studying the Books of the Bible Chronologically 11

It is true, of course, that the Bible is *one* book, having *one* Author. Nevertheless, it is correct to say that this glorious book represents an entire library and that it has ever so many human authors. Now, in a library the books must be arranged according to a definite system. Sometimes all the volumes on poetry will be placed in one section, on one shelf, or in one bookcase; those on history, in another; etc. That, as we have seen on p. 33, is the manner in which the books of our Bible have been arranged. In the Old Testament we find three groups (historical, poetical, and prophetical); similarly, in the New (historical, epistolary, and prophetical). Now, this arrangement is excellent for devotional reading. When one uses the Bible for this purpose, the interest is generally riveted on one small section: this or that particular chapter or paragraph, and its spiritual meaning for the soul. The relation in which the *books* stand to one another is not then of primary concern. And inasmuch as the Bible is the reliable, inspired handbook for devotional reading, and this use of Scripture is perhaps the most popular one, we have no fault to find with the arrangement of the books in our English Bibles. In fact, we deem it an excellent arrangement—and providential.

The question now arises: Should we *always* and *for every purpose* adhere to that order? Must we follow it even when we study Old or New Testament Introduction or when we take up Bible Survey? There are various views:

1. Many conservative scholars, in their works on Old or New Testament introduction, cling to this arrangement. As we see it, this is probably not the best procedure. *Reading* a small section of Scripture for a devotional purpose is one thing; *studying* the Bible as a whole and its books in their relation to one another is quite a

different matter. It may require a different arrangement of the books. Let us see what happens when for the purpose of introduction the books are treated one by one according to the order found in our English Bibles. The reader is asked to make a long distance jump from Isaiah, about 700 B.C., to Jeremiah, about 600 B.C.; then, after a few more books have been discussed, he must hurry *back* to the time of Hosea and Amos, about 750 B.C. Moreover, Ezra-Nehemiah, which tells us what happened during the sixth and fifth centuries B.C. and was probably not completed until the fourth, is studied long before the prophets which preceded it by centuries (Amos, Hosea).

What happens in the case of the New Testament? First, one studies the Gospels. With this procedure we find no serious fault; for it can be argued that although at least two of them were composed after most of Paul's epistles had gone forth, they, nevertheless, record the events which occurred prior to that great apostle's conversion. It all depends upon the question whether one wishes to arrange the books according to their date of composition or according to their material content. Either makes sense. It need hardly be added that, whatever the date of composition, the Synoptics (Matthew, Mark, and Luke) must be studied together or, at least, in close succession. Still following the arrangement of the books in our English Bibles, Acts is studied after the Gospels. Again—and for the same reason—we offer no objections. But from here on the real difficulties begin. It is, of course, immediately clear that, with respect to the Epistles, the date of composition and material content coincide for all practical purposes. Hence, it would seem to be hardly correct to discuss Romans before I Corinthians, for in actual fact the latter was written before the former. Similarly, it seems hardly the best procedure to discuss Galatians after II Corinthians, unless one is prepared to accept a late date for Galatians. Matters become worse, however, when after Ephesians, Philippians and Colossians, which belong to the period 60/61-63, one has to turn *back* suddenly to the period 50-53, in order to study the historical conditions which prevailed when Paul wrote I and II Thessalonians. There follows another *forward* jump to the period intervening between Paul's first imprisonment and his death, 63-67, to which we ascribe I and II Timothy and Titus (and, of course, Titus actually preceded II Timothy!). Next comes Philemon, which should have been studied in connection with Colossians. The mind has now traveled *back* once more to the period of the first Roman imprisonment, 60/61-63.

Hebrews is next; hence *forward* again, to the period 67-96. There follows James, which carries one *back* to the very earliest times (perhaps to the year 50 or even earlier). Then *forward* again in order to reach the period 63-67 to which belong I and II Peter, and again *forward* to 67-96 for I, II, and III John. Here, however, occurs another "*about face*," unless one accepts a very late date for Jude. Finally, proceeding once more in a *forward* direction, we reach the year 96 or thereabout when Revelation was written.

This method does not impress us as being the best. It requires too much mental zigzagging.

2. Shall we follow the order accepted by liberal scholars? In their opinion the Hexateuch (Genesis-Joshua) was not completed until the fourth century B.C. Amos stands first in their list. This tallies with their evolutionistic conception of the history of religion. In the New Testament, Revelation is not placed last but before the Pastoral Epistles and before II Peter. On the basis of faith in Scripture's infallibility there is no room for this arrangement. The Pastoral Epistles claim to have been written by Paul. II Peter opens with the words: "*Simon Peter*, a servant and apostle of Jesus Christ. . . ." Now Peter and Paul died long before John wrote Revelation. It is not necessary, therefore, to discuss this liberal re-arrangement of the books at any greater length. No person who claims to be a conservative can accept it.

3. Which order shall we follow in this book? For the *New* Testament the chronological order immediately commends itself. The difficulties are not insurmountable. Each book is placed in its proper setting. The study of the books begins to resemble the reading of a continued story. We have, accordingly, arranged these sacred scriptures in the order of their date of composition as far as this can be determined. We have allowed two *possible* exceptions: the Synoptics have been discussed as a unit; II Peter and Jude, because of their close resemblance, have been included in the same chapter. Accordingly, the New Testament books are arranged thus:

As already indicated, 6, 7, and 8 can be made 1, 2, and 3. However, here one encounters a slight difficulty: if the Synoptics are placed first because of their material content (e.g., with a view to the study of what is known as Biblical theology), should not the Gospel of John, for the same reason, be treated immediately after Matthew, Mark, and Luke? But if this be done, John's *Gospel* is separated from his *Epistles*, though the two (Gospel and Epistles) have much in common.

For the *Old* Testament the same chronological method can be used to a considerable extent. It is our conviction that the Pentateuch not only describes events which happened first but was also actually first in date of composition. Joshua and Judges carry the story forward and belong to the same general period of composition, i.e., they, too, as we see it, were brought to completion before the year 1000 B.C. I and II Samuel follow a little later and present no difficulty in this connection. It is only when we reach I and II Kings that we must depart somewhat from the classification according to date of composition, for many other Old Testament books were completed before Kings. Nevertheless, because in the original these four—Joshua, Judges, Samuel, Kings—form a unit and tell a continuous story, we shall leave them in that order. As we see it, the best procedure for the Old Testament will be to follow the grouping found in the Hebrew. Accordingly, we shall discuss the three groups—Law, Prophets, and Writings—in that order. In the interest of chronological arrangement however, we shall depart from the order found in the Hebrew (printed edition) and English Bibles with respect to the Latter Prophets (Isaiah to Malachi). Instead of first discussing the larger books (the "major" prophets) and then the smaller ones (the "minor" prophets), we shall rearrange them so that they can be studied in their chronological order, just like the Epistles in the New Testament. Whereas many of the

Writings are of uncertain date, we shall simply adhere to the arrangement which was *finally* (it's a long story!) given to these books in the Hebrew. Hence, we follow the *original* order for The Law (Pentateuch), The Former Prophets (Joshua-Kings), and The Writings, while we rearrange The Latter Prophets.

Accordingly, in the chapters which follow the Old Testament books are arranged as follows:

Rugged mountain terrain as
seen from the slopes of Mount Sinai.
Wolfe Worldwide

12
The Law or Pentateuch: Genesis, Exodus, Leviticus, Numbers, and Deuteronomy

The Pentateuch or Fivefold (i.e., Fivefold *Book*) is the oldest inspired document. It has always been associated with the name of Moses. He was a man with a versatile mind, able to write legislation, history, and poetry. His life was spent in intimate fellowship with Jehovah (Deut. 34:10).

For this very reason it is not hard to believe that Jehovah told Moses what to write. In fact, it is even *necessary* to believe that at least the Creation account was based upon direct divine revelation, for whatever happened during the first five days (and part of the sixth) of Creation Week was not witnessed by human eyes. With respect to the remainder of the Book of Genesis, there is nothing wrong with the firm belief that Moses was the author and that he was divinely guided in his selection of sources, both oral and written, as well as in the choice of words which could serve as vehicles of the divine ideas. There is certainly considerable merit in the position of men like Yahuda and Van der Valk that even the language of the first book of the Bible presupposes an Egyptian background. Everything points to Moses!

As to Exodus, we know that it was Moses who wrote the Book of the Covenant; i.e., all or most of the contents of chapters 20-23. See Exodus 24:4-8; cf. also Exodus 34:27. Why can he not have written other similar sections? Moreover, that his literary activity was not confined to the writing of laws but included also narration is clear from Exodus 17:14.

The Book of Leviticus not only definitely presupposes a desert environment but begins with the words: "And Jehovah called Moses, and spoke unto him out of the tent of meeting, saying. . . ."

The story of Israel's desert journeyings described in the Book of Numbers is expressly ascribed to Moses (Num. 33:2).

Finally, with respect to Deuteronomy, one is forced to the conclusion that almost the entire contents of the book can be traced directly to the man "whom Jehovah knew face to face." Study the evidence contained in such passages as Deuteronomy 31:9, 22, 24; Daniel 9:11-13.

Accordingly, when anyone says that Moses was the author of the Pentateuch, he is correct![1] This statement, however, must not be interpreted to mean that Moses wrote *every letter* of the Bible's first five books, including even the account of his own death (Deut. 34:5-12). Among the remaining passages which some thoroughly conservative scholars regard as not having been written by Aaron's brother are the following:

Genesis 14:14: "Abraham . . . pursued as far as Dan." According to many scholars, this statement implies the previous conquest of Canaan.

Genesis 36:31: "And these are the kings that reigned in the land of Edom, before there reigned any king over the children of Israel." Scholars whose conservative position is not in doubt for even a moment are of the opinion that this passage was written after there was a king in Israel.

Genesis 50:10, 11; Numbers 35:14; Deuteronomy 1:1, 5; 4:46. These passages use the expression "beyond the Jordan" to indicate the region east of the river. Accordingly, many conclude that the one who wrote these passages must have lived west of the Jordan, which was not true with respect to Moses.

Exodus 11:3; Numbers 12:3: "Moreover, the man Moses was very great in the land of Egypt. . . ." Also: "Now the man Moses was very meek, above all the men that were upon the face of the earth." Would Moses have said this concerning himself?

Personally, we are not interested in lengthy argumentations which aim to show that also all of these and similar passages must be ascribed directly to Moses. We doubt whether anything is gained. One conclusion must, however, be maintained: whatever in Scripture—be it Old or New Testament—is directly or by clear implication ascribed to Moses should be assigned to his authorship. But nowhere does Scripture either state or imply that Moses wrote

1. Recommended reading for everyone is O.T. Allis, *The Five Books of Moses*, Presbyterian and Reformed Publishing Company, Nutley, N. J.

every word of the Pentateuch! Of *one* fact, however, we can be certain: the Pentateuch is inspired and has the Holy Spirit as its Author!

Every attempt has been made to assign a very late date to large sections of the Pentateuch. However, the effort has not met with general acceptance. It is at variance with the facts; e.g., the contents of Deuteronomy presuppose an environment different from that of the days of King Josiah; see p. 116. The counter-argument, according to which all statements which do not harmonize with the preconceived late date are to be considered interpolations, impresses one as being a subterfuge. By means of that type of reasoning one always has the better of the debate, according to the maxim: "Heads I win, tails you lose."

It has not pleased God to reveal to us the name of the inspired author who gave the Pentateuch its final form. From Genesis 36:31 one may probably conclude that this man, whoever he was, did not live before the days of King Saul. Also, he must have lived before David became king over all Israel. Before that event the Book of Judges appeared. Now in that document (as well as in the later Old Testament books) we find echoes not only of the ideas but even of the phraseology of various parts of the Pentateuch, proving that much (if not all) of the Fivefold was already in existence. Note these parallel passages: Genesis 50:24 and Judges 2:1; Exodus 1:8 and Judges 2:10; Numbers 20:17 and Judges 11:17; etc. In these and many similar passages the original often indicates an even closer resemblance than the English translation.

Conservative scholars, accordingly, are of the opinion that the Pentateuch reached its final form before the year 1000 B.C. See pp. 35, 100.

We shall close this chapter with a few remarks about each of the five books.

Genesis

Apart from Genesis it would be impossible to understand the contents of later revelation. To be sure, the Gospels tell us that Jesus came into the world to save sinners, but it is the Book of Genesis which records the story of the fall. It was not Paul in Romans and Galatians but Moses in Genesis who first deposited to writing the revealed doctrine of justification by faith (Gen. 15:6). Again and again the inspired New Testament authors go back in their reasoning beyond Israel to Genesis; see Galatians 3:17; Hebrews 6:20. It is not to be denied, of course, that the ideas appear in a more amplified form in the New than in the Old. The gist, nevertheless, is already present in Genesis!

The Book of Genesis gravitates toward the fulfillment of Genesis 3:15. The patriarchs are separated from the rest of humanity in order that in their seed *all the nations of the earth* may be blessed. The entire Bible is, indeed, a missionary book! These patriarchs also receive the promise of (a) an abundant posterity, and (b) a fertile country.

For the contents of Genesis see also pp. 83-93, 447, 451.

The outline that follows is easily committed to memory:

Genesis

BEGINNINGS

1, 2	**I. Material Universe and Man.**
3-5	**II. Sin and Salvation.**
6-9	**III. Devastation and Deliverance.**
10-50	**IV. Confusion and Covenant.**
10, 11	A. The line of confusion.
12-50	B. The line of the covenant.
12-24	1. Abraham
25, 26	2. Isaac.
27-36	3. Jacob.
37-50	4. Joseph and his brothers.

(Note: the chapter indications for Genesis and also for the other books are often approximate. Consult the Bible to see exactly where one section ends and another begins.)

Exodus

This book continues the story begun in Genesis. It reveals the fulfilment of the first element in the twofold promise (abundant posterity). Moreover, not only in the history which is recorded here—see pp. 93-95—but also in the tabernacle which is described in this book the coming Christ stands revealed. In the court stood the altar of burnt offering and the laver, pointing forward to Christ through whose blood we are justified and through whose Spirit we are sanctified. In the holy place were to be found the table of shewbread, the seven-branched candlestick, and the altar of incense, respectively foreshadowing Christ as our Bread of Life, our source of Light, and our Intercessor. Finally, there was the Holy of Holies with its ark of the covenant, containing the law. But between the Glorious Presence and God's holy law which man had transgressed was the blood-sprinkled cover, the "mercy seat," an appropriate symbol and type of Christ, our Atonement. The holy of holies was the image of heaven itself; the ark, a symbol of God's throne. The entire tabernacle, being the abode of Jehovah, was a beautiful and most appropriate prophecy of Christ, in whom all the fulness of the godhead dwells bodily.

For the contents of Exodus see also pp. 93-95, 447, 451.

Outline:

Exodus

ISRAEL CALLED AND CONSECRATED

1-19	**I. Israel Called out of Egypt.**
1-6	A. Persecution (of God's people).
7-12	B. Plagues (upon Egypt).
13-19	C. Passage from Egypt to Sinai.
20-40	**II. Israel Consecrated at Sinai.**
20-23	A. The covenant established (beginning with the Ten Commandments).
24-31	B. The tabernacle designed.
32-34	C. The covenant renewed.
35-40	D. The tabernacle made.

Leviticus

Closely connected with Exodus is Leviticus, an evident fact when one compares the last paragraph of the former with the opening words of the latter: "Then the cloud covered the tent of meeting, and the glory of Jehovah filled the tabernacle. . . . And Jehovah called Moses, and spoke to him out of the tent of meeting. . . ." The book contains regulations for worship. These laws indicate how a sinner may attain fellowship with Jehovah (chs. 1-16) and how the believer maintains this fellowship (chs. 17-27).

For the New Testament believer the teaching (always in the light of the New Testament) may be summarized as follows:

Leviticus 1-7

(1) "Apart from shedding of blood there is no remission" (cf. Heb 9:22).

(2) The offender's guilt is removed by means of the suffering and death of a substitute. Study Leviticus 17:11; then also Matthew 26:28; John 1:29; I Peter 1:18, 19; Hebrews 9:6-14, 24, 25; 10:1-18

(3) Sin offering, burnt offering, and peace offering follow one another in that order; i.e., when the offender's sins have been removed (symbolized by the sin offering), and his life has been wholly consecrated to Jehovah (indicated by the burnt offering) nothing now prevents him from exercising blessed fellowship with his God (pictured by the peace offering); cf. Rom. 5:1.

Leviticus 8-10

(4) Man needs a mediator in order to approach God: the priesthood in Israel foreshadowed the word of Christ, our Highpriest.

Leviticus 11-15

(5) Not only the removal of the *guilt* of sin is necessary but also the removal of its *pollution*. Sin is loathsome to Jehovah. Death symbolizes sin. Hence, in Israel those animals were considered "clean" which do not bring about death and/or do not clearly show the work of death (the process of deterioration) in their bodies Thus, e.g., land animals that are carnivorous are unclean.[2] Leprosy too, pictures the hideousness of sin.[3] Only when the loathsomeness of sin is grasped will there be an ardent yearning for the Messiah.

Leviticus 16

(6) "Being sorry" is not enough; sin cannot be removed without an atonement.

2. There are many theories concerning the criterion according to which some animals were considered clean, others unclean. I am indebted to J. P. Van Haitsma for the view defended in this paragraph.
3. This fact is brought out clearly by Lee S. Huizenga in *Unclean, Unclean,* pp 135-150.

(7) As Israel's Highpriest entered the Holy of holies and sprinkled the blood, so our Highpriest, Jesus Christ, has entered the heavenly Holy of holies with the merits of his own blood atonement. However, there are important differences: Israel's highpriest had to offer a bullock for his own sins first of all; Christ had no personal sins. The highpriest sprinkled the blood of a goat; Christ shed his own blood. The highpriest made atonement *symbolically* and *typically*; Christ, *really*. The highpriest had to repeat the Atonement Day ritual every year; Christ shed his blood *once for all*. The highpriest made atonement by sprinkling the blood of *one* goat, while the other goat symbolically "carried away" sin. Christ did both at the same time: he made atonement and thereby removed sin. Read Hebrews 9.

Leviticus 17-22

(8) In order to maintain fellowship with God the believer should adhere to this rule: "Whether, therefore, you eat or drink or whatever you do, do it all to the glory of God" (I Cor. 10:31). The believer should dedicate his food to God and receive it back from him on the basis of an accepted atonement.

(9) The believer must not only avoid practices which are wrong in themselves but also those which are characterized by evil associations and tendencies.

(10) Also with respect to the matter of the sexual relationship God should be glorified, his laws obeyed. Sexual relationship between close blood relatives is contrary to God's will.

Leviticus 23-25

(11) Just as Israel had its "appointed seasons" which were periods of special religious solemnity and rejoicing—the three great feasts (Unleavened Bread, Weeks or Pentecost, and Ingathering or Tabernacles) and the sabbatic cycle (seventh day, seventh month, seventh year, the year which followed the seventh sabbatic year, etc.)—so also we of the new dispensation should observe our festal commemorations of the great facts of redemption, in order that these may not fade from the memory (I Cor. 5:7, 8).

Leviticus 26, 27

(12) Jehovah's law needs constant ratification in our lives. That law speaks not only about covenant blessings but also about "the vengeance of the covenant." Those who know the way but do not

walk in it are punished sevenfold. On the contrary, the believer who lives in fellowship with his God strives to make this evident in every way, including generous and systematic giving, in the measure in which the Lord has blessed him.

As ceremonial requirements, these laws are no longer valid. Their *underlying principles* are as valid today as during the old dispensation. Every believer should study Leviticus.[4] He should do so before he starts with Hebrews!

Outline:

Leviticus
JEHOVAH'S LAWS OF WORSHIP

Chapters	
1-16	**I. How the sinner attains fellowship with Jehovah.**
1-7	A. Oblation (offerings).
8-10	B. Mediation (priestly).
11-15	C. Separation (between clean and unclean, etc.)
16	D. Expiation (the Day of Atonement).
17-27	**II. How the believer maintains fellowship with Jehovah.**
17-22	A. Sanctification (holiness in eating, drinking, the sexual relationship).
23-25	B. Celebration (religious festivals).
26, 27	C. Ratification (promises and threats).

Numbers

Whereas Leviticus contains the laws which Jehovah gave to Moses at Sinai, Numbers describes the manner in which Jehovah led his people from Sinai to the plains of Moab. The book is full of the Christ. It may be called the gospel in the Old Testament, as is clear from the outline (see below). Spiritual lessons for everyday life may be drawn from every chapter. Let us give a few examples:

Chapter 1: The "numbering" which takes place is, in reality, a

4. The interpretation of Leviticus in *The Expositor's Bible* is, to say the least very interesting and instructive.

registration for service. It shows us that every believer is a soldier, and that every soldier has something to do.

Chapter 2: There is strength in *organization.*

Chapter 3 and 4: Specialization: each man has his *special* task to perform in the kingdom of God.

Chapter 6: Special tasks require special *consecration,* which is even more necessary than mental or physical qualification.

The story content of the Book of Numbers is summarized on p. 95; see also p. 448.

Remember that *The Serpent Lifted Up* supplies the key to the interpretation of the whole book.

Outline:

Numbers
ISRAEL'S JOURNEY FROM SINAI TO THE PLAINS OF MOAB: A LESSON IN SIN AND GRACE

1-9	**I. Preparations for leaving Sinai.**
10-21	**II. Journey from Sinai to the plains of Moab:** a story of repeated *sin* and resulting *failure* until Jehovah in his *grace* causes the *serpent to be lifted up.* Thereupon mainly,
22-36	**III. Blessing and victory in the plains of Moab.**

(See especially 23:7-12, 23, 24; 24:3-10, 15-25; 31; 32.)

How would you expand this outline?

Deuteronomy

This book is a rehearsal of the law. It is not a mere repetition, however. Since the law was given at Sinai a new generation had arisen. On the eve of taking possession of Canaan this new generation must be shown why it should obey the law. The purpose of the book is clearly stated in the outline (see below). In Exodus, Leviticus, and Numbers, Jehovah is represented as speaking to Moses or through Moses to Israel. In Deuteronomy, Moses himself is addressing Israel. The style is hortatory and very impressive. The leading ideas are these: Jehovah is a *unique* God, the God of heaven and earth, spiritual in his being (4:35; 6:4; 7:25; 10:17; etc). Israel is a *unique*, peculiar people, especially beloved of Jehovah, as is clear from the manner in which he has led them (4:31; 29:13). The relation between this unique God and the unique people is *unique*: Jehovah is Israel's father (32:6); hence, Israel must love Jehovah and not merely fear him as do the nations round about (4:10; 5:29; 6:5; 10:12; etc). Israel *owes* Jehovah a debt of gratitude. On Deuteronomy see also what is said on p. 47, 115, 143, 211, and 451.

Outline:

Deuteronomy
JEHOVAH'S GRACIOUS DEALINGS: AN INCENTIVE UNTO GRATEFUL OBEDIENCE

1-4	**I. Jehovah has dealt graciously with you** (from Sinai to Moab).
5-26	**II. Observe, therefore, his law** (the law reviewed beginning with the Ten Commandments).
27, 28	**III. In order that you may be blessed, not cursed.**
29-34	**IV. Conclusion.**
29, 30	A. The covenant made in Moab.
31-34	B. Moses' farewell and death.

Excavation at the Old Testament site of Jericho and the traditional "Mount of Temptation" in the background.
George A. Turner

The Former Prophets: 13
Joshua, Judges, Samuel, and Kings

Joshua

The patriarchs received the promise of a) an abundant posterity and b) a fertile country. See Genesis 15:5, 18; 28:13, 14. Exodus shows us the fulfilment of the first promise; Joshua, of the second. There is also a very close connection between Joshua and the immediately preceding Book of Deuteronomy. Deuteronomy records Moses' death and immediately introduces Joshua. The Book of Joshua opens with a reference to Moses. We read,

> *So Moses the servant of Jehovah died there in the land of Moab. . . . And Joshua the son of Nun was full of the spirit of wisdom. . . . Now it happened after the death of Moses, the servant of Jehovah, that Jehovah spoke to Joshua, the son of Nun, Moses' minister, saying . . .* (Deut. 34:5, 9; Josh. 1:1).

Joshua was a great general: he possessed the qualities of leadership and enjoyed the respect of the people. Nevertheless, his real greatness consisted in this, that he, like Moses, was Jehovah's servant (Josh. 24:29). The real commander-in-chief who led the Israelites into Canaan was "the Prince of the host of Jehovah," introduced in 5:14. Joshua was, moreover, a type of the coming Messiah (Heb. 4:8), who leads his people into that true Land of Rest of which the earthly Canaan was a type.

No one knows who gave the Book of Joshua its present form. That the book rests on written sources composed by Joshua himself is clear from 24:26. Conservative scholars, however, are not agreed with respect to the extent of Joshua's authorship. That he himself cannot have been the one who gave the document its final form is clear from Joshua 24:29-33. A comparison of 15:63 and II Samuel 5:6-10 seems to indicate that the book was brought to completion before David smote the Jebusites and took the stronghold of Zion hence, before the year 1000 B.C.

The theme and the division are clearly suggested by the book itself. Throughout, the idea is emphasized that it was *Jehovah* who fulfilled his promise to the fathers in establishing Israel in the land of Canaan. The author gives us not only the theme but also the outline of his book. He does so in the very first paragraph of the first chapter:

Verse 2: "Arise, go over this Jordan." This is the center of the discussion found in chapters 1-4. Joshua instructs the people to prepare themselves with a view to this crossing of the Jordan (ch. 1) the spies cross over and return (ch. 2); the people cross and set up memorial stones (chs. 3 and 4); and after the crossing the Old Testament sacraments (circumcision and passover) are administered (ch. 5).

Verse 5: "There shall not a man be able to stand before you." This indicates the contents of chapters 5-12: the enemies are defeated; the land (a large portion of it) is conquered.

Verse 6: "Be strong and of good courage; for you shall cause this people to inherit the land which I swore to their fathers to give them." This refers to chapters 13-22: the actual inheritance of the land; i.e., its division among the tribes and families of Israel.

Verse 7: ". . . do according to all the law which Moses, my servant commanded thee." This is the gist of chapters 23 and 24; see 23:6 24:15, 24. For the contents of Joshua see also pp. 95, 448.

Outline:

Joshua
JEHOVAH ESTABLISHES ISRAEL IN THE PROMISED LAND

1-5 | **I. Jehovah causes Israel to <u>enter</u> the land (West Palestine); i.e., to cross the Jordan.**

6-12 | **II. Jehovah causes Israel to <u>conquer</u> the land.**

6-8 | A. Central Campaign (Jericho, Ai, etc.)

9, 10 B. Southern Campaign (the five kings, etc.)

11, 12 C. Northern Campaign (Hazor, etc.) and summary.

13-22 **III. Jehovah causes Israel to inherit the land** (its division among the tribes).

23, 24 **IV. Joshua, in his farewell address, emphasizes Israel's resulting obligation to worship and love Jehovah.**

Judges

The Book of Judges records Israel's history from the conquest of Canaan to the judgeship of Samuel. It was a period of probation: Jehovah has been faithful to his promise. Will Israel remain faithful to Jehovah? See also pp. 95-97. The people's repeated failure emphasizes the need of salvation from without and creates in the hearts of the ever-present godly remnant a yearning for the promised Seed.

Judges was written at a time when Israel already had a king but before David had established himself as ruler over all Israel (Judg. 1:21; cf. II Sam. 5:3-9; see further Judg. 17:6; 18:1). There are those who lean to the opinion that Samuel was the author, but no one knows.

Outline:

Judges
JEHOVAH PROVES ISRAEL IN THE DAYS OF THE JUDGES

1, 2 **I. Israel forsakes Jehovah.**

3-16 **II. Outward result: oppression.** Observe the oft-repeated cycle:

A. Relapse.

B. Retribution.

C. Repentance.

D. Rescue (by means of a "judge").

17-21	**III. Inward Result: Corruption:**
17, 18	A. Idolatry.
19-21	B. Immorality.

I and II Samuel

Originally I and II Samuel were one book; thus also I and II Kings. The Septuagint divided these two books into four: First, Second, Third, and Fourth Kingdoms. The Vulgate substituted the term "Kings" for "Kingdoms." In *Samuel* the story of the judges is continued, Samuel himself being the last judge. He was, moreover, the one who anointed the first two kings, Saul and David, whose story is also told in this work. Hence, this inspired volume received its name from him. That he himself cannot have been the author of the entire work is clear from the fact that his death occurred long before the events recorded in II Samuel; see I Samuel 25:1. In fact, from the well-known story of Saul and the witch at Endor it is clear that Samuel died before Saul (I Sam. 28). It has not pleased the Lord to inform us who was the author of what we today call I and II Samuel, neither does it matter as long as we believe that what was written is the very Word of God. From I Samuel 27:6 it would appear that the work was brought to completion sometime after the division of the kingdom. It is altogether probable that the inspired author made use of earlier sources; see II Samuel 1:18. He tells us the story of the establishment of the kingdom. He pictures Samuel as *the man of prayer*; Saul, as *the king who played the fool*; and David, as *the man after God's heart.* On the contents of I and II Samuel see also pp. 96-101, 451.

Summary outline:

I and II Samuel
JEHOVAH'S WAY WITH HIS PEOPLE IN THE DAYS OF SAMUEL, SAUL, AND DAVID

I Sam. 1-7	**I. Samuel, the man of prayer.**
I Sam 8-31	**II. Saul, the king who played the fool.**
II Sam 1-24	**III. David, the man after God's heart.**

A more complete and detailed outline would be:

I and II Samuel
JEHOVAH'S WAY WITH HIS PEOPLE IN THE DAYS OF SAMUEL, SAUL, AND DAVID

I Sam. 1-7	**I. Samuel, the man of prayer.**
I Sam. 1, 2	A. Samuel and his mother (he is born in answer to her prayer).
I Sam. 2, 3	B. Samuel and his Lord (he ministers to Jehovah–in contrast with the wicked sons of Eli–and from Jehovah he receives the prophetic call).
I Sam 4-7	C. Samuel and his people (though ignored by them when they rely upon the ark to give them victory in battle, he prays for them and leads them back to God: Ebenezer).
I Sam 8-31	**II. Saul, the king who played the fool.**
I Sam. 8-12	A. His Early Success (anointed king; victory over Ammonites; acclaimed king).
I Sam. 13-15	B. His Grievous Sins (ill-advised sacrifice; disobedience).
I Sam. 15-31	C. His Lack of Genuine Sorrow (embitterment against David whom he pursues; the tragic end of his life).
II Sam. 1-24	**III. David, the man after God's heart.**
II Sam. 1-10	A. His Early Success (king over Judah; then, over all Israel; makes Jerusalem his religious and political capital; gains victory over Philistines).
Sam. 11, 12	B. His Grievous Sins (Bathsheba; Uriah). Cf. also 24.
I Sam 13-24	C. His Genuine Sorrow (hence, pardon; but his sins have sad results: four children die). Cf. also I Kings 1, 2.

I and II Kings

The writings of the Former Prophets form a continuous narrative of the long period–more than eight hundred years for Judah, almost seven hundred years for all the tribes–during which Israel lived in

Canaan. In other words, they cover the era *Conquest to Exile.* The events are evaluated from the prophetic standpoint. Thus, the prophetic spirit of Moses rests upon Joshua; and it is he who, as it were, introduces the period of the judges. Again both Saul and David are anointed by the prophet Samuel and are judged by his high standard. And similarly, the narrative contained in I and II Kings (originally *one* book; see p. 34) is that of history as evaluated by God's inspired prophets. Moreover, the prophetic point of view does not clash with the priestly. On the contrary, the two are in beautiful harmony. The "best" kings are those who not only banish all idolatry but also refuse to sanction the worship of Jehovah under a foreign and compromising symbolism. They are those kings (Hezekiah, Josiah) who tear down the "high places" and honor the divinely ordained ritual at Jerusalem. The prophet and the devout priest in Jerusalem are in complete accord.

The period covered in I and II Kings extends from the death of David in 972 to the death of Nebuchadnezzar in 561; hence, more than four hundred years. It was therefore necessary for the author or redactor to make use of sources such as *The Book of the Acts of Solomon* (I Kings 11:41), *The Book of the Chronicles of the Kings of Israel* (I Kings 14:19), *The Book of the Chronicles of the Kings of Judah* (I Kings 14:29), etc. It is considered probable that the main body of the work was brought to completion before the exile, and that II Kings 25 (do I Kings 4:24; 6:37, 38; 8:1-5; 12:1-20 also show traces of a later hand?) was added during the period of captivity.

For the contents of I and II Kings see also pp. 69-70, 72, 105-119.

Summary outline:

I and II Kings

JEHOVAH'S WAY WITH HIS PEOPLE FROM THE REIGN OF SOLOMON TO THE BABYLONIAN EXILE

I Kings 1-11	I. **The United Kingdom** (under Solomon).
I Kings 12–II Kings 17	II. **The Divided Kingdoms.**
II Kings 18-25	III. **The Remaining Kingdom** (Judah).

A more detailed outline would be:

I and II Kings
JEHOVAH'S WAY WITH HIS PEOPLE FROM THE REIGN OF SOLOMON TO THE BABYLONIAN EXILE

I Kings 1-11	I. **The United Kingdom** (under Solomon).
I Kings 1-4	A. Rising (accession to the throne; wisdom).
I Kings 5-8	B. Shining (crowning work: the temple; etc.).
I Kings 9-11	C. Declining (polygamy and consequent idolatry). Result:
I Kings 12–II Kings 17	II. **The Divided Kingdoms.**
I Kings 12–II Kings 14	A. The kings, to Uzziah of Judah, and to Jeroboam II of Israel. The Mission of the prophets (Elijah and Elisha and others) to an idolatrous people.
II Kings 15-17	B. The kings, to Hezekiah of Judah, and to Hoshea of Israel. The Assyrian Exile.
II Kings 18-25	III. **The Remaining Kingdom** (Judah).
II Kings 18-23	A. Jehovah's blessing upon the reigns of the king-reformers Hezekiah and Josiah (contrast Manasseh).
II Kings 23-25	B. Jehovah's punishment upon wicked Judah and its wicked kings (Jehoahaz to Zedekiah); the Babylonian Exile.

Sheep and children on a rocky,
barren hillside at Tekoa.
George A. Turner

The Latter Prophets: Amos, Jonah, and Hosea 14

Amos[1]

It is not at all difficult to make the transition from Kings to Amos. This prophet lived in the days of the Divided Kingdom, which is discussed in I Kings 12–II Kings 17. More precisely, he prophesied during the long and prosperous reigns of Jeroboam II of Israel and Uzziah of Judah; see II Kings 14, 15; II Chronicles 26. He was a rustic, one of the "herdsmen of Tekoa," situated about six miles south of Bethlehem. Although he belonged to the Kingdom of Judah, he had been called to proclaim the word of Jehovah in the kingdom of Israel. He prophesied at Bethel (Amos 7:13), where Jeroboam I had established the worship of Jehovah under the image of a calf. From this type of worship to outright idolatry was but one step, which many had taken. Yet, Bethel was the very place where Jehovah had given his glorious promise to Jacob! See Genesis 28. On pp. 111-112 we have given the historical background which one must study in order to appreciate the prophecies of Amos. See also p. 454. In a day when many were "at ease in Zion" and "secure in the mountain of Samaria," this man of God spoke out fearlessly and boldly. Amaziah, the idolatrous priest at Bethel, "sent to Jeroboam, king of Israel, saying, Amos has conspired against you in the midst of the house of Israel: the land is not able to hear all his words" (Amos 7:10). To the prophet he addressed these words: "O you seer, go, flee away into

1. We shall not try to present any bibliography on the Minor Prophets. Among those consulted are the following: E. Henderson, *The Book of the Twelve Minor Prophets;* C. Von Orelli, *The Twelve Minor Prophets;* C. F. Keil and F. Delitzsch, *The Twelve Minor Prophets;* E. B. Pusey, *The Minor Prophets;* B. D. Cohon, *The Prophets;* and F. E. Gaebelein, *Four Minor Prophets.*

the land of Judah and there eat bread, and prophesy: but prophesy not again at Bethel; for it is the king's sanctuary and a royal house" (7:12). The priest received the reply which he deserved (vss. 14-17).

The main thrust of the prophecy of Amos is this: Jehovah deals with the nations according to a strictly ethical standard; he punishes them for their transgressions. But whereas Israel has sinned *knowingly* and in spite of the fact that Jehovah had lavished his special kindness upon this people, its punishment would be much more severe; see 3:2.

The style of the book is vivid, graphic, startling. Every word is an arrow aimed at the very heart of his hearers, many of whom must have been aristocrats who had grown fat upon the substance of the poor! Courageously, almost *bluntly*, Amos tells them that they are going to be carried away into captivity. The impassioned words which flew from his lips must have dismayed his audience. Here is a sample of his style:

> *Hear this word, you cows of Bashan, who are in the mountain of Samaria, who oppress the poor, who crush the needy, who say to their husbands, Bring and let us drink. The Lord Jehovah has sworn by his holiness that lo, the days are coming upon you, when they shall take you away with hooks, and your remnant with fish hooks* (Amos 4:1, 2).

Nevertheless, the book is by no means devoid of tender appeal, as is clear from chapter 5:

> *For thus says Jehovah to the house of Israel, Seek me, and you shall live. . . . Seek Jehovah and you shall live. . . . Seek him who made the Pleiades and the Orion, and turns the shadow of death into the morning, and makes the day dark with night; who calls the waters of the sea, and pours them out upon the face of the earth (Jehovah is his name). . . . Seek good and not evil, that you may live; and so Jehovah, the God of hosts, will be with you, as you say. Hate the evil, and love the good, and establish justice in the gate: it may be that Jehovah, the God of hosts, will be gracious to the remnant of Joseph.*

It is hardly necessary to add that the message of the Book of Amos—and of James, his New Testament counterpart; see p. 318—is thoroughly up-to-date. Churches that neglect their social duties and place a one-sided emphasis upon individualistic salvation clearly indicate that they have not yet caught up with Amos—nor with Christ! And when we say this, we are by no means endorsing the theology of the social gospel.

Observe how Amos first gains his audience by condemning and pronouncing woe upon the surrounding nations in the name of Jehovah. But the fire of his withering denunciations approaches closer and closer, until it finally reaches Ammon, then Moab, then Judah, and then—without the least hesitation—Israel itself! Be sure to use a map in studying chapters 2 and 3.

The manner in which the prophet reaches his target may be graphically represented as follows:

THE SPIRAL OF JUDGMENTS IN AMOS
Chapters 1 and 2

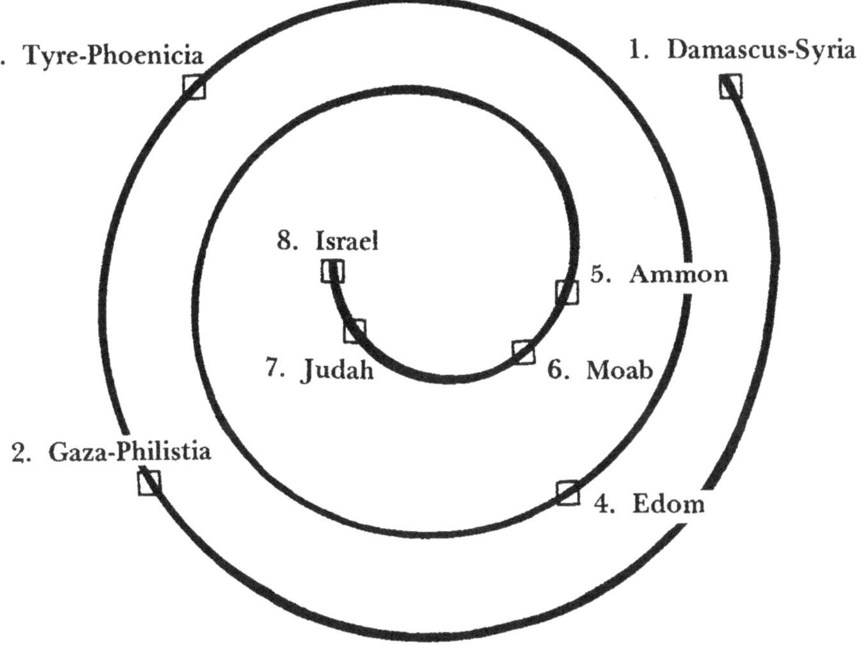

Summary outline:

Amos
WOE AND WEAL FOR ISRAEL

1, 2 | I. Woe is at hand for the nations that have committed cruel, inhuman deeds.

3-6 **II. Therefore, woe is at hand for highly-favored Israel.**

7-9:10 **III. Visions of threatening woe.**

9:11-15 **IV. Promises of weal.**

This brief outline can be expanded thus:

Amos
WOE AND WEAL FOR ISRAEL

1, 2 **I. Woe is at hand for the nations that hav committed cruel, inhuman deeds.** Key phrase "for three transgressions, yes, for four. . . ."

A. Syria: savage cruelty.

B. Philistia: slave-trade.

C. Phoenicia: slave-trade and treaty-breaking.

D. Edom: irreconcilability.

E. Ammon: sadism and mad aggression.

F. Moab: vengefulness.

G. Judah: departure from Jehovah.

H. Israel: exploitation of the poor, sham religior

3-6 **II. Therefore, woe is at hand for highly-favorec Israel.** Key phrase: "Hear this word. . . ."

A. The verdict.

B. Its justice.

C. Exhortation to repentance.

D. Woes to be visited upon the impenitent.

7-9:10 **III. Visions of threatening woe.** Key-phrase: "Thu the Lord Jehovah showed me."

A. The locust plague.

B. Fire (drought?).

C. The plumbline.

D. The interruption: Amos accused by Amaziah

E. Basket of ripe fruit.

F. The sanctuary trembling to its foundations.

9:11-15 | **IV. Promises of Weal.**

A. The Davidic dynasty to flourish once more.

B. The people to be restored to their country with wonderful prosperity.

Jonah

See also p. 454.

Another prophet of the Glamor Age was Jonah, a son of Amittai. He was from Gath-hepher near Nazareth. It was he who predicted that "the Lord would restore the border of Israel from the entrance of Hamath to the sea of the Arabah," a prophecy which was fulfilled during the days of Jeroboam II. See II Kings 14:25; cf. Jonah 1:1. When Israel rejected Jehovah—as we learned from the prophecy of Amos—Jonah was commissioned to carry the word of God to Nineveh, the capital of that very nation which was even now expanding its boundaries until, after about half a century, it would destroy the kingdom of the ten tribes! The prophet, probably fearing that Jehovah would transfer his love from Israel to Assyria, disliked his commission and boarded a ship which sailed in the opposite direction from Nineveh. A storm overtakes the ship, and the prophet, having confessed his guilt, is thrown into the sea. He is swallowed up by a great fish. From the fish's belly he utters a stirring prayer. He is vomited out upon the dry land. His commission is renewed. Accordingly, he walks through the streets of the great city proclaiming: "Yet forty days, and Nineveh shall be overthrown."

The people "repent." This greatly disturbs Jonah, so that he becomes angry. He hopes against hope that the city will still be destroyed. Moreover, he "went out of the city, and sat on the east side of the city, and there made him a booth, and sat under its shade, till he might see what would become of the city" (4:5). Jehovah causes a plant to spring up, which protects him against the scorching rays of the sun. But in the morning a worm kills the plant. The prophet becomes very angry. The book closes with the touching words:

And Jehovah said, You feel grief over the plant, on which you did not bestow labor, nor did you make it grow; which came up in a night, and perished in a night. Then should not I feel grief over Nineveh, that great city, in which are more than a hundred and twenty thousand persons who do not know their right hand from their left, and also much livestock?

Scripture nowhere states who wrote the book which tells the story of Jonah. It does definitely inform us that chapter 2 contains the very prayer which the prophet uttered "out of the fish's belly." We have placed this prophecy in a group with Amos and Hosea because these three prophets performed their task during the Glamor Age (though Hosea continues into the next period). Not all conservative scholars are agreed on the date when the Book of Jonah was written. Though some contend that the entire book was composed by the prophet whose story it relates, other thoroughly conservative scholars admit that there is considerable merit in the arguments which seem to support an exilic or even post-exilic date. They point especially to the grammatical characteristics of the book (the Aramaic constructions) and to the passage: "Now Nineveh *was* an exceeding great city, of three days journey (3:3b). This sounds as if, when the book was written, the city no longer existed. It was destroyed in the year 612.

What really matters is the fact that the book is fully inspired and conveys valuable lessons for every age. It shows us that Jehovah's mercy is not limited to one nation; also, that it is the duty of God's elect to "show forth the excellencies of him who called them out of darkness into his marvelous light" (I Pet. 2:9).

Jonah is not a myth; he was a real person. What is written in the book *really* happened. Our Lord clearly teaches this in Matthew 12:39, 40; Luke 11:29, 30, passages which also indicate that Jonah was a type of the Christ.

Outline:

Jonah

JONAH'S MISSION TO NINEVEH: JEHOVAH'S LOVE CONTRASTED WITH JONAH'S ANGER

1 | **I. Jonah's mission to Nineveh; his disobedience and its results.**

2 | **II. His prayer from the belly of the fish and his release.**

3 | III. His preaching to the people of Nineveh and their repentance.

4 | V. Jehovah's love contrasted with Jonah's anger.

Hosea

Hosea—the name means salvation—was in all probability a citizen of the Northern Kingdom (7:5). He was a contemporary of Amos and also of Isaiah; in other words, he belonged to the *Glamor Age* and also to the *Growth of Assyria* Period. See pp. 111-114. In his beautiful book he pours out his heart. He speaks out of the fulness of his own bitter experience. This experience was used by the Lord as a dramatic portrayal of Jehovah's relation to Israel.

The prophet had married a certain woman by the name of Gomer. But his wife was not true to him. She became "a wife of whoredom." She went after other lovers and conceived "children of whoredom": Jezreel, Lo-ruhamah, and Lo-ammi (son, daughter, son). For the meaning of these symbolic names see II Kings 9:17, 37; 10:30; Hosea 1:4, 6, 9. If the "woman" of chapter 3 who is called an "adulteress" is Gomer, then the rest of the story is as follows. Hosea, instead of completely rejecting his unfaithful wife, slips away to the haunt of shame, buys Gomer back for fifteen pieces of silver and a homer and a half of barley, and mercifully restores her to her former position of honor.

Although there are those who believe that this story of Gomer's unfaithfulness was merely a vision, the arguments upon which that conclusion is based are unconvincing. The entire narrative is presented as actual history; see 1:2, 3. Nevertheless, the facts in the story have symbolical significance, somewhat as follows:

(1) Just as Hosea had married Gomer, so Jehovah had become Israel's "Husband."

(2) Just as Gomer had become untrue to Hosea, so Israel had become unfaithful to Jehovah.

(3) Just as Gomer was enslaved by her paramours, so the Israelites would be enslaved by those very nations in which it was putting its trust.

(4) Just as Hosea restored Gomer, so Jehovah would restore Israel's remnant.

(5) Just as Hosea, in order to restore Gomer, redeemed her with the

price of silver and barley, so Christ would redeem the true Israel with the price of his own blood.

The story of Gomer can be summed up in three words: *sin, punishment, restoration.* And that is also the cycle which is found in this beautiful prophecy. Sin, punishment, restoration is the theme of chapters 1-3, of chapters 4:1–6:3, of 6:4–11:12, and of 12-14. Nevertheless, there is no "vain repetition." See the outline below. One might compare this cyclical arrangement with that of I John; see pp. 429-430.

In Hosea's later days Assyria's chariot wheels had already been set in motion. Israel was heading straight for disaster. Jehu's dynasty came to an end, and political chaos resulted, in fulfilment of the prophecy of II Kings 10:30. Israel as a nation was about to perish. Kings were being assassinated in regular order (Hos. 8:4; see p. 112). Nevertheless, Jehovah's heart was filled with tender, yearning love for his own (11:8). Said he, in wondrous compassion: "I will heal their backsliding. I will love them freely" (14:4).

Summary outline:

Hosea

GOMER'S SIN, PUNISHMENT, AND RESTORATION: A SYMBOL OF ISRAEL'S SIN, PUNISHMENT, AND RESTORATION

1-3	I. Gomer's sin, punishment, and restoration considered as a symbol.
4:1–6:3	II. Those (in Israel) who sin; those who are punished. Restoration.
6:4–11:11	III. Their sins; their punishments. Restoration.
12-14	IV. The grievous character of the sins; the severity of the punishments. Restoration.

Expanded outline:

Hosea

GOMER'S SIN, PUNISHMENT, AND RESTORATION: A SYMBOL OF ISRAEL'S SIN, PUNISHMENT, AND RESTORATION

1-3	I. Gomer's sin, punishment, and restoration considered as a symbol. A. Gomer's sin: unfaithfulness to her husband.

B. Her punishment: she is deserted by her lovers; sold into slavery.

C. Her restoration: "So I bought her to me. . . ."

4:1–6:3 **II. Those (in Israel) who sin; those who are punished. Restoration.**

A. Those who sin.

B. Those who are punished.

C. Restoration: "he has torn, and he will heal us. . . ."

6:4–11:11 **III. Their sins; their punishments. Restoration.**

A. *Their sins.*

1. Trusting in burnt offerings (dead ritualism).
2. Trusting in kings of their own choosing.
3. Trusting in Egypt and in Assyria.
4. Trusting in idols.

B. *Their punishments.*

1. Away to Assyria and Egypt the people and treasures shall go.
2. Barren and Bereaved of children they shall be.
3. Carried away shall be their idols.
4. Destroyed shall be their fortresses.
5. Exchanged for wrath shall be Jehovah's love.

C. *Restoration*: "How shall I give thee up, Ephraim?"

12-14 **IV. The grievous character of the sins; the severity of the punishments. Restoration.**

A. *The grievous character of the sins.*

1. In spite of Jehovah's faithfulness, Israel has become unfaithful.
2. In spite of Jehovah's revelation (to Jacob) at Bethel, Israel worships idols at Bethel.
3. In spite of the fact that Jehovah led Israel out of Egypt, Israel copies the morals of Egypt and of the nations.

B. *The severity of the punishments.* They will be:

1. Swift.

2. Terrible.

3. Relentless.

C. *Restoration:* "I will heal their backsliding; I will love them freely."

It is held by many that these prophecies were delivered during the following reigns:

1-3	I. The reign of King Jeroboam II of Israel.
4:1–6:3	II. The reign of King Menahem.
6:4–11:11	III. The reigns of King Pekah and King Hoshea.
12-14	IV. The reign of King Hoshea.

NOTE: 11:12 should begin a new chapter (12).

The Cyrus Cylinder records the Persian monarch's edict allowing captured peoples to return to their homelands. Under this policy, many Jews resettled in Jerusalem and rebuilt their temple. ***British Museum***

The Latter Prophets: 15
Isaiah and Micah

Isaiah

To Amos, Jehovah is the God of unflinching, universal justice; to Jonah, of tender, ocean-wide compassion; to Hosea, of sovereign, reclaiming love; and to Isaiah, of sublime, incomparable majesty (Isa. 6:3; 57:15). None among the gods resembles Jehovah; none can be compared to him (Isa. 40:18). Jehovah is the only God who saves! Accordingly, his people must put their trust in him and in no other object. That is the central theme of this great hero of faith who has been called the king of all the prophets. His name is indicative of his message, for it means *Jehovah Has Saved.*

He was the son of Amoz (not to be confused with Amos). He belonged to a family of rank and was intimate with royalty. He was a married man and had two sons: Shear Jashub ("a remnant shall return") and Maher-shalal-hashbaz ("hastening to the spoil; hurrying to the prey"). In the year of Uzziah's death Isaiah received his call to the prophetic office (ch. 6).

For majesty and versatility of expression as well as for brilliancy of imagery this prophet has no equal. In his book are to be found the most tender pleadings (1:18 ff.), the most vivid portrayals (ch. 3), the most touching parables (ch. 5), the most profound visions (ch. 6), the most startling prophecies (ch. 7), the most jubilant psalms of praise (ch. 12), the most graphic predictions of woe (ch. 13), the most cheering consolations (ch. 40), and the most complete delineations of the coming, the suffering, and the subsequent glory of the Messiah (ch. 53).

For the historical background of the prophecies of Isaiah and Micah we refer to what is found on pp. 112-115; see also pp. 448,

453. When the ruthless Assyrian conqueror was terrorizing the nations, and Judah, unwilling to join in a coalition against him, was attacked by Israel and Syria, and, therefore, was thinking seriously of inviting Assyrian help, it was Isaiah who, in the name of Jehovah, admonished his king and people to trust only in Jehovah. King Ahaz disregarded this advice and asked Assyria to come to his assistance. The Assyrian wolf accepted only too gladly, and in 722 Samaria fell. As everyone could easily see, Judah was next! Accordingly, Judah now turned to Egypt for help. Once more it is Isaiah who, in the name of his Sender, says, "No, God's people must place their trust in Jehovah alone, not in Egypt." This preaching finally bears fruit in the life of Hezekiah, and Jehovah rewards the faith of this king by destroying the Assyrian host (chs. 36, 37). But the people, as a whole, continue their leaning on the arm of flesh. Even Hezekiah, in a moment of weakness, shows the ambassadors from Babylon "the house of his armor" (39:2), whereupon Isaiah predicts that the king's treasures and also his descendants shall be "carried to Babylon." This prediction forms a fitting introduction to chapters 40-66, in which the prophet speaks from the standpoint of the Babylonian exile and predicts pardon, deliverance, and restoration.

Many are of the opinion that Isaiah himself could not have written chapters 40-66.[1] They present linguistic (different grammar and style characteristics), theological (a different conception of God, etc.), and historical arguments for their position. Some of the men who take this position are, however, willing to admit that the linguistic and theological arguments do not really *prove* their contention, and that the *historical* argument is the strongest. This, briefly, is as follows: Whereas chapters 40-66 assume the exile as already present, Isaiah, who died long before it occurred, could not have written them. Other scholars, however, have shown that the real situation is on this order:

1. Chapters 40-66 contain many passages which view city and temple as having been destroyed, the people as being in captivity, and Cyrus as already present upon the scene of history (41:2; 42:22, 24; 44:26-28; 45:1; 47:6; 51:3; 58:12; 61:43; 63:18; 64:10).

2. These same chapters also contain another series of passages which represent city and temple as existing, and Cyrus as a person who is going to make his appearance in the future (40:9; 41:25; 43:28; 46:11; 48:2; 52:1, 7, 8; 56:5-7; 62:6 ff.)

1. See R. H. Pfeiffer, *Introduction to the Old Testament,* p. 452ff. Also S. R. Driver, *An Introduction to the Literature of the Old Testament,* p. 243.

3. The suggestion that in addition to a Second (or Deutero-) Isaiah, who supposedly lived in Babylonia shortly before the Return and wrote chapters 40-55, there was also a Third (or Trito-) Isaiah, who prophesied in Palestine after the Return and wrote chapters 56-66, solves nothing; for also in chapters 56-66 there are references to city and temple as having been laid waste and no longer existing.

4. Hence, we must choose between these alternatives: either, an unknown author of the captivity era composed chapters 40-66 and at times wrote as if Jerusalem and the temple were still in existence, though he knew full well that this was not the case; or else, Isaiah himself wrote these chapters and, being fully assured that the events which God had predicted would come to pass, used the present tense in order to indicate this certainty.

5. Whereas the book itself again and again declares that Jehovah predicts the distant future and that the ability to do so is his alone, this second position is to be preferred see 41:22-29; 42:9; 44:7; 46:10 ff.; 48:6.

Summary outline:

Isaiah
SALVATION IS OF JEHOVAH

1-39	**I. Prophecies based on events which happened during Isaiah's own time.** Trust neither in Assyria nor in Egypt but in Jehovah, who rewards those who trust in him.
40-66	**II. Prophecies based on the event that happened after Isaiah's own time;** namely, the predicted Babylonian captivity. Jehovah will deliver his people from Babylonian and from spiritual captivity and will make Zion glorious.

Expanded outline:

Isaiah
SALVATION IS OF JEHOVAH

1-39	**I. Prophecies based on events that happened in Isaiah's own time.**
1-5	A. Judah's departure from Jehovah (formalism, materialism, vanity) condemned.

6-12 B. The Book of Immanuel, beginning with Isaiah's ordination vision. *Trust not in Assyria but in Jehovah,* who will provide salvation through his Immanuel.

13-24 C. Judgments upon the nations that are hostile to those who *trust* in Jehovah.

25, 26 D. Hymns of *trust.*

27-35 E. *Trust in Jehovah, not in the shadow of Egypt.*

36-39 F. The reward given to those who *trust* in Jehovah (as does Hezekiah).

36, 37 1. Deliverance from the Assyrian foe.

38, 39 2. Deliverance from death. Babylonian Captivity predicted as a punishment for lack of *trust.*

40-66 II. **Prophecies based on the event that happened after Isaiah's own time**; namely, the predicted (see ch 39) Babylonian Captivity.

40-48 A. Jehovah, incomparable in greatness, will redeem his people. He will deliver them from *Babylonian captivity* through his "anointed" Cyrus.

49-57 B. Jehovah will deliver his people from *spiritual captivity* through "the Servant of Jehovah" ("Servant of Jehovah" passages: 49:1-9 50:4-9; 52:13–53:12; *but also 42:1-7;* cf Matt. 12:17-21; Acts 8:35).

58-66 C. The glory of redeemed Zion.

We might add that the nations upon whom judgments are pronounced in chapters 13-24 are: Babylonia, Assyria, Philistia Moab, Syria, Ethiopia, Egypt, Arabia, Edom, and Phoenicia.

Micah

Micah was a contemporary of Isaiah. Although he addresses the people of Judah, his words concern all Israel. We find in these rophecies combinations of theology and ethics, of Hosea and Amos, f emphasis upon the first and upon the second tables of the Law.

The prophet denounces Israel's idolatry and hollow ritualism (1:7; :6-8) as well as the exploitation of the poor by the rich (2:2). 'hese denunciations pass into prophecies of impending doom upon amaria and Jerusalem. The book may be divided into three sections, ach of which begins with the expression "Hear" (1:2; 3:1; 6:1) nd ends with a message of hope and cheer for the remnant (1:12, 3; ch. 5, especially vss. 7-15; ch. 7, especially vss. 18-20). The pening of the prophecy very impressively describes *Jehovah's 'ontroversy:*

> *Hear, you peoples, all of you; listen O earth, and all that is in it; and let the Lord Jehovah be witness against you, the Lord from his holy temple. For behold, Jehovah comes forth out of his place, and will come down, and tread upon the high places of the earth. The mountains shall be melted under him, and the valleys shall be cleft, as wax before the fire, as waters that are poured down a steep place. . . .*

Thus, Samaria and Jerusalem are brought to trial before the ations. Jehovah first appears as Accuser, but soon as Judge. The ations form, as it were, a circle to see the judgment upon the two apitals. Notice also the play upon words in 1:10-16; example: "In he House of Dust [Beth-le-aphrah] roll yourself in the dust."

The most well-known passage of Micah's prophecy is, of course, :2: "But you, Bethlehem Ephrathah . . ." That it refers to Christ is lear from Matthew 2:6. Micah predicts the coming of the Messiah, he exact place of his birth, the nature of his work, his influence over he nations, and his victory over all his enemies. The prophet lives in is message. Everywhere he reveals deep personal interest. It is as if e himself experiences that which he predicts. The love of Jehovah or his remnant, as pictured in this prophecy, may be characterized s tender, yearning, and intensely personal. He who says that love is bsent from the Old Testament has never read Micah! In 7:18 the nan from Moresheth-gath (in Judah, near Philistia) asks the question, 'Who is like Jehovah [literally, who is a God like thee]?" There was ever a moment when the prophet did not ask this question, for it is he very meaning of his name (*Micah*—who is like Jehovah?). He tells s that Jehovah is a God *"who delights in lovingkindness."*

Outline:

Micah
JEHOVAH'S CONTROVERSY

1, 2 **I. With the capitals**: Jerusalem and Samaria.

A. Idolaters and those who exploit the poor shal be punished.

B. The remnant shall be blessed: "their king i passed on before them, and Jehovah at the heac of them."

3-5 **II. With the rulers**: prophets, priests, and princes.

A. Those who "skin" the needy (see 3:3) shall gc into Babylonian exile.

B. The *remnant,* rescued from Babylon, shall b blessed, when he comes who "shall be a Rule: in Israel; whose goings forth are from of old from everlasting."

6, 7[2] **III. With the people.**

A. Ritualists should consider the question: "Wha does Jehovah require of you, but to do justly and to love kindness, and to walk humbly witl your God?"

B. The *remnant* shall be blessed when "all thei sins are cast into the depths of the sea."

2. Do these chapters belong to Micah's prophecies? We believe they do. Th unity of the book is assailed by R. H. Pfeiffer, *Introduction to the Ol Testament,* p. 592ff., and defended by J. Ridderbos, *De Kleine Profeten,* vol II, pp. 102-104.

The southeast corner of the Old
City wall of Jerusalem.
George A. Turner

The Latter Prophets: Nahum, Zephaniah, and Habakkuk 16

Nahum[1] See also p. 454.

Micah had predicted:

(a) The destruction of Samaria (Mic. 1:6). It occurred in 722.

(b) The destruction of Jerusalem (3:12). This prophecy was fulfilled in 586.

(c) In connection with b, the Babylonian Captivity (4:10); date of fulfilment: 586-536.

(d) The Return (4:10). This took place in 536 and following years.

(e) The coming, task, and victory of the Messiah (ch. 5). The fulfilment of this prediction pertains to the New Dispensation.

In the time of Nahum the first of these prophecies had been fulfilled. Accordingly, this prophet lived in the period between the fall of Samaria, 722, and that of Jerusalem, 586. More precisely, he appeared upon the scene after the fall of Thebes in 663 (No-Amon, 3:8) and before the destruction of Nineveh in 612. To Nahum Jehovah was the God of vengeance; that is, of retributive justice. At the same time he is also a God of tender compassion. The very name Nahum means *compassionate*. Though slow to anger, Jehovah will most certainly pour out his wrath upon those who hate him and oppress his people. On the other hand, those who take refuge in him have nothing to fear.

Observe the striking contrast between 1:2 and 1:7, which may be translated as follows:

1. In connection with this book one should read C. J. Gadd, *The Fall of Nineveh.*

A jealous God and an Avenger is Jehovah;
An Avenger is Jehovah, full of wrath;
An Avenger is Jehovah for his adversaries,
And he reserves wrath for his enemies.

. . . .

Good is Jehovah,
A stronghold in the day of trouble;
And he knows those who take refuge in him.

For poetic strength and beauty Nahum has no peer, unless it be Isaiah. His prophetic utterances are full of rhythm: they roll and rumble just like the chariots of war which he describes. The prophet lived during the dark days in which Judah was tributary to Assyria. This was the time of foreign domination; see p. 115. Heavy was the Assyrian yoke, and Judah's king was Manasseh before his conversion! It was Nahum's glorious task to predict that the days of the oppressor's capital were numbered. His theme is *Jehovah's Vengeance Revealed in Nineveh's Overthrow.* He predicts the downfall of *every* Nineveh that shall seek to destroy or seduce God's people. Accordingly, this prophecy forms the background of Revelation 17.

Outline:

Nahum
JEHOVAH'S VENGEANCE AND GOODNESS REVEALED IN NINEVEH'S OVERTHROW

1:1-8	**I. Hymn contrasting Jehovah's vengeance upon his adversaries with his goodness toward his people.**
1:9–3:19	**II. Nineveh's overthrow.**
1:9-15	Nineveh's Overthrow means Judah's freedom.
2:1-10	Account (graphic and prophetic) of Nineveh's siege and fall.
2:11–3:7	How Nineveh earned its fall.
3:8-11	Unlike No-Amon (Thebes) is Nineveh? It shall likewise be destroyed!
3:12-19	Marked for destruction are all its defenses.

Zephaniah

See also p. 454.

Nahum's prophetic activity was followed by that of Zephaniah, who, according to some interpreters, was the great-great-grandson of King Hezekiah (this is by no means certain, however); see Zephaniah 1:1. This prophet was living in the days of Josiah; see pp. 115, 116 for the historical background. It is held by many that he prophesied during the early part of the reign of this king; i.e., before the days of the great reformation; see II Chronicles 34:3. If so, he may have encouraged Josiah to undertake this religious transformation. Everything points to the fact, however, that the reformation did not reach the *heart* of the masses. Judah, as a nation, was getting ripe for the judgment. Zephaniah foresees this Day of Wrath. It is in store not only for Nineveh and (later) Babylon but also for Jerusalem, whose people are intoxicated with the desire to oppress the poor; whose princes, like hungry wolves, prey upon those in distress; whose judges are gluttonous robbers, evening wolves that leave nothing till the morning; whose prophets are lighthearted deceivers; and whose priests, the very guardians of the sacred precincts, profane the sanctuary. And all this in spite of the constant and stirring pleading of Jehovah (3:1-7). Hence, the Day of Wrath is coming, not only upon all the nations but also upon Zion. That Day is near, full of terror, irrevocable, and universal (ch. 1).

Nevertheless, the real theme of Zephaniah's prophecy is not *The Day of Wrath* as such but this: *In that terrible day Jehovah will hide his people, his faithful remnant.* The meaning of the name *Zephaniah* as well as the main thrust of his book is this: "Jehovah has hidden or treasured" his own, even "the remnant of Israel," those who "take refuge" in him (3:12, 13; cf. 2:3—"it may be you will be hidden in the day of Jehovah's anger"). This pious remnant, in turn, will be a blessing to the nations among whom Judah will be scattered. Gentiles will "call upon the name of Jehovah, to serve him with one consent" (3:9; cf. vs. 20).

The Day of Wrath of which the prophet spoke lies buried in the now long forgotten past. Nevertheless, it is typical of a day which is still future, even the Judgment Day. But then as well as in the past, the true and faithful remnant will be hidden and treasured and will have nothing to fear.

Outline:

Zephaniah
JEHOVAH HIDES HIS PEOPLE IN THE DAY OF WRATH

1:1–3:8	**I. The day of wrath.**
1:1-3	A. Zephaniah announces Zero Hour–the Day o Wrath–for the whole earth.
1:4-13	B. Even Judah shall not be spared.
1:14-18	C. Picture of the Day of Wrath.
2:1-3	D. Humble yourselves before Jehovah.
2:4-15	E. All the surrounding nations shall be punished.
3:1-4	F. Neither shall Jerusalem be spared.
3:5-8	G. I said: "Oh that she would fear me."
3:9-20	**II. Jehovah hides and exalts his people.**
3:9	A. All the nations shall serve Jehovah.
3:10-20	B. He will hide and exalt "the remnant of Israel."

Habakkuk

See also p. 454.

Nahum probably carried on his prophetic activity about the yea 650; Zephaniah, about the year 630 (though some believe that h prophesied during the last years of Josiah). The next prophet i Habakkuk, who appears upon the scene a little later; i.e., during th reign of wicked Jehoiakim; see p. 116, and II Kings 23; 24 The rich are still oppressing the poor. Moreover, what arrests th prophet's attention is that they seem to be getting away with i Jehovah seems to tolerate the exploitation of the needy. He is no doing anything about it. So, Habakkuk begins to ask questions. H addresses them to Jehovah. Whereas elsewhere Jehovah speaks to th prophet, here the prophet speaks to Jehovah. He complains, ask questions, advances objections and–waits for an answer.

Habakkuk's first question is on this order: "Why does Jehova allow the wicked in Judah to oppress the righteous?" Jehova answers: "Evil-doers will be punished. The Chaldeans [Babylonians are coming." But this answer leads to another question: "Why does Jehovah allow the Chaldeans to punish the Jews, who, at least, are more righteous than these foreigners?" The prophet stations himself upon his watchtower and awaits an answer. The answer arrives. It amounts to this: "The Chaldeans, too, will be punished. In fact, *all sinners* will be punished . . . but the righteous shall live by his *faith.*" It is his duty and glory to trust, even when he is not able to "figure out" the justice of Jehovah's doings. In this humble trust and quiet confidence he shall *live* (cf. Rom. 1:17; Gal. 3:11).

But Jehovah does more than merely tell the prophet that he should exercise faith. He also strengthens that faith by means of a most marvelous, progressive vision (ch. 3). Habakkuk sees the symbol of Jehovah's presence descending from Mt. Paran. Having descended, he stands firm and shakes the earth. The tent hangings of Cushan and Midian are trembling and are being torn to shreds. One question worries the prophet: "Upon whom is Jehovah's wrath going to fall? Merely upon the realm of nature? Upon Judah?" Finally, the answer arrives: Jehovah destroys the Chaldeans and delivers his people.

So fearful and terrifying had been the appearance of Jehovah, so alarming the sound of the tempest, of crumbling mountains, etc., that the prophet was trembling in every part of his body. Nevertheless, he no longer questions the ways of Jehovah's providence. From now on he is going to "wait quietly." He expresses his gratitude in a beautiful psalm of trust, which begins with the words: "For though the fig tree shall not flourish . . . " (3:17-19).

Outline:

Habakkuk
THE RIGHTEOUS SHALL LIVE BY HIS FAITH

1, 2 | **I. Faith tested: the prophet's questions and Jehovah's answers.**

- A. Why does Jehovah permit the wicked in Judah to oppress the righteous?
- B. Answer: The Chaldeans will come as a punishment for the wicked.
- C. But the Chaldeans are worse than the Jews.
- D. Answer: The Chaldeans also will be punished: *all* sinners will be punished; but the righteous shall live by his *faith.*

3 | **II. Faith strengthened by a vision shown in answer to the prophet's prayer.**

A. Habakkuk's prayer.

B. The vision in answer to this prayer: Jehovah appears for the destruction of the Chaldeans and the salvation of Zion.

C. The effect of this vision upon the prophet: his gratitude expressed in a beautiful psalm of trust and rejoicing.

Under I D one can, if he wishes, arrange the sins of the Chaldeans, for which they are punished, as follows:

2:4-8	Avidity.
2:9-11	Boastfulness.
2:12-14	Cruelty.
2:15-17	Delight in the misery of their victims.
2:18-20	Expecting deliverance from idols.

Air view of Anathoth (modern Anata), hometown
of the prophet Jeremiah. Anathoth is two and
one-half miles northeast of Jerusalem.
Matson Photo Service

The Latter Prophets: 17
Jeremiah, Obadiah, and Ezekiel

Jeremiah

See also p. 453.

One will never be able to understand the Book of Jeremiah unless he has made a study of the life of the prophet and the conditions of the times in which he lived. Moreover, as Jeremiah carried on his activity during the reigns of Josiah, Jehoahaz, Jehoiakim, Jehoiachin, and Zedekiah, the reader should review what is said on pp. 115-118.

Jeremiah prophesied during a period of at least forty years, the last forty years of Judah's existence, 626-586. In fact, he even continued his work after the fall of Jerusalem among those Jews who had fled to Egypt.

This lengthy period of prophetic activity may be divided as follows:

1. 626-621. *From the call of Jeremiah to the finding of the Book of the Law.*

The man of Anathoth, northeast of Jerusalem, received his divine commission in the thirteenth year of Josiah (1:1, 2), just one year after the king had begun to "purge Judah and Jerusalem from the high places, and the Asherim, and the graven images, and the molten images" (II Chron. 34:3).

Observe that the reformation had only made its beginning: the land was still full of idolatry as a result of the very long and very wicked reign of Manasseh; see p. 115. And the prophet was very young. Moreover, he was by nature very sensitive and tenderhearted. He has been called "the weeping prophet." He would never have *enlisted* as a prophet. He was *drafted.* Nevertheless, he was ever faithful to his charge though this very faithfulness resulted in a constant inner conflict: he desired to predict weal, but he was ordered to prophesy woe, even the approach of the Babylonian captivity for the sins of the people (1:6, 13, 14):

> *Then said I, Ah, Lord Jehovah! behold, I do not know how to speak; for I am a child. . . . And the word of Jehovah came to me a second time, saying, What do you see? And I said, I see a boiling caldron; and its face is from the north. Then Jehovah said to me, Out of the north evil shall break forth upon all the inhabitants of the land.*

During this first period of his prophetic activity Jeremiah probably uttered the predictions found in chapters 1-3, testifying against the idolatry which was rampant (2:13):

> *For my people have committed two evils: they have forsaken me, the fountain of living waters, and hewed out cisterns for themselves, broken cisterns, that can hold no water.*

As Jehovah's prophet he earnestly pleads with Judah to acknowledge its iniquity and to return to Jehovah. He promises the salvation of the penitent remnant ("one from a city and two from a family") and, in one of the most glorious and far-reaching prophecies, sees the time coming when a spiritual people shall worship Jehovah spiritually, the ark of the covenant (the symbol of the entire ceremonial liturgy) being no longer in existence (3:11-18).

2. **621-608.** *From the Finding of the Book of the Law to the Death of Josiah and Accession (After Jehoahaz) of Jehoiakim.*

With the discovery of the book of the Law the reformation began to be pushed vigorously. But though idolatrous shrines, altars, etc., disappeared everywhere, the change was outward rather than inward. The Jehovah-ritualism of the book of the Law was superimposed upon the old sinful ways and selfish habits. What we find in chapters 4, 5, and 6, condemning religious formalism, was probably uttered during this period. Very striking is the prophet's illustration: "For thus says Jehovah to the men of Judah and to Jerusalem, Break up your fallow ground and sow not among thorns" (4:3).

That was exactly what they were doing: sowing the newly discovered Jehovah-religion among the thorns of the old idolatry. *The heart of the people was evil still* (5:23-25).

And then, in 608, Josiah the Reformer, met his tragic death, and with his death the reformation also passed away.

3. 608-605. *From the Accession of Jehoiakim to the Year of the Battle of Carchemish.*

This was the period of Egyptian rule. Wicked Jehoiakim was leading Judah back to idolatry. Whatever Jehovah worship was left had generally deteriorated into mere superstition and outward formalism. "As long as the temple is standing in Jerusalem, we are perfectly safe" was the people's slogan. Here, accordingly, belongs Jeremiah's famous temple sermon, chapters 7 and 26; see 7:1-7:

> *The word that came to Jeremiah from Jehovah, saying, Stand in the gate of Jehovah's house, and proclaim there this word, and say, Hear the word of Jehovah, all you men of Judah, who enter these gates to worship Jehovah. Thus says Jehovah of hosts, the God of Israel, Amend your ways and your doings, and I will cause you to dwell in this place. Trust not in lying words, saying, The temple of Jehovah, the temple of Jehovah, the temple of Jehovah are these. For if you thoroughly amend your ways and your doings; if you thoroughly execute justice between a man and his neighbor; if you oppress not the sojourner, the fatherless and the widow, and do not shed innocent blood in this place, neither walk after other gods to your own hurt: then will I cause you to dwell in this place, in the land that I long ago gave to your fathers, for a lasting possession.*

Now read 26:8, 9.

> *And when Jeremiah had made an end of speaking all that Jehovah had commanded him to speak to all the people, the priests and the prophets and all the people laid hold on him, saying, You shall surely die. Why have you prophesied in the*

> *name of Jehovah, saying, This house shall be like Shiloh, and this city shall be desolate, without inhabitant? And all the people were gathered about Jeremiah in the house of Jehovah.*

Jeremiah was rescued. The changes which, in the course of time, would bring about the fulfilment of his prophecies were rapidly taking shape. These were the days of shifting empires. The Battle of Carchemish sealed the fate of Egypt and of Judah as well. The seventy years of Babylonian sovereignty (605-536) began. In the reign of Jehoiakim three periods may be distinguished: a) vassal of Egypt, 608-605; b) more or less willing puppet king rendering tribute to Babylon, 605-601; c) in rebellion against Babylon, 601-597.

No longer able to appear in the temple, Jeremiah was ordered to put his prophecies (chs. 1-7) into writing. This roll, read to the princes by Jeremiah's faithful pupil Baruch, was afterward read "in the ears of the king," wicked Jehoiakim. What happened when these words of terrible rebuke and impending judgment were heard is vividly described in Jeremiah 36:22, 23:

> *Now the king was sitting in the winter-house in the ninth month: and there was a fire in the brazier burning before him. And when Jehudi had read three or four leaves, the king cut it with the penknife, and cast it into the fire that was in the brazier, until the entire scroll was consumed in the fire that was in the brazier.*

The roll was rewritten at the command of Jehovah, and certain additions were made at this time, so that the complete roll of which Jeremiah 36:32 speaks is probably to be found in chapters 1-10. Also, a terrible curse was uttered upon Jehoiakim (36:29 ff.).

4. **605-597.** *From the Year of the Battle of Carchemish to the Accession of Zedekiah.*

During the remainder of the reign of the wicked king, Jeremiah probably uttered the prophecies found in chapters 11-17. In this section it is made clear that Judah is going to be judged because of its idolatry and greed, and that this punishment can no longer be averted; see 15:1:

Then said Jehovah to me, Though Moses and Samuel stood before me, yet my heart would not be inclined toward this people: cast them out of my sight and let them go forth.

5. 597-586. *From the Accession of Zedekiah to the Fall of Jerusalem.*

Zedekiah was a weakling. Deep down in his heart he knew that Jeremiah was Jehovah's servant and that his predictions were going to be fulfilled. In fact, he was filled with a kind of superstitious respect for the prophet and sought his advice again and again. This advice was ever the same: "Submit to the king of Babylon to whom you have sworn allegiance, and do not join any rebellious movement." But Zedekiah was afraid of his nobles and generals, and did not dare to oppose their clamor for revolt. In a word, he was a ruler without a fixed and definite foreign policy. The counsel of the prophet may be gathered from the words of Jeremiah 27:12, 13:

. . . Place your necks under the yoke of the king of Babylon, and serve him and his people, and live. Why should you and your people die by the sword, by famine, and by pestilence, as Jehovah has spoken concerning any nation that will not serve the king of Babylon?

Cf. Jeremiah 21:8, 9; 23:1, 5.

The prophet also wrote a letter to the exiles in Babylon urging them to expect a long captivity, to reject the lies of the false prophets, and to settle down to a normal life (29:5-7).

But when, about the year 589, a new king began to rule over Egypt, the anti-Babylonian intrigues were resumed with vigor. Soon Jerusalem was besieged. In order to gain the favor of Jehovah, Jewish nobles began to release their Hebrew slaves. But as soon as Nebuchadnezzar's army withdrew "for fear of Pharaoh's army" (Jer. 37:11), the slaves were compelled to return to their former masters. During the breathing spell which Judah enjoyed when the siege was raised, Jeremiah was regarded as a false prophet and a traitor. On the way to Anathoth one day, he was arrested and thrown into a muddy cistern, from which the pity of an Ethiopian eunuch, Ebed-melech, rescued him (ch. 38).

A secret meeting of king and prophet now took place. Very vivid is the account found in Jeremiah 38:14-28; see especially verses 17-19:

> *Then said Jeremiah to Zedekiah, Thus says Jehovah, the God of hosts, the God of Israel: If you will go to the king of Babylon's princes, then your soul shall live, and this city shall not be burned with fire; you and your house shall live. But if you will not go to the king of Babylon's princes, then shall this city be given into the hand of the Chaldeans, and they shall burn it with fire, and you shall not escape out of their hand. And Zedekiah the king said to Jeremiah, I am afraid of the Jews that are fallen away to the Chaldeans, lest they deliver me into their hand, and mock me.*

Jeremiah was taken to the court of the guard where he remained until Jerusalem was taken.

When the fall of the city was already in sight, he was permitted to speak words of comfort and deliverance. Babylon's sovereignty would not last forever (29:10):

> *For thus says Jehovah, After seventy years are accomplished for Babylon, I will visit you, and perform my good word toward you, in causing you to return to this place.*

The prophet envisions the day when a new covenant will be established with the house of Israel and with the house of Judah, the glorious New Testament period (31:31 ff.).

As to the chapters of the Book of Jeremiah which can be ascribed to the period 597-586 (the reign of Zedekiah), it should be noted that they are not arranged consecutively: chapters 27-29 have reference to the early part of this king's reign; chapters 21 (1-10), 30-34, and 37-44 refer to his last years, and even to the events which happened after the fall of the city. (In chapters 25, 26, 35, and 36 we are brought back to the days of Jehoiakim, especially to his fourth year, the year 605, Battle of Carchemish.)

6. 586 and afterward. *The Fall of Jerusalem and Subsequent Events.*

When Jerusalem was taken, Jeremiah, who had consistently urged surrender to Babylon, was treated with every mark of respect by the conquerors and given the choice of going to Babylon or remaining with the wretched remnant in Jerusalem. He chose the latter alternative. He placed himself under the protection of the good governor Gedaliah. When the latter was murdered, Jeremiah was compelled to accompany the Jews who, fearing vengeance, fled to Egypt. The prophet continued his work in their midst. There are conflicting reports concerning his death.

We have given a rather lengthy (though necessarily incomplete) review of the life of Jeremiah because, as already indicated, his prophecies can be understood only when they are studied in the light of the entire historical background. The division of the book—and here we depart from the usual outlines of Jeremiah—must needs be in accordance with the facts given above. Accordingly, it becomes apparent that the section which comprises chapters 18-36 cannot be placed under a specific heading, for it contains prophetic utterances on various themes scattered over many years. There is, however, one characteristic which distinguishes chapters 18-51: the prophet is often referred to in the third person; in other words, though whatever is found is thoroughly inspired, it is not all from the "pen" of Jeremiah; many sections and historical notes may be ascribed to Baruch, Jeremiah's pupil.

Chapter 52 is a historical appendix not written by Jeremiah. It is clear from verse 31 that this chapter must be dated about the middle of the sixth century B.C. It should be compared with II Kings 25, from which it was probably derived.

In harmony with the historical background given above and on pp. 115-118 we present the following outline:

Jeremiah
JUDAH'S APPROACHING DOWNFALL, A DIVINE JUDGMENT

1-3 | **I. Jeremiah's call; Judah's idolatry condemned.**

4-6 | **II. Evil heart condemned.**

7-10, 45 | **III. Remaining chapters of the Roll of Baruch:** chapter 7 containing the famous Temple Discourse; chapters 8-10, additional prophecies of Jeremiah which were included in the roll when it was rewritten. Chapter 45 is held by some to have been a subscript of Baruch at the end of chapters 1-7 (the original roll, which was burned by Jehoiakim).

11-17 | **IV. Even Moses and Samuel cannot avert Judah's approaching doom.**

18-36 | **V. Miscellaneous prophecies pertaining to different periods.** (chs. 25, 26 and 35, 36, pertain to the early period of the reign of Jehoiakim). **Messiah's coming predicted** (ch. 23, the Righteous Branch); **the seventy years and Judah's Restoration** (chs. 30, 31); **the New Covenant** (ch. 31).

37-44 | **VI. Interesting and consecutive account of Jeremiah's activities and experiences during the last part of Jerusalem's siege and thereafter.**

46-51 | **VII. Against the nations, oracles.**

52 | **VIII. Historical Appendix** (cf. II Kings 25).

Obadiah

See also pp. 116-118.

Jeremiah experienced the fulfilment of his own prophecies: the Jews were scattered among the nations just as he had predicted. Now at the time when Jerusalem was destroyed, the Edomites, hereditary enemies of the Jews, rejoiced in its downfall. They gloated over the people in distress and cut off the refugees. Like vultures they devoured whatever was left of the prey which the Babylonians had brought down. It is for this reason that Obadiah pronounces Jehovah's curse upon Edom. He predicts that this nation will be completely destroyed, while, on the other hand, Judah will be restored. The prophecy was fulfilled in every way. Not only was Edom conquered by Babylonia but its country was also invaded by the Arabians. Afterward John Hyrcanus ravaged the land of the Edomites; see p. 126. Thus also shall every enemy of God's people be destroyed, particularly, the covenant-breaker Esau.

In the foregoing we have assumed that the prophecy of Obadiah was written very shortly after the events of 586 and refers to the destruction of Jerusalem by Nebuchadnezzar. We have carefully read and studied the arguments of those worthy exegetes who believe that the calamity which is described occurred earlier; e.g., during the days of Jehoram, when Philistines and Arabians invaded Judah (II Chron. 21:16, 17). Though we are willing to admit that the matter is somewhat uncertain, we regard the events of 586 to be a much more probable historical setting for the following reasons:

(1) Of a rejoicing by the Edomites at the time of the invasion which occurred during the reign of Jehoram Scripture says not a word.

(2) Of a rejoicing by the Edomites when Jerusalem was destroyed in 586, Scripture gives vivid and numerous accounts (Lam. 4:21; Ezek. 25:12-14; 35:5, 10-15; 36:5; Ps. 137:7).

(3) The "destruction" of Judah to which Obadiah refers, resulting in a numerous host of captives who were scattered everywhere, is of a too comprehensive character to refer to anything less than the great disaster of 586.

Obadiah

JEHOVAH WILL HUMBLE THE PRIDE OF EDOM WHO REJOICED IN HIS BROTHER'S DISTRESS

Read the prophecy several times. What outline do you suggest?

Ezekiel

See also pp. 116-119, 453-454.

Ezekiel was a priest who had been carried away from Judah with Jehoiachin in the year 597. He lived on the Chebar, a canal in Babylonia. He prophesied during the period 593/2–570 (Ezek. 1:2–29:17). He was a man of great influence and authority. The elders of the Jewish community would gather in his house to hear the words of Jehovah.

Ezekiel's prophecies abound in visions and symbolisms. These visions, far from being the fancies of a wandering mind, make excellent sense, as many commentators have shown. Yet theological magazines never seem to tire of publishing articles in which the advocates of this theory, in one form or another, seem to vie with each other in exhibiting their knowledge of psychiatric terms. One does not always receive the impression that the men who write these learned articles have first of all made a thorough exegetical study of the prophecies of Ezekiel in their historical setting.

Probably the most famous of all these visions is the one of "The Wheel Within a Wheel," that is, "The Throne Chariot." It is a very comforting vision, exactly the kind which was needed by the captives in Babylonia. They had been cruelly deported. Far away from Jerusalem and its temple they were prone to wonder whether they were also far away from Jehovah. Was not Jehovah's presence linked inseparably with the holy city? But then Ezekiel receives his vision: out of the thunder and the lightning there emerges God's throne chariot. It comes from the north; that is, from Jerusalem (consult a map). It indicates that Jehovah has established his presence in Babylonia among the captives. He has not forsaken them.

The Book of Ezekiel is very beautifully arranged, as will appear immediately from the outline below. Before the actual fall of Jerusalem in 586 it was Ezekiel's duty to demolish the false hopes of those who expected a speedy return. Accordingly, his theme was annihilation: the state of Judah will cease to exist. Chapter 33 is the dividing point: Ezekiel receives the report that Jerusalem has fallen. The entire tone of his message now changes: he predicts resurrection of Judah's statehood, restoration of its remnant, a glorious future for Israel re-established in its own country.

Outline:

Ezekiel
ANNIHILATION AND RESURRECTION

1-32	I. **Annihilation** (twelve prophecies).
1-24	A. For the state of Judah (five prophecies).
25-32	B. For the surrounding nations (seven prophecies).
33 (dividing point)	*Jerusalem falls.*
34-48	II. **Resurrection** (twelve prophecies).
34-39	A. For Judah (seven prophecies).
40-48	B. For the temple, in a new form (five prophecies).

This may be expanded as follows:

Ezekiel
ANNIHILATION AND RESURRECTION

1-32	I. **Annihilation** (twelve prophecies).
1-24	A. For the state of Judah (five prophecies).
1:1–3:15	1. Appearance of the glory of Jehovah on his throne chariot.
3:16–7:27	2. National distress for national wickedness.
8:1–19:14	3. Noah, Daniel, and Job unable to avert the disaster.
20:1–23:49	4. Iniquity of Judah to be punished by the instrument of Jehovah: Babylon.
24:1-27	5. Heart's desire of the exiles (Jerusalem and its sanctuary) to be destroyed, as symbolized by the death of Ezekiel's wife.
25-32	B. For the surrounding nations (seven prophecies–*consult a map*).
25:1-7	1. "I will deliver you (Ammon) to the children of the east."
25:8-11	2. Like destiny for Moab.
25:12-14	3. Anger to be revealed to vengeful Edom.
25:15-17	4. Total destruction for cruel Philistia.
26:1–28:19	5. Isles to shake at the sound of Tyre's destruction.
28:20–28:26	6. Outright destruction (by sword and plague) of Sidon.
29-32	7. Nebuchadnezzar to receive Egypt.
33 (dividing point)	*Jerusalem falls.*
34-48	II. **Resurrection** (twelve prophecies).
34-39	A. For Judah (seven prophecies), etc.
34	1. Righteous Shepherd "David" to replace unrighteous shepherds.
35	2. Envious Edom to be punished.
36:1-15	3. Shameful treatment by the nations to be reversed.

36:16-38	4. Uncleanness of Israel to be removed when it returns to its land.
37:1-14	5. Resurrection (or Revival) of Israel by God's Spirit.
37:15-28	6. Reunion of Israel and Judah under "David."
38, 39	7. Enemies (Gog and Magog) to be destroyed.
40-48	B. For the temple, in a new form (five prophecies).
40:1–43:12	1. Contour of the temple.
43:13–46:21	2. Temple and altar ordinances.
47:1-12	3. Issuing (from the temple) waters.
47:13–48:29	4. Oblation for priests and Levites; landmarks for the tribes.
48:30-35	5. Names of the twelve gates.

Mount Gerizim, in the region of Samaria.
Levant Photo Service

18 The Latter Prophets: Haggai, Zechariah, Joel, and Malachi

Haggai

See also p. 454.

The prophets whose books we discuss in this chapter performed their task after the Return from the Exile. Haggai was contemporary with Zechariah (cf. Hag. 1:1 with Zech. 1:1); Joel may have been contemporary with Malachi, but this is by no means certain.

When, about the year 536, a Jewish remnant returned from Babylon, they set up the altar of burnt offering and laid the foundation of the temple (Ezra 3:3, 10). Due to circumstances—see p. 120—the work of rebuilding ceased so that for at least fifteen years no progress was made. After this long recess Haggai and Zechariah urged the leaders, Zerubbabel and Joshua, as well as the people, to resume the work.

The prophecies of Haggai are dated—see 1:1; 2:1, 10, 20; they were delivered within the space of four months. The prophet destroys the people's syllogism, which must have been on this order:

(1) Building the temple requires material wealth.

(2) At the present time we do not possess material wealth. Accordingly,

(3) This is not the proper time to build.

He attacks the minor premise and the conclusion by indicating that their present poverty and crop failure are the results of their sinful neglect with respect to Jehovah's house (1:9):

> *You looked for much, and lo, it came to little; and when you brought it home, I blew upon it. Why? . . . Because of*

my house that lies in ruins, while each of you busies himself with his own house.

Haggai, in arousing the people to resume their work, appealed to the will, the emotions, and the reason (1:7-11); and his exhortation had the desired effect: three weeks after the first prophecy was uttered everybody was busy rebuilding the temple (1:15). It was finished four years later, about the year 516 B.C. (Ezra 6:15). A second prophecy was necessary in order to encourage those who deplored the insignificant aspect of the new building, even in its beginnings, as compared with the temple of Solomon. The prophet declares that Jehovah will shake the nations so that their precious things, silver and gold, shall fill the house. In fact, "the latter glory of this house shall be greater than the former, says Jehovah of hosts; and in this place will I give peace, says Jehovah of hosts" (2:6-9).

The third prophecy is really a supplement to the first: the present crop failure is the result of former negligence with respect to Jehovah's house; from this day on things are going to take a turn for the better (2:10-19).

Similarly, the fourth prophecy is a supplement to the second: in the day when Jehovah will shake the nations, he will honor Zerubbabel. It is probable that this leader of the Return was the ancestor of both Joseph and Mary; see pp. 121, 135-137.

Outline:

Haggai
EXHORTATION TO REBUILD JEHOVAH'S HOUSE

1	**I. Condemnation of sinful neglect:** "Is it a time for you yourselves to dwell in your ceiled houses, while this house is in ruins?" The work of rebuilding is resumed.
2:1-9	**II. Encouragement: Jehovah will shake the nations, etc.:** "And I will shake . . . all nations; and the precious things of all nations shall come; and I will fill this house with glory."
2:10-19	**III.** (Supplement to I) **Explanation of present crop failure: the result of the former, sinful neglect;** but: "From this day will I bless you."

2:20-23 — IV. (Supplement to II) **Promise to be fulfilled when Jehovah shakes the nations**: "I will take you, O Zerubbabel . . . and will make you as a signet [seal ring]."

Zechariah

See also pp. 120-121, 454.

Zechariah warned the returned exiles that they should not walk in the ways of their fathers (1:4), but should return to Jehovah and trust in his promises. This introductory exhortation is followed by a series of visions, as follows:

(1) **The man among the myrtle trees and those who follow him**: though at present the nations are at rest, there is going to be a change in the interest of Judah, for Zion has an Intercessor.

(2) **The four horns and four blacksmiths**: destruction is in store for the nations that have afflicted the Jews.

(3) **The young surveyor and the angel**: Zion will expand among the nations; Jerusalem will be inhabited as villages without walls (cf. Acts 2).

(4) **Joshua, the high-priest, pardoned and clothed with beautiful garments**: the priesthood, though defiled, is cleansed and accepted by Jehovah.

(5) **The golden candlestick and the olive-trees**: God's people derive their strength to accomplish great things from the enabling, illumining, and never-failing Spirit of Jehovah.

(6) **The flying roll and the woman in the ephah**: sanctification; i.e., wickedness will be destroyed and removed from the land.

(7) **The four horse-drawn chariots**: the land will enjoy Jehovah's protection from every direction. (It must be admitted, however, that the meaning of this vision is by no means clear. There are ever so many widely varying interpretations.)

These visions are followed by a symbolic act (see the outline).

The third section of the book contains a question concerning the propriety of continuing the fasts. In the answer it is pointed out that Jehovah desires obedience first of all, that the woes which have befallen the Jews should be viewed as means unto a glorious end, and that fasts shall be turned into cheerful feasts.

Chapters 9-14 constitute a section by itself, with a historical background that is different from the one which is basic to chapters 1-8. There are those who cling to the view that the entire section or a part of it is of pre-exilic date. They base this belief upon passages such as 9:1, 10, 13; 10:2, 6, 7, 10; 11:14; etc. (references to Damascus as still existing; to Ephraim, Joseph, Israel; to idols; etc.). But not any of these passages, when correctly interpreted, is in conflict with a much later date. On the contrary, 9:13 points in the direction of the post-exilic period: Greece is already on the horizon as a mighty power. We are in agreement with those who see in this section—chapters 9-14—several extended references to the mighty conflict between Antiochus Epiphanes and the Maccabees. However, we regard these references not as *descriptions* of already existing conditions but as *prophecies* based upon divine revelation regarding events which *began* to take shape even in the days of their inspired author (think of the significant Grecian victories of 490 and 480 B.C.).

Whatever be the proper division of chapters 9-14—see the many and conflicting schemes in commentaries, Bible encyclopedias, and introductions—it is at least probable that among the predicted events the following are to be recognized:

1. The further progressive return of the captives from the lands of the captivity (10:8-12).
2. The defeat of the countries which surround Judah in a day when Judah itself will be protected (9:1-8).
3. The victories of the Maccabees over Antiochus Epiphanes (9:11-17; 12:1-9); see also p. 125.
4. The coming of the Righteous King, the True Shepherd (9:9); also his rejection (11; 13:7); see Matthew 21:5; 26:14-16.
5. The election of the Remnant throughout the new dispensation (13:8, 9; cf. this with other *remnant* passages: Jer. 3:14; 23:3; Amos 3:12; 5:15; Mic. 2:12; 5:3, 7, 8; 7:18-20; Hab. 2:4; Zeph. 3:12, 13; Hag. 1:12, 14; Zech. 8:6, 12).
6. The outpouring of the Spirit and the blessings of the Messianic Age, with the total disappearance of the dispensation of shadows and ceremonies (most of ch. 14).

Special attention should be called to the beautiful and startling Messianic prophecies contained in this book. Be sure to study them: 3:8-10; 6:12-14; 9:9, 10; 11:12; 12:10; 13:1, 7. Observe that the coming, rejection, and future glory of the Branch or Shepherd King are predicted.

Needless to say, all these prophecies should be studied in their proper contexts. Moreover, in certain cases the possibility of progressive fulfilment should be recognized. Also, it should be constantly borne in mind that Christ is the very heart and center of prophecy, so that the Old must constantly be interpreted in the light of the New; see p. 83.

Summary outline:

Zechariah

THE FUTURE GLORY OF ZION
AND OF ITS SHEPHERD-KING
revealed by means of

1:1–6:8	**I. Visions.**
6:9-15	**II. A symbolic act.**
7, 8	**III. An answer to a question.**
9-14	**IV. Predictions and promises.**

This may be expanded as follows:

Zechariah

THE FUTURE GLORY OF ZION
AND OF ITS SHEPHERD-KING
revealed by means of

1:1–6:8	**I. Visions and ideas indicated by them.**	
1	A. The man among the myrtle-trees and those who follow him.	Intercession
1	B. The four horns and the four blacksmiths.	Destruction of the enemy.
2	C. The young surveyor and the angel.	Expansion
3	D. Joshua, the high-priest, pardoned and clothed with beautiful garments.	Absolution

4	E. The golden candlestick and the olive trees.	Spirit-effusior Hence:
5	F. The flying roll and the woman in the ephah.	Sanctification and
6	G. The four horse-drawn chariots.	Shelter
6:9-15	II. A symbolic act (the coronation of Joshua as priest-king; a symbol and a type of the Branch).	
7, 8	III. An answer to a question (whether the fasts should be continued).	
9-14	IV. Predictions and promises regarding the future of Zion, and the rejection and subsequent glory of its Shepherd-King.	

Joel

See page p. 454.

Those who favor a post-exilic date for Joel[1] do so for th following reasons:

1. Babylonia and Assyria are no longer mentioned as threatenin Judah.
2. The captivity is evidently a thing of the past. The Holy Land ha been parted. The people have been scattered among the nation (2:19, 27; 3:1, 2).
3. The Phoenicians and Philistines, the Egyptians and the Edomite have given assistance to Judah's tormentors. They have sold th children of Judah to the Greeks and have robbed God's people o silver and gold (3:5).
4. No longer do kings rule in Judah but priests and elders (1:1, 13 2:17).
5. The pouring out of Jehovah's vengeance upon those who hav oppressed Judah is promised (ch. 3) as well as the day whe Judah once more will be glorious.
6. The Northern Kingdom, having ceased to exist, is no longe mentioned, nor is there any reference to its idolatry.

---

1. See art. "Joel" in *Westminster Dictionary of the Bible.* J. H. Raven in *Ol Testament Introduction,* pp. 212-215, defends the pre-exilic date.

7. The language is full of Aramaisms.

It is possible that Joel and Malachi delivered their prophetic messages *about* the same time; i.e., about a century after the Return under Joshua and Zerubbabel.

The people are beginning to lose courage. Does Jehovah really love Zion? Shall his promises ever reach fulfilment? Besides, there is the locust plague (Joel 1 and 2; Mal. 3:11—but it is not at all certain that these passages refer to the same plague). Joel and Malachi assure God's people that Jehovah's protecting love for those who really trust in him remains ever unchanged (Joel 2:18, 25; 3:16; Mal. 1:1; 3:6). Malachi predicts the coming of the "Messenger of the Covenant" and of his forerunner (3:1), while Joel foresees the effusion of the Holy Spirit to usher in the Messianic Age.

The entire Book of Joel centers around three subjects: plague, penitence, promise. Very vivid is the description of the *devastation* (ch. 1) and the *devastator* (ch. 2). (The graphic details should be compared with articles on the locust plague which have appeared in various journals and encyclopedias.) This is followed by a call to repentance and to prayer. The glory of Jehovah is at stake (2:17). Promises of material prosperity follow repentance. This outpouring of physical blessings, in turn, is a symbol and type of the effusion of the Holy Spirit in the Messianic Age (2:28-32, cf. Acts 2). The nations which have afflicted Zion will be punished in the day of Judah's exaltation (ch. 3).

Outline:

Joel
LOCUST PLAGUE, PENITENCE, DIVINE PROMISES

1:1–2:11	I. **Plague** (of locusts).
2:12-17	II. **Penitence** (the people's).
2:18–3:21	III. **Promises** (divine).
	A. Disappearance of the locusts; abundance of crops.
	B. Outpouring of the Holy Spirit.
	C. Judgment upon the nations which have afflicted God's people.
	D. Judah's future glory and blessedness.

Malachi

See also pp. 448, 454.

"Rend your heart, and not your garments," was Joel's call to repentance. That repentance was indeed necessary is emphasized by Malachi. The people were lacking in gratitude (1:1-5). They dishonored Jehovah by presenting blemished offerings, gifts which they would not have dared to present to the governor, and in this they were assisted by profane priests (1:6–2:9). The land was full of adulterers, those who married foreign wives, having put away their own (2:10-16). Meanwhile, there were those who doubted whether Jehovah would ever take vengeance. They said, "Where is the God of justice?" Accordingly, the coming of the Messenger of the Covenant and of his forerunner is predicted (2:17–3:6). Again, there were those who withheld the tithe, robbing God (3:7-12). Just as some entertained doubts with respect to Jehovah's punitive righteousness so there were also those who had misgivings with respect to his remunerative (rewarding, in the favorable sense) righteousness. In this connection 1:16-18 is indeed most comforting. The *contrast* between the future of the wicked and the righteous is vividly described in 4:1-3. The touching prophecy closes with the exhortation of 4:4-6: "Remember the law of Moses, my servant. . . . Behold I will send you Elijah the prophet. . . ." On this passage see p. 143; on historical background of Joel and Malachi see pp. 122-123.

Outline:

Malachi
JEHOVAH'S LOVE UNREQUITED

1	**I. By an ungrateful people.**
2:1-9	**II. By profane priests.**
2:10-16	**III. By adulterous individuals.**
2:17–3:6	**IV. By those who doubt Jehovah's punitive righteousness.**
3:7-12	**V. By those who rob God.**
3:13–4:3	**VI. By those who doubt Jehovah's remunerative righteousness.**
4:4-6	**VII. (Closing exhortation and promise.)**

Main entrance of the Cave of Adullam
in the Judean Wilderness, where Saul
interrogated David from the opposite slope.
Levant Photo Service

The Writings: 19
Psalms, Proverbs, and Job

Psalms

We have discussed the Law and the Prophets. And now we come to the Writings, sometimes simply called the Psalms, employing the title of the first book as a designation of the entire group to which that book belongs.

There is a very close connection between the Law and the Prophets on the one hand, and the Psalms (proper) on the other. Psalm 1 pronounces a blessing upon the man "whose delight is in the *law* of Jehovah" and who meditates on it day and night. Psalm 2 is a *prophecy* of the reign of Jehovah's Anointed.

In the Psalms the believer pours out his heart before Jehovah. Accordingly, expressions of repentance, communion, hope, faith, love, etc., abound. There are psalms for every occasion in life and for every spiritual condition, so that the Psalter is universal in its appeal to believing hearts. Some of the best-known psalms are listed on pp. 448, 451-453. The student should become thoroughly familiar with this list and, if possible, with many other psalms not found in it.

Originally the Psalms were grouped differently than in our present Bible. In very ancient times collections were made of psalms which were ascribed to one author or of those which could be grouped about one central idea. Thus, there was a collection of the psalms of David, 1-41; another, of the psalms of Asaph, 50, 73-83 (twelve); another, of the psalms of the sons of Korah, 42-49, 84, 85, 87, and 88 (twelve); another, of processional hymns (used by pilgrims on their way to Jerusalem), 120-134; and, finally, of the Hallelujah psalms, 105-107; 111-114; 116-118; 135, 136; 146-150.

After several regroupings the Hebrew Psalter was finally divided into five books, each one ending with a doxology; see Psalm 41:13; 72:18 ff; 89:53; 106:48; and Psalm 150. These doxologies (except Psalm 150) were added after the collections had been completed. From I Chronicles 16:36 it may probably be inferred that the author of Chronicles was already acquainted with this fivefold division of the Hebrew Psalter.

In each of the five books one may find:

1. Cries for rescue from sin and misery, sometimes accompanied by a confession of sin;
2. Songs commemorating divine deliverance; and
3. Psalms of praise and gratitude.

Not only that, but in many cases the three ideas—misery, deliverance, praise and gratitude—are present in the same psalm, e.g., 51. Hence, any attempt to give a material outline of the entire Psalter with a different descriptive phrase or title for each book, would necessarily fail. The only division that can be made is the merely formal one, into the five recognized books.

Nevertheless, there is a measure of progress in the Psalter, taken as a whole. The songs do, indeed, lead to a gradual climax. There are, however, many detours and regressions. The idea of *misery* (from which the poet seeks deliverance) is especially evident in Book I. Books II and III, although devoted in large measure to the same theme, also contain several well known songs of *deliverance*, e.g., 46, 48, 66, 68, 76, 77, 78, 81. *Thanksgiving and praise* abounds in Books IV and V, although also in these books the ideas of misery and deliverance occur again and again. We repeat what was said in the preceding: in many cases, all through the Psalter, the three ideas or two of them are found alongside each other or follow one another in the same psalm.

For a typical plaint or lament see Psalm 7 and Psalm 51 (penitential psalm).

For a song which commemorates divine deliverance see Psalm 48.

For psalms of praise and thanksgiving see Psalms 93-100; 113-118; 144-150.

It should be added, however, that these three ideas—misery, deliverance, gratitude—do not exhaust the fund of religious experiences to which the Psalter gives expression. The Psalter is as rich and varied as is sanctified human life itself. One should become thoroughly acquainted with it. On Messianic psalms see p. 133. In the final analysis, the Spirit of Christ is the Author of this collection of collections.

The experiences of David are often so clearly typical of him that apart from him they cannot be correctly and fully interpreted; study, e.g., Psalm 8 in the light of Matthew 21:15, 16; I Corinthians 15:27; and Hebrews 2:9.

Outline:

Psalms

CRIES FOR RESCUE FROM SIN AND MISERY, SONGS COMMEMORATING DIVINE DELIVERANCE, ANTHEMS OF PRAISE AND GRATITUDE, ETC.

Book I	Psalms 1-41
Book II	Psalms 42-72
Book III	Psalms 73-89
Book IV	Psalms 90-106
Book V	Psalms 107-150.

Proverbs

Every nation has its witty sayings in which the knowledge gained by experience is summarized. There is a tendency to view the Book of Proverbs as being nothing more than a collection of such aphorisms. According to this rather common idea these "proverbs" of Scripture hardly excel the sayings of Amen-em-ope, the Egyptian. But this is an error. If it were true, Proverbs would have no claim to a place in Holy Scripture. Underneath the superficial resemblance there is a fundamental difference between the witticisms of the nations and the proverbs of God's Word. The proverbs included are not only *tersely expressed deductions from daily experience* but also *divine precepts* (whether expressed or implied). Moreover, they point to *the fear of Jehovah* as the basic principle of all true knowledge. Only when we bear in mind these distinctions is it proper to speak of Proverbs as belonging to the realm of wisdom literature. The wisdom literature found in Scripture, though similar in some of its aspects to that which is found elsewhere, is in reality in a class by itself. It points to the true Wisdom who was "set up from everlasting . . . before the earth was" (Prov. 8:23). Whoever practices the wisdom precepts contained in this book is using the best means to achieve the highest goal.

From the following outline it will become apparent that the term *proverb* has a very wide connotation:

Proverbs
THE FEAR OF JEHOVAH IS THE BEGINNING OF WISDOM

These proverbs are not easy to arrange in groups; e.g., section III, Exhortations (or precepts) and Warnings, also contains some Observations. Nevertheless, as a general characterization, the following will be an approximation to the truth:

	Wisdom's
1-9	I. **Commendation** (i.e., the Praise of Wisdom).
10-22	II. **Contrasts and Observations.**
22-24	III. **Exhortations** (or Precepts) **and Warnings.**
25-29	IV. **Comparisons** (or Similitudes) **and Contrasts.**
30, 31	V. **Descriptions** (ending with the description of the worthy woman).

An illustration of each of these follows:

1. *Commendation or Praise of Wisdom:* "Happy is the man who finds *wisdom*, and the man who obtains *understanding*" (3:13).

2. *Wisdom's Contrasts:* "The fear of Jehovah prolongs days; *but* the years of the wicked shall be shortened" (10:27). Also, "Scoffers set a city in flame, *but* wise men turn away wrath" (29:8).

3. *Wisdom's Observations:* "Children's children are the crown of old men; and the glory of children are their fathers" (17:6).

4. *Wisdom's Exhortations (or Precepts):* "*Apply* your heart unto instruction, and your ears to the words of knowledge" (23:12).

5. *Wisdom's Warnings:* "*Rejoice not* when your enemy falls, and *let not* your heart be glad when he is overthrown" (24:17).

6. *Wisdom's Comparisons (or Similitudes):* "*As* in water face answers face, *so* does the heart of man to man" (27:19).

7. *Wisdom's Descriptions:* "The ants are not a strong people, yet

hey provide their food in the summer" (30:25). Also, "She [the vorthy woman] opens her mouth with wisdom, and the law of indness is on her tongue" (31:26).

Sections I, III, and V are written, for the most part, in connected tyle. Sections II and IV are written mostly in disconnected style.

Another division of the same five sections is as follows:

Proverbs

THE FEAR OF JEHOVAH IS THE BEGINNING OF WISDOM

1-9	**I. The proverbs of Solomon, the son of David, the king of Israel.**
10-22	**II. The proverbs of Solomon.**
22-24	**III. The words of the wise.**
25-29	**IV. Proverbs of Solomon which the men of Hezekiah, king of Judah, copied out.**
30, 31	**V. The words of Agur . . . the words of King Lemuel.**

If one wishes, he can, of course, combine the two outlines given above into one. We regard the first one as being valuable because it ndicates the material contents and also the style of the proverbs ncluded in each section. The second one, given in the Book of Proverbs itself, is valuable because it indicates the author or editor in each case.

Job

See also p. 448.

The Book of Job also belongs to the wisdom literature of the Old Testament. It embodies the product of the desire, created by the Holy Spirit, to shed light on the problem of the suffering of God's children. The solution of this problem is presented in a very nteresting and largely poetic manner, and is connected with the personal history of Job. No one knows *when* he lived; *that* he lived is he clear teaching of Scripture (Ezek. 14:14-20; James 5:11). Many evidences have been presented in favor of this or that date when the

Book of Job was written. The very fact that even among conservative scholars there is such a wide diversity of opinion would seem to prove that it is impossible, on the basis of the available evidence, to establish the date.

Far more important is the fact that the solution of the problem of suffering which is presented in this beautiful book is thoroughly up-to-date. It is a solution for every age, as seen in the outline which follows:

Job
WHY DOES A JUST GOD AFFLICT GOD-FEARING JOB?

1, 2 | **Prologue: God accepts Satan's challenge ("touch all that he has, and he will renounce thee to thy face"), and Job suffers terrible calamities.**

3 | **II. In the presence of his three "friends" (Eliphaz, Bildad, and Zophar) Job curses the day of his birth, but he does not renounce God.**

4-31 | **III. The discourses of Job and his friends.**

- A. First cycle of discourses.
  1. Eliphaz.
  2. Job.
  3. Bildad.
  4. Job.
  5. Zophar.
  6. Job.
- B. Second cycle of discourses.
  1. Eliphaz.
  2. Job.
  3. Bildad.
  4. Job.
  5. Zophar.
  6. Job.
- C. Third cycle of discourses.
  1. Eliphaz.
  2. Job.

3. Bildad.
4. Job (this includes a poem in praise of wisdom).

32-37 **IV. The discourses of Elihu.**

38-41 **V. Jehovah's address to Job.**

42:1-6 **VI. Job's answer to Jehovah.**

42:7-17 **VII. Epilogue: Job prays for his friends and receives twice as much as he had before.**

Sections I and VII are prose; the other sections are mostly poetry.)

The outline above is formal and tells us very little about the *naterial content* of the book. A brief indication of the material ontent—short enough to be committed to memory—would be as ollows:

Job
WHY DOES A JUST GOD AFFLICT GOD-FEARING JOB?

1, 2 **I. Prologue: Sorely afflicted Job struggles with this question.** Stages of the struggle:

A. He "sins not nor charges God foolishly."

B. He does not sin "with his lips." Later:

3 **II. In the presence of his three "friends"** (Eliphaz, Bildad, and Zophar) **Job curses the day of his birth, but he does not renounce God.**

4-31 **III. The discourses of Job and of his friends.**

A. How his friends answer the question.

1. God afflicts you because you are a very wicked man.
2. God afflicts you because you have not helped those in distress.
3. God afflicts you in order that, being chastened, you may be healed.

B. How Job answers his friends.

In answer to 1 above: Then how is it that God allows many wicked people to prosper?

Besides, I am not wicked but righteous.

In answer to 2 above: This is not true: I have always helped those in distress.

In answer to 3 above: Does this require that suffer so very grievously?

C. Job rebukes his friends because they fail to comfort him, and in his grief turns to God as his Vindicator.

32-37 **IV. Elihu rebukes the three friends because they condemn Job though they cannot answer his arguments. He rebukes Job because the latter claimed to be righteous.**

(This leaves the fundamental question—Why does a just God afflic the righteous?—still largely unanswered. The real answer follows.)

38-41 V. **Jehovah's address to Job.** The reason why Jehovah afflicts the righteous cannot be *fully* grasped by mere man, who is not even able to understand the created universe; e.g., behemoth (the hippopotamus) and leviathan (the crocodile). *Hence, because Jehovah is so very great and infinitely wise, man must not expect to understand him fully but must TRUST* him. (This is clearly implied.)

42:1-6 VI. **Job's answer to Jehovah**: "I have heard of thee by the hearing of the ear; but now my eye see thee: Therefore I abhor myself, and repent in dust and ashes."

42:7-17 VII. **Epilogue**: Job prays for his friends and receive twice as much as he had before.

As in the case of Proverbs so here: if one wishes, he can combine the formal with the material outline.

It may be well here to give some quotations from the book itsel so that section III (the discourses of Job and of his friends) may stand out more clearly:

A. How Job's friends answer his question.

1. *God afflicts you because you are a wicked man.*

"Remember, I pray you, whoever perished being innocent?

Or where were the upright cut off?" (4:7).

"Behold God will not cast away a perfect man, Neither will he uphold the evil-doers" (8:20).

"Know therefore that God exacts of you less than your iniquity deserves (11:6).

"Is not your wickedness great?
Neither is there any end to your iniquities" (22:5).

2. *God afflicts you because you have not helped those in distress.*

"For you have taken pledges of your brother for nought,

And stripped the naked of their clothing.
You have not given water to the weary to drink,
And you have withheld bread from the hungry.

. . . .

You have sent the widow away empty,
And the arms of the fatherless have been broken.
Therefore snares are round about you,
And sudden fear troubles you" (22:6-10).

3. *God afflicts you in order that, having been chastened, you may be healed.*

"Behold, happy is the man whom God corrects:
Therefore, despise not the chastening of the Almighty.

For, he makes sore and binds up;
He wounds, and his hands bring healing" (5:17, 18).

B. How Job answers his friends.

1. *In answer to 1 above: Then, how is it that God allows many wicked to prosper? Besides, I am not wicked but righteous:*

"Wherefore do the wicked live,
Become old, wax mighty in power?
. . . .
Their houses are safe from fear,
Neither is the rod of God upon them.
Their bull breeds without fail,
Their cow calves and does not cast her calf.
They send forth their little ones like a flock,
And their children dance.
They sing to the timbrel and harp,
And rejoice at the sound of the pipe" (21:7-12).

"My foot has held fast to his steps;
His way have I kept, and have not turned aside" (23:11).

"My righteousness I hold fast, and will not let it go:
My heart shall not reproach me so long as I live" (27:6).

2. *In answer to 2 above: This is not true. I have always helped those in distress:*

"If I have withheld the poor from their desire,
Or have caused the eyes of the widow to fail,
Or have eaten my morsel alone
And have not shared it with the fatherless

If I have seen any perish for want of clothing,

Or that the needy had no covering

. . . .

Then let my shoulder blade fall from the shoulder,
And let my arm be broken from its socket" (31:16-22).

3. *In answer to 3 above: Does this require that I suffer so grievously?*

"Oh that my vexation were but weighed,
And my calamity laid in the balances!" (6:1).
"I was at ease and he broke me apart,
He has taken me by the neck and dashed me to pieces:
He has also set me up as his target.
He breaks me with breach upon breach;
He runs upon me like a warrior.

. . . .

My face is red with weeping,
And on my eyelids is the shadow of death;
Although there is no violence in my hands,
And my breath is pure.
O earth, cover not my blood,
And let my cry find no resting-place" (16:12-19).

C. Job rebukes his friends because they fail to comfort him, and in his grief he turns to God as his vindicator.

"No doubt, but you are the people,
And wisdom shall die with you" (12:1).

"But you are fabricators of lies;
You are worthless physicians" (13:4).

"I have heard many such things:
Miserable comforters are you all.
Will your empty words never end?
Or what incites you to answer?
I also could speak as you do,
If your soul were in my soul's stead,

I could join words together against you,
And shake my head at you.
But I would strengthen you with my mouth
And the solace of my lips would assuage your grief" (16:2-5).

"How long will you vex my soul,
And break me in pieces with words?
These ten times have you reproached me
You are not ashamed to hurt me" (10:1-3).

"Even now, behold, my witness is in heaven,
And he that vouches for me is on high.
My friends scoff at me:
But my eye pours out tears to God" (16:19-20).

"Oh that my words were now written!
Oh that they were inscribed in a book!
That with an iron pen and lead
They were graven in the rock forever!
For I know that my Redeemer lives,
And at last he will stand up upon the earth
And after my skin, even this body be destroyed,
Then without my flesh shall
I see God;
Whom I, even I, shall see on my side,
And my eyes shall behold, and not as a stranger.
My heart is consumed within me" (19:23-27)

Built on the site of Solomon's temple,
the Dome of the Rock in its present form
dates back to A.D. 691.
George A. Turner

20 The Writings: Song of Solomon, Ruth, Lamentations, Ecclesiastes, and Esther

The three great poetical books, Psalms, Proverbs, and Job, are followed by the five smaller rolls which form a group by themselves and were read in connection with the feasts and fasts of the Jews.

The order in which these books are arranged in the Hebrew Old Testament can more easily be retained in the memory if one forms the habit of mentally linking each book with the occasion and date on which it was *read*, as follows:

1. **The Song of Solomon**, which by the Jews was interpreted as picturing the love of Jehovah for Israel, a love manifested in a most emphatic and tender manner when he led his people out of Egypt, was read at the Feast of Passover (April), which commemorated that event.

2. **Ruth**, since its scenery is that of a harvest festival, was read during the Feast of Pentecost, when the firstfruits of the wheat harvest were presented (May-June).

3. **Lamentations**, in which the capture of Jerusalem and its dreadful results for Israel are bemoaned, was read on the day set aside to commemorate the burning of the temple (August). According to tradition the first temple was destroyed upon this day (the 9th of Ab) by Nebuchadnezzar, and the second temple on the same day of the year by Titus.

4. **Ecclesiastes**, which imparts strength and consolation to the children of God in the midst of their trials and hardships, was read at the Feast of Tabernacles (October), which was a kind of pageant of the hardships which the Israelites experienced when they lived in booths during their desert journey.

5. **Esther**, which gives a vivid account of the deliverance of the

Jews in the days of wicked Haman and of the institution of the Feast of Purim, was read at every celebration of that feast (March).

Accordingly, the books simply follow the order of the above-mentioned solemn occasions in the Jewish religious year.

Even among scholars of undoubted orthodoxy there is great diversity of opinion with respect to questions of date and authorship of these five books. In a Bible survey we cannot devote adequate space to a discussion of these questions: a mere summarizing statement will have to suffice.

Concerning the title of the first of the five, many scholars have pointed out that the rendering "The Song of Songs *which has reference to* Solomon" (instead of "The Song of Songs *which is* Solomon's") is also possible. They call attention to the fact that in this inspired book Solomon is often referred to in the third person, which, as they see it, would be rather unnatural if he himself wrote the book (1:5; 3:7, 9, 11; 8:11; cf. also 8:12, second person). Others, however, reject this translation and defend the Solomonic authorship.[1]

No one knows who wrote the Book of Ruth. It is clear from the mention of David in 4:21 that it cannot have been composed much earlier than the year 1000. The opinion that the book originated in post-exilic times, a belief based upon the fact that Ruth 4:7 describes a custom (already ancient when Ruth was written) ordained in Deuteronomy 25:9, is rooted in the presupposition that Deuteronomy was *composed* (not merely *found*) in the year 622/21 B.C. But this presupposition is in conflict with the meaning of II Kings 22:3 ff. The notion—it hardly deserves a more favorable designation—that the Book of Ruth is a protest against the rigid exclusivism of Ezra, who obliged the Jews to put away their foreign wives (Ezra 9 and 10),[2] is hardly deserving of consideration, as it does not rest upon even a shred of evidence.

The original (Hebrew) text does not tell us who wrote Lamentations, whether Jeremiah or others. II Chronicles 35:25 does not settle the matter either way. The book must have been written after the beginning of the Exile.

With respect to Ecclesiastes, there are those who view the

1. J. H. Raven, *Old Testament Introduction,* p. 283.
2. See. E. J. Goodspeed, *The Story of the Bible,* p. 97. Even R. H. Pfeiffer refuses to go as far as that, *Introduction to the Old Testament,* p. 719.

grammatical peculiarities and the vocabulary of this book (as well as other characteristics) to be definite indications of its late date.[3] Some interpret 1:1 as being best explained by the theory that the Preacher, whoever he was, tells us what, according to his inspired judgment, Solomon at the close of his earthly life *would have said* as he viewed life in retrospect.[4] Others are of the opinion that this hardly does justice to the passage. They believe that "the son of David" (whom they regard as Solomon, on the basis of 1:13; 2:1-12; etc.) was himself, *in some real sense,* the author of this book; e.g., that he was the originator of that type of inspired wisdom literature which flourished during later generations among *the wise men* (Eccl. 12:11).

The Book of Esther is of anonymous authorship. One of its sources was a narrative composed by Mordecai (9:20). From 1:1 it would seem that Xerxes was dead when Esther was written, and from 9:19 it is clear that Purim had become an established festival. On the basis of the vivid manner in which the Persian empire and its customs are described it is held that the book was written before the conquests of Alexander the Great.

Song of Solomon

The first of these five books bears the title or superscription, "The Song of Songs, which is Solomon's." The term "Song of Songs" indicates *the most beautiful song.*

Concerning the interpretation of this book opinions vary widely.[5]

1. There is, first of all, the literal method of explaining the Song. It occurs in ever so many forms. One of these is the shepherd hypothesis, according to which there are three main characters: Solomon, the Shulamite maiden, and her shepherd lover. Solomon does everything in his power to win the heart of the maiden, but she remains loyal to her rustic lover. The theory has not found general acceptance. One reason for this is the fact that the hypothesis is not supported by clear and consistent analysis of the book.

---

3. J. H. Raven, Old Testament Introduction, p. 305ff; W. J. Beecher, art. "Ecclesiastes" in *I.S.B.E.*
4. Cf. art. "Ecclesiastes" in the *Westminster Dictionary of the Bible.*
5. See the summary of interpretations given by R. H. Pfeiffer, *Introduction to the Old Testament,* p. 714ff.

2. There is also the allegorical explanation, which also occurs in many variations. In its most popular form it considers the poem to be *directly* descriptive of the love between Christ and the church (or Christ and the believer). It has often led to the most fanciful spiritualizations of various passages. Thus, according to a running chapter head of the Authorized (King James) Version the "little sister" who "shall be spoken for" (7:8), indicates the Gentiles who shall be called. Such fanciful allegorizations hardly commend themselves.

On the positive side it may be stated that most conservative scholars will perhaps be able to endorse the following propositions:

1. The Song of Songs does not bear its name in vain. It is, indeed, a most beautiful book, as fully inspired as any of the others.

2. The book is a unit, not an anthology of unconnected love lyrics.[6] The unity of the poem is clear from the repeated refrain, "I adjure you, O daughters of Jerusalem, by the roes, or by the hinds of the field, that you do not stir up or awake love, until it please" (2:7; 3:5; 8:4).

3. Canticles extols real, pure, unquenchable love between two human lovers: a bridegroom and a bride. This must be our starting point in the interpretation.

4. This love between bridegroom and bride is a symbol not only of the love between Jehovah and Israel (Isa. 50:1; 54:5; 62:4; Jer. 2:2; 3:1-13; Ezek. 16; 23), but also of the love between Christ and his church. Not only is Solomon a type of Christ (II Sam. 7:12-17; Ps. 72; Matt. 12:42; Luke 11:31), but the love between husband and wife is a symbol of the close relationship which exists between our Lord and his church (Eph. 5:31, 32). Moreover, the progress in our experience of this relationship is sometimes illustrated by the various elements that pertain to an Oriental wedding (Rev. 19:7; 21:9). See the author's *More Than Conquerors*, pp. 214-217. What is true of every Old Testament book holds also with respect to the Song of Solomon: it is never interpreted fully until it is viewed in the light of New Testament revelation.

Hardly two commentators agree on all the details of division. Nevertheless, many are of the opinion that there is a certain progress of thought which—whatever be the interpretation and the exact verse at which one section ends and another begins—may be represented in its simplest form somewhat as follows:

6. Pfeiffer, p. 716.

Outline:

Song of Solomon
LOVE STRONG AS DEATH: A FIT SYMBOL AND TYPE OF THE LOVE OF JEHOVAH FOR ISRAEL, AND OF CHRIST FOR HIS CHURCH

1, 2	I. The lovers sing of their love for one another. He bids her rise and come away. She rejoices in the fact that they belong to one another.
3:1-5	II. In a dream she loses him but finds him again.
3:6–5:1	III. They fetch her, and the wedding takes place.
5:2–6:12	IV. In another dream she scorns his love but they are reconciled.
6:13–8:14	V. Closing love songs.

It is clear that there are three "speakers" in this Song: she, he, and the daughters of Jerusalem (by some interpreted as the chorus). Commentators are not in agreement as to the exact number of verses that should be assigned to each of these.

Ruth

See also pp. 448, 451.

In the days when the judges judged—see pp. 60, 95-99, 223-224—a certain man of Bethlehem in Judah, Elimelech by name, and his wife Naomi, together with two sons, emigrated to the country of Moab. They were driven there by famine. Soon Elimelech died. The sons, Mahlon and Chilion, married Moabite women. After about ten years these sons also died. Naomi and her daughters-in-law, Orpah and Ruth, prepared to return from the country of Moab. Having traveled a little distance, Naomi bade her daughters-in-law to return each of them to her mother's house. Orpah returned, but Ruth insisted upon remaining with Naomi. Very touching are her words as recorded in Ruth 1:16, 17:

> *And Ruth said, Entreat me not to leave you, and to return from following after you; for, wherever you go I will go; and*

> *wherever you lodge I will lodge; your people shall be my people, and your God my God; where you die, will I die, and there will I be buried: Jehovah do so to me and more also, if anything but death part you and me.*

Arriving in Bethlehem, Ruth finds favor in the eyes of Boaz, in whose field she had been gleaming. Boaz takes her to wife, and she becomes an ancestress of David; hence, of Christ.

The purpose[7] of the book is twofold: first, it indicates how Jehovah rewards those who make the wise spiritual choice and who show stedfast filial loyalty; secondly, it shows us the universal significance of the Mediator, Jesus Christ; i.e., his significance for men of every nation, tribe, and tongue.

Outline:

Ruth
RUTH'S WISE CHOICE AND FULL REWARD

1	**I. Ruth's wise choice:** "your people shall be my people, and your God my God."
2-4	**II. Her full reward.**
2	A. Material support.
3, 4	B. A good marriage through which she becomes an ancestress of the Christ.

Lamentations

In this book the destruction of Jerusalem in the year 586 and the lot of its population are bewailed. It is well to notice that not only the *wretched condition* of the people is lamented, but also the *sin* which had brought it about (3:40 ff.).

Outline:

Lamentations
DIRGES AND PLAINTS IN CONNECTION WITH JERUSALEM'S FALL

I. Dirges (i.e., funeral songs: Jerusalem—"the daughter of Zion"—has died).

7. Pfeiffer, p. 719, expresses his opinion that the author of Ruth simply desired to tell an interesting story of long ago.

1 A. Zion's desolate condition.

2 B. The Author of this desolate condition: Jehovah.

4 C. The bitter siege which resulted in this desolate condition.

II. Plaints (songs of personal or collective sorrow).

3 A. Personal sorrow with hope of relief.

5 B. Collective sorrow with a prayer for relief.

In the *dirge* or *elegy* (funeral song) the lot of the city of Jerusalem is bewailed. In the *plaint* or *lament* the poet relates his own consequent suffering (ch. 3) or that which he shares with others (ch. 5). We have an example of the dirge in II Samuel 1: David's dirge over Saul and Jonathan: "How are the mighty fallen." When a city is personified and viewed as having "died," the dirge is employed in a *figurative* sense. That is what we have here in the first, second, and fourth songs of Lamentations. See also Amos 5: "The virgin of Israel is fallen; she shall no more rise."

Of the *plaint* or *lament* we find numerous instances in the Psalms; e.g., Psalm 3: "Jehovah, how are my adversaries increased."

It is well to distinguish between dirges and plaints, and to remember that the Book of Lamentations has three dirges and two plaints. The plaint which we find in chapter 3 refers to personal sorrow as does also Psalm 3. The plaint found in chapter 5 refers to collective suffering as does also Psalm 79:

We are become a reproach to our neighbors,
A scoffing and derision to those that are round about us.
. . . .
Help us, *O God of* our *salvation, for the glory of thy name;*
And deliver us, *and forgive* our *sins, for thy name's sake.*

Ecclesiastes

See also pp. 448, 453.

The Book of Ecclesiastes contains "the words of the Preacher [Qoheleth] the son of David, king in Jerusalem." The term "Qoheleth" indicates a person (or group of persons) of rank who meets with the congregation (in this case) in order to impart instruction; accordingly, a preacher.

To interpret the book is not at all an easy task. At the close of his very instructive article in *Christelikjke Encyclopaedie*, Dr. G. Ch. Aalders ventures the suggestion that the Preacher repeatedly introduces *problems* of various kinds and then describes his struggle to arrive at *solutions* of these problems.

This theory, according to which the book contains problems followed, in each case, by a solution, is also held by Martin J. Wyngaarden. I am indebted to him for the following excerpts from a paper which he read before The Society of Biblical Literature and Exegesis. It is hardly necessary to add that these few excerpts fail to do justice to the elaborate discussion which the subject received in Dr. Wyngaarden's paper.

He based his interpretation upon Ecclesiastes 12:11 (cf. 8:1) and is of the opinion that the *"goads"* represent the *problems* which serve as incentives to investigation, and that the *"nails"* indicate the *solutions* to these problems. He divides Ecclesiastes into four discourses. Concerning the fourth or last of these he states:

"We now come to the fourth and last discourse, including chapters 8-12, beginning with the inquiry: 'Who is the wise man and who knows the interpretation of the thing?' Then follow seven 'goads' and 'nails' or seven 'puzzling things' each followed by an 'interpretation from the higher, authoritative standpoint.'

"We have the first 'goad' in the question, 'Who is the wise man?' (8:1) followed by the 'nail' or 'interpretation': 'The wise man's heart discerns time and judgment' (8:2-5).

"The second 'goad' appears in the words 'The misery of man is great upon him' (8:6-8). But it is followed by the 'nail': 'I know that it shall be well with them that fear God' (8:9-13).

"The third 'goad' is indicated by the words: 'There are righteous unto whom it happens according to the words of the wicked' (8:14, 15). But the 'nail' follows promptly: 'The righteous and the wise and their works are in the hand of God' (8:16–9:1).

"The fourth 'goad' looms up in the words: 'All things come alike to him who sacrifices and him who does not sacrifice' (9:2-6). But the 'nail' is right at hand: 'God has already accepted your works, let your garments be always white' (9:7-10)."

Continuing in this fashion Wyngaarden views the contents of 9:11–10:20 as the fifth goad, and the solution found in 11:1-6 as its nail. He finds the sixth goad in 11:7-10, and its nail in 12:1-7; the final goad (implied) in 12:8-10, and its nail in 12:11.

We wish to express our appreciation to the author of the above-mentioned article. His summary outline of Ecclesiastes is as follows:

Ecclesiastes

GOADS AND NAILS: THE LIFE UNDER THE SUN CONTRASTED WITH THE LIFE UNDER GOD WHO MADE THE SUN

1, 2	I. **First Discourse.**
1:1–2:23	A. *Goad:* Man and nature are subject to vanity; the striving after earthly wisdom and selfish pursuits is unsatisfactory.
2:24-26	B. *Nail*: The grateful acceptance of the present good constitutes a boon from the hand of God.
3-5	II. **Second Discourse.**
3:1-15	A. *Nail*: Life is a gift of God to the man who pleases God. It is to be viewed not only in the light of the present but also of the future age or eternity.
3:16–4:16	B. *Goad*: That which befalls the sons of men befalls beasts—all go unto one place (immortality doubted by the man who views matters from the lower standpoint, "under the sun").
5	C. *Nail*: The highest good should be sought at "the house of God" and by obeying his ordinances.
6, 7	III. **Third Discourse.**
6	A. *Goad*: Who knoweth what is good for man in life?
7	B. *Nail*: Wisdom is as good as an inheritance; more excellent is it for them that see the sun.
8-12	IV. **Fourth Discourse** (already analyzed; see pp. 302-303).

Esther

Esther, whose story is related in the book named for her, was a beautiful Jewish maiden, a cousin of Mordecai, who had adopted her. Some years after King Xerxes had rejected his wife Vashti, who refused to permit herself to be displayed to revelers at a banquet, Esther was chosen to take her place. In this high position she availed herself of the opportunity to frustrate the plot of Haman, the king's favorite, which he had devised against the Jews. As a result of the glorious deliverance of Jehovah's people, the Purim Feast was instituted. The book indicates, in a most striking manner, the overruling providence of God in rendering possible the execution of God's plan with respect to the Jews, from whom the Christ was to be born. For the historical background of the Persian Age see pp. 119-123; especially p. 121.

Outline:

Esther
PROVIDENCE AT WORK IN THE DAYS OF ESTHER THE QUEEN

1, 2	**I. Esther, a beautiful Jewish maiden, made queen in the place of Vashti.**
3-6	**II. Her life, that of her foster-parent, Mordecai, and that of all the Jews threatened by wicked Haman, the king's favorite.**
7, 8	**III. The Jews triumph over Haman.**
9, 10	**IV. This triumph commemorated in the Feast of Purim.**

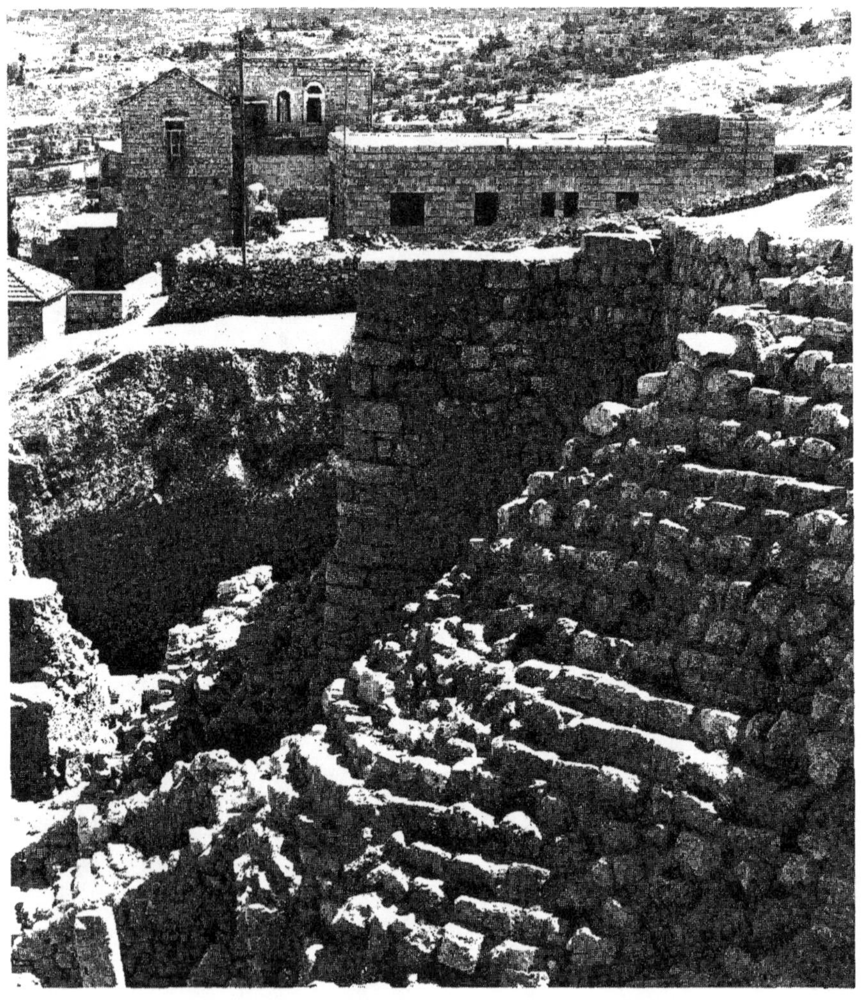

A section of Nehemiah's wall uncovered
at the hill of Ophel, near Jerusalem.
The excavation was done by Kathleen Kenyon.
Levant Photo Service

21 The Writings: Daniel, Ezra, Nehemiah, and Chronicles

Daniel

See also pp. 46-47, 454.

The Book of Daniel bears the name of its chief character.

Conservative interpreters are probably agreed with many, if not all, of the following propositions, which express our own view[1]:

1. The sections in which Daniel is introduced as speaking in the first person—"I saw, understood, was mourning," etc.—were written by Daniel himself and afterward included in the book which bears his name (7:2 ff.; 8:1 ff.; 9:1 ff.; 10:2 ff.; cf. Matt. 24:15).

2. The fact that the use of the third person with reference to Daniel occurs side by side with the use of the first person (7:1; 10:1) and that in the entire historical section of the book (chs. 1-6), he is referred to in the third person is probably best explained by assuming that another inspired person collected the prophecies of Daniel and also wrote the narrative portion of the book. Proclamations by Nebuchadnezzar were also included in the book (3:29; 4:34-37; cf. 6:26, 27). This view of the matter is also in harmony with what is found in Daniel 6:28: "So this Daniel prospered in the reign of Darius, and in the reign of Cyrus the Persian," a statement which one would hardly ascribe to the "pen" of Daniel himself.

3. Daniel was a real, not a legendary, person who belonged to a princely family of Judah and was carried away to Babylon by

1. One need not agree with the theological ideas of J. A. Montgomery in order to appreciate the valuable information—especially philological—which he presents in his *Critical and Exegetical Commentary on the Book of Daniel*, a volume in the *I.C.C.*

Nebuchadnezzar about the year 605 (Dan. 1:1; Jer. 25:1). Ezekiel 14:14, 20 refers to him, and not to some other individual by that name about whom we know nothing.

4. Daniel continued his recorded prophetic activity until the "third year of Cyrus, king of Persia" (10:1). For the historical background see pp. 116-119. It is not necessary to believe that the Book of Daniel, in its supposedly original Hebrew form, was written several centuries after the prophet's death.

5. In its present form, Daniel 2:4b–7:28 is written in Aramaic, the remainder of the book in Hebrew. Accordingly, the Aramaic ends in the midst of the record of prophetic revelation. Serious consideration should be given to the theory that originally the entire book was written in Hebrew; that in the days of Antiochus Epiphanes, the persecutor who tried his utmost to destroy the sacred writings of the Jews, some sections of this original were lost; and that the lost sections were replaced by the corresponding translations in the popular language of the Jews (Aramaic). II Maccabees 2:14 reads: "And in like manner Judas also gathered together for us all those writings that had been scattered by reason of the war that befell, and they are still with us."

6. If one accepts the theory according to which the prophecies which occur in this book are to be regarded as *vaticinia ex eventu* (predictions that grow out of the event), the question whether the book does not become a fraud cannot be suppressed.

7. That Daniel was, indeed, a "prophet" is the teaching of Matthew 24:15. Nevertheless, his prophecies are of a different type from those which are found in the books of the Later Prophets. Whereas in the case of the latter the thrust of the message pertains to the present, Daniel predicts the future (8:26; 12:4, 9); whereas they discuss Jehovah's relation to his people, he describes the never-failing character of the execution of God's plan in the history of Israel's relation to the nations of the world. The Book of Daniel also contains a large *historical* section: such chapters as 1, 3, and 6 are history rather than prophecy. Accordingly, it evokes no surprise that the book is included among the Writings rather than among the Prophets.

Outline:

Daniel
GOD'S SOVEREIGNTY IN HISTORY AND PROPHECY

1-6 **I. In history: the story of Daniel and his three friends.**

1 A. The four refuse to defile themselves with royal food and are rewarded, Daniel receiving the ability to interpret dreams and visions.

2 B. He interprets Nebuchadnezzar's dream about the image with its four parts, is rewarded, and secures for his friends high political positions.

3 C. This leads to jealousy and the fiery furnace for the three, but their wonderful deliverance causes the king to glorify the Most High God.

4 D. The king soon forgets, glorifies himself, and, in fulfilment of his dream about the tree which was hewn down, is deposed for a season.

5 E. This divine judgment is disregarded by his "son" Belshazzar, who at a feast exalts himself against the God of Heaven and is slain, so that Darius the Mede receives the kingdom and promotes Daniel.

6 F. As a result of this promotion enemies plot against Daniel so that he is cast into the lion's den, but God delivers him.

7-12 **II. In prophecy.**

7 A. Prophetic vision of the four beasts (cf. I B above): the lion, bear, four-headed leopard, beast with iron teeth. See pp. 70-71, 116-129.

8 B. Vision of the ram and the he-goat whose horn was replaced by four others (cf. four-headed leopard above), and the relation of this vision to "the glorious land." See also pp. 123-124.

9 C. Daniel's penitent prayer for the glorious land and its people, and the vision (of the seventy sevens) which he receives.

10-12 D. Conflicts between Persia and Greece (cf. ram and he-goat, II B above) and their significance for "the glorious land."

Chronicles
Ezra
Nehemiah

Chronicles, Ezra, and Nehemiah form a unit. They tell one story. Observe how the Return decree of Cyrus, the first part of which is found in the very last verse of II Chronicles, is continued in the first chapter of Ezra. Moreover, in the Book of Nehemiah we read how Ezra read the law to the people (ch. 8). The language of Chronicles, Ezra, and Nehemiah is similar. Moreover, various references in these books—such as the genealogy in I Chronicles 3 and Nehemiah 12:10, 11, 22—would seem to indicate that they were brought to completion about two hundred years after the Return. Accordingly the date 336 B.C. for this group is probably approximately correct. It is very well possible that one inspired author, incorporating in his document various original sources—such as the memoirs of Ezra (Ezra 7:27—9:15), official decrees of Persian kings (II Chron. 36:23; Ezra 1:1-4; 6; 7:11-26), and the memoirs of Nehemiah (Neh. 1:1—7:5; 12:31-43; 13)—and making extensive use of the earlier books of the Old Testament and probably of other sources, wrote (or, if you prefer, edited) these books.

In the printed editions of the Hebrew Old Testament, Chronicles follows Ezra-Nehemiah and is the last book of the canon. We have shown on p. 19 that this was the arrangement of the books as Jesus knew it. It is, however, considered probable by many scholars that *originally* Chronicles was followed by Ezra-Nehemiah. At any rate, the story begun in Chronicles is continued in Ezra-Nehemiah.

The holy men of God whose words are recorded in this group of books clearly show us the repeated failure of man to achieve salvation and the urgent necessity of the coming of the Messiah, whose line of descent is traced in Chronicles.

While Kings is written from the prophetic point of view—see p. 225—Chronicles-Ezra-Nehemiah is written from the priestly. This is probably also one of the reasons why Chronicles omits the history of Saul and of the kingdom of Israel, and records only that of Judah with its capital Jerusalem, where stood the temple.

Originally Ezra and Nehemiah formed one book. We find a trace of this in article 4 of The Belgic Confession, where Ezra is called "the *first* of Ezra." Ezra-Nehemiah clearly indicates that Jehovah is a God who ever fulfils his promise. The Return from the Exile and the re-establishment of the Jews in their land in order that they may bring forth the Christ, "as concerning the flesh," is clear proof of this fact.

For the content of Chronicles-Ezra-Nehemiah see also pp. 99-123.

Outlines:

I and II Chronicles

A HISTORY OF JUDAH'S KINGDOM AND OF ITS KINGS: THE ROYAL ANCESTORS OF THE MESSIAH

I Chron. 1-10	I. Introduction: Genealogies from Adam to Saul.
I Chron. 11-29	II. David and his reign.
II Chron. 1-9	III. Solomon and his reign.
II Chron. 10-36	IV. Judah's history from the division of kingdom to the restoration from Babylonian exile.

Ezra

JEHOVAH STIRS UP CYRUS AND ARTAXERXES TO PROMOTE THE RE-ESTABLISHMENT OF THE JEWS IN THEIR LAND

Ezra 1-6	I. The return under Zerubbabel: the temple is rebuilt and dedicated. (Date of the period covered: about 536-516.)
Ezra 7-10	II. The return under Ezra: reforms are instituted. (Date of these reforms: about 458/457.)

How would you expand this outline?

Nehemiah

JEHOVAH'S GOODNESS TO THE JEWS IN THE DAYS OF NEHEMIAH

displayed during

Neh. 1-12	I. Nehemiah's first visit to Jerusalem. (Date of Nehemiah's first stay in Judah: about 444-432.)
Neh. 13	II. Nehemiah's second visit to Jerusalem.

A more complete and detailed outline would be:

Nehemiah

JEHOVAH'S GOODNESS TO THE JEWS IN THE DAYS OF NEHEMIAH

displayed during

1-12 **I. Nehemiah's first visit to Jerusalem.**

1-7 A. *In* answer to his prayer to Jehovah, Nehemiah gains permission from Artaxerxes to rebuild Jerusalem's walls, which is done amid sever opposition.

8-12 B. *In* the seventh month and afterward there ar special solemnities.

1. *Convocation* to listen to the reading of the law.
2. *Feast* of Tabernacles.
3. *Fast* (confession of sin and covenanting to observe the law of Moses).
4. *Dedication* of the wall.

13 **II. Nehemiah's second visit to Jerusalem.**

A. Tithes enjoined.

B. Trespass of the sabbath ordinance and of th marriage ordinance condemned.

The past still meets the present at the Pool of the Sultan, just outside the walls of the Old City of Jerusalem. Here animals are traded and sold every Friday. ***Religious News Service***

James 22

The Epistle of James may have been the first New Testament book. See p. 188. A glance at the chart below will indicate what may have been the order in which the New Testament writings appeared. Notice the resemblance between the figures which indicate the dates: 50, 53, 57; 60, 63, 67. The listing should be compared with the chronological chart on p. 24.

The Books of the New Testament in Probable Chronological Order

A. Probably written before or about the year 50
   - James
   - Perhaps Mark (see p. 373f)

B. 50/51-53/54
   - Galatians
   - I and II Thessalonians

C. 53/54-57/58
   - I and II Corinthians
   - Romans

D. 60/61-63
   - Colossians
   - Philemon
   - Ephesians
   - Philippians

E. 63-67
   - I and II Peter
   - Matthew
   - Luke
   - Acts
   - I Timothy
   - Titus
   - II Timothy
   - Jude

F. 67-96
   - Hebrews
   - Gospel of John
   - I, II, and III John
   - Revelation

There is a close resemblance between the words of Jesus, a recorded by Matthew, and those of James:

Jesus	James
7:7: *Ask, and it shall be given you. . . .*	1:5: *Let him ask God, wh gives. . . .*
7:11: . . . *how much more shall your Father, who is in heaven, give good things to them that ask him?*	1:17: *Every good gift and ever perfect gift is from above, com ing down from the Father o light. . . .*
7:24: *Every one, therefore, who hears these words of mine, and does them. . . .*	1:22: *But be doers of the wor and not hearers only. . . .*
5:3: *Blessed are the poor in spirit, for theirs is the kingdom of heaven.*	2:5: *Did not God choose thos who are poor as to the world t be . . . heirs of the kingdom . . .*
7:12; cf. 22:39: *All things, therefore, whatsoever you would that men should do unto you, even so do also to them; for this is the law and the prophets. . . . You shall love your neighbor as yourself.*	2:8: *Howbeit if you fulfil th royal law, according to the scrip ture, you shall love your neigh bor as yourself, you do well.*
5:7: *Blessed are the merciful, for they shall obtain mercy.*	2:13: *For judgment is withou mercy to him who has shown n mercy.*
7:16: *By their fruits you shall know them. Do men gather grapes of thorns, or figs of thistles?*	3:12: *Can a fig tree, my broth ers, yield olives, or a vine figs?*
5:9: *Blessed are the peacemakers. . . .*	3:18: *And the fruit of righteous ness is sown in peace for them that make peace.*
7:1: *Judge not, that you be not judged.*	4:11: . . . *He that judges hi brother . . . judges the law. . . .*
6:19: *Lay not up for yourselves treasures upon the earth, where moth and rust consume. . . .*	5:2: *Your riches are corrupted and your garments are moth eaten.*

:12: . . . *so persecuted they the rophets who were before you.*	5:10: *Take, brothers, for an example of suffering . . . , the prophets. . . .*
:34, 35: . . . *Swear not at all; either by the heaven . . . nor by he earth. . . .*	5:12: . . . *swear not, neither by the heaven, nor by the earth. . . .*

We are not at all surprised to find such striking similarity between he Sermon on the Mount (Matt. 5-7), uttered by Jesus, and the pistle of James; for Jesus and James were brothers, according to the lesh. Nevertheless, it is not that physical tie which James desires to mphasize. Rather, he calls himself "a servant of God and of the ord Jesus Christ."

There is also a very close resemblance between the phraseology of his epistle and the words of James recorded in Acts 15. This is specially apparent in the original: cf. Acts 15:23 with James 1:1; Acts 15:13 with James 2:5; Acts 15:14 with James 1:27; Acts 15:19 vith James 5:19, 20; and Acts 15:25 with James 1:16, 19; 2:5.

James had once disbelieved the claims of Jesus (John 7:5). But the isen Lord had appeared to him (I Cor. 15:7). Hence, before Pentecost we find him with the disciples of Jesus in the upper room Acts 1:14). He was a married man (I Cor. 9:5). He became a eader—some say, *the* leader—of the church at Jerusalem. He was a levout man, known as "the Just." The same title is also given to his ather (Matt. 1:19) and to Jesus himself (James 5:6).

To represent him as Paul's opponent is unfair. This unjust verdict ests partly upon an erroneous interpretation of Galatians 2:12. Though he observed the Old Testament ordinances, he was not a Judaizer: he did not try to impose these institutions upon the Gentiles. Nowhere is he pictured as Paul's opponent. On the contrary, he very clearly championed the cause of Paul (Acts 15:13-29). To the very end he remained Paul's friend (Acts 21:18-25). The opinion of Luther that James wrote a downright "strawy" epistle is regrettable. Paul and James are not at all in conflict. They faced different issues. James values genuine faith very highly (1:3, 6; 2:1, 5, 22-24; 5:15). The "faith" which he condemns is that of dead orthodoxy and of demons (2:19). Paul would condemn that just as vehemently. On the other hand, Paul is a firm believer in the necessity of good works as a fruit of faith (Rom. 2:6-10; II Cor. 9:8; Eph. 6:23; Col. 1:4; I Thess. 1:3; II Thess. 2:17). When we reject James, we are rejecting the very teachings of our

Lord; for, as we have already shown, there is the closest resemblance.

James addressed this epistle to "the Twelve Tribes which are of the Dispersion." In all probability, he thus characterizes the Jewish Christians scattered everywhere. They were in danger of losing their patience, oppressed as they were by the wicked rich. Losing courage, they were also in danger of drifting into the condition of a merely intellectual "belief" devoid of the practice of Christian virtues. In writing to them the author is deeply conscious of his authority. In the 108 verses of the epistle he uses 54 imperatives. His style is simple and straightforward. Images are constantly being drawn from the realm of nature, just as in the discourses of Jesus. James deals with the ethical implications of Christianity. Hence, his letter has an up-to-date ring. Its interest in social justice strikes a responsive chord in the hearts of the people of our day and age. The thrust of the epistle reminds us again and again of the prophecies of Amos, who also was direct in his approach, drew his images from nature, and rebuked social injustice. James has been styled "the Amos of the New Testament." He desires that his readers, having been redeemed by their Lord Jesus Christ, shall make manifest their faith in *deed, word,* and *thought* (discussed in that order) and that they shall endure amid trial and temptation until the coming of the Lord.

A superficial glance at this epistle may easily leave the impression that every attempt to outline it must fail. There is, first of all, the duadiplosis, by which we mean that some of the sentences are joined to one another like overlapping shingles. One clause is added to another by the repetition of a leading word. The most striking examples of this characteristic are 1:3-6 and 1:12-15. See also 3:2-8, which presents a more involved illustration of the same peculiarity.

The proving of your faith works *patience.*
And let *patience*
have its *perfect* work,
that you may be *perfect* . . . *lacking* in nothing.
But if any *lacks* wisdom
let him *ask* of God . . .
let him *ask* . . . without *doubting;*
for he that *doubts,* etc.
James 1:3-6

Now, this type of discourse, superficially viewed, reminds one of a person who in conversation changes his subject constantly. We call him a rambler. If that is what James does, it would be just as impossible to outline his epistle as it would be to outline a dictionary. Closer study, however, reveals that this is not at all the case. In the entire section 1:1-18 he rivets our attention upon one central thought: he is admonishing the sorely oppressed and afflicted readers of his epistle *to exercise endurance in the midst of trials and temptations.* If they lack this grace, they should, with confidence, ask God to supply it. Instead of losing all courage, they should reflect on their high estate. That the necessity of exercising endurance in the midst of trials and temptations is, indeed, uppermost in the mind of the author is evident also from the fact that in the paragraph beginning at verse 12 the blessedness and the reward of such endurance are indicated. Moreover, the fact that it—as well as every grace—is the gift of God is again emphasized (see vs. 17). All this is beautiful unity. James has not wandered away from his subject at all. Moreover, he ends his epistle as he begins it; namely, with an exhortation unto endurance (cf. 1:3, 4, 12 with 5:11).

The objection may be raised: "Does not 1:19-27 prove that this epistle is lacking in logical unity?" We answer that although when one reads these verses it may seem as if the author is wandering aimlessly from one subject to another, so that outlining his epistle would become an impossibility, in reality this is not the case. The facts are these:

In verse 22 James says: "Be doers of the word, and not hearers only," and this thought continues through verse 25.

Then, in verse 26 he suddenly turns his attention to the necessity of the bridled tongue: "If anyone considers himself religious, while he bridles not his tongue . . . his religion is futile" (cf. also vss. 19, 20).

Finally, in verse 27 he gives us a brief description of "pure religion and undefiled." In this connection he speaks about keeping oneself "unspotted from the world." See also verse 21, which contains a similar emphasis upon purity: "Wherefore, putting away all filthiness and overflowing of wickedness, receive with meekness the implanted word, which is able to save your souls."

This again looks like rambling. But looks deceive. It is, in fact, the very opposite of rambling. James is, as it were, preaching a sermon—and what he presents in his epistle bears so many resemblances to a well-organized sermon that some interpreters have regarded it to be just that—and before he dwells at length on certain "points," he first states them. He is going to enlarge on the fact that genuine faith, which far excels mere intellectual belief, is demonstrated by *deeds* of kindness and impartiality (ch. 2), by *words* of restraint (the bridled tongue) and wisdom (ch. 3), and by *thoughts* or inner attitudes of purity and meekness (ch. 4). These three points are first *mentioned* or *introduced* in the paragraph 1:19-27, as already indicated. Then, in chapters 2, 3, and 4 they are dwelt on at length. We find something very similar in the manner in which Joshua opens his story. See pp. 221-222.

Accordingly, we present the following summary outline:

James
GENUINE FAITH DEMONSTRATED

1* | I. **Endurance.** Subjects of the next three chapters introduced.
2 | II. **Deeds.**
3 | III. **Words.**
4 | IV. **Thoughts (inner attitudes).**
5 | V. **Endurance.**

**Chapter indications are approximate.*

Expanded outline:

James
GENUINE FAITH DEMONSTRATED

1* | I. **Exercising endurance in the midst of trials and temptations.** Subjects for the next three chapters introduced.
2 | II. **Being doers of the word;** i.e., practicing *deeds* of impartiality and kindness.
3 | III. **Bridling the tongue;** i.e., using *words* of restraint and wisdom.
4 | IV. **Being pure and humble in thought and attitude.**
5 | V. **Exercising endurance unto the coming of the Lord;** so that, instead of using profanity when oppressed, prayer is uttered, especially for the sick and for those who have wandered away from the truth.

**Chapter indications are approximate.*

WHO WERE THE GALATIANS?

see pp. 324-325

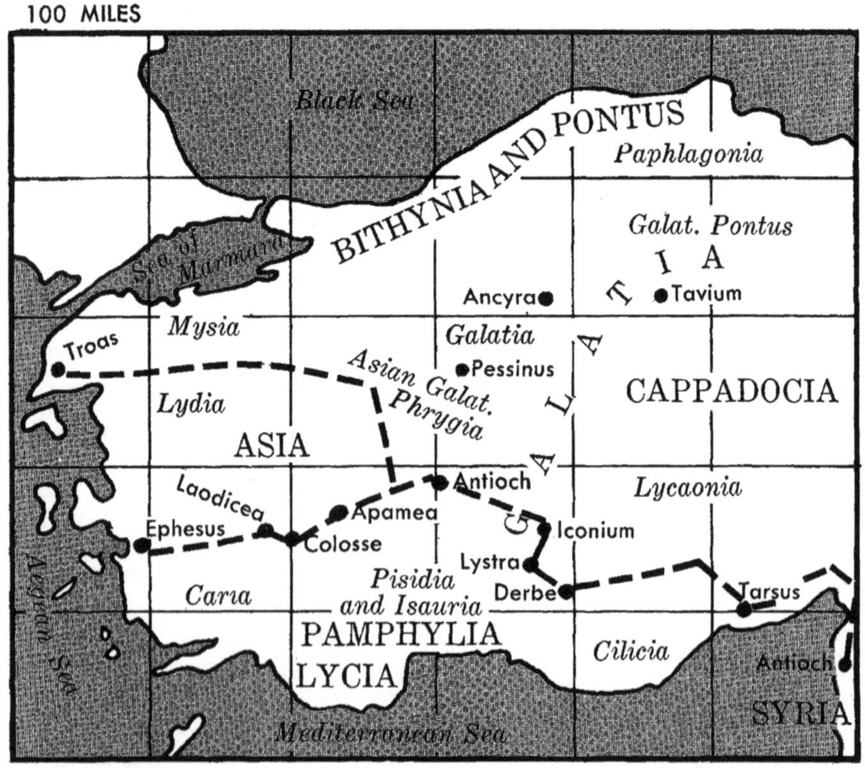

ASIA, GALATIA, etc.: Roman Provinces
Mysia, *Galatia*, etc.: Geographic Regions
— — — — — — — — — — : Beginning of second Miss. Journey: Antioch (Syria) to Troas; and of third: Antioch (Syria) to Ephesus

Galatians, 23
I and II Thessalonians

;alatians

ee also p. 456.

From the Epistle of James we proceed to Galatians. It has often been tated that there is a marked contrast between these two and hat Galatians affirms what James in his epistle denied. But this is ot true. In fact, it would be possible to defend the proposition that ;alatians is the defense of the motion which James made at the erusalem Conference, when he said, "Wherefore my judgment is, that ve *trouble not* them that from among the Gentiles turn to God" (Acts 5:19).

In Galatians the doctrine of justification by faith—salvation apart rom submission to the ceremonial law—is defended over against the eaching of exactly the same *troublemakers* who had made it ecessary to convene the Jerusalem Conference.

Of all the epistles of Paul which have come down to us, Galatians nay well be the oldest. It was probably written during the apostle's econd Missionary Journey; see also pp. 189-194. The Judaists had uffered defeat at the Jerusalem Conference. Wherever Paul went he "delivered them the decrees," which amounted to a kind of charter of liberty: the Gentiles were told that they did not need to submit to ircumcision in order to be saved, that they were free from any obligation to keep the ceremonial law. So, the Judaists got busy. These were Jews who had accepted Jesus as the Messiah but ontinued to attach such great significance to the ceremonial laws hat they said *to the Gentiles:* "Except you be circumcised after the ustom of Moses, you cannot be saved" (Acts 15:1).

These Judaists spread the lie that Paul was nothing but a self-styled apostle and that his Gospel had not come by special revela tion. Hence, in order to vindicate not only his own apostolic callin and authority but especially the glorious doctrine which h proclaimed—justification by faith, not by law-works—the apostl now writes an epistle which he addresses to the churches of Galatia

Now, the Roman province of Galatia consisted of two parts: (a) territory in northern Asia Minor which had been invaded by certai Keltic tribes; (b) certain districts to the south of this Keltic territory

Whereas Paul was in the habit of using the official names o Roman provinces to indicate the location of his churches (I Cor 16:19; II Cor. 1:1; 8:1) we believe that also here in Galatians 1:2 h employs the term in that same sense; that is, as indicating the entir Roman province of Galatia.

This raises the question: "Did the readers inhabit Northern o Southern Galatia?"[1] (Be sure to consult a Bible-map at this point. Having carefully reviewed all the arguments on both sides, we d not hesitate to endorse the Southern Galatian theory for the follow ing reasons:

1. The Book of Acts does not indicate that Paul ever founded an churches in Northern Galatia. But it does relate at some length th establishment of churches in Southern Galatia: Pisidian Antioch Iconium, Lystra, and Derbe (Acts 13; 14). Moreover, it clearly state that on his Second Missionary Journey the apostle revisited at leas some of these very churches (Acts 16:1). Now, this fits exactly int the picture as drawn by the Epistle to the Galatians (see 4:13).

2. It would seem that the great missionary-apostle hurried awa from the marshy lowlands surrounding Perga and traveled towar "Galatia" for reasons of health (Gal. 4:13). The invigorating climat of Southern Galatia suited this purpose far better than that o Northern Galatia.

3. From Galatians 2:5 it is clear that the churches which Paul i addressing in this epistle had been established *before* the Jerusalem Conference. In fact, at this conference the apostle was thinking o the welfare of these already-established churches, their future prog ress in grace. The passage is as follows: ". . . to whom we gave place i the way of subjection, no, not for an hour; *that the truth of the gospe might continue with you.*"

It is clear, therefore, that the apostle is addressing churches tha

1. See W. Hendriksen, *N.T.C.*, Galatians, pp. 4-14 for a thorough discussion o this question.

had been established during his First Missionary Journey; hence, the churches of Southern Galatia (see Acts 13 and 14).

4. It was at Lystra in Southern Galatia that Paul had circumcised Timothy, whose mother was a Jewess and whose father was a Greek. In the light of that event, recorded in Acts 16:3, we can understand (though we cannot justify) the false charge of the Judaists that Paul's deeds were in conflict with his preaching (Gal. 5:11).

5. According to Galatians 2:10 and I Corinthians 16:1, Paul asked the Galatians to contribute toward the relief of the needy in Judea. This "bounty" was to be carried to Jerusalem by approved individuals appointed severally by the contributing churches (I Cor. 16:3). In the list of those persons recorded in Acts 20:4, we also find men from Derbe and Lystra in Southern Galatia; namely, Gaius and Timothy. We do not find anyone from Northern Galatia!

6. The epistle contains *specific* references to Barnabas (2:1, 9, 13). Now, it is clear from the Book of Acts that Barnabas accompanied Paul on the First Missionary Journey when the churches of Southern Galatia were founded.

As we see it, the *Northern* Theory is not supported by the evidence. Also improbable is the idea that this letter was sent while the apostle was staying at Ephesus. A look at the map will convince anyone that in that case he could hardly have said what we find in Galatians 4:20: "But I could wish to be present with you now. . . ." To a great traveler like Paul, a trip from Ephesus to Northern Galatia would not have appeared a formidable obstacle. All the evidence points to Corinth as the place from which the apostle wrote this epistle. And the time? In all likelihood, it was just before Silas and Timothy rejoined the apostle (Acts 18:5), bringing good news from the congregation of Thessalonica. Paul seems to have been alone when he wrote Galatians. When he wrote the Epistles to the Thessalonians, the two helpers had joined him.

Note the salutation of Galatians, "*Paul* . . . to the churches of Galatia," and those in I and II Thessalonians, "*Paul, and Silvanus, and Timothy,* to the church of the Thessalonians. . . ."

Paul follows a definite plan in his letter writing:

(1) salutation,

(2) thanksgiving and prayer—sometimes with a doxology,

(3) a discussion—often doctrinal presentation, followed by practical application, and

(4) conclusion—greetings (not always present) and benediction. From our outlines we generally omit items 1 and 4. See the Bible for these. Are all four present in Galatians? In Titus?

Brief outline:

Galatians
JUSTIFICATION BY FAITH

1, 2 **I. Its origin**: this doctrine is not of human but of divine origin.

3, 4 **II. Its vindication**: both Scripture (the Old Testament) and experienee bear testimony to its truth.

5, 6 **III. Its application**: it produces true liberty which glories in the cross of Christ.

Expanded outline:

Galatians
JUSTIFICATION BY FAITH

1, 2 **I. Its origin**: this doctrine is not of human but of divine origin.

A. There is only one, true Gospel.

B. This Gospel was revealed to Paul by God, not by man. Historical evidence:

1. Rescued by God's grace from intense Judaism, Paul had not gone to Jerusalem to seek the advice of men, but had gone to Arabia.
2. True, he had visited Jerusalem, but not until three years later, and then for only fifteen days.
3. Leaving Jerusalem he had gone far away—to Syria and Cilicia—where he had been proclaiming the gospel independently for fourteen years.
4. Then, on a visit to Jerusalem, its "pillars" had imparted nothing to him, but seeing the

grace given him, had approved his mission to the Gentiles.

5. Far from receiving anything from Jerusalem's "pillars," he had even rebuked Peter (for his temporary vacillation) in words ending with: "For I through the law died to the law, that I might live unto God. I have been crucified with Christ; and it is no longer I that live, but Christ lives in me," etc.

3, 4 **II. Its vindication**: both Scripture (the Old Testament) and experience bear testimony to its truth.

A. Argument from experience: had the Galatians received the Holy Spirit as a result of law works or as a result of faith in Christ?

B. Arguments from Scripture.

1. Scripture declares that Abraham's *faith* was reckoned to him for righteousness (Gen. 15:6) and that the righteous shall live by *faith* (Hab. 2:4).
2. This promise to (or covenant with) Abraham is still in force. The law, which came later, far from annulling the promise, serves it, being the tutor to faith in Christ.

C. Arguments from experience.

1. Have the Galatians forgotten their former bondage (to heathendom) that they now wish to exchange it for another kind of bondage (to Judaism)?
2. Have they forgotten the joy with which they had received the gospel when Paul first proclaimed it to them?

D. Argument from Scripture: Scripture teaches that children of the promise should cast out bondage (Gen. 21:10, 12).

5, 6 **III. Its application.**

A. Do not become entangled in bondage to the law.

B. Neither try to combine both principles. They cannot be combined: those who would be justified by the law are severed from Christ.

C. The only right principle is active faith. This is true liberty.

D. Such liberty, however, does not mean license. It means *love*. It does not welcome the fruits of the flesh, but of the Spirit.

E. Hence, it never grows weary of well-doing toward all men, especially to those that are of the household of faith.

F. It glories not in self but in the cross: "Far be it from me to glory save in the cross of our Lord Jesus Christ," etc.

I Thessalonians

See also p. 456.

From Galatians to I Thessalonians is but a small step. Paul is still at Corinth on his Second Missionary Journey. One day his soul is gladdened by the arrival of Silas and Timothy. The report which Paul received with respect to conditions in the church at Thessalonica was, on the whole, cheering (Acts 18:5; I Thess. 3:6 ff.) Spiritually the church was making fine progress. But there was also bad news. The Jews, filled with prejudice and hatred, were casting insinuations at the character and ministry of Paul (2:3-10), so that the apostle's influence for good was being undermined. Base opponents were interfering with the comfort of his message. And comfort was badly needed. Some members of the church had fallen asleep. Would they share in the glory of Christ's return? (4:13 ff.) Moreover, if this return was imminent, why work any longer? Why toil for the things which would soon perish? (4:11).

It is clear that Paul is concerned about this congregation, so recently established. Very tactfully he stresses the fact that the new faith demands a complete break with the immoral conduct which characterizes heathendom (4:1-8). Moreover, fully realizing the importance of proper respect for the offices, especially in a newly organized congregation, and of love among all the members, Paul writes:

But we beseech you, brothers, to appreciate those who labor among you, and are over you in the Lord and admonish you; and to esteem them very highly in love because of their work. Be at peace among yourselves . . . admonish the disorderly, encourage the fainthearted, support the weak, exercise patience toward everyone," (5:12-14).

The apostle's purpose in writing this epistle has, accordingly, become abundantly clear: to express his gratitude for the news which Timothy had brought with reference to the spiritual condition of the congregation as a whole; to defend himself over against those who had called his motives into question; to re-emphasize the necessity of a complete break with heathendom and its immorality; to strengthen the offices for the welfare of the entire church; and last but not least, to shed further light upon the doctrine of Christ's Return and to warn the brothers against a misapplication of this doctrine in daily life.

Outline:

I Thessalonians

HOW, THROUGH THE MINISTRY OF PAUL, THE GOSPEL HAD COME TO THESSALONICA, AND HOW CHRIST WILL COME AGAIN

1:1–4:12	**I. How, through the ministry of Paul, the Gospel had come to Thessalonica.**
4:13–5:28	**II. How Christ will come again.**

Expanded outline:

I Thessalonians

HOW, THROUGH THE MINISTRY OF PAUL, THE GOSPEL HAD COME TO THESSALONICA, AND HOW CHRIST WILL COME AGAIN

1:1–4:12	**I. How, through the ministry of Paul, the gospel had come to Thessalonica.**
1, 2	A. Paul's *past* connection with the church at Thessalonica: how (in the Spirit and in power, etc.) he had brought the gospel to Thessalonica

	and how (joyfully, etc.) the Thessalonians had received it.
3	B. Paul's *present* connection: how having been prevented from making a personal visit, he had sent Timothy and how the latter had gladdened the apostle's heart with his report.
4:1-12	C. Paul's hope for the *future:* he exhorts them to abound more and more in sanctification and all its fruits, such as love for the brothers and honorable conduct toward outsiders.
4:13–5:28	**II. How Christ will come again.**
4:13-18	A. In such a manner that those who will have survived until the coming of the Lord will have no advantage over those who have fallen asleep.
5:1-28	B. In such a *sudden* manner that believers should always be vigilant, and should manifest, with respect to all classes, and at all times, that work of sanctification whose Author is God himself and his Spirit.

II Thessalonians

See also p. 456.

We can imagine with what joy I Thessalonians was read by the members of the newly established congregation. But did it solve everything? Apparently not. Tidings reached Paul—by means of the very men who had delivered the letter to its destination and had now returned?—that some members were still confused, thinking that the Lord's *sudden* coming (I Thess. 5:3) implies his *immediate* coming. Idleness and disorderly conduct were the results on the part of a few of the members (II Thess. 3:6-14). To add to this confusion someone seems to have sent a forged letter purporting to come from Paul (2:2; 3:17). Hence, while still at Corinth Paul writes II Thessalonians in order to correct the errors with respect to the doctrine of Christ's Return, to admonish every member to conduct himself in an orderly manner, and to comfort the church in the midst of continued persecution.

Read the epistle carefully and see whether you are able to expand the following brief outline:

II Thessalonians
THE REVELATION OF THE LORD JESUS FROM HEAVEN

1 I. It has a twofold purpose.

A. To render vengeance to the disobedient.

B. To be glorified in the saints.

2:1-12 II. It shall be preceded by the falling away and the revelation of "the man of sin."

2:13–3:17 III. Its contemplation should result not in disorderliness, idleness, and excitement; but in sanctification, comfort, and peace.

The temple of Apollo at Corinth. Erected in 590 B.C., the structure was an impressive tourist attraction even in New Testament times.

I and II Corinthians, 24 and Romans

Corinthians

ee also pp. 194-195, 449, 455-456.

It was at Corinth during the Second Missionary Journey that Paul 'rote the epistles which we studied in the last chapter: Galatians and and II Thessalonians. The apostle remained at Corinth a long time nd became closely attached to this congregation. Therefore, it does ot surprise us that on his Third Missionary Journey, during his stay t Ephesus, he was in constant contact with the church across the .egean Sea. We know that to this congregation he sent a letter hich, for some reason, has not come down to us (I Cor. 5:9). At nother time he personally visited Corinth (II Cor. 12:14; 13:1). lso, just before writing the epistle which we call I Corinthians, the postle sent Timothy to Corinth for the confirmation of the church Cor. 4:17). As Timothy went by the land route—by way of lacedonia (Acts 19:22)—Paul expected that his fellow-worker would rrive in Corinth after I Corinthians had reached its destination Cor. 16:10).

It was toward the close of Paul's stay at Ephesus that those that ere of the house of Chloe (I Cor. 1:11) reported to the apostle that he congregation at Corinth was being torn by party strife. Some ere saying: "I am of Paul." Perhaps these were people who had egard for the contents of the Gospel rather than for the form in hich it was presented. Others said: "I am of Apollos." Were these eople lovers of oratory? Still others: "I am of Cephas [Peter]." This lass may have been composed of individuals who adhered to certain eremonial requirements (cf. Gal. 2:11 ff.), but we cannot be sure. nd finally, there were those who said, "I am of Christ," as if they were the only ones who had a right to that distinction. Also, it was being commonly reported that a member of the congregation was living in open sin with his father's wife and that believers were bringing their mutual quarrels before heathen courts (I Cor. 5, 6). These evils needed *correction.*

About this same time Paul received a letter from Corinth—probably brought by the three persons mentioned in I Corinthians 16:17—in which he was asked to impart advice on several problems which very naturally arose when the gospel of light and salvation had made its impact upon the low moral life of this thoroughly pagan city. Accordingly, not only *correction* but also *instruction* was badly needed. Hence, the apostle now writes I Corinthians, which was probably carried to Corinth by Titus, Paul's spiritual son.

Brief outline:

I Corinthians
CORRECTION AND INSTRUCTION FOR THE CHURCH AT CORINTH

1-6	I. **Correction**, with respect to:
1-4	A. Contention (party strife).
5	B. Fornication.
6	C. Litigation.
7-16	II. **Instruction,** with respect to:
7	A. Marriage problems.
8-10	B. Meats which have been offered to idols.
11	C. Meetings: proper conduct at public worship. (Should women be covered? How should the Lord's Supper be celebrated?)
12-14	D. Manifold gifts.
15	E. Mystery (the mystery of the resurrection and the changing in a moment).
16	F. Material assistance for the needy in Judea.

After committing to memory this brief summary, be sure to study the following expanded outline:

I Corinthians
CORRECTION AND INSTRUCTION FOR THE CHURCH AT CORINTH

1-6 I. **Correction,** with respect to:

1-4 A. Contention (party strife).

1. It glories in *men,* saying: "I am of Paul; I of Apollos; I of Cephas; I of Christ."
2. The gospel glories in *Christ crucified.*
3. It teaches that "all things are yours, whether Paul or Apollos or Cephas . . . ; and you are Christ's; and Christ is God's."
4. To establish you in this doctrine "I have sent Timothy to you . . . I (myself) will come to you shortly."

5 B. Fornication.

1. "It is reported that . . . one of you has his father's wife."
2. "Put away the wicked man from among yourselves."
3. "I wrote to you in my epistle to have no company with fornicators. . . ."

6 C. Litigation.

1. Litigation before worldly courts is unworthy of believers.
2. Quarrels between members should be settled within the congregation.
3. Those who defraud and live in sin will not inherit the kingdom of God.

7-16 II. **Instruction,** with respect to:

7 A. Marriage Problems.

1. Because of the temptation to immorality each man should have his own wife, each woman her own husband. The husband should give his wife her conjugal rights, and vice versa.

2. It is well for unmarried persons and fo widows to remain single. But it is better to marry than to be consumed by passion.

3. The wife must not leave her husband; but i she does, she should remain single or els be reconciled to her husband. The husband similarly, should not divorce his wife.

4. One should not separate himself from a unbelieving marriage partner who consent to remain with the believer. If th unbeliever departs, the brother or sister i not "under bondage."

5. Because of persecution in store for th church it is well for girls not to marry; yet if persons who are single marry, it is no sin A father must not refuse to give hi daughter in marriage if this refusal woul expose her to the danger of seduction.

6. A wife is bound to her husband as long a he lives; but if her husband has fallen asleep she is free to marry whom she will, but onl in the Lord.

8-10 B. Meats which have been offered to idols.

1. One should show consideration for th brother who would stumble if a believe were to eat such meats.

2. One should eat whatever is sold in the mea market without asking whether it (or par of it) has first been consecrated to idols However, one should not do so if he woul be giving offence to a brother. When one i invited to eat in the home of an unbeliever he should follow the same course.

3. "Whether therefore you eat, or drink, o whatever you do, do all to the glory o God," . . . in order that sinners may b saved.

11 C. Meetings: proper conduct at public worship.

1. Women should be covered (proper hairdo) as a sign of an obedient and reverent spirit.
2. The "love feasts," to which the rich carry much food and the poor little, must be abolished. Let every member eat at his own home. Then let him celebrate the Lord's Supper in church, according to Christ's commandment.

12-14 D. Manifold Gifts.

1. These gifts—the power to perform miracles, to speak in tongues, to prophesy—are imparted by one and the same Spirit, and should be used for the common welfare.
2. The greatest gift of all is love. Make this your aim.
3. To prophesy is better than to speak in tongues.

15 E. Mystery (the mystery of the resurrection and the changing in a moment).

1. Some, though believing that Christ arose, do not believe that men in general will be raised from the dead. But if the dead are not raised, Christ did not arise either. Then all is lost.
2. Christ was raised from the dead as "the first fruits of them that are asleep."
3. The resurrection body in comparison with the body which descends into the grave: "it is sown in dishonor; it is raised in glory," etc.
4. "We all shall not sleep, but we shall all be changed, in a moment, in the twinkling of an eye, at the last trump."

16 F. Material assistance for the needy in Judea.

1. Believers at Corinth should contribute toward this cause according to their ability, in an orderly, systematic manner.

2. When Paul arrives, he will send that bounty to Jerusalem by the hands of men appointed by the church. The apostle announces his own coming and requests that Timothy be received cordially and sent back to Ephesus.

II Corinthians

See also p. 456.

Before we begin a discussion of II Corinthians it is necessary to state clearly and emphatically that we have made careful study of all the arguments—linguistic and other—advanced by those learned scholars, both liberal and orthodox, who maintain that there is no direct connection between our First and Second Epistle. These scholars assume that between the writing of these two letters the apostle made a visit to Corinth, a very painful visit, and also wrote an epistle which has not been preserved. They believe that II Corinthians was written with that painful visit and lost epistle in mind. They base their theory upon what they consider the correct translation of II Corinthians 2:1, and they appeal to other passages for additional support: II Corinthians 2:3, 4; 7:8, 12; chapters 10-13 (which by some are regarded as part of the "lost" epistle); etc. In a Bible survey we do not have the space to enter into these arguments. We have not been convinced by them. As we see it, there is the closest possible connection between I and II Corinthians. There is no substantial evidence to show that either a visit or a letter intervened between the two epistles which are found in our Bibles. The connection between I and II Corinthians was, in all likelihood, somewhat as follows:

Shortly after sending I Corinthians Paul left Ephesus and went to Troas. Originally the apostle had planned to go directly by sea from Ephesus to Corinth, from there to Macedonia, then back again to Corinth, and so to Jerusalem (II Cor. 1:15, 16). It is possible that in the very first letter which Paul sent to Corinth—a letter which preceded even our I Corinthians; see p. 333—he had so informed the congregation. But for good reasons (II Cor. 1:23) he changed his plan and conveyed this information to the church (I Cor. 16:5). For this change in his plans Paul was criticized severely (II Cor. 1:15-23).

The apostle carried out his revised plan. From Ephesus he traveled o Troas. Here he had expected to meet Titus with news from 'orinth. When the latter did not appear, Paul was filled with alarm (II Cor. 2:12, 13; 7:5). He began to reflect on the letter which he ad written, especially on the severe reproof or *correction* of chap-ers 1-6. He wondered whether the church at Corinth had taken to eart the necessary admonitions. Having crossed the sea, he was verjoyed when he not only met Titus in Macedonia but also eceived good news about Corinth (II Cor. 7:6-15). Though favor-ble, for the church as a whole had repented, the report was not ltogether of that character. Enemies of Paul had not taken kindly to he rebuke which they had received. They assailed Paul's apostleship nd charged that he was fickle because he had changed his traveling lans (1:15-24); that he displayed a boastful courage which veiled an nner cowardice–his letters were "terrifying" (at a distance he roars ke a lion), but his bodily presence "weak" (when present he purrs ke a kitten); and that even when he preached the gospel at Corinth vithout financial remuneration his motives were not pure (11:7-12); tc.

Accordingly, from Macedonia (Philippi?) Paul now writes II Corin-hians. His purpose was threefold: (a) to express his gratitude for the nanner in which the church, as a whole, had taken to heart the ontents of I Corinthians; (b) to urge that the collection for the eedy saints in Judea be carried forward energetically; and (c) to lefend himself against the false charges which had been made by his nemies.

In connection with the following brief outline for memorization, e sure to consult a map of Paul's Third Missionary Journey and to ead carefully pp. 194-197.

II Corinthians

THE APOSTLE PAUL, THE MINISTER OF GOD, WRITES ANOTHER LETTER TO THE CHURCH AT CORINTH

1-7 | **I. The past:** he reviews his past (i.e., recent) experiences in their bearing upon the church at Corinth. Paul had traveled from Ephesus, by way of Troas, to Macedonia on his Third Missionary Journey.

8, 9 | **II. The present:** he expresses his (present) desire that the collection for the needy saints at

Jerusalem shall be carried forward energetically Paul is now in Macedonia.

10-13 **III. The future**: by defending himself against fals charges he makes preparation for a visit t Corinth in the near future.

This outline may be expanded as follows:

II Corinthians

THE APOSTLE PAUL, THE MINISTER OF GOD, WRITES ANOTHER LETTER TO THE CHURCH AT CORINTH

1-7 **I. The past**: he reviews his past (i.e., recent experiences in their bearing upon the church a Corinth. Paul had traveled from Ephesus, vi Troas, to Macedonia, on his Third Missionar Journey.

1:1-11 A. Having been at death's door in "Asia," he i able to comfort the afflicted people o Corinth.

1:12–2:4 B. He had changed his traveling plans and ha delayed his coming in order to spare them.

2:5-11 C. He had ordered that the Corinthian offende be disciplined; but whereas the latter ha repented, he should be forgiven and restore to full fellowship.

2:12, 13 D. He had found no relief for his spirit when h failed to meet Titus at Troas. Hence, thoug Troas offered an "open door," he ha departed to Macedonia.

2:14–7:15 E. This open door in Troas and also the goo news concerning Corinth, which he had hear in Macedonia where he had met Titus, ha riveted his attention upon the triumphs an glories of the Christian ministry even ami suffering ("we are pressed on every side") an death ("the dismantling of the earthly ten dwelling").

8, 9 **II. The present**: he expresses his (present) desir that the collection for the needy saints a

Jerusalem shall be carried forward energetically. Paul is now in Macedonia.

8:1-11 A. The pattern for this offering: the self-sacrificing spirit of Macedonia, and the example of Christ who "for your sake became poor though he was rich."

8:12–9:5 B. Its character and the method of collecting it.

9:6-15 C. Its results.

1. With respect to the givers: an abundance of every possible grace.
2. With respect to the recipients: their wants amply supplied.
3. With respect to God: by means of their (the recipients') thanksgiving God is glorified.

10-13 **III. The future**: by defending himself against false charges he makes preparations for a visit to Corinth in the near future.

10 A. The opponents must remember that Corinth is within the *province* of his apostleship.

11:1–12:13 B. They must know that Paul is far from being a sham apostle; the *proofs* of his apostleship (i.e., his apostolic credentials) have been furnished in suffering, revelations, and signs. See pp. 181-182.

2:14–13:14 C. They must consider that the *purpose* of his apostleship is not to destroy but to edify.

Romans

See also pp. 449, 455.

So Paul arrived at last in Corinth on his Third Missionary Journey. It does not at all surprise us that from here he wrote his Epistle to the Romans. The apostle had been thinking of Rome for a long time (Rom. 1:13), and even during his lengthy ministry at Ephesus he had purposed in the spirit: "After I have been in Jerusalem, I must see

Rome" (Acts 19:21). See p. 195. He cannot proceed at once from Corinth to Rome, for he must first journey to Jerusalem in order to fulfil his ministry of mercy (Acts 24:17; Rom. 15:25, 26; I Cor. 16:1; II Cor. 8:1, 2). From Jerusalem he will go to Rome. That was his plan. And it was carried out, though in a manner which the apostle while at Ephesus and at Corinth did not realize. If Jerusalem may be called historically the first capital of Christianity, Antioch in Syria the second, Ephesus the third, then certainly Rome was going to be the fourth. From this strategic center the glorious gospel would spread to still more distant regions. See pp. 191, 406. It is very well possible that the church at Rome had been established by converts from the Gentiles, members of influential congregations that had been founded by Paul. This would account for the fact that in Rome the apostle had many personal acquaintances to whom he wished to be remembered. However, it is not at all necessary to suppose that Paul had personally met all of the individuals mentioned in chapter 16. His friends in Rome may have written him about some of the members of their church with whom the apostle had not become personally acquainted but who were, nevertheless, his brothers and sisters in the Lord. Most of the names that are mentioned have been found in the sepulchral inscriptions on the Appian Way. Some are specifically Latin names. Accordingly, we accept chapter 16 as a genuine part of the Epistle to the Romans.

Paul's purpose in writing a letter to this predominantly Gentile congregation (1:5, 6, 13; 11:13; 15:15) may well have been to pave the way for his intended visit, and also to give a clear and full exposition of his gospel, in view of the fact that Rome was destined to be a strategic center. Accordingly, we find that in this epistle the doctrine of salvation by sovereign grace—justification by faith apart from law works—is set forth in detail. Questions and objections are answered, and the glorious fruits of justification in the life of the believer are brought to light. The epistle was probably carried to Rome by sister Phoebe (Rom. 16:1).

Brief outline of Romans:

Romans
JUSTIFICATION BY FAITH

1-11 | **I. Exposition.** Justification by faith, apart from the works of the law, is:

1-3 | A. Necessary.

4 B. Scriptural.

5-8 C. Effectual.

9-11 D. Historical.

12-16 II. **Significance for every sphere.** The attitude of the justified believer toward:

12 A. God and the brotherhood.

13 B. The higher powers (the state).

14-16 C. Those who are weak. Salutations.

Expanded outline for careful study:

Romans
JUSTIFICATION BY FAITH

1-11 I. **Exposition.** Justification by faith, apart from the works of the law, is:

1-3 A. Necessary.

1. Theme stated (1:16, 17): "the gospel is the power of God unto salvation to every one who believes . . . as it is written, But the righteous shall live by faith" (cf. 3:24).
2. The Gentiles need this justification "because that, knowing God, they glorified him not as God, neither gave thanks" (1:21).
3. The Jews also need it, for they "practice the same things" (2:1). Accordingly, "there is none righteous, no not one" (3:10).

4 B. Scriptural.

1. "What does the scripture say? And Abraham *believed* God and *it was reckoned* unto him for righteousness" (4:3).
2. David speaks similarly in Psalm 32:1 ff.; cf. Rom. 4:6, 7.

5-8 C. Effectual; i.e., possessing adequate power to produce the desired spiritual blessings, such as:

1. Peace: "Being therefore justified by faith we have (or: let us continue to have) peace with God through our Lord Jesus Christ" (5:1).
2. Holiness: "We who died to sin, how shall we any longer live in it?" (6:2).
3. Spiritual joy: "For I delight in the law of God after the inward man" (7:22).
4. Super-invincibility (the "more than conqueror" frame of mind): "No, in all these things we are more than conquerors
9-11 through him that loved us" (8:37).

D. Historical: In the course of past history the promises of God were intended not for the nation but for the *believing remnant.* Thus it is always; see p. 274.

1. The nation was rejected because of its unbelief and disobedience (9:32; 10:21).
2. "All Israel" (i.e., the entire believing remnant throughout the ages) shall be saved (11:26; cf. 11:5, 7, 23).

12-16 **II. Significance for every sphere.** The attitude of the justified believer toward:

12 A. God and the brothers: "Present your bodies a living sacrifice, holy, acceptable to God . . ." (12:1). "In love of the brothers be tenderly devoted to one another" (12:10; cf. also 13:8-14).

13 B. The higher powers: "Let every soul be in subjection to the higher powers" (13:1).

14-16 C. Those that are weak: "Now we who are strong ought to bear the infirmities of the weak, and not to please ourselves" (15:1; cf. 14:1). Salutations: "Salute Urbanus our fellow worker in Christ" (16:9) and similar greetings.

The theater at Ephesus, scene of the
riot of the silversmiths. Seating capacity
was approximately 25,000.
Levant Photo Service

Colossians, Philemon, Ephesians, and Philippians 25

Colossians

See also pp. 195-199, 456.

From Corinth, where we last saw Paul in the act of dictating to Tertius the Epistle to the Romans (Rom. 16:22), the apostle traveled by way of Philippi, Troas, Tyre, and Caesarea to Jerusalem. A delegation, consisting of duly chosen representatives of the churches of Macedonia, Galatia, and Asia also went to Jerusalem, accompanying Paul (and Luke, who joined the apostle at Philippi) during a considerable part of the journey. To this delegation had been entrusted the task of carrying to Jerusalem the contribution which, with so much earnestness and zeal, Paul had caused to be collected in the various churches for the relief of the needy in Judea. The apostle and his companions probably arrived in Jerusalem just before Pentecost of the year 57 or 58 (Acts 20:16).

But this ministry of mercy resulted in Paul's imprisonment. From Jerusalem the apostle was brought to Caesarea, and from there to Rome, as "the prisoner of the Lord."

During his first imprisonment in Rome both Luke and Mark—and many others—are in Paul's company (Col. 4:10, 14). From Epaphras, who was probably the founder of the predominantly Gentile church at *Colosse*, the apostle hears about the subversive teachings which were plaguing the Colossian congregation. Paul is convinced that a letter must be dispatched to these friends who are in danger of being led astray. At the same time, the recently converted fugitive slave, Onesimus must be returned to his master *Philemon,* who was a member of the Colossian church. Moreover, a person journeying from Rome to Colosse would probably try to reach that city by way of the port of *Ephesus*, where the apostle had labored a long time and had established a flourishing church.

Accordingly, from Rome Paul writes three epistles: Colossians, Philemon, and Ephesians. It is at least possible that Tychicus was the bearer of all three, delivering them to their respective destinations and bringing Onesimus back to his master. It does not surprise us that Colossians and Ephesians resemble each other so closely, though their themes are not the same (see below). This man Tychicus was a very close friend and most useful assistant of Paul, who calls him "the beloved brother and faithful minister in the Lord" (Eph. 6:21 cf. Col. 4:7).

The church at Colosse had probably been established during Paul's lengthy ministry at Ephesus (Acts 19:10). The speculative heresy which threatened to lead this congregation astray is difficult to describe even upon the basis of the original. That it was a kind of Judaistic ceremonialism can hardly be questioned. It is also clear that certain elements of speculative philosophy and of morbid asceticism had been incorporated into this false religion. Was angel worship also advocated? Our answer affects the translation of 2:18. Is it "worship of the angels" or "angelic piety"? On this passage see *N.T.C.* on Colossians, pp. 125, 126. As interpreted by many conservative scholars these errorists not only proclaimed that the ceremonial law must be kept as a means unto *perfection* (fulness) but also that the body is the seat of evil; that, accordingly, material beings must not approach God directly but through the intermediation of higher spirits (angel worship); and that Christ was one of these spirits. We cannot be sure about the correctness of all the elements in this interpretation. One thing, however, is certain: the false teachers failed to proclaim Christ as the Only and All-Sufficient Savior. Faith in Christ and in his atoning work had to be *supplemented* by ascetic beliefs and practices; otherwise a person would never attain to "fulness."

It would seem that the apostle, in combating the error, employs certain terms which had endeared themselves to the false teachers, such as *rudiments* (or elements) of the world, *fulness*, *self-abasement*, etc. Paul probably uses these terms in the spirit of ridicule. Over against the dangerous untruth which threatens to undermine the doctrinal purity and spiritual life of the congregation at Colosse the apostle stresses the fact that Christ is Pre-eminent, the One and Only and All-Sufficient Savior, the One who leads men to fulness and in whom all the fulness dwells. This letter probably greatly strengthened the hands of Archippus, who, in the opinion of many, was temporarily taking the place of Epaphras until the latter would return from Rome. That Archippus was a "lazy" person cannot be justly inferred from Colossians 4:17 (cf. Philem. 2 and I Tim. 4:16).

Brief outline:

Colossians
CHRIST, THE PRE-EMINENT ONE,
THE ONLY AND ALL-SUFFICIENT SAVIOR

1, 2	**I. Christ, the Pre-eminent One, the Only and All-Sufficient Savior:** <u>**the object of our faith.**</u>
1	A. This truth expounded positively.
2	B. This truth set forth negatively (i.e., over against heresies).
3, 4	**II. Christ, the Pre-eminent One, the All-Sufficient Savior:** <u>**the source of our life.**</u>
3:1-17	A. This truth applied to all believers.
3:18–4:18	B. This truth applied to special groups.

Expanded outline:

Colossians
CHRIST, THE PRE-EMINENT ONE,
THE ONLY AND ALL-SUFFICIENT SAVIOR

1, 2	**I. Christ, the Pre-eminent One, the Only and All-Sufficient Savior:** <u>**the object of our faith.**</u>
1	A. This truth expounded positively: thanksgiving to the Father, whose Son is:
	1. The image of the invisible God.
	2. The firstborn of all creation.
	3. The head of his body, the church, its hope of glory; the One through whom all things are reconciled to God.
2	B. This truth set forth negatively: whereas in him all treasures of wisdom and knowledge

are hidden; hence, be not deceived by systems which detract from his pre-eminence and all-sufficiency, such as:

1. False philosophy, which denies that the believer attains to perfection apart from worldly wisdom.
2. Judaistic ceremonialism, which denies that the believer attains to perfection apart from submission to Jewish ceremonies; e.g., regulations dealing with circumcision, food and drink, sabbaths, etc.
3. Angelolatry, which denies that the believer attains to perfection apart from the worship of angels. (This, however, is not certain; see above.)
4. Asceticism, which denies that the believer attains to perfection apart from submission to negative ordinances: "do not taste; do not touch."

3, 4 **II. Christ, the Pre-eminent One, the Only and All-Sufficient Savior: the source of our life.**

3:1-17 A. This truth applied to all believers:

1. Because Christ is our life, both now and at his manifestation, we should do away with ("put to death") sinful attitudes and practices.
2. Because Christ is our life, we should adopt ("put on") Christian attitudes—compassion, kindness, etc.—and practice Christian virtues, in order that the word and the peace of Christ may rule in us.

3:18–4:18 B. This truth applied to special groups, that all may do what is pleasing to Christ, whose mystery Paul, in answer to prayer, hopes again to proclaim.

1. *Wives and husbands*: wives should be in subjection to their husbands; husbands should love their wives.

2. *Children and fathers*: children should obey their parents; parents should not provoke their children.
3. *Servants and masters*: servants should obey their masters; masters should treat their servants justly.

Philemon

Philemon was one of the pillars of the church at Colosse. He loved the Lord and the brothers, and had given concrete evidence of this fact again and again (7). He was Paul's spiritual son, for the Lord had used the preaching of Paul to change his heart (19). The new life had affected not only himself but also his household. It is considered probable that Apphia was his wife, and Archippus their son. See p. 349. Friends who had accepted the Lord regularly gathered for worship at their home (2). In the absence of Epaphras Archippus would probably have charge of the service (Col. 4:17). He may have been a young man who, like Timothy, was in need of encouragement (cf. I Tim. 4:12).

Now, Onesimus—the name means "useful" or "beneficial"—was one of the slaves of Philemon's household. This slave ran away, journeying all the way to Rome. In Rome he came into contact with Paul. Just as the Lord had formerly blessed the sermons of the great missionary to the heart of the master so he now blessed them to the heart of the slave. So dear did the latter become to the apostle that Paul calls him "my child, whom I have begotten in my bonds" (10), "my very heart" (12) "a brother beloved . . . both in the flesh and in the Lord" (16), "the faithful and beloved brother" (Col. 4:9). Gladly would Paul have kept Onesimus at his side as an assistant, for his character had finally caught up with his name. Notice the play on the name of this slave in Philemon 11: "Onesimus [i.e., useful, beneficial] who was once *useless* to you but now is *useful* to you and to me" (cf. also verse 20 in the original).

But Paul does not deem it right to keep Onesimus in Rome. He decides to send him back to his master with the very carefully and politely worded request that the latter accord him a hearty welcome as one who is no longer merely a slave but a brother beloved. If he in any way has defrauded his master, Paul is ready to assume ful responsibility for the payment of the debt. With unsurpassable tac the great apostle adds: "not to mention that you owe me your ver self besides" (19).

Paul does not command, though, as he himself states, he has *right* to do so; he rather *appeals* to the heart of Philemon (9). He i fully confident that the latter will do "even beyond" what is aske of him (21). The apostle entertains hopes of being released from hi present imprisonment and trusts that Philemon will "prepare lodging" for him (22).

It is hardly necessary to add that although this fully inspire epistle does not in so many words condemn the institution c slavery, it strikes at its very spirit and transforms the slave into brother beloved.

We propose the following theme:

Philemon
PAUL'S REQUEST FOR THE KIND RECEPTION OF THE FUGITIVE SLAVE ONESIMUS

Read the epistle several times in different translations. Then mak your own outline and commit it to memory.

Ephesians

See also p. 449.

A third epistle written by Paul during his first Roman impriso ment was that to the Ephesians.[1] There are many scholars—bot liberal and conservative—who believe that this letter was not prima ily intended for the congregation at Ephesus but for an entire grou of congregations, Ephesus being one of them. Some of those wh hold this opinion would identify this letter with the one "fro Laodicea" mentioned in Colossians 4:16. Other interpreters, howeve reject this entire "circular letter" theory. The arguments o both sides may be summarized as follows:

Those who favor the idea that Ephesians was a circular lette advance the following reasons for this view:

1. The position that Ephesians was addressed to the particular congregation Ephesus is defended by R. C. H. Lenski in his commentary on that book.

(1) The words "in Ephesus," (Eph. 1:1) are omitted in the best and most ancient manuscripts.

(2) In Ephesians 1:15 we read: "For this cause I also *having heard* of the faith in the Lord Jesus which is among you. . . ." This means that the apostle had never become personally acquainted with the readers; he had only *heard* about them. Therefore, the epistle cannot have been intended for the congregation at Ephesus, which Paul himself founded and where he labored for such a long period.

(3) In every epistle addressed by Paul to a congregation which he had founded or with which he had become personally acquainted there is a reference to the fact that he was the spiritual father of the church and had labored in its midst (I Cor. 1:14; 2:1; 3:5 ff.; 11:23; 15:1 ff.; II Cor. 3:3; Gal. 1:8; 4:13 ff.; Phil. 1:27 ff.; I Thess. 1:5; 2:1 ff., etc.). No such reference occurs in Ephesians. On the contrary, the epistle is completely lacking in any intimate touches, items of personal information, or allusions to the work of the apostle in the congregation at Ephesus as recorded in the Book of Acts. If it was never intended as a letter to a particular church but rather as a circular letter, this is understandable.

(4) The epistle contains no personal greetings; yet, if it had been intended for the congregation at Ephesus, these would not have been lacking.

Those who believe that the epistle was addressed to the church at Ephesus and was not a circular letter answer as follows:

In answer to (1): In all ancient manuscripts (except the one which was corrupted by the heretic Marcion) the epistle has the title: *To the Ephesians*. All the ancient versions have "in Ephesus" in verse 1. How shall we explain that title and those versions if the letter was not originally intended for the congregation at Ephesus? As to the absence of "in Ephesus" from verse 1 of the most ancient manuscripts, is it not possible that someone tampered with the text as Marcion did with the title?

In answer to (2): Does it not often happen that one "hears" about people from whom he has been separated for a number of years? It was about five years since the apostle had been at Ephesus. Why, then, would it have been impossible for him to say: "I have heard of the faith which is among you"?

In answer to (3): It is not true that there is no connection between the record of Paul's work at Ephesus as we find it in Acts and the contents of this epistle. On the contrary, of which letter can it be said more truly than of Ephesians that it proclaims "the whole counsel of God" (cf. Eph. 1:3-14)? Now, according to Acts 20:27, that is exactly the characterization of Paul's preaching at Ephesus. Absence of major local problems that troubled the congregation may explain why Paul does not in this letter refer to the manner in which he had been received when he founded the church. Moreover, as to intimate touches and news with respect to himself, he explains this in 6:21, 22:

> *But that you may also know my affairs, how I am getting along, Tychicus, the beloved brother and faithful minister in the Lord, shall make known to you all things; whom I am sending to you for this very purpose, that you may know our circumstances and that he may comfort your hearts.*

Finally, *in answer to (4)*, II Corinthians, Galatians, I and II Thessalonians also lack greetings, although they were addressed to congregations which had been founded by Paul.

My own view is that the letter was sent to the churches of "Ephesus and surroundings."

On one point no disagreement is possible: the Epistle to the Ephesians is a most beautiful, a most comforting epistle. It is characterized throughout by the apostle's passion for the absolute. He is never satisfied with halfway conclusions. He pushes every line of thought to its very limit and seeks the ultimate basis for every principle. Thus, he is not satisfied until he has discovered the foundation of our redemption in God's eternal plan (1:4, 11), until he has included both Gentile and Jew in the sphere of Christ's redeeming love (2:11-14). He does not rest until he has made it clear that Christ, the Head of the church, also governs the entire universe in behalf of the church (1:20-22). He also pushes the ethical ideal to the utmost limit: he is not content when people are "saved" or "converted." No, they must be brought to "the measure of the stature of the fulness of Christ" (4:13). And, finally, his ideal is that his readers, together with all the saints, "may be strong to apprehend what is the breadth and length and height and depth" and may "*know* the love of Christ *which passes knowledge*." O glorious paradox! See 3:18, 19.

We suggest the following outline:

Ephesians
THE UNITY OF ALL BELIEVERS IN CHRIST

1-3 **I. The truth expounded** (seven sections).

A. It is a oneness in Christ (three sections).

B. It is a fellowship with one another (three sections).

C. It is a oneness in Christ and a fellowship with one another in order that believers may strive *to know* the love of Christ *which passes knowledge* (one section).

4-6 **II. The truth applied** (ten sections).

A. To all believers (five sections).

B. To particular groups. Conclusion: the panoply of God (five sections).

Expanded outline:

Ephesians
THE UNITY OF ALL BELIEVERS IN CHRIST

1-3 **I. The truth expounded** (seven sections).

1:1-14 A. It is a oneness *in Christ*, resulting in every spiritual blessing for the believer.

1:15-22 B. It is a fellowship *with one another*, expressed in prayer and thanksgiving for one another.

2:1-10 C. It is a oneness *in Christ*, resulting from the great facts of redemption which center in Christ.

2:11-18 D. It is a fellowship *with one another*, implying the reconciliation of Jew and Gentile through the cross.

2:19-22 E. It is a oneness *in Christ* as chief cornerstone (progressively realized).

3:1-13 F. It is a fellowship *with one another* now revealed to all men.

3:14-21 G. It is a oneness *in Christ* and a fellowship *with one another* in order that believers together

	may strive to know the love of Christ which passes knowledge!
4-6	**II. The truth applied** (ten sections).
4:1–5:21	A. To all believers (five sections).
4:1-16	1. This unity is a unity amid diversity.
4:17-24	2. Admonition to maintain this unity by *attachment to Christ* and *detachment* from the world.
4:25-32	3. Admonition to maintain this unity by exercising truth and love toward one another.
5:1-14	4. Admonition to maintain this unity by self-sacrifice versus self-indulgence.
5:15-21	5. Admonition to maintain this unity by subordinating ourselves to one another out of reverence for Christ.
5:22–6:24	B. To particular groups. Conclusion: the panoply of God (five sections).
5:22-24	1. In this fellowship the church is subject to Christ, this subjection symbolized by the wife's subjection to her husband.
5:25-33	2. Also, the Christ loves the church this love symbolized by the husband's love for his wife.
6:1-4	3. In this fellowship believers are embraced together with their children; hence, both parents and children must reveal a conduct in harmony with their membership in this fellowship.
6:5-9	4. In this fellowship believing servants are embraced together with their believing masters; hence, both must make manifest a conduct in harmony with this fellowship.
6:10-24	5. Conclusion. This glorious unity or fellowship of all believers in Christ *over against the forces of evil* necessitates the employment of the entire panoply of God.

For a different Outline see *N.T.C.* on Ephesians, pp. 62-66.

'hilippians

ee also pp. 449, 456.

The church at Philippi, never slow in the business of sending gifts o help Paul in his need (Phil. 4:16), had heard about the apostle's mprisonment and decided to send him another bounty. It is lelivered by Epaphroditus, who may have been the pastor of the :ongregation. Paul, pleased with this manifestation of a genuine, :hristlike spirit, now sends a letter of appreciation and gratitude. It nay have been written a little later than the trio: Colossians, 'hilemon, Ephesians. In this beautiful epistle he thanks the 'hilippians for their evidence of generosity and admonishes them to row in Christlikeness and in the joy that results, a joy which must ot be changed to sadness by the knowledge of the apostle's bonds. Ie warns them not to give any encouragement to the party spirit hat was being fostered in certain quarters. Paul rejoices in the fact hat even his bonds have "fallen out unto the progress of the gospel" 1:12-14). Epaphroditus, who had been ill but had been graciously estored to health, carries the letter with him to Philippi. Paul hopes 'to send Timothy shortly" and significantly adds, "But I trust in the ord that I myself also shall come shortly" (2:23-24).

The epistle does not have a theme or anything which would pproach a logical outline (see p. 45). It is, nevertheless, a true gem. It may be summarized as follows:

Philippians
PAUL POURS OUT HIS HEART TO THE PHILIPPIANS

1:1-11	**I. The joyful servant of Christ Jesus** *revealing* his warm affection for the Philippians by means of salutation, thanksgiving, and prayer.
1:12-30	**II. The optimistic prisoner** *rejoicing* in his imprisonment for the gospel and in the fact that Christ will be magnified by him in life and in death.
2:1-18	**III. The humble cross-bearer** *exhorting* the Philippians to live the life of oneness, lowliness, and helpfulness, *after the example of Christ Jesus*, and to shine as lights.
2:19-30	**IV. The thoughtful administrator** *promising* to send Timothy to the Philippians as soon as possible,

and even now *sending* Epaphroditus back to them.

3:1-21 V. **The indefatigable idealist** *warning* against the *concision* party, as contrasted with the true *circumcision* people; e.g., with Paul, who could boast of many prerogatives but has rejected them all, trusting completely in Christ' righteousness; and *exhorting* the Philippians to copy him and to remember that heaven is thei homeland.

4:1-9 VI. **The tactful pastor**, in general, *exhorting* the Philippians to remain firm; in particular, *entreating* Euodia and Syntyche to be of the same mind and Syzugus to help them; *urging* the Philippians to rejoice in the Lord, to be generous, to bring al their needs to God in prayer, and finally to meditate only on praiseworthy things, practicin these in imitation of Paul, with promise of rich reward.

4:10-23 VII. **The grateful recipient** *rejoicing* in the generosity of the Philippians, *confessing* his faith in God who will supply every need, and *concluding* his letter with words of greeting and benediction.

The southern end of the Sea of Galilee,
from an elevated site looking eastward
to the mountains of Syria.
Three Lions, Inc.

I and II Peter, and Jude 26

I Peter

See also p. 456.

During his first Roman imprisonment Paul wrote Colossians, Philemon, Ephesians (these three belong together), and Philippians. In these letters he indicates that he expects to be released soon (Phil. 2:24; Philem. 22). This hope was realized, according to the testimony of Clement of Rome, Eusebius, Jerome, etc. (cf. also Acts 28:30, 31).

While Paul was absent from Rome, Peter reappears upon the scene. We find him in "Babylon" (I Peter 5:13) together with Silas and Mark (5:12, 14). Whereas Mark was with Paul during his first imprisonment at Rome (see p. 347) it seems natural to assume that, when the apostle was released, the author of our second Gospel simply remained for a while in the world capital. It is altogether probable, therefore, that the designation "Babylon" means Rome, as it does in Revelation 17:5, 9.

In Rome Peter receives information about the churches of Asia Minor. The membership of these congregations was of predominantly Gentile origin (cf. I Peter 1:14, 18; 2:9, 10; 3:6; 4:3). These people were experiencing severe persecution, perhaps mainly at the hands of their associates in daily life (believing servants being oppressed by their infidel masters; believing wives by their unbelieving husbands; entire Christian families by their heathen neighbors, etc.; 4:12). They were becoming discouraged (1:13). Some were beginning to show a tendency to follow the course of least resistance and to drift back into heathendom and its immorality (1:13, 14; 2:11, 12). Accordingly, the apostle in his First Epistle places before his readers the "living hope" and admonishes them to conduct themselves in harmony with this hope. They must realize that they are "sojourners" here below. Their real home is in heaven. They are, accordingly, not *mere* sojourners but *elect* sojourners (1:1), a most glorious designation!

The following brief outline is easy to memorize:

I Peter
THE LIVING HOPE

1:1-12	**I. Praise to the Father for the living hope.**
1:13–2:10	**II. Exhortation unto a conduct in harmony with this hope.**
2:11–3:22	**III. This holy conduct should become manifest in every sphere.**
4	**IV. Example of Christ** (through suffering to glory).
5	**V. Rules for particular groups.**

Expanded outline for careful study:

I Peter
THE LIVING HOPE

1:1-12	**I. Praise to the Father for the living hope.**
1:13–2:10	**II. Exhortation unto a conduct in harmony with this hope.**
	A. This conduct should be *holy*; for
	B. Pilgrims are a *holy* nation, etc.
2:11–3:22	**III. This holy conduct should become manifest in the relation of:**
	A. Believers to the Gentiles.
	B. Subjects to rulers.
	C. Servant to master.
	D. Wife to husband.
	E. Husband to wife.
	F. Brother to brother.
	G. Friend to foe.

4 IV. **Example of Christ** (through suffering to glory).
   A. Arm yourselves with the same mind, inasmuch as
   B. You are partakers of Christ's sufferings.

5 V. **Rules for special groups.**
   A. For *pastors:* Feed the flock.
   B. For *youth:* Obey your superiors.
   C. For *all:* Cast all anxiety upon God and withstand the evil one.

II Peter

See also p. 456.

The apostle Peter wrote his Second Epistle when he was about to depart from this life (II Peter 1:14); hence, probably very soon after he had written I Peter. It is, therefore, reasonable to suppose that this letter, too, was written from Rome and was addressed to the same readers. The apostle says:

> *This is now, beloved,* the second epistle *that I write to you; and* in both of them I stir up your sincere mind *by reminding you that you should recall the words which were spoken by the holy prophets, and the commandment of the Lord and Savior through your apostles: knowing this first that in the last days mockers shall come with mockery, walking after their own lusts, and saying, Where is the promise of his coming? . . .*" (II Peter 3:1-7).

It has been claimed that this statement cannot possibly refer to anything which Peter has said in the epistle which is known to us as I Peter, that it must refer to some other letter which the apostle had written but which was lost, and that there are good reasons for assuming that II Peter actually preceded I Peter.

We do not agree with this reasoning; for, although I Peter does not contain the very *words* which are found in II Peter 3:1-7, it does, indeed, contain the *substance*, and that is all that is necessary. The apostle says that in both epistles he is *stirring up the mind;* he intends to arouse the readers from their spiritual lethargy, to rive their attention on *the promise of his coming,* to remind them of th words spoken before by *the holy prophets,* etc. This is exactly what w find in the First Epistle: exhortation to "gird up the loins of you mind" (I Peter 1:13); emphasis on the coming or "revelation of Jesu Christ" (same verse), references to what the "holy prophets" hav spoken (I Peter 1:16, 24; 2:6-8); etc. There is, accordingly, goo reason to regard I Peter as the very epistle to which the apostle refe in II Peter 3:1-7. If this be granted, then the two letters of Pete which we possess were addressed to the same readers: th predominantly Gentile churches of Asia Minor. Against this positio it cannot be urged that, were this the case, II Peter would hav gained as early and universal recognition as did I Peter, for this is nc at all *necessarily* the case. Ever so many things may have happene e.g., the person who had been charged with the task of bringing th epistle (II Peter) to its destination may have failed to do so, an others, finding the letter, may not have been able to determine i destination inasmuch as 1:1 is very general and indefinite. Moreove there are phrases in the earliest patristic writings which remind on of certain similar words and passages in II Peter, and which ma indicate that at least in certain quarters this epistle was known an recognized at a very early time. We also believe that Jude refers to i See pp. 366-367.

There are those who affirm that whoever wrote I Peter cannc possibly have written II Peter, which is so different in style an diction. We admit that there is a difference, but this may be due t the change in subject matter (though not in general purpose) or to th possibility that Peter employed a different amanuensis (cf. I Pet 5:12, which has no parallel in II Peter). While stressing th *difference* in style and vocabulary, some forget the strikin similarities. The two epistles have several words which are rarely not at all found in other New Testament books; in both, believers ar designated as "called" and "elect"; both emphasize the significanc of prophecy; both testify to the author's habit of presenting a matt positively and negatively, etc.

We believe that the author of this as well as of the First Epistl was the apostle Simon Peter. In a Bible survey we do not have th space to enter into the arguments which have been presented again the Petrine authorship. Our reasons for believing as we do are th following:

(1) The author calls himself Simon Peter (II Peter 1:1).

(2) He vigorously condemns falsehood and hypocrisy (2:1-3). It is, therefore, difficult to believe that he himself would be a deceiver who would write a spurious letter.

(3) He was a witness of the transfiguration (1:16-18; cf. Matt. 17:1).

(4) He tells us that from Christ he had received a prediction regarding his death (1:14; cf. John 13:36; 21:18, 19).

(5) He is well acquainted with Paul (II Peter 3:15; cf. Gal. 1:18).

When Peter wrote his Second Epistle he knew that false teachers were spreading their sinister doctrines and that this danger would increase in the future. Accordingly, II Peter contains both an exhortation to grow in the full practical knowledge of the truth as it is in Christ and a warning against false prophets.

We present the following brief outline:

II Peter
AN EXHORTATION AND A WARNING

1	**I. Exhortation to grow in the knowledge of Christ.**
2, 3	**II. Warning to beware of false prophets.**

Notice the parallelism in parts I and II of the following expanded outline:

II Peter
AN EXHORTATION AND A WARNING

1	**I. Exhortation to grow in the knowledge of Christ.**
1:1-8	A. *Its character:* practical, experiential, fruitful.
1:9-11	B. *Its (positive) reward:* it prevents one from stumbling; it supplies entrance into Christ's kingdom.
1:12-21	C. *Its witnesses.*
	1. Eye witnesses, including Peter, soon to die.
	2. The Father.
	3. The word of prophecy.

1:19 — D. *Its affirmation of the second coming*: "until the day dawn, and the dayspring arise in your hearts."

2, 3 — **II. Warning to beware of false prophets.**

2:1-3a — A. *Their character:* destructive and covetous.

2:3b-17 — B. *Their (negative) reward.*

1. Like that of the angels who fell.
2. Like that of the ancient world in the days of Noah.
3. Like that of Sodom and Gomorrah.
4. Like that of Balaam.

2:18-22 — C. *Their witnesses.* Cf. verse 14.

1. Unstedfast souls.
2. Those who know the way but turn back.

3 — D. *Their denial of the second coming.*

1. Their mockery.
2. Their errors.
3. What their example should teach us by contrast: to sanctify ourselves and to long for the second coming.

Jude

What Peter predicted was fulfilled shortly afterward, in the days of Jude, "a servant of Jesus Christ and brother of James," hence, a brother of Jesus (Matt. 13:55). Jude does not tell us where the readers of his epistle were living or who they were. It is not improbable, however, that they lived in Asia Minor, to which also I and II Peter had been addressed. Many able scholars are of the opinion that the Epistle of Jude preceded II Peter, which it resembles so closely. However, others have shown that this is improbable. We have been convinced by their arguments. Let the reader judge for himself by comparing the following excerpts:

II Peter 3:3: *Knowing this first that in the last days mockers*

Jude 17, 18: *But you, beloved must remember the words that*

shall come with mockery, walking after their own lusts.	*were spoken beforehand by the apostles of our Lord Jesus Christ. They said to you, In the last times there will be mockers, walking after their own ungodly lusts.*
II Peter 2:1: . . . *among you also there shall be false teachers, who will secretly introduce seductive heresies, denying even the Master who bought them, bringing swift destruction upon themselves.*	**Jude 4:** *For certain men secretly slipped in among you. Their condemnation was predicted long ago; ungodly men, who turn the grace of our God into an excuse for licentiousness, and deny our only Master and Lord, Jesus Christ.*

The reasoning of the loudmouthed boasters who are condemned by Jude may have been, "Whatever is done in the body is not chargeable to the soul." This falsehood, in turn, may have been based upon a kind of paganistic and speculative soul-versus-body (spirit-versus-matter) dualism. At any rate, the errorists wallowed in all kinds of sinful excess. By their daily conduct they denied "our Master and Lord, Jesus Christ" (4). The danger to believers was so great that while Jude was planning to write on a large subject—"our common salvation"—he suddenly felt it necessary to write this letter in which he urges the readers to remain stedfast and to "keep themselves in the love of God" (21).

It is held by many that in verses 9, 14, and 15 Jude is quoting from apocryphal books, the *Assumption of Moses* (vs. 9) and the *Book of Enoch* (vss. 14, 15). This, however, cannot be proved. All we can say is that according to the testimony of the ancients Jude confirms (or reminds one of) a statement in the *Assumption of Moses* and that he also uses language which is remarkably similar to that which is found in the *Book of Enoch*. Of course, this does not mean that Jude "quotes" either of these sources. Entirely reliable oral tradition may be the source of the statements in all three (*Assumption of Moses, Book of Enoch, Jude*). We simply do not know where Jude received his information. It does not matter. The fact is that what Jude wrote was inspired, true!

Inasmuch as there is a very close resemblance between the second division of II Peter and the Epistle of Jude, we have chosen as the theme:

Jude
A WARNING TO BEWARE OF FALSE PROPHETS

Read the epistle carefully, not once but at least three times. What outline do you suggest?

Bethlehem from the area today
referred to as "Shepherd's Fields."

The Synoptics: 27
Matthew, Mark, and Luke

See also pp. 131-175, 448-449, 455.

In the preceding chapter we discussed I and II Peter (also Jude). Now, there is a close connection between Peter and the Gospels. There are commentators who believe that Peter in his Second Epistle promises that he will provide a Gospel. They are of the opinion that our Gospel of Mark was the one which redeemed Peter's promise. The passage to which we have reference is II Peter 1:15: "I will indeed make every effort to see to it that after my departure you will always be able to call these things to remembrance."

Others, however, reject this interpretation. Even so, it remains a fact that there is a close traditional connection between Peter and the Gospels, especially between Peter and the Gospel of Mark.

This is, therefore, the proper place to introduce the Synoptics: Matthew, Mark, and Luke. We may conceive of the historical background which led to their formation somewhat in the following manner:

Our Lord was addressing the multitudes, and they were "all ears." They were saying such things as: "Where does this man get this wisdom?" They wondered at the words of grace that were flowing from his lips. They were astonished. This man did not quote authorities, as the scribes were constantly doing. He was himself, in very person, the Authority. He was original, and his words were "from the heart to the heart."

The people had come from all over the country. They had brought their sick and demon-possessed. He had cured the sick and cast out the demons. And now he was uttering words of life and beauty. His disciples were with him. They, too, were listening. Were some of these listeners doing something besides listening? Was

Matthew taking notes of *the oracles* of the Lord? And was he addin other notes about Christ's *deeds? Did these notes become an impor tant Gospel source*?

After a ministry of slightly more than three years our Lord wa crucified. He arose triumphantly and ascended to heaven. The di ciples, gathered for prayer and worship, would often discuss th words which the Lord had spoken while he was still with them. Now as never before, they began to discern the meaning of those ver words which before had seemed so mysterious to them. He ha spoken about his approaching death on the cross. But at that tim this instruction had impressed them as being absurd. What? . . . th Messiah . . . suffer and die? On a cruel, shameful, accursed cross Impossible! Peter—how well he remembered it!—had taken him asid and had even made an attempt to rebuke him.

But now everything had become different. Due to the illumin tion of the Holy Spirit, shedding the light of heaven on all thes wondrous words and happenings, all had become plain, at leas much plainer than at first. How they now loved those very word which had baffled them formerly.

And so—but here we begin to enter the realm of theory— collection was made of the oracles of the Lord. The man who mad this collection—or shall we say, one of the men?—was Matthew, one-time collector of customs, who was able to tell a wonderful stor about the manner in which the Lord had called him (Mark 2:13 ff. A variously interpreted ancient tradition relates that Matthew com piled the *Logia* in the Hebrew (i.e., Aramaic) language. But what meant by *Logia*? Considerably more than the discourses and saying which the Lord had uttered?

Was the document which Matthew is said to have drawn u largely a collection of oracles or was it the entire Gospel? If th former be correct, then it is conceivable that Matthew afterwar embodied these oracles, translated into Greek, in his complete Gospe The *Logia,* then, would become a source for the Gospel, nc only for the Gospel of Matthew but perhaps even for that of Luk Matthew and Luke contain much common material that is not foun in Mark. This material consists mainly of sayings of Jesus. Th symbol Q—the first letter of the German *Quelle*, meaning *source* may be used, in a non-committal, purely algebraic manner, to ind cate this extra-Marcan Matthew-Luke material. Whether Q is, i reality, tantamount to Matthew's "oracles" is debatable. Those wh favor the view that the *Logia* and *the entire Gospel* according t Matthew are one and the same emphasize the fact that this Gospel i a well organized, beautifully arranged book which gives every evidence of being an organic unit.

Whereas Matthew quotes the Old Testament again and again, his book very properly follows Malachi. Although Matthew is the first book of the *New Testament*, it is firmly rooted in the *Old*. It was the former publican's purpose to persuade the Jews that Jesus of Nazareth was the Messiah promised in the Old Testament.

Another Gospel was written by Mark. In biblical usage the term *gospel* refers to the good news itself. Later on, however, it began to be employed to indicate the four books which contain that good news. Whenever we employ the term in the former sense, we can speak of only *one* gospel (cf. Gal. 1:6-9). Whenever we use it in the latter sense, we have the perfect right to speak about four Gospels. The home of Mark was in Jerusalem (Acts 12:12). It was he who deserted Paul and Barnabas on the First Missionary Journey (see p. 185). Paul, therefore, refused to take Mark with him on the second tour. Subsequently, however, we find Mark again in the company of Paul at Rome during the apostle's first imprisonment (Col. 4:10; Philem. 24). We also find him in the company of Peter, his spiritual father (I Peter 5:13). During Paul's second imprisonment in Rome the apostle to the Gentiles asks Timothy to bring Mark with him to Rome "for he is profitable to me in the ministry."

The church fathers call Mark "the interpreter of Peter." Some of them almost leave the impression that Mark's Gospel is nothing else than the record of Peter's preaching. Clement of Alexandria tells this interesting story:

> *So charmed were the Romans with the light that shone in upon their minds from the discourses of Peter, that, not content with a single hearing and the* viva voce *proclamation of the truth, they urged with the utmost solicitation on Mark, whose Gospel is in circulation, and who was Peter's attendant, that he would leave them in writing a record of the teaching which they had received by word of mouth. They did not give up until they had prevailed on him; and thus they became the cause of the composition of the so-called Gospel according to Mark.*

If the recent discovery of a papyrus scrap in cave #7 near Qumran has been *correctly* (a) *dated* about A.D. 50, and (b) *identified* as being part of Mark 6:52, 53, the conclusion that this Gospel itself was composed considerably earlier than that date would be right. But this matter is still being debated. We are probably safe in stating that of the Gospels in their present form Mark was the oldest and originated sometime during the period A.D. 40-65.

Internal evidence supports the idea that there was a close connection between the preaching of Peter and the Gospel of Mark. The vivid little touches which are found in Mark and nowhere else presuppose the account of an eye-witness (1:20, 29, 31; 2:1-4, 27; 3:5-12; 4:35-41; 5; 6:14-29, etc.). Then, too, incidents in which Peter figured prominently are often omitted by Mark; as, Peter's walking on the water (Matt. 14:29); his appearance in the incident of the tribute money (Matt. 17:24-27); Christ's statement that he had made supplication for Simon, i.e., Peter (Luke 22:31, 32); and the prophecy of Jesus "And I also say unto you that you are Peter, and upon this rock will I build my church . . ." (Matt. 16:18). At times also Peter's name is suppressed in Mark but expressed by Matthew or Luke. Compare Matt. 15:15 with Mark 7:17; Luke 22:8 with Mark 14:13; or vice versa: Mark 16:7 ("But go, tell his disciples *and Peter . . .*") with Matthew 28:7. See also Mark 5:37; 11:21. Moreover, in the vivid, dramatic, fast-moving action of Mark's Gospel many see a reflection of the spontaneous and impulsive personality of Peter.

Mark writes his Gospel for the Romans and pictures the Messiah as the miracle worker, the mighty one, the great king and conqueror. That was language which Rome could understand.

The third Gospel was written by Luke. This is the testimony of the title and also of early tradition. Luke was the beloved physician, the friend and associate of Paul. The latter mentions Luke in two epistles of his first imprisonment (Col. 4:14, Philem. 24) and in the epistle of the second imprisonment (II Tim. 4:11). Luke was in very close association with Mark. They were together in Rome. It is not at all surprising but gratifying that, in spite of the lengthy arguments that have been presented to the contrary, thoroughly conservative scholarship is more and more arriving at the conclusion that Luke made use of Mark's Gospel.

Luke has himself stated the purpose of his Gospel in these words:

> *Since many have undertaken to draw up a narrative of the things that have been fulfilled among us, just as those who from the beginning were eyewitnesses and servants of*

the Word handed them down to us, it seemed good to me also, having traced the course of everything accurately from the beginning, to write an orderly account for you, most excellent Theophilus, so that you may know the exact truth about the things you have been taught.

Luke, then, writes his Gospel with the purpose of convincing Theophilus and, in general, the Greeks, that Jesus is the Christ, the sympathetic High Priest, the Savior of the world. This book, accordingly, abounds in stories in which our Lord's mercy toward the less privileged, the sick, the needy, social outcasts, sinners, women, children, all nations, etc., comes to expression (1:48; 2:7, 8, 24, 36; 3:6; 4:18; 6:20; 7:2, 6, 12, 37; 8:42; 10:38; 13:11; 14:13, 23; 17:16; 18:3, 15; 21:3; 24:47).

The first three Gospels resemble each other in several respects. They present the same general view of the life and teachings of our Lord, and are therefore called Synoptic Gospels. They are similar, yet different.

Their *similarity* is evident. (a) *In material content* or subject matter one finds, upon examination, that Matthew's Gospel contains, in substance, almost all of the Gospel of Mark. This material which is common to Matthew and Mark constitutes a little less than one-half of Matthew's Gospel. Luke's Gospel contains about half of the material of the Gospel of Mark. Besides this, a little less than one-fourth of Matthew's Gospel consists of extra-Marcan material—mostly words of Jesus—which, in substance, is also found in Luke. (b) The similarity is also evident *in the order of events* as recorded. Thus, if a person has committed to memory the main topics of Mark's short Gospel, he is able to find much of this *Marcan material* in Luke's Gospel by employing a very simple device: Mark 1 (add 3) cf. Luke 4; Mark 2 (add 3) cf. Luke 5; Mark 3 (add 3) cf. Luke 6; Mark 4 and 5 (add 3) cf. Luke 8; and Mark 6 (add 3) cf. Luke 9. And now add 8, as follows: Mark 10 cf. Luke 18; Mark 11 cf. Luke 19; Mark 12 cf. Luke 20; Mark 13 cf. Luke 21; Mark 14 cf. Luke 22; Mark 15 cf. Luke 23; and even for some of Mark 16 cf. Luke 24. At this point we advise careful reading of the expanded outlines of Mark and Luke found on pp. 389-395. The exceptions will then also become evident. Mark's order of events should also be compared with that of Matthew. It will then become apparent that Matthew and Mark have the same general sequence of events, though here, too, there are frequent exceptions. Moreover, in Matthew thi sequence is interrupted by six (not five!) great discourses: chapter 5-7, 10, 13, 18, 23, 24-25. Even more interesting is the fact tha generally where Matthew's order of events differs from that of Mark Luke agrees with Mark; and where Luke's sequence differs fror Mark, Matthew agrees with Mark. (c) Finally, this similarity is eviden *in the identical or almost identical Greek words employed in paralle accounts* (cf. Matt. 3:7 ff. with Luke 3:7 ff. both in English and i Greek).

Nevertheless, there are also differences: (a) Each of the three ha *material* not found in the others (consult expanded outlines on pp 386-396 for examples). (b) The difference *in the order of events* ha already been indicated: sometimes Matthew agrees with Mark agains Luke, or Luke with Mark against Matthew. (c) There is at time considerable *variation in wording* (cf. Matt. 8:2-4; Mark 1:40-45 Luke 5:12-15).

Hence, the Synoptic Problem is this: how shall we account fo such remarkable unity amid such striking diversity? A complet solution has not been found. In fact, every attempt at a solutio gives rise to several new problems and difficulties (see pp. 376-378)

Those who believe that Matthew's *Logia* (see pp. 372-373) wer not much more than a collection of sayings or oracles view them as written source of his Gospel. Some think that Matthew himsel afterward embodied the *Logia* in his Gospel and that Luke, too used them or a similar list. All this is merely a theory. Anothe question would be: Is there a literary relation of some kind betwee Matthew and Mark? The striking differences between the two hav already been partly explained: Mark was Peter's interpreter. But how shall we account for the striking similarities? Compare, e.g., Mar 1:16-19 with Matthew 4:18-21. The well-known theory according t which there was a fixed and rigidly uniform (not merely harmonious oral tradition, so that the stories with respect to the words and work of our Lord were repeated over and over again in almost or quit *identical* verbal form, has failed to carry conviction. Not only liber but also conservative authors have seen its inadequacy. What then Shall we assume very early written source material of narrativ character used by both Matthew and Mark? See. Diagram A, p. 378 Or shall we have recourse to the theory that Mark used Matthew' Gospel in writing his own? See Diagram B. Objections have bee advanced against both of these assumptions. Another widely hel view, which would solve many problems but would create man thers, is this: Matthew's own part in the composition of the Gospel amed after him was limited to the work of compiling the sayings nd discourses of Jesus with perhaps a minimum of narrative framevork. Afterward Mark wrote his largely narrative Gospel. (Some, owever, reverse this order.) And then some unknown person very kilfully interwove the discourse material of Matthew into the narraive material of Mark, thereby producing the Gospel "according to Matthew" which we possess today. The sequence of Gospel composiion, accordingly, would be as follows: (a) Aramaic Matthew, aftervard translated into Greek, (b) Mark, (c) our present Greek Matthew, d) Luke. See diagram C. (Here some would add narrative sources rior to Mark and used by all three.) Can you mention some bjections that can be advanced against this popular theory? We shall imply have to admit that the question of the literary connection etween Matthew and Mark has not been completely solved.

The problem of the literary connection between Mark and Luke s probably easier. See also p. 374. It is not only possible but robable that Luke, who not only was with Mark in Rome during 'aul's first imprisonment but probably also afterward (II Tim. 4:11), nade use of Mark's Gospel. We do not believe that it has been onvincingly shown that this is excluded by what Luke says in 1:1-3. n fact, we believe that these verses rather argue in favor than against he idea that Luke used Mark. Says the beloved physician: "Since nany have undertaken to draw up a narrative of the things that have een fulfilled among us . . . it seemed good to me also . . . to write an rderly account for you. . . ." Moreover, no convincing arguments ave as yet been presented which would cause us to depart from the iew, strongly supported by external and internal evidence, that the rder in which Mark and Luke are arranged in our Bibles—Luke following Mark—is correct. Literary comparison, as well as Luke 1:1-4, would seem to indicate that it was Luke who used Mark, and ot vice versa.

The three theories of literary dependence which we have discussed may be indicated graphically. Observe that in all three diagrams Mark and Q (the non-Marcan discourse material which is common to Matthew and Luke) are considered factors which, taken together, make an important contribution to the formation of Luke's Gospel. With Matthew the case is different: three different theoretical possibilities are suggested by the diagrams, clearly indicating, as stated earlier, that the problem of the literary relation between Matthew and Mark has not been solved.

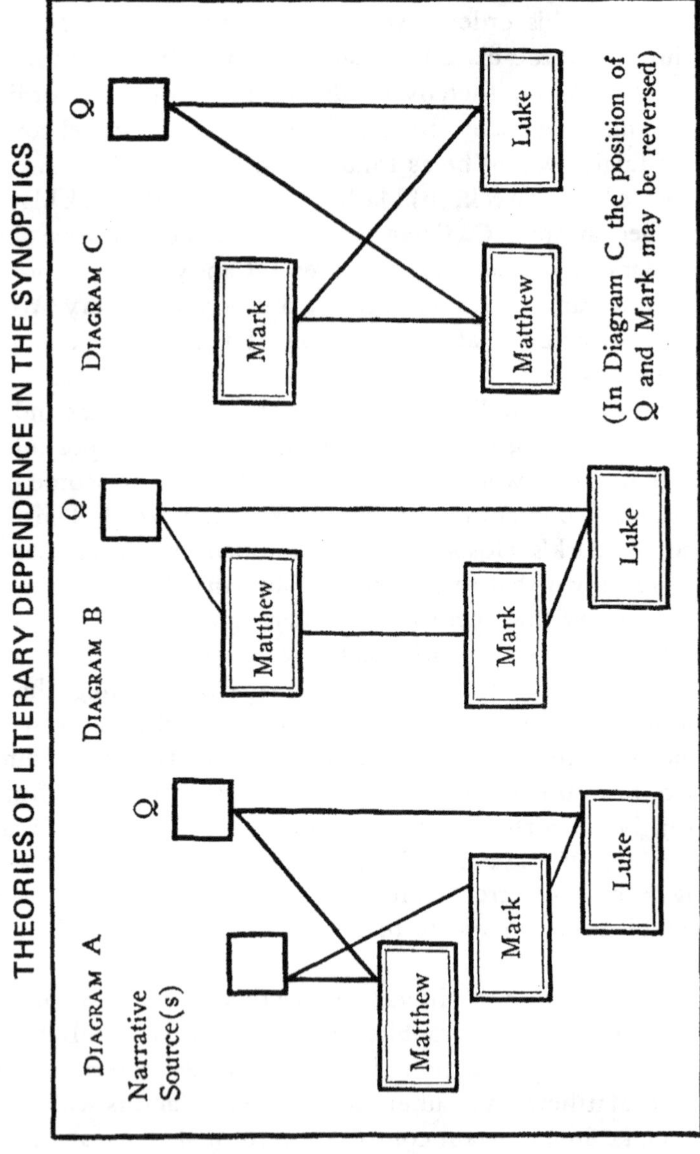
THEORIES OF LITERARY DEPENDENCE IN THE SYNOPTICS
DIAGRAM A
Narrative Source(s)
Q
Matthew
Mark
Luke
DIAGRAM B
Q
Matthew
Mark
Luke
DIAGRAM C
Q
Mark
Matthew
Luke
(In Diagram C the position of Q and Mark may be reversed)

However, even if one of these three diagrams should present a correct picture, it would not yet account for the *entire* contents of any Gospel; both Matthew and Luke have considerable material which can be traced neither to Mark nor to Q. Moreover, as we have seen, there are other important differences. *And do not forget the probability of Matthew's notes (p. 372) as a source for all three synoptics!*

This brings us to a *concluding summary.* It is reproduced here from my *N.T.C., Matthew,* pp. 53, 54. In that same work the reader can find a far more extensive treatment of the Synoptic Problem, pp. 6-54. The quoted summary is as follows:

"On the basis of literary comparison, Luke 1:1-4, and ancient tradition (for example, with reference to the relation between Mark and Peter), the following would seem to be a fair statement embodying a partial solution of the Synoptic Problem:

(1) *Why are the three so similar?*

(a) Because the same Primary Author, the Holy Spirit, inspired them all, and they all record the words and deeds of the same Lord Jesus Christ.

(b) Because the three are based on observation of many of the same facts.

(c) Because the observed facts were transmitted accurately, so that the three Gospels rest upon a thoroughly harmonious oral tradition.

(d) In part also because of literary relationship, both Matthew and Luke having probably used Mark's Gospel; all three having utilized Matthew's earlier notes, Luke perhaps also using Matthew's Gospel.

(2) *Why are the three so different?*

(a) Because Jesus himself proclaimed the "gospel of the kingdom" in different ways at different places, and because he performed similar deeds in various places.

(b) Because different witnesses of the works and words of Jesus made different observations. When three intelligent and honest men see the same miracle or hear the same sermon, what they see and hear will generally not be *exactly* the same thing, but will vary in accordance with the respective personality of each of the three witnesses.

(c) Because the oral transmission of these observations, though harmonious, was multiple in character.

(d) Because *more* or *less* extensive use could be made of Matthew's notes, and their contents could be inserted in various places, according to the judgment of the individual evangelist.

(e) Because in the use of sources, whether oral or written, each evangelist exercised his Spirit-guided judgment, in accordance with his own character, education and general background, and with a view to the realization of his own distinct plan and purpose."

What a glorious all-sided view these Gospels present with respect to the Christ! Matthew pictures him as the Great Prophet. Think of the six discourses. Mark pictures him as the Mighty King; Luke, as the sympathetic High Priest. All three proclaim him as being the long-expected Messiah, the Christ of God, the all-sufficient Savior.

The Church of All Nations, on the slopes
of Mount of Olives. The church stands next
to the Garden of Gethsemane.
Levant Photo Service

The Synoptics: 28
Matthew, Mark, and Luke (continued)

'he following summary outline of the Synoptics should be com-ıitted to memory. It should be carefully compared with the outline f John's Gospel, especially with the indication of the various minis-:ies (p. 427), and with the chronological table, p. 73.

THE SYNOPTICS

The Gospels According to Matthew, Mark, and Luke

JESUS, THE CHRIST

Matthew: Jesus, The Christ, The Great Prophet

Mark: Jesus, The Christ, The Mighty King

Luke: Jesus, The Christ, The Sympathetic High Priest

'hat he is indeed the Christ (the Great Prophet, Mighty King, ympathetic High Priest) is evident from:

ſatt. 1:1–4:11 nd parallels ı Mark and uke	**I. The preparation for, and the inauguration of his ministry.** A. *The Preparation.* Probably Dec., 5 B.C.–Dec., A.D. 26. B. *The Inauguration.* Probably Dec., A.D. 26–April, A.D. 27 (The Synoptics skip the Early Judean Ministry, April-Dec., A.D. 27, for which see John 2:13–4:32.)
ſatt. 4:12–20:34 ıd parallels	**II. The ministry itself.** A. To the *multitudes,* mainly in Galilee. This is the Great Galilean Ministry. Dec., A.D. 27–April, A.D. 29.

B. To the *disciples* (but see what is said on Luke p. 393f), in (1) the surrounding regions; (2 Judea; and (3) Perea. Accordingly, this sub division (B) comprises (1) the Retiremen Ministry, April–Oct., A.D. 29; immediatel followed by (2) the Later Judean Ministry Oct.–Dec., A.D. 29, recorded only in Joh 7:1–10:39; and (3) the Perean Ministry, Dec. A.D. 29–April, A.D. 30.

Matt. 21:1–28:20 and parallels — **III. The glorious conclusion of his ministry.**

A. From the triumphal entry into Jerusalem t the death on the cross. This is the Passio Week, April, A.D. 30

B. The Resurrection, April, A.D. 30

To indicate the same three main divisions, similarly subdivide slightly different phraseology may be used, as in *N.T.C., Matthew* pp. 99, 103, 237, 757:

The Gospel of Matthew
The Work Which Thou Gavest Him To Do

1:1–4:11	**I. Its beginning or inauguration.**
4:12–20:34	**II. Its progress or continuation.**
21:1–28:20	**III. Its climax or culmination.**

Each division in the abbreviated outline of Matthew has parallel in Mark and Luke.

We favor this kind of summary outline for the followin reasons:

1. Such an outline is indicated by the Synoptics themselves Thus, the boundary between I and II is clearly marked in all thre Gospels. See Matthew 4:12-14; Mark 1:14, 15; and Luke 4:14, 15 our Lord begins his great Galilean Ministry. The same holds wit respect to the boundary between II and III: Jesus approaches Jerusa lem and is about to make his triumphal entry into that city. Se Matthew 21:1, 2; Mark 11:1, 2; Luke 19:28, 29. Even the subdivi

ions under the main divisions are rather clearly evident. It must, however, be understood that to the multitudes (II A—first outline) does not mean *exclusively*, but *especially* to the multitudes. Similarly, II B means *especially* to the disciples, but see what is said on Luke below.

2. Such an outline shows that the three—Matthew, Mark, and Luke—proceed along the same general lines: they present one pattern. They see things together, as the name *Synoptics* implies. Three separate outlines, one for each Gospel, will never indicate this, unless preceded by *one* summary outline for all three. Such an outline, followed by the others, emphasizes the unity amid diversity.

3. It also harmonizes with the historical scheme of our Lord's earthly sojourn, found on p. 73. The two—summary outline and historical scheme—should be studied together and compared.

4. It is memorizable and should be used as a basis for the study of the expanded outlines found on pp. 386-396.

Subdivision II B of Luke's Gospel requires special attention. It has three sections: (1) 9:18-50, the Retirement Ministry. This section has its parallel in Matthew and Mark. It is followed by (2) 9:51—13:21, which may include incidents belonging to the Later Judean Ministry; (compare *N.T.C.* on it). The last section is (3) 13:22—19:27, which includes events pertaining to the Perean Ministry. See John 10:22, 40-42; Luke 13:31; 18:35. Toward the close of this section—see 18:15-43—Luke returns for a moment to the material found in Matthew and Mark, then leaves it again (Luke 19:1-27). It is clear, therefore, that these nine chapters (9:51—18:14, 19:1-27) except for such discourse material which is also found in Matthew but not in Mark, are largely peculiar to Luke. In all, Luke has 27 parables, 18 of which are peculiar to his Gospel. They are addressed not only to the disciples but also to the multitudes. Section II A in Luke is, in the main, a ministry of *deeds*. Section II B is, in the main, a ministry of *words or teachings*.

The brief summarizing outlines of the Synoptics which we have given can be expanded for each of these three Gospels. For a more thorough discussion of the contents of the Gospels see pp. 131-173. For the Gospel of Matthew we suggest the following expanded outline. It should be carefully compared with the summary outline, pp. 383-384, and with the expanded outlines of Luke and Mark, especially the latter.

Matthew

JESUS, THE CHRIST, THE GREAT PROPHET

That he is indeed the Christ, the Great Prophet, is evident from:

1:1–4:11	**I. The preparation for, and the inauguration of his ministry.**
1, 2	A. *The Preparation.*
ch. 1	1. The legal ancestry and supernatural conception, according to *prophecy* (see 1:23).
2	2. His birth in Bethlehem, where he is adored by the wise men; flight into Egypt; and home in Nazareth, according to *prophecy* (2:6, 18, 23).
3:1–4:11	B. *The Inauguration.*
3	1. His baptism by John, who was himself the fulfilment of *prophecy* (3:3).
4:1-11	2. His victory over Satan in the temptation.
4:12–20:34	**II. The ministry itself.**
4:12-15:20	A. To *the multitudes*, mainly in Galilee: the Great Galilean Ministry.
4:12–7:29	1. He calls four disciples, teaches, preaches, and heals; and by means of the Sermon on the Mount (the first great discourse, chs 5-7) he proclaims the Gospel of the Kingdom.
	a. The citizens of the kingdom.
	b. The righteousness of the kingdom.
	c. Exhortation to enter the kingdom.
8, 9	2. He performs kingdom miracles (call Matthew, etc.).
	a. He controls the physical universe.
	b. Also, the realm of evil spirits.
	c. And even the realm of the dead.
10	3. He sends forth the Twelve as kingdom ambassadors (the second great discourse).
11	4. He extols the herald of the kingdom, John the Baptist.

12 (cf. also 16:1-12) 5. He condemns the enemies of the kingdom (impenitent cities, Pharisees).

13 6. He utters kingdom parables (the third great discourse) and is rejected at Nazareth. (This is probably the same rejection as the one to which Luke 4 refers: there was probably only one rejection at Nazareth.)

4:1–15:20 7. His kingdom miracles cause Herod to surmise that John the Baptist is risen from the dead. Our Lord dispenses kingdom blessings: the feeding of the five thousand (both real and symbolical), etc.

5:21–20:34 B. To *the disciples*, in the surrounding regions and in Perea: the Retirement Ministry and (after the later Judean Ministry; see especially John 7:1–10:39, and perhaps Luke 9:51–13:21) the Perean Ministry.

15:21–16:12 1. During the Retirement Ministry he answers the lovelessness of his disciples ("send her away") by healing the daughter of the Canaanitish woman, their cold calculation ("Where in this uninhabited region would we get bread enough to feed such a crowd?") by miraculously feeding the four thousand, and their blindness by explaining to them that his warning against the "leaven" of the sign-seeking Pharisees was a warning against their teaching.

16:13–20:34 2. During the Retirement Ministry and the Perean Ministry, in addition to performing a few miracles, he teaches his disciples, especially *the lesson of the cross;* i.e., of his coming suffering, death, etc.

16:13-28 a. Its necessity, in answer to Peter's rebuke, "Be it far from thee, Lord," a rebuke which followed his great confession.

17 b. Its glory; i.e., the glory to which it leads, as foreshadowed by the transfiguration. This is followed by the miracle of the healing of the epileptic boy.

18 c. Its blessings, limited to those of childlike and forgiving spirit (the fourt great discourse) and

19:1–20:16 d. Distributed according to God's sovereig will. See especially 19:30 and 20:15. Thi section includes Christ's teachings on d vorce and on "little children," as well a the story of the rich young ruler.

20:17-34 e. Its self-sacrificing motive and substitu tionary character. See especially 20:25 28. This section ends with the story of th blind men at Jericho.

21:1–28:20 **III. The glorious conclusion of his ministry. Th Passion Week and the Resurrection.** By means c his suffering, death, and resurrection, he prove himself to be the Christ, the great and tru Prophet, over against Jerusalem's prominent bu false religious leaders.

21:1–27:66 A. From the triumphal entry into Jerusalem t the death on the cross: the Passion Week.

21:1–22:14 1. By his triumphal entry into Jerusaler according to prophecy (see 21:4, 5, 42), b cleansing the temple according to prophe cy (21:13) after having cursed the fig tre and by means of three parables—the Tw Sons, the Wicked Husbandmen, the Ma riage Feast—he intensifies the opposition o Jerusalem's leaders.

22:15-45 2. By answering their questions—Is it lawfu to give tribute to Caesar? Is there resurrection? (an implied question) an Which is the great commandment?—and b asking them a question—What do you thin of the Christ?—he confutes them, in all thi fulfilling prophecy (22:32, 43, 44).

23 3. In a sevenfold woe he condemns them an utters a prophetic lamentation with respec to their impenitent city (the fifth grea discourse).

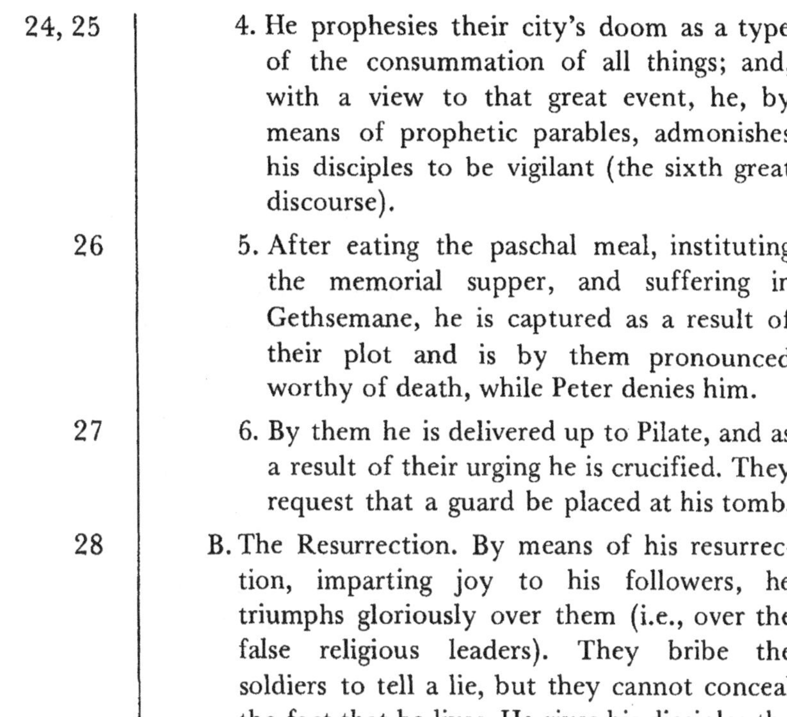

24, 25 4. He prophesies their city's doom as a type of the consummation of all things; and, with a view to that great event, he, by means of prophetic parables, admonishes his disciples to be vigilant (the sixth great discourse).

26 5. After eating the paschal meal, instituting the memorial supper, and suffering in Gethsemane, he is captured as a result of their plot and is by them pronounced worthy of death, while Peter denies him.

27 6. By them he is delivered up to Pilate, and as a result of their urging he is crucified. They request that a guard be placed at his tomb.

28 B. The Resurrection. By means of his resurrection, imparting joy to his followers, he triumphs gloriously over them (i.e., over the false religious leaders). They bribe the soldiers to tell a lie, but they cannot conceal the fact that he lives. He gives his disciples the Great Commission.

Similarly, for the Gospel of Mark the summary outline found on pp. 383-384, can be expanded as follows. Compare this longer outline with the shorter (Synoptic) one, as well as with the expanded outlines of Matthew and Luke.

Mark
JESUS, THE CHRIST, THE MIGHTY KING

That he is indeed the Christ, the Mighty King, is evident from:

1:1-13 I. **The inauguration of his ministry** (notice that the thirty years of preparation are not discussed in Mark).

1:1-11 A. His baptism by John, who was himself the fulfilment of prophecy.

1:12, 13 B. His mighty victory over Satan in the temptation.

1:14–10:52 **II. The ministry itself.**

1:14–7:23 A. To the *multitudes*, mainly in Galilee: th Great Galilean Ministry.

1:14–3:35 1. He calls four disciples, later Matthew an the Twelve; and he performs might miracles chiefly in and around Capernaur

4, 5 2. He speaks in parables, including the secre growth of the seed (4:26-29), and perforr other mighty miracles in the same gener region.

6 3. He is rejected at Nazareth, sends forth th Twelve (whose miracles in his Name caus Herod to surmise that John the Baptist risen from the dead), and feeds the fiv thousand.

7:1-23 4. He points out the contrast between re and merely ceremonial defilement, betwee the tradition of men and the comman ment of God.

7:24–10:52 B. To the *disciples*, in the surrounding regior and in Perea. This section, accordingl describes the Retirement Ministry and (aft the Later Judean Ministry see especially Joh 7:1–10:39, and perhaps Luke 9:51–13:21 the Perean Ministry.

7:24–8:26 1. During the Retirement Ministry he pe forms deeds of might: he heals th daughter of the Canaanitish woman and th deaf mute. He answers the cold calculatio of his disciples ("Where in this uninhabite region can anyone get bread enough to fee them?") by miraculously feeding the fou thousand, and he answers their blindne by explaining to them that his warnin against the "leaven" of the sign-seekin Pharisees was a warning against the teaching. He heals the blind man who sa men "as trees, walking."

8:27–10:52 2. During the Retirement Ministry and th Perean Ministry, in addition to performir deeds of might, he teaches his disciples, especially the lesson of the cross.

8:27-38 a. Its necessity, in answer to Peter's rebuke, which followed his confession.

9:1-32 b. Its glory; i. e., the glory to which it leads, as foreshadowed by the transfiguration. This is followed by the cure of the epileptic boy.

9:33-50 c. Its blessings, limited to those of a childlike spirit and

10:1-31 d. Distributed according to God's sovereign will (see especially 10:31). This section includes Christ's teachings on divorce, on "little children," as well as the story of the rich young ruler.

10:32-52 e. Its self-sacrificing motive and substitutionary character. See especially 10:42-45. At Jericho, on the way to Jerusalem, blind Bartimaeus is healed.

11:1–16:20 **III. The glorious conclusion of his ministry. The Passion Week and the Resurrection.** By means of his victorious suffering, death, and resurrection he proves himself to be the Christ, the mighty King.

11:1–15:47 A. From the triumphal entry into Jerusalem to the death on the cross: the Passion Week.

11:1–12:12 1. By his triumphal entry into Jerusalem he proclaims the coming of his kingdom (11:10; cf. Zech. 9:9). By cleansing the temple, after having cursed the fig tree, and by uttering the parable of the Wicked Tillers, he fills the hearts of his adversaries with fear.

12:13-37 2. By answering their questions—Is it lawful to give tribute to Caesar? Is there a resurrection? (the question is implied) and What commandment is first of all?—and by asking them a question—How can the scribes say that the Christ is the *Son* of David?—he confutes them.

12:38-44	3. He condemns them, but he commends the poor widow and her generous gift.
13	4. He announces their city's doom, as a type of the consummation of all things.
14	5. After eating the paschal meal, instituting the memorial supper, and suffering in Gethsemane, he is captured as a result of their plot and is by them pronounced worthy of death, while Peter denies him.
15	6. By them he is delivered to Pilate, and as a result of their urging he is crucified.
16	B. The Resurrection. As a result of his mighty and glorious resurrection, his disciples are filled with amazement and fear. He manifest himself to Mary Magdalene, to two disciples and to the eleven to whom he gives the Great Commission and power to perform mighty deeds. He is received up to heaven and sits down at the right hand of God. (For the authenticity of Mark 16:9-20 see *N.T.C.* on that Gospel.)

For the Gospel of Luke we suggest the following expanded outline. It should be carefully compared with the condensed outline on pp. 383-384, and with the expanded outlines of Matthew and of Mark, especially the latter.

Luke
JESUS, THE CHRIST, THE SYMPATHETIC HIGH PRIEST

That he is indeed the Christ, the Sympathetic High Priest, is evident from:

1:1–4:13	**I. The preparation for and the inauguration of his ministry.**
1, 2	A. *The preparation.*
1	1. The annunciation of the birth of the herald and of his own birth. The birth of the herald, John the Baptist.

2 — 2. The birth of Jesus in Bethlehem; his circumcision, presentation in the temple, visit to Jerusalem, and advance in wisdom and stature and favor with God and men.

3:1–4:13 — B. *The inauguration.*

3 — 1. His baptism by John, who was himself the fulfilment of prophecy. His natural ancestry.

4:1-13 — 2. His victory over Satan in the temptation.

:14–19:27 — **II. The ministry itself.**

4:14–9:17 — A. To the *multitudes*, mainly in Galilee: the Great Galilean Ministry. *It is, in the main, a ministry of deeds.*

4:14–6:49 — 1. At Nazareth he clearly declares himself to be the Messiah; he is rejected. He calls his first disciples, later Matthew and the Twelve; and he reveals his sympathy by performing miracles—including the catch of fishes—in and around Capernaum. On a level spot (on a mountain; cf. Luke 6:17 with Matt. 5:1) he delivers what has come to be known as the Sermon on the Mount.

7, 8 — 2. He reveals his sympathy to the centurion by healing his servant, to the widow at Nain by raising her son, to John the Baptist by answering his question of doubt, and to the sinful woman by forgiving her sins. He speaks in parables and reveals his sympathy by performing more miracles in the same general region.

9:1-17 — 3. He sends forth the Twelve, whose miracles in his Name cause Herod to be perplexed because it was said by some that John was risen from the dead. He feeds the five thousand.

:18–19:27 — B. To the *disciples* in the surrounding region, and to both disciples and multitudes in Perea and elsewhere. After describing the Retirement Ministry (9:18-50), this section has as its basis the Perean Ministry but is often in definite as to time and place. *It is mainly ministry of words and teachings.*

9:18-50 1. The Retirement Ministry. In addition t performing a few miracles, he teaches hi disciples, especially *the lesson of the cross.*

9:18-27 a. Its necessity, in answer to Peter's rebuke which followed his confession.

9:28-45 b. Its glory; i.e., the glory to which i leads, as foreshadowed by the trans figuration. (This is followed by the stor of the cure of the epileptic boy.)

9:46-50 c. Its blessings limited to those of childlike spirit.

9:51–13:21 2. Scenes from various ministries, basicall the Perean.

9:51-62 a. He journeys toward Jerusalem and i rejected by the Samaritans.

10 b. He sends out the seventy. The parable o the Good Samaritan. He is entertaine by Mary and Martha at Bethany.

11 c. He teaches his disciples to pray. Parabl of the Embarassed Host. He denounces hi adversaries and discourses on anxiety.

12 d. Parable of the Rich Fool and simila parables.

13:1-21 e. Parables of the Barren Fig tree, of th Mustard Seed and of the Leaven. He heal a crippled woman on the sabbath.

13:22–19:27 3. The Perean Ministry (continued).

13:22-35 a. On a journey through Perea he speak about "the narrow door," and answer the warning: "Herod wants to kill you."

14 b. He reveals his sympathy by healing th man afflicted with dropsy. Parable of th Slighted Invitation.

15 c. Parables of the Lost Sheep, Lost Coin Lost (Prodigal) Son.

16	d. Parables of the Cautious Steward (i. e., the steward who had foresight). Parable of the Rich Man and Lazarus.
17	e. Ten Samaritan lepers healed, of whom only one returns to offer thanks. Discourse on the future coming of the Son of Man.
18:1-14	f. Parable of the Widow who Persevered. Parable of the Pharisee and the Publican.
18:15-34	g. Christ's teaching on "little children" and the story of the rich young ruler. The lesson of the cross continued (cf. 9:18-50).
18:35-43	h. At Jericho, on the way to Jerusalem, a blind man is healed.
19:1-27	i. Jesus visits Zacchaeus. The Parable of the Pounds.

19:28–24:53 **III. The glorious conclusion of his ministry. Th Passion Week and the Resurrection.** By means o his vicarious suffering, death, and resurrectior he proves himself to be the Christ, th sympathetic High Priest, who offers himself as sacrifice.

19:28–23:56 A. From the triumphal entry into Jerusalem t the death on the cross: *the Passion Week.*

19:28-20:19 1. In connection with his triumphal entry int Jerusalem he reveals his tender sympath by weeping over the city. He cleanses th temple. Parable of the Wicked Tenants.

20:20-44 2. By answering the questions of his adve saries—Is it lawful to give tribute to Caesar Is there a resurrection? (the question implied)—and by asking them a question How can they say that the Christ is David Son?—he confutes them.

20:45–21:4 3. He condemns them, but he commends th poor widow and her generous gift.

21:5-38 4. He announces their city's doom, as a typ of the consummation of all things.

22 5. After eating the paschal meal, institutir the memorial supper, and suffering i Gethsemane, he is captured as a result c their plot and is by them pronounce worthy of death, while Peter denies him.

23 6. By them he is delivered to Pilate, and as result of their urging he is crucified. On th way to the cross he is bewailed by th daughters of Jerusalem.

24 B. *The Resurrection.* The Christ, risen from th dead, reveals himself to two disciples; then t the ten, addressing them in tender sympathy "Why are you troubled? . . . See my hanc and my feet, that it is I myself." Later, in th presence of his disciples, he ascends. He carried up into heaven.

The Arch of Titus, in Rome, was erected to commemorate the victory of Titus over the Jewish revolt (A.D. 70). One panel depicts Roman soldiers carrying booty taken from the temple at Jerusalem. ***Levant Photo Service***

Acts 29

ee also pp. 449, 455.

From Luke's Gospel to Acts is but a small step. We have already ntroduced the author of the third Gospel and of Acts. See pp. 74-375. To be sure, both books are anonymous. Nevertheless, the vidence which links Luke with Acts is conclusive:

1. It is evident both from the style of the books and from Acts :1 (cf. Luke 1:1-4) that whoever wrote the Gospel also wrote the cts. Now, according to its caption and according to the testimony f the earliest witnesses the Gospel was written by Luke.

2. The author of Acts was a companion of Paul, as is indicated by he "we" sections (Acts 16:10-17; 20:6-16; 21; 27; 28). He was, ccordingly, with Paul on his Second Missionary Journey, at Troas nd at Philippi. He was evidently left behind at the latter place 16:17-19). Toward the close of the third tour he again joins Paul at hilippi (20:6). It seems probable that he was with Paul throughout he latter's stay in Caesarea. At any rate he is in Paul's company on hat long and eventful journey to Rome (27:1). Now, from Paul's pistles we gather information about one very faithful companion, a eloved physician, Luke, who was with the apostle during both his irst and his second imprisonment (Col. 4:14; Philem. 24; II Tim. :11). Hence, the question arises: Is the author of the "we" sections n Acts–hence, the author of the entire Book of Acts; for the style, n general, is the same throughout–the same person as "the beloved hysician" of Colossians 4:14? The very fact that Luke's name is ever mentioned in Acts strengthens the position that he was the uthor. But also the name of Titus, another companion of Paul, is ever mentioned in Acts. It would seem, however, that the medical anguage of both the third Gospel and of Acts favors the conclusion

that the author was, indeed, the beloved physician. To be sure, serious endeavor has been made to show that many of the so-calle medical terms which are said to occur in the third Gospel and in Act belong to the language of general culture.[1] But the question is nc one of *terms* (in the original) only, such as those used in Luke 5:18 (c Mark 2:3) and Luke 18:25 (cf. Mark 10:25), but also of medic interest cropping out in many incidental ways (cf. Luke 4:35 wit Mark 1:26; Luke 4:38 with Mark 1:30; Luke 6:6 with Mark 3:1 Luke 8:43 with Mark 5:25, 26; Luke 8:55 with Mark 5:42; Luk 9:38 with Mark 9:17; Luke 22:50 with Mark 14:47; and see Act 28:1-6). The evidence points unmistakably to Luke as the author c the third Gospel and of Acts.

3. Early tradition also bears abundant testimony to the fact tha Luke wrote Acts.

4. The point of view of the Book of Acts is distinctly Pauline (c Acts 13:46 with Eph. 3:1, etc.).

So wonderfully accurate a historian is Luke that critics wh formerly doubted the historicity of some of his accounts have, aft more careful study and investigation, arrived at the opposite co clusion and have openly confessed their change of mind. There hav been those who challenged Luke's statement in his Gospel (2:2) tha the registration decreed by Augustus was made when Quirinius wa governor of Syria. It is known that Quirinius was governor in A.D. and that at that time a census was taken which angered the Jews. Di Luke make a mistake by connecting the governorship of Quiriniu with a census held many years before A.D. 6? However, Sir W. M Ramsay cleared up this difficulty. Near Antioch in Pisidia he foun inscriptions which show that shortly before the time of our Lord' birth Quirinius was *military* governor of Syria. Moreover, in a probability the actual execution of the census decree was delayed few years in Herod's realm (see p. 139).

Luke 3:1 presents another difficulty. Here Luke tells us tha John the Baptist's preaching began in the fifteenth year of the reig of Tiberius Caesar. But Tiberius began to reign in A.D. 14 upon th death of Augustus. His fifteenth year would bring us to A.D. 28 a the year when John began to preach. But whereas Jesus probabl began his ministry in the year A.D. 26 (see chart, p. 73) and John first appearance upon the public scene preceded that of the Lord, i

1. See H. J. Cadbury, *The Style and Literary Language of Luke*, but the corre view is probably found in A. T. Robertson, *Luke the Historian in the Lig of Research*, p. 11.

s evident that there is a mistake somewhere. However, the error is not in what Luke wrote but in our own calculation. It has been shown that Tiberius was associated with Augustus in the administration of the provinces from the year A.D. 12. From that year Tiberius actually reigned. Hence, John's preaching began in A.D. 26. It is the *actual* administration which Luke has in mind, as is also clear from the synchronism which we find in Luke 3:2: "in the highpriesthood of Annas and Caiaphas." Technically, Annas was no longer the high priest; *actually*, he ruled together with Caiaphas.

And so Luke's accounts, both in the Gospel and in Acts, have been vindicated again and again. The use of the term *proconsul* instead of *propraetor* in Acts 13:7 is one of the clearest illustrations. The island of Cyprus was a senatorial province (hence, the term *proconsul*) for only a short time. But just at that time when on his first missionary journey Paul and Barnabas visited this region it was, indeed, ruled by a proconsul, as is also evidenced by an interesting inscription. So also the rulers of the city of Thessalonica are called *politarchs.* An inscription found in that city has that very term. Additional examples are easily furnished.[2]

Luke, moreover, had abundant sources to draw from, both written and oral. He could draw upon his own observations (think of the "we" sections of Acts), upon the direct and personal information to be derived from his great friend Paul, perhaps upon Paul's epistles (though it is not certain that he had seen them) and upon other trusted witnesses, such as Philip the Evangelist, the friends at Jerusalem, James (the Lord's brother), Mark, copies of letters (Acts 15:23 ff.; 23:26 ff.). There are those that hold that he had an Aramaic written source for Acts 1-15. The main fact is that he was infallibly guided by the Holy Spirit, both in the selection of his material and in the actual composition of his books.

Luke's two books belong together. They are both addressed to the same person, Theophilus. The latter was, in all probability, a Greek. He had a Greek name. He must have been a person of high distinction, for he is addressed as "most excellent Theophilus" (Luke 1:3) in the same manner in which Felix and Festus are addressed (Acts 23:26; 24:3). The beloved physician sends his messages to him and, in general, to all the Greeks, that they may come to believe in Christ or, believing in him, may be confirmed in their faith. Now, when we say that Luke's Gospel and his Book of Acts belong together we do

---

2. See A.T. Robertson's work mentioned in Note 1; also W.M. Ramsay, *The Bearing of Recent Discovery on the Trustworthiness of the New Testament.*

not merely mean that they were addressed to the same person. Ther is also material continuity. For, whereas in his first book Luke ha written about the things which Jesus *began* to do and to teach (Act 1:1), in his second book he describes *the continuation* of the worl and teaching of the Lord. That same Christ who, when he was o earth, performed miracles and imparted instruction, is doing s today; but now from heaven. Hence, the story which is here recorde is that of the work of Christ in the extension of the church. Th theme is, therefore, suggested in 1:1. And the outline is clearl indicated in 1:8: ". . . and you shall be my witnesses both in Jeru salem [chs. 1-7] and in all Judea and Samaria [chs. 8-12] and to th uttermost parts of the earth [chs. 13-28]." *Be sure to consult a ma when studying this outline!* For a more thorough discussion of th contents of Acts, see pp. 175-199.

Acts
THE WORK OF JESUS CHRIST IN THE EXTENSION OF THE CHURCH (Cf. p. 74)

1-12	**I. The extension of the church in and from Jeru salem.**
13-28	**II. The extension of the church from Antioch.**

Expanded Outline:

Acts
THE WORK OF JESUS CHRIST IN THE EXTENSION OF THE CHURCH

1-12	**I. The extension of the church in and fro Jerusalem.**
1-7	A. In Jerusalem.
1, 2	1. Christ's Ascension. Choice of Matthias t replace Judas. The outpouring of the Ho Spirit. Results:
3:1–4:31	2. Wonders and signs; particularly the cure the lame beggar.
4:32–5:11	3. Witness bearing and voluntary sharing; als its perversion in the case of Ananias an Sapphira.

5:12–7:60 4. Winning of souls; the rapid growth of the church, which results in persecution—imprisonment of the Twelve and martyrdom of Stephen, which in turn results in further growth.

8-12 B. From Jerusalem, into all Judea and Samaria and the surrounding regions.

8 1. Philip's missionary labors.

9:1-30 2. Saul's conversion.

9:31–11:18 3. Peter's missionary labors.

1:19–12:25 4. Results of these labors: the further growth of the church, which results in further persecution: martyrdom of James, the son of Zebedee; imprisonment of Peter.

13-28 **II. The extension of the church from Antioch, mainly through the labors of Paul.**

13:1-15:35 A. Paul's First Missionary Journey and the Jerusalem Conference.

5:36–18:22 B. Second Missionary Journey.

8:23–21:16 C. Third Missionary Journey.

1:17–26:32 D. Paul in Jerusalem and Caesarea.

27, 28 E. Voyage to Rome, arrival, and first Roman imprisonment.

Nero, the Roman emperor at the time
of Paul's imprisonment, trial, and martyrdom.

The Pastoral Epistles: I Timothy, Titus, and II Timothy 30

ee also p. 456.

The Book of Acts closes with the statement:

> *And he [Paul] remained two whole years in his own rented house, and welcomed all who came to him, preaching the kingdom of God, and teaching the things concerning the Lord Jesus Christ with all frankness unhindered.*

Where did the apostle go after his release? We simply do not know ith any degree of certainty. However, the Pastoral Epistles imply a umber of journeys which cannot be fitted into the itineraries of aul which are recorded in the Book of Acts. It is probable that these urneys must be dated between the apostle's release and his death. owever, even the Pastorals fail us at this point, for they do not rnish complete information with respect to these travels. They erely furnish the "links" which can be joined together in ever so any different ways. Among the many possible combinations the llowing is, perhaps, as good as any (be sure to consult a map):

1. Immediately after his release Paul sends Timothy to Philippi ith the good news that he also plans to come (Phil. 2:19-23).

2. Paul himself starts on his journey toward Asia Minor and on e way to that destination leaves Titus on the island of Crete to ring to completion the organization of the churches which had been stablished on that island (cf. Acts 2:11; Tit. 1:5).

3. The apostle arrives at Ephesus, travels on until he reaches olosse just as he had intended to do (Philem. 22), and returns to phesus.

4. At Ephesus he is joined by Timothy, who brings news from th congregation at Philippi (see 1 above). Paul asks Timothy to remai at Ephesus, which was in need of his ministry (I Tim. 1:3, 4).

5. Paul himself goes to Macedonia, just as he had planned (Ph 2:24; I Tim. 1:3). He hopes to return to Ephesus at a later date (I Tin 4:13). From Macedonia (Philippi?) he writes two epistles whic resemble each other rather closely: I Timothy and Titus. (This is ju a *possibility*. There are many who think that Titus was written little later from Ephesus.)

6. The apostle journeys to Nicopolis (in Epirus), located on th east coast of the Ionian Sea. Here he spends the winter and is joine by Titus (Tit. 3:12).

7. Paul (and Titus?) journeys to Spain (Rom. 15:24).

8. Having returned to Asia Minor (see 5 above), he leaves Troph mus sick at Miletus, south of Ephesus (II Tim. 4:20).

9. At Troas he visits Carpus, at whose home he leaves his cloak (Tim. 4:13). He is rearrested. Cruel Nero was reigning (see p. 75). Th was the monster of iniquity who had murdered his step-brother, *h own mother*, his wife (Octavia), his tutor (Seneca), and many other When Rome was burned in 64, the people accused Nero of having s the city on fire. He sought to turn attention from himself and place the blame on the Christians. It is held by many that Peter suffere martyrdom about this time, hence, very shortly after having sent h two epistles (see pp. 361, 363). Paul, having been released earlie was traveling to various places (see 1-7 above). In the meantin Christianity had become a forbidden religion. Accordingly, sometin between 65 and 68 the apostle was again made a prisoner, perhaps Troas.

10. By way of Corinth, where Erastus remained (Rom. 16:2 II Tim. 4:20), Paul is brought to Rome. His second imprisonment w severe and brief (II Tim. 1:16, 17; 2:9). He was condemned to dea and beheaded on the Ostian Way, about three miles outside of th capital. Just before he died he wrote II Timothy, death alread staring him in the face. His shout of triumph was:

> *For I am already being poured out as a drink-offering, and the time of my departure has arrived. I have fought the good fight, I have finished the race, I have kept the faith; for the future there is in store for me the crown of righteousness, which the Lord, the righteous Judge, will award to me on*

> *that day: and not to me only, but to all who have longed for his appearing* (II Tim. 4:6-8).

Luke remained with him to the end (II Tim. 4:11). Whether Timothy and Mark reached Rome before the apostle's death we do not know.

Let us return now to 4 above. At Ephesus the Judaists were spreading their strange errors, placing great stress upon such things as endless genealogies, "profane and old wives' fables," and posing as "teachers of the law" (I Tim. 1:4, 7; 4:7). According to many interpreters—and they may be right!—these errorists also assumed that matter was evil (or at least the seat of evil) and therefore prohibited marriage, advocated abstinence from certain foods, and recognized only a spiritual resurrection (I Tim. 4:3; cf. II Tim. 2:18). Others, however, view I Timothy 4:3 as a prophecy of things to come rather than a description of things as they were at the time.

The "minister" at Ephesus was Timothy. We purposely surround the term "minister" with quotation marks, for Timothy's office was not exactly identical with that of the present day local pastor, whose main duties are limited to just one congregation to which he is bound until he accepts a call to go elsewhere. Timothy occupies a special office: he is Paul's special emissary, representing the apostle now in this, then in that congregation. Moreover, such men would often "minister" to an entire group of churches.

Timothy was of a rather timid disposition and also rather young. His task was difficult, for prominent church members—perhaps even church officers—were spreading the errors to which we referred in the preceding. Accordingly, Paul now sends him a letter, encouraging him, warning him with respect to the heresies which he will have to combat, and stressing the great importance of a spiritually well organized church, with church officers who are sound in doctrine and life. In this connection the apostle also gives directions for public worship.

There are those who think that I Timothy and Titus were written about the same time (perhaps even on the same day!) from the same place. It is impossible either to prove or to disprove this. The apostle, knowing that the reputation of the Cretans was none too good and earnestly desirous of rendering assistance to Titus in his attempt to raise the spiritual level of these people, writes an epistle in which the necessity of a sanctified life, a genuinely godly conduct, is emphasized. Specific directions—touching also the spiritual qualifications of the leaders—are given. Moreover, Titus is instructed to join Paul a Nicopolis. See 5 and 6 above.

For II Timothy see 10 above. The great apostle, realizing that h is about to depart from this life, asks Timothy to visit him and als to bring Mark; but, being in doubt whether these assistants will b able to reach Rome before his death, Paul admonishes Timothy tha whatever happens, he must keep clinging to the sound doctrine an must defend it unceasingly against every adversary.

The three Pastorals are similar, but each places emphasis upon certain aspect of the church's welfare: I Timothy, upon the publi worship and proper organization of the church; Titus, upon th sanctified life or conduct of the church; II Timothy, upon the soun doctrine of the church.[1]

I Timothy
THE APOSTLE GIVES DIRECTIONS FOR PUBLIC WORSHIP AND FOR THE PROPER ORGANIZATION OF THE CHURCH

1 **I. The apostle.**

A. He had journeyed to Macedonia, leavin Timothy in Ephesus to combat prevaler heresies.

B. He thanks God who made him—the chief c sinners—a minister of the Gospel.

2 **II. Directions for public worship.**

3-6 **III. The proper organization of the church (and th proper relation among its members).**

Expanded outline:

I Timothy
THE APOSTLE GIVES DIRECTIONS FOR PUBLIC WORSHIP AND FOR THE PROPER ORGANIZATION OF THE CHURCH

1 **I. The apostle.**

A. He had journeyed to Macedonia, leavir

1. R. Erdman, *An Exposition of the Pastoral Epistles,* p. 10.

Timothy in Ephesus to combat prevalent heresies.

B. He thanks God who made him—the chief of sinners—a minister of the gospel.

2 **II. Directions for public worship.**

A. *Men* must lift up holy hands in prayer for all classes of people, for it is the will of God the Savior that all be saved.

B. *Women* must dress in becoming attire and must not teach but learn in quietness with all submissiveness.

3-6 **III. The proper organization of the church (and the proper relation among its members).**

3 A. *Elders, deacons,* and *women who render auxiliary service* in the congregation must be spiritually and morally qualified for the good order of the church of the living God, the church of Jesus Christ, "he who was manifest in the flesh . . . received up in glory."

4 B. *The "minister"* (Timothy) must diligently combat (Judaistic) heresy and attend to the public reading of Scripture, preaching, and teaching. He must be an example to all. He must know how to deal judiciously with old and young of either sex.

5 C. *Lone widows* (i.e., those without children) must be "honored" by the church. *Widows who have children* or grandchildren should receive a return from them. *Widows who perform an auxiliary function in the church* must have the necessary qualifications. *The congregation* must consider the elders to be worthy of double honor, particularly those who labor in the Word and in teaching. These rules must be kept without discrimination.

6:1, 2 D. *Slaves* must honor and serve their masters, especially when the latter are believers.

6:3-21 E. *Those who strive after riches* and regard godliness a means of gain know nothing, etc.

Those who are rich in material possession must be admonished not to place their hop on earthly riches but on the bountiful God Timothy is exhorted to discharge faithfull the mandate which he has received.

Titus
THE SANCTIFIED LIFE (or CONDUCT) OF THE CHURCH

1 **I. Precepts for congregational life.**

2 **II. Precepts for family (and individual) life.**

3 **III. Precepts for social (i.e., public) life.**

Expanded outline:

Titus
THE SANCTIFIED LIFE (or CONDUCT) OF THE CHURCH

1 **I. Precepts for congregational life.**

A. Elders are to be appointed in each town.

B. They should be well qualified, for Crete is no lacking in disreputable individuals and Juda izers.

2 **II. Precepts for family (and individual) life.**

A. All classes of individuals that compose th home circle should conduct themselves i such a manner that by their life they ador the doctrine of God, their Savior.

B. Reason: to all classes of individuals the grac of God has appeared unto sanctification an unto joyful expectation of the gloriou appearance of their great God and Savio Jesus Christ.

3 **III. Precepts for social (i.e., public) life.**

A. Believers should be obedient to the rulin authorities.

B. They should be kind to all men, whereas it was the kindness of God, the Savior, which brought about salvation. Those who are not kind but quarrelsome and factious should be rejected after one or two admonitions.

The following brief outline is not only true to the actual contents f II Timothy but also memorizes easily (it rhymes):

II Timothy
THE SOUND DOCTRINE OF THE CHURCH

1 I. Hold onto it.

2 II. Teach it.

3 III. Abide in it.

4 IV. Preach it.

This can be expanded as follows:

II Timothy
THE SOUND DOCTRINE OF THE CHURCH

1 I. **Hold onto it** (i.e., follow its pattern).

A. As did grandmother Lois and mother Eunice, Onesiphorus; and as I do.

B. Though it causes you to suffer hardship and desertion.

2 II. **Teach it** (i.e., cause it to be taught).

A. For it brings great reward: "If we endure, we shall also reign with him," but vain questionings breed quarrels.

B. For its contents are glorious: "Jesus Christ, risen from the dead, of the seed of David"; "The Lord knows those who are his"; and "Let every one who names the name of the Lord depart from unrighteousness."

3 III. **Abide in it** (i.e., remain faithful to it).

A. Don't be misled by people who have its forr not its power.

B. It is based on Scripture, God-breathed.

4 IV. **Preach it** (i.e., proclaim, herald it).

A. In season, out of season, as long as men a willing to listen, for they will not always c so.

B. In view of the fact that I (Paul) am about "set sail." Hence visit me soon, for Demas h forsaken me. Bring Mark along. Bring m travel cloak, books, parchments. Alexande the metal worker, opposed me, but I w rescued from the lion's mouth, and I will saved for God's heavenly kingdom.

Chapel of the Ascension on the Mount of Olives. The dome is Islamic, but the lower part is of Crusader architecture.
Levant Photo Service

Hebrews 31

ee also pp. 449, 456.

The historical background of Hebrews is probably as follows: eter had received his inheritance in the heavens; Paul, his crown. 'hese deaths shocked believers everywhere. Two great leaders had een removed from the earthly scene.

In Rome a church had been established even long before Paul ntered that city for the first time as a prisoner. It consisted largely f converts from the *Gentile* world; see p. 342. To that church Paul ad addressed an epistle. However, when he arrived in Rome, he nmediately proclaimed the gospel to the *Jews*. The result was that some believed . . . some disbelieved" (Acts 28:24); see p. 199. It is ltogether probable that when persecution arose (see p. 406) it was t first directed against the old, established congregation of chiefly ;entile believers. The Jews, being the more recent converts and in a lass by themselves, escaped for a while (Heb. 12:4). Soon, however, ll this began to change. Christianity became a forbidden religion, nd the threat of imminent persecution faced everyone who vorshiped the Christ. Moreover, this persecution was of the most itter variety.

It is not surprising, therefore, that among the more recent :onverts–i.e., the body of Jewish believers who did not belong to he old predominantly Gentile church and continued to meet by hemselves–the tendency became apparent to desert the cause of :hrist. Apostasy was the paramount danger. See Hebrews 2:1-3; 3:6, .2; 4:14; 6:3-6; 10:24-26, 29, 35; 12:12, 13, 25; 13:9. \ccordingly, God moved one of his servants to write a "word of :xhortation" (Heb. 13:22), in order that the Jewish believers whom ıe addressed might adhere stedfastly to their faith in Jesus, whom he described as being infinitely superior to the Jewish prophets, th angels, Moses, Joshua, Aaron, etc.

No one knows who wrote this epistle. That it was not Paul is clear

1. Hebrews is anonymous, unlike Paul's epistles.

2. Hebrews is completely different in form from Paul's epistles The latter, with slight variations, follow a certain pattern—salutatio followed by thanksgiving (or by doxology and thanksgiving)—which i completely absent in Hebrews.

3. About the last thing Paul would ever say is found in Hebrew 2:3. He emphasized the fact that he had received his gospel directl from Christ (Gal. 1:11 ff.; I Cor. 9:1 ff.; 15:8 ff.).

4. The calm, balanced style of Hebrews is not at all similar to th deeply emotional, abrupt style which characterizes Paul's epistles.

5. The Greek which the author of Hebrews employs belongs t the literary *Koine*, while the Greek employed by Paul approaches th vernacular *Koine*. It is, however, incorrect to say that Hebrews use "better" Greek than is found in Paul's epistles. The Greek, in bot cases, is good, but of a different kind.

6. In Hebrews we find the antithesis of "antitype" (see th peculiar use of that term in Hebrews 9:24; contrast its use in I Pete 3:21) versus type, earthly versus heavenly things, shadow versu reality. In the Pauline epistles the antithesis is that between faith an law works, spirit and flesh, grace and sin, etc.

7. When the author of Hebrews quotes the Old Testament, he use the LXX version. Paul shows no such preference for this version.

8. Paul uses the title "the Lord Jesus Christ" with grea frequency. Hebrews, on the contrary, prefers the simple "Jesus" o at times, "Jesus Christ."

9. The characteristically Pauline phrase "in Christ" does not occu in Hebrews.

10. There are many other differences. Paul uses the term *faith* in slightly different sense than does Hebrews. He often asks his reade to become imitators of him in his willingness to endure persecutio for the sake of Christ. Contrast with this Hebrews 10:32; 13:3. An so one could continue.

Who, then, is this Jewish Christian, with a Hellenistic backgroun thoroughly at home in the Scriptures, who has heard the gospel fro the lips not of Christ but of the first witnesses, and is acquainte with Timothy (13:23)? Many answers have been given even in th rliest centuries. The strongest arguments have been advanced in vor of Barnabas and Apollos. The best answer to the question is at we simply do not know.

The readers, as we see it, were in all probability—one cannot be *re* about it!—the Jewish Christians in Rome who formed distinct ody and had been brought to Christ long after the founding of the edominantly Gentile church in that city. This belief that the aders lived in *Rome*, not in Jerusalem, is favored by Alford, Dods *xpositor's Greek Testament*), Erdman, Greydanus, Grosheide, unter, Lenski, Rees (*I.S.B.E.*, art. "Hebrews"), and many other able holars. In our opinion, it deserves the preference. Among the many asons which have been advanced in favor of this position are the llowing:

1. The most natural (though not the only possible) interpretation Hebrews 13:24 is: "Those who come from Italy wish to be membered to you." The original uses the preposition *from*. This rase would seem to place the author somewhere outside of Italy. his company there are believers "from Italy" who are tendering eir cordial regards to their friends who have remained in the other country. This makes good sense. Now, let us imagine for a oment that the author is writing from Italy to Jewish Christians in rusalem. In that case he would probably have written: "Those in *ome* (or some other definite city) convey their greetings." Certainly ot everybody in Italy was sending best regards!

2. According to Hebrews 2:3 the readers seem not to have heard e Lord himself but only the early witnesses. But Jerusalem and idea had been the scene of Christ's Early and Later Judean Minis- y. Here, too, he suffered and died. Hence it would seem that the aders either belonged to the second generation of Jewish Christians in rusalem and to the period after the beginning of the Jewish War, or at they lived elsewhere; i.e., outside of Jerusalem. The first alterna- ve is, however, most improbable: we know that about the time of e Jewish War the Christians fled the city, and we do not find a ody of Jewish Christians in Jerusalem for many, many years. It is, erefore, logical to seek the readers elsewhere.

3. Before A.D. 70 the temple was still standing in Jerusalem. ow, if the epistle had been intended for Jewish Christians in erusalem, why did not the author refer to that temple and its ritual? e never does. He constantly refers to the original tabernacle as escribed in the Book of Exodus. See Hebrews 8:5; 9; etc. The fact

that the author uses the present tense (8:4; 9:6, 9; 10:1 ff.; 13:1 cannot possibly prove that the temple services were still being co ducted. One would first have to prove that the author is speaki about temple ritual at all. If, as is very evident, he is discussing t tabernacle service and its significance, then these present tenses mu of course, be taken as historical presents. These occur in gre abundance in the New Testament. Hebrews 10:2 is not difficu Read it in the light of the preceding verse: the sacrifices never ceas at the end of a given year; they had to be repeated the next year.

4. It is hard to believe that argumentation based upon the LX version of the Old Testament would be very convincing to *Jewi* believers *in Jerusalem* who were in danger of falling away from t faith.

5. The mention of almsgiving as one of the chief graces of t "Hebrews" (6:10; 10:34) tells against Jerusalem. As pictured in t Book of Acts, the church in Jerusalem was poor and in need of he from elsewhere (Acts 11:29, 30; 24:17; Rom. 15:25; I Cor. 16:1- II Cor. 8, 9; Gal. 2:16).

6. It could hardly be charged against the mother church in Jeru lem that it had produced no teachers (Heb. 5:12).

7. The earliest recognition of this epistle was in Rome, just as would expect if we believe that it was addressed to people living that city. Clement of Rome makes use of Hebrews. So does t Shepherd of Hermas.

8. Timothy was well known in Rome (Phil. 1:1; Col. 1:1; II Ti 3:9; Philem. 1; cf. Heb. 13:23).

9. The Jews in Rome and elsewhere were "Hebrews" as well those in Jerusalem. Paul of *Tarsus* calls himself "a Hebrew of t Hebrews" (Phil. 3:5; cf. II Cor. 11:22).

Even among those who believe that the epistle was addressed Jewish Christians in Rome there is a difference of opinion wi respect to the exact occasion which made this letter necessary. are agreed that the readers were in danger of deserting the cause Christ. The question, however, remains: does the author warn agair a turning to *infidelity* or does he point out the danger of a retu to *Judaism*? Some favor the former position, on the basis of Hebre 3:12. Others, however, accept the second alternative, which al commends itself to us: the Jewish Christians in Rome were in dang of returning to their synagogues in order that they might esca persecution. This position finds support not so much in isolat assages (e.g., Heb. 13:9-13) as in the entire argumentation of the pistle. The author throughout proves that the Christian religion is finitely superior to the Jewish.

In attempting to outline this beautiful New Testament book one act must be borne in mind: the author again and again *intersperses* is reasoning with definite warnings against apostasy. Sometimes ese admonitions *follow* the argument; sometimes, they *precede* it. ometimes the warning consists of a sentence or two. Sometimes it onsists of a lengthy paragraph. In studying the following outline, one ust bear this fact constantly in mind.

Hebrews

A WORD OF EXHORTATION: JESUS IS WORTHY OF YOUR FAITH. HAVE FAITH IN HIM, THEREFORE, AND DO NOT FALL AWAY.

:1–10:18	**I. Jesus is worthy of your faith.** *(This section is interspersed with warnings against apostasy).*
1, 2	A. As a Revealer he is greater than the prophets and the angels.
3	B. As a Mediator he is greater than Moses (the "son" versus the "servant").
4:1-13	C. As a Rest-Provider he is greater than Joshua.
:14–10:18	D. As a High Priest he is greater than Aaron.
	1. He belongs to a better order, namely, that of Melchizedek.
	2. He is the minister of a better tabernacle.
	3. He has brought a better sacrifice.
:19–13:25	**II. Have faith in him, therefore, and do not fall away.**
10:19-39	A. The indispensable character of unwavering faith.
11	B. Its nature and its heroes.
12, 13	C. Its fruits, such as endurance, peace, love, obedience, stedfastness, prayerfulness.

The site of Jacob's Well, as seen through an opening in the unfinished church built at the site.
Levant Photo Service

32 The Gospel and Epistles of John

The Gospel of John

See also pp. 449-451, 456.

After the death of Peter and a little later of Paul, the Lord provided another great leader who took upon himself the care of some of the churches formerly served by the two departed leaders. We refer, of course, to the apostle John. He was the son of Zebedee and Salome (Mark 1:19; 16:1, 2; cf. Matt. 27:56). Zebedee was probably a prosperous fisherman. He employed hired servants (Mark 1:20). It is supposed that Salome was a sister of the virgin Mary (Matt. 27:56; cf. John 19:25). If this be correct, Jesus and John were cousins. John's brother James is usually mentioned first and was probably the elder of the two.

Before he became a follower of Jesus the apostle John was a disciple of John the Baptist. In his later years the apostle vividly recalled the moment when he first met Jesus and decided to become his follower. Says he: "It was about the tenth hour," (John 1:39). That first meeting of which we have any record was followed after an interval by the decision to become a regular disciple (Mark 1:16 ff.; Luke 5:10) and then an apostle (Matt. 10:2) sent forth and charged by Jesus.

John and James appear to have been men with pent-up emotions, flashing forth on occasion. Jesus calls them "sons of thunder" (Mark 3:17). When Jesus is on his way to Jerusalem and the inhabitants of a Samaritan village refuse to lodge him, the fiery anger of the sons of Zebedee flashes forth in the words: "Lord, do you want us to call down fire from heaven and consume them?" (Luke

9:54). Surely, John was "the disciple of love." Love and flashin anger are not mutually exclusive. It was genuine love for Jesus which manifested itself in this ill-conceived utterance. It was love als which caused John to interfere with the man who, though castin out demons in the name of Jesus, was not a regular disciple (Luk 9:49, 50).

It is a mark of John's genuine humility that he never mentions b name those who belong to the inner circle of his relatives. Althoug he loved the Master intensely, it is not his love for Christ bu the latter's love for the apostle that is emphasized in the Fourth Gospel. John styles himself "the disciple whom Christ loved" (John 13:21).

Jesus clearly predicted that John's death would be different fror that of Peter (John 21:18-23), a passage which disposes of the ide that John suffered martyrdom at an early date.

In the Gospels and Acts we often find John in the company o Peter, both before and after Christ's resurrection (John 1:35-42 13:23, 24; 18:15, 16; 20:2; 21:20; Acts 3:1; 4:19; 8:14). After th resurrection John is one of the pillars of the church at Jerusaler (Gal. 2:9; Acts 15:6). He probably left Jerusalem at the beginning o the Jewish War, A.D. 66. According to the testimony of many earl witnesses the apostle went to Ephesus, where he lived many years was banished to the island of Patmos during the reign of Domitia (see p. 75), was allowed to return to Ephesus by Nerva, and die at the beginning of Trajan's reign, having reached a very advance age.

It was Irenaeus who said: "Afterward John, the disciple of th Lord, who also leaned upon his breast, published a Gospel during hi residence at Ephesus in Asia." Both external and internal evidenc support this view. According to the information furnished by th Gospel itself the author was a Jew, as is evident from his style, hi constant reference to Old Testament prophecy (John 2:17; 7:38 10:34; 12:15; 12:38-41; 13:18; 17:12; 19:24, 36, 37), his acquain tance with Jewish customs (2:6, 13; 3:25; 11:55; 13:5; 18:28 19:31), references to the Jewish Messianic expectation (7:27, 42 12:34) and to the Jewish feasts (7:37; 10:22, 23; 18:39), et Moreover, he was a Palestinian Jew who possessed detailed know edge of Palestinian topography (1:28; cf. 11:1; 2:14, 20; 5:1; 8: 10:22, 23; 11:18, 49; 18:1, 10). Finally, he was an eyewitness, on of the Twelve, one of the earliest disciples (1:35-42). The other tw ry early disciples were Andrew and Peter. A comparison with Mark 16-20, 29 indicates that the disciple who is never mentioned by ame and who was the author of the Fourth Gospel (John :20-24) must have been either James or John. But it is evident om John 21:19 that the author of the Fourth Gospel survived eter. This was not true with respect to James, who was put to eath in the year 44. Hence, the anonymous author must have een John.

The purpose of this Gospel is clearly stated in 20:31: ". . . these igns are written that you may believe that Jesus is the Christ, the on of God, and that believing you may have life in his name."

In distinction from the Synoptics, John's Gospel discusses not so nuch the kingdom as the king himself; reveals that Jesus from the ery beginning asserted his Messianic claim (see p. 144); describes, vith few exceptions, Christ's work in Judea; dwells at great length on he events and discourses which belong to a period of less than wenty-four hours (chs. 13-19); unmistakably indicates that the ctive ministry of our Lord extended over a period of at least three ears; and, in general, places great emphasis upon the spiritual haracter of Christ's task on earth. Nevertheless, John and the ynoptics, far from contradicting one another, supplement each ther.

The plan of John's Gospel is, indeed, beautiful. The arrangement s superb. We see the Word in his pre-incarnate glory, so that we may ppreciate his condescending love in coming to earth in order to save inners. In his earthly ministry he reveals himself to ever-widening ircles (see the outline below), and is rejected both in Judea and in Galilee. Nevertheless, he does not at once destroy those who have ejected him, but, instead, makes his tender appeal to sinners, that hey may believe in him. By two mighty deeds he reveals himself learly as the Messiah. But, though the Greeks seek him, the Jews, vho have seen such clear tokens of his character, love, and power, eject him. He turns to his "inner circle" and tenderly instructs them n the Upper Room just before his final suffering and death. In his ery death he overcomes the world and by means of his resurrection ne reveals the meaning of his cross. For a discussion of the contents of John's Gospel, see also whatever on pp. 131-173 is based on this Gospel.

Brief outline:

Gospel of John
JESUS, THE CHRIST, THE SON OR WORD OF GOD

1-12 **I. His public ministry.**

1-6 A. Before the final Feast of Tabernacles: th glory of the Word; the Word revealing himse to ever-widening circles; the Word rejected.

7-10 B. At the Feast of Tabernacles and at the Fea of the Dedication: the Word making h tender appeal to sinners.

11, 12 C. After the Feast of the Dedication: the Wo revealing himself clearly as the Messiah b two mighty deeds: the raising of Lazarus an the triumphal entry into Jerusalem.

13-21 **II. His private ministry.**

13 A. The Supper: the Word issuing and illustratin his new commandment.

14-17 B. Supper discourses and prayer: the Wo tenderly instructing his disciples and in pray committing them to his Father's care.

18, 19 C. Gethsemane to Golgotha: the Word dying as substitute for his people.

20, 21 D. Resurrection and appearances: the Word, b means of his resurrection, triumphing glo ously.

Expanded outline:

Gospel of John
JESUS, THE CHRIST, THE SON OR WORD OF GOD

1-12 **I. His public ministry.**

1-6 A. Before the final Feast of Tabernacles: th glory of the Word; the Word revealing himse to ever-widening circles; the Word rejected.

1:1-14 1. The glory of the Word.

1:1, 2 — a. The Word in the beginning.

1:3, 4 — b. The Word at the creation.

1:5-13 — c. The Word after the fall.

1:14 — d. The Word at the incarnation.

1:15–4:54 — 2. The Word revealing himself to ever-widening circles.

1:15-34 — a. To John the Baptist who testifies concerning him.

1:35–2:12 — b. To his immediate disciples (their testimony; their faith when they witness the first miracle; cf. 2:11).

2:13–4:42 — c. To Jerusalem (cleansing of the temple: reformation; Nicodemus: regeneration), Judea, and Samaria.

4:43-54 — d. To Galilee (the healing of the nobleman's son).

5, 6 — 3. The Word rejected.

5; see esp. v. 18 — a. In Judea (miracle at Bethesda).

6; see esp. v. 66 — b. In Galilee (feeding the five thousand, etc.).

7:1–10:39 uke 9:51–21) — B. At the Feast of Tabernacles and at the Feast of the Dedication: the Word making his tender appeal to sinners.

7 — 1. To the multitudes in the temple: "If anyone is thirsty, let him come to me and drink."

8 — 2. To the woman taken in adultery: "Go your way; from now on sin no more." Also to the multitude: "I am the light of the world."

9 — 3. To the man born blind whom he healed: "Do you believe in the Son of God? . . . You have both seen him, and he it is who speaks with you."

10:1-39 — 4. To the Pharisees, disciples, etc.: "I am the

good shepherd. . . . My sheep hear my voic
and I know them, and they follow me."

10:40–12:50 C. After the Feast of the Dedication: the Wor
revealing himself clearly as the Messiah b
two mighty deeds:

10:40–12:11 1. Having gone beyond the Jordan, *h*
afterward returns to Judea and rais
Lazarus of Bethany. He withdraws t
Ephraim. Returning again, he is anointe
by Mary at Bethany.

12:12-50 2. *He makes his triumphal entry int*
Jerusalem. The Greeks seek him but th
Jews reject him.

13-21 **II. His private ministry.**

13 A. The Supper: the Word issuing and illustratir
his new commandment.

14-17 B. Supper discourses and prayer: the Wo
tenderly instructing his disciples and in pray
committing them to his Father's care.

14-16 1. The instruction (Upper Room discourses

14 a. A word of comfort.

15 b. A word of admonition.

See 15:4 (1) Abide in me (our relation to Christ

See 15:12 (2) Love one another (our relation to or
another).

See 15:27 (3) Also bear witness (our relation to th
world).

16 c. A word of prediction.

17 2. The prayer: the Word praying for himse
and his own.

17:1-5 a. For himself.

17:6-19 b. For his immediate disciples.

17:20-26 c. For the church at large.

18, 19 C. Gethsemane to Golgotha: the Word dying a
substitute for his people.

18:1-11 1. The arrest.

18:12–19:16 2. The trial and denial.

19:17-37	3. The crucifixion.
19:38-42	4. The entombment.
20, 21	D. Resurrection and appearances.
20:1-18	1. Appearance to Mary Magdalene.
20:19-25	2. Appearance to the ten, Thomas being absent.
20:26-31	3. Appearance to the eleven. Purpose of this Gospel stated.
21	4. Appearance to the seven at the Sea of Tiberias (Peter's restoration). Conclusion.

Whereas it is the purpose of John's Gospel to select only those events from the life of our Lord in which his deity becomes most strikingly evident and whereas in doing this he enlarges on Christ's work and teachings in Judea, it is impossible to give a logical division of the book according to the chart of ministries. The logical dividing point is at the end of chapter 12, just as we gave it. Nevertheless, for the sake of chronological clarity and of showing more plainly how this Gospel is related to the others, we give below an indication of the various ministries as referred to in this Gospel. It should be compared with the summary outline of the Synoptics on pp. 383-384 and also with the chronological chart on p. 73.

In John the Preparation begins in eternity, and is described in I A 1 of the expanded outline (John 1:1-14).

The Inauguration is described in I A 2 a and b (John 1:15–2:12).

The Early Judean Ministry, which is not given in the Synoptics, is described in I A 2 c (John 2:13–4:42). (Here we include our Lord's work in Samaria.)

The period of the Great Galilean Ministry is described in I A 2 d–I A 3 b (John 4:36–6:71).

The Retirement Ministry is omitted in John. The Later Judean Ministry is described in I B (John 7:1–10:39).

The Perean Ministry is described in I C 1 (John 10:40–12:11). Observe, however, that while the raising of Lazarus occurred *during* the Perean Ministry, it actually took place in Judea, a fact on which John loves to dwell. So also the anointing by Mary occurred when Jesus returned to Judea (Bethany) from his Perean Ministry and was about to enter his week of suffering and death.

Ten chapters are devoted to the Passion Week and the Resurrection. This is I C 2–II D 4 (John 12:12–21:25).

The Epistles of John (with emphasis on I John)

Tradition informs us that the first readers of John's Gospel wer the churches in Asia Minor. A strange heresy was threatening thei purity and spiritual progress. It is very difficult to determine its exac nature, but from a close study of the Epistles of John and some c the early fathers we arrive at the conclusion that it was probably kind of incipient gnosticism. It was probably characterized by mos if not all, of the following features:

1. **Spirit-matter dualism**: matter is the source of evil; spirit, of th good.

2. **Docetism**: whereas the material body (the flesh) is the sourc and seat of evil, a real coming-into-the-flesh (or incarnation) i impossible. God is too pure to become united with the human body

3. **Cerinthianism**: whereas a real incarnation is unthinkable, w must distinguish between a heavenly Christ and an earthly Jesus. Th former never fully united with the latter but merely descended upo him at his baptism and left him again on the eve of his Passion Accordingly, the heavenly Christ did not suffer.

4. **Antinomianism** (a life that is contrary to God's holy law) whereas soul and body have nothing to do with each other, the sou cannot be held responsible for the deeds of the body; hence, let th body do whatever it pleases. "Sin" is an inherent quality of bodil existence: "*I*" do not commit sin.

5. **Knowledge, not love, is the highest virtue.**

In the light of this summary we are able to understand some of th statements which occur in the Epistles of John:

II John 7: *"For many deceivers have gone out into the world, eve those who do not confess Jesus Christ as coming in the flesh."*

I John 4:2: *"This is how you can recognize God's Spirit: ever spirit that confesses that Jesus Christ has come in the flesh is from God"* Contrast (1) and (2) above.

I John 5:5, 6: *"And who is he that overcomes the world, but he wh believes that Jesus is the Son of God? This is the one who came b water and blood, even Jesus Christ; not with the water only, but wit the water and with the blood"*; i.e., the historical Jesus is the Chris not only in his baptism ("the water") but also in his Passion ("th blood"). Contrast (3) above.

I John 1:8, 10: *"If we say that we have no sin, we deceive ourselve* *ıd the truth is not in us. . . . If we say that we have not ıned, we make him a liar and his word is not in us."*

I John 3:4, 6: *"Every one who practices sin also practices wlessness; in fact, sin is lawlessness . . . no one who continues to sin ıs seen him or known him.* Contrast (4) above.

I John 3:13-18: *"We know that we have passed out of death into ˈe, because we love the brothers. . . . But whoever has the world's ods, and sees his brother in need but closes his heart against him, ɔw can the love of God remain in him? My dear children, let us not ve with words or tongue, but with deeds and in truth."* Contrast) above.

John was fully aware of the fact that when the errorists or antichrists" denied that the Jesus of history was and is the Christ, ıey attacked the very foundations of the Christian faith. Hence, he oldly declares that this heresy is "of the devil." But he writes his irst Epistle not only in order to warn against this error and to ɔndemn it, but also in order that the marks of those who have ːllowship with God and are his children may be clearly described so ıat true believers may have peace and joy. For a fuller statement of ıe apostle's purpose in writing this beautiful epistle study the ɔllowing passages: 1:3, 4; 2:12-14, 21; 5:13.

That the Gospel and the Epistles of John have much in common is greed on every side. Let the reader compare for himself. It is not so ːadily granted that also the Book of Revelation and the Epistles have ıuch in common; nevertheless, this is, indeed, the case. Neither ıoves in a straight line: the contents of both must be arranged along ıe lines of parallelism. What we mean is this: just as in Revelation he "seer" describes the conflict between Christ and Satan (or etween the church and the world) until the Judgment Day is eached *and then turns back to cover the same ground once more ntil the Judgment Day has again arrived*, so also the First Epistle, aving discussed the three marks of the true believer, *returns again to ˈs starting point, and,* having reviewed them again, *returns once ıore!* Both Revelation and I John are definitely *cyclic* or *arallelistic* in their arrangement. The resemblance is even closer: in oth cases the cycles do not merely repeat what has been said before. here is definite *progress,* i.e., something is added; see the outline elow—so that we can apply the term *progressive parallelism* to the rain of thought in both books. See also p. 236 and p. 443.

This Epistle of John is truly a gem! It is full of teaching and comfort for every age. The following outline is sufficiently concise be committed to memory. Besides, it is very easy and becomes easi after one has read I John several times.

I John
THE MARKS OF THOSE WHO HAVE FELLOWSHIP WITH GOD

Prologue: We proclaim the Word of Life, whom we have seen a heard, in order that you may have fellowship with us and with t Father and the Son, and may rejoice, vss. 1-4.

1, 2	**I. God is Light and sheds light on our pat** Therefore,
1:5–2:6	A. God's children *walk in the light*: they confe their sins and obey his commandments.
2:7-17	B. *They love the brothers,* not the world.
2:18-29	C. *They confess* that *Jesus* is the Christ.
3:1–4:6	**II. God is Life and imparts life to us** (see especial 3:1, 2, 9). Therefore,
3:1-10a	A. "God's children"—how glorious is the lo which the name implies!—*do what is right a purify themselves.*
3:10b-24	B. *They love the brothers* in answer to the lo of the Son, who laid down his life for us.
4:1-6	C. *They confess* that *Jesus Christ* has come the flesh.
4:7–5:21	**III. God is Love and has manifested his love to u** Therefore,
4:7–5:3	A. *God's children love the brothers* (cf. B unde and II above) in answer to the love of *t Father*, who gave *his Son*, and of *the Spir* who bears witness.
5:4-12	B. *They confess* that *Jesus Christ* is the Son God, and believing in him, have eternal life.
5:13-21	C. Conclusion: the certainties of the Christi faith ("we know"); the final admonitio Summary of certainties:

1. Certainty of possessing everlasting life.
2. Certainty of answered prayer.
3. Certainty of the believer's life of sanctification.
4. Certainty of the absolute antithesis between believers and the world.
5. Certainty of the fact that our convictions correspond with reality.
6. Final admonition: "Little children, guard yourselves from idols."

II and III John

In II John "the elder," who, as both tradition and style would seem to indicate, was the apostle John, is writing to "the elect lady," probably a particular congregation in Asia Minor. The author, probably writing from Ephesus, rejoices greatly that there are those who are "walking in the truth." But whereas he has heard that some deceivers have gone forth into the church who deny that Jesus Christ had come in the flesh (see p. 428), he bids believers shun such teachers: "If any one comes to you, and does not bring this teaching, do not receive him into your house, and do not give him a greeting: for he who gives him greeting shares in his evil work" (vss. 10, 11).

The "boss" of the congregation resisted the authority of the apostle and instead of refusing to extend hospitality to false teachers, refused to welcome John's own messengers: "Diotrephes, who loves to have the pre-eminence among them, will have nothing to do with us" (III John 9). This evil individual even expelled from the congregation those who would welcome them. But Gaius, another church member, received the apostle's missionaries and showed them every kind of hospitality. John praises his conduct and, by implication, expresses the hope that Gaius will bestow the same love upon Demetrius, the bearer of the letter, whom he warmly recommends (III John 12).

The contents of II John and III John, which belong together, can be summarized as follows:

II John
DO NOT SHOW HOSPITALITY TO THOSE WHO REJECT THE TRUTH

III John
SHOW HOSPITALITY TO THOSE WHO PROCLAIM THE TRUTH

How would you expand these brief summarizing statements int an outline?

The altar of Zeus at Pergamum, to which the apostle John referred when he spoke of "Satan's Throne." This reconstructed model stands in the State Museum at Berlin.
Staatliche Museen Zu Berlin

Revelation 33

:e also pp. 449, 456-457.

Beautiful beyond description is the last book of the Bible. It is :autiful in form, in symbolism, in purpose, and in meaning. Where literature do we find anything that excels the majestic description f the Son of Man walking in the midst of the seven golden lamp-ands (1:12-20)? Where in Scripture do we find a more vivid and cturesque portrayal of the Christ, Faithful and True, going forth nto victory, seated upon a white horse, arrayed with a garment rinkled with blood, followed by the armies of heaven (19:11-16)? here, again, do we find a sharper contrast than that between the oom of Babylon on the one hand and the felicity of Jerusalem the olden on the other (chps. 18, 19, 21, 22)? And where are the rone in heaven and the blessedness of heavenly life depicted in a anner more simple, yet beautiful in its very simplicity (4:2–5:14; :13-17)? What a wealth of comfort; what an insight into the future; ove all, what an unveiling of the love of God is contained in the ords of the prophecy of this book!

What is the purpose of this book?

The Book of Revelation seeks to impart comfort. That is its main urpose—to comfort the militant church in its struggle against the rces of evil. It abounds in consolation for afflicted believers. To em is given the assurance that:

God sees their tears (7:17; 21:4).

Their prayers rule the world! (8:3, 4).

Their death is precious in his sight, and their soul immediately ascends to heaven. A heaven whose glory far surpasses the intensity of earthly suffering (14:13; 20:4).

Their final victory is assured (15:2).

Their blood will be avenged (6:9; 8:3).

Their Christ lives and reigns forever and forever! It is he wh governs the world in the interest of his church (5:7, 8). He coming again to take his people to himself in "the Marriage Supp of the Lamb" and to live with them forever in a rejuvenat universe (chps. 21, 22).

Thinking of that glorious hope, that Second Coming, our hear begin to throb with joy; our souls are consumed with yearning, wi breathless impatience; our eyes attempt to pierce the dark, treme dous sea of clouds, hoping that the glorious descent of the Son Man may burst upon the view. It is a longing which gushes in words: "And the Spirit and the bride say, Come, And he that hear let him say, Come."

But what do our eyes behold? Already he is with us—with us *the Spirit,* walking in the midst of the seven golden lampstan (1:12-20). "And he laid his right hand upon me, saying, Fe not; I am the first and the last, and the living one; and I w dead, and behold, I am alive for evermore, and I have the keys Death and Hades." More than conquerors are we through him wh loved us!

What is the theme of this book?

The theme of this book is: *The Victory of Christ and of H Church over Satan and His Helpers.*

The Apocalypse intends to show us that things are not what th *seem.* The beast that comes up out of the abyss *seems* to victorious. He

> *. . . will make war with them, overcome them, and kill them. And their dead bodies will lie in the street of the great city, which spiritually is called Sodom and Egypt, where also their Lord was crucified. For three days and a half men from every people, tribe, language, and nation will gaze on their dead bodies and refuse to let them be buried. And those who live on earth will gloat over them and will indulge in celebrations. They will send each other gifts, because these two prophets had tormented these earth-dwellers"* (11:7b-10).

But this rejoicing is premature. In reality it is the believer wh triumphs:

> *But after the three days and a half a breath of life from God entered them, and they stood upon their feet; and great fear fell upon those who saw them . . . the dominion over the world has become the dominion of our Lord and of his Christ; and he shall reign forever and ever (11:11, 15b).*

Throughout the prophecies of this wonderful book the Christ is ever pictured as the Victor, the Conquerer (1:18; 2:8; 5:9ff.; 6:2; 11:15; 12:9ff.; 14:1, 14; 15:2ff.; 19:16; 20:4; 22:3). He conquers death, Hades, the dragon, the beast, the false prophet, the men who worship the beast, etc. *He* is victorious; hence, so are *we*—even when we seem to be hopelessly defeated!

Do you see that band of believers?

Are their garments splashed and filthy? They wash their robes and make them white in the blood of the Lamb (7:14; 22:14). Are they "in great tribulation"? They come out of it (7:14). Are they killed? They stand upon their feet (11:11). Are they persecuted by the dragon, the beast, and the false prophet? In the end you see them standing victoriously on Mount Zion. Rather, you see the Lamb, and with him a hundred and forty-four thousand, having his name and the name of his Father written on their foreheads (14:1). They triumph over the beast (15:2).

Does it *seem* as if their prayers are not heard? (6:10). The judgments sent upon the earth are God's answer to their prayers (8:3-5). Why, these very prayers constitute the real key that will unlock the mysteries of any sound philosophy of history.

Do they seem to be defeated? In *reality* they *reign!* Yes, they reign upon the earth (5:10), in heaven with Christ a thousand years (20:4), and in the heaven and earth for ever and ever (22:5).

And what happens to those who *seem* to be conquerors? We see them arise out of the abyss, the sea, and the earth. Yes, we see the dragon (12:3), the beast (13:1), the false prophet (13:11), and Babylon (14:8), in that order! And then? We see them go down in defeat—Babylon (18:2), the beast and the false prophet (19:20), and the dragon (20:10), in that (exactly reversed) order!

Agaln, do you wish to know the theme of the book? Let the book speak for itself. Its theme is stated most gloriously and completely in 17:14:

> *These shall war against the Lamb, and the Lamb shall overcome them, for he is Lord of lords, and King of kings; and*

they also shall overcome that are with him, called and chosen and faithful.

Who wrote this book?

The author tells us his name is *John* (1:1, 4, 9; 22:8). Th question is: Which John? The apostle or another? Some deny th John, the beloved disciple, wrote the Apocalypse. They point out striking *difference* between the grammar, the style, and the gener tone of John's Gospel and his Epistles on the one hand and Revel tion on the other. These differences must be admitted. But does th mean that John the Apostle did not write the Apocalypse? In ou opinion, it does not. There are various ways in which these diffe ences can be explained. Besides, we should not exaggerate them There is also a strong body of *resemblance* between John's Gosp and the Apocalypse. There are certain similarities even in peculi grammatical constructions and characteristic expressions (cf. Joh 7:37 with Rev. 22:17, John 10:18 with Rev. 2:7, John 1:29 wit Rev. 5:6, John 20:12 with Rev. 3:4, and John 1:1 with Rev. 19:13

The early church is almost unanimous in ascribing Revelation t the apostle John. That was the opinion of Justin Martyr, Irenaeu (who was a disciple of a disciple of the apostle John), the Muratoria Canon, Clement of Alexandria, Tertullian, Origen, and Hippolytu

When we add to this that according to a very strong tradition th apostle John was banished to the isle of Patmos (1:9), and that h spent his closing years at Ephesus, to which the first of the seve epistles of the Apocalypse was addressed (2:1), the conclusion th the last book of the Bible was written by "the disciple whom Jesu loved" is inescapable.

When did John write the book? In the year 69 (or even earlier), must we reverse the digits and make it 96? We have not found single really cogent argument in support of the earlier date.

How is the book arranged?

A careful reading of Revelation makes it clear that *the boo consists of seven sections. These seven run parallel.* They span th entire dispensation from the First Coming to the Second Coming Christ. Usually, whenever the author reaches the Judgment Day it clearly evident that he returns again to describe the same length period—First Coming to Second Coming of Christ—from a differen aspect. The reader should see this for himself. The very first sectio chapters 1—3, appears to span the entire dispensation, from Christ

irst Coming to shed his blood for his people (1:5), to his Second
oming unto judgment (1:7). Chapters 4–7 constitute the next
atural division of the book. Here the very first reference to Christ
ictures him as having been slain and now ruling from heaven (5:5,
). That description takes us back to the purpose of the First
oming. Toward the end of the section the final judgment is intro-
uced (6:12-17; 7:9-17). The next section consists of chapters 8–11.
lso at the close of this section there is a very clear reference to the
inal judgment (11:15, 18). This brings us to the fourth section,
hapters 12–14. It begins with a very clear reference to the First
oming. The birth of our Savior and his ascension to heaven is
learly mentioned (12:5). The section closes with a stirring descrip-
ion of Christ's Second Coming unto judgment (14:14ff.). Moreover,
hen one compares chapter 12 with chapter 20 (12:3, 9 with 20:2,
), it becomes clear that also at the beginning of chapter 20 we are
tanding on the threshold of the new dispensation; i.e., we have
eturned to the First Coming of Christ. Revelation 20:11ff. clearly
escribes the Second Coming and the judgment. In Revelation 21
nd 22 the new heaven and earth are described. Moreover, if, as we
ave indicated, the section on the seven seals, chs. 4–7, spans the
ntire dispensation, it would seem natural to conclude that the
ections on the seven trumpets and the seven bowls do also (chs.
–11, 15, 16). Indeed, it seems probable that all seven sections are
o be interpreted as spanning the entire dispensation.

What we have here is *parallelism* or *cyclic arrangement,* just as in I
ohn (see p. 429). Remember that I John and Revelation come
rom the same author. Nevertheless, the cycles are no mere repeti-
ions. Each one adds to the thought of the preceding one. Every
ection, moreover, is exactly where it should be. There is no confu-
ion anywhere. Thus the church always functions as a *lampstand*
"candlestick"), a light-bearer, causing the light of the gospel to shine
orth into the darkness of the world, (chs. 1–3: the seven lamp-
tands). What is ever the result? This, that the world always, again
nd again throughout history, persecutes the church. And that is the
neaning and substance of the seven seals of persecution (chs. 4–7).
But does God allow this persecution to go unpunished? Indeed not!
Ie is ever sending upon the world his initial judgments, symbolized
nder the figure of the seven trumpets of judgment (chs. 8–11).
Moreover, if at any time the world does not take these initial
udgments to heart but continues impenitent, it receives the outpour-
ng of the seven bowls of final wrath (chs. 15, 16). The struggle

between the church and the world (chs. 1–11–the first three sec tions–ever indicates a deeper conflict between the dragon (Satan and Christ (chs. 12–22, the last four sections). The devil alway employs the three allies mentioned in chapters 12–14: 1) the beas out of the sea, i.e., the world as center of persecution, 2) the beas out of the earth or the false prophet, i.e., world as center of fals religion and false philosophy, and 3) Babylon, i.e., world as center o seduction. The three aim their attacks respectively against the bodies minds, and hearts of believers. These allies of Satan always—agai and again throughout the entire dispensation—go down in defeat. I chapters 17–19 the two beasts and Babylon are defeated; in chapte 20 the dragon (Satan) himself is "cast into the lake of fire an brimstone." Over the ruins of Babylon there hovers the vision o Jerusalem the Golden (chs. 21, 22). God's people are ever victorious

What we have here, therefore, is a most beautiful and comfortin philosophy of history, which shows us that God himself through hi Christ is ruling over the affairs of men in the interest of his churc which, though seemingly defeated, is ever victorious.

The teaching of these seven sections, which reveal such a glorio unity and gradual thought progression, is in agreement with th entire Bible:

Rev. 1–3: The lampstands of witness-bearing. Compare Mat 5:14: "You are the light of the world."

Rev. 4–7: The seals of persecution. Compare John 16:33: "In th world you have tribulation: but be of good cheer; I have overcom the world."

Rev. 8–11: The trumpets of judgment or initial vengeance. Com pare Lk. 18:7: "And shall not God avenge his elect that cry to hi day and night?"

Rev. 12–14: The Lamb (Christ) versus the dragon (Satan) and h helpers. Compare Gen. 3:15: "And I will put enmity between yo and the woman, and between your seed and her seed: he sha bruise your head, and you shall bruise his heel."

Rev. 15, 16: The bowls of final wrath upon impenitent persec tors. Compare Rom. 2:5: "But because of your hardness an impenitent heart you are storing up wrath. . . ."

Rev. 17–19: The fall of Babylon and of the beasts. Compare John 2:17: "The world and its desires pass away."

Rev. 20–22: The dragon's doom. Jerusalem the Golden. Compa

Rom. 8:37: "We are more than conquerors through him who loved us," and Jude 6.

To this conception of the Apocalypse we give the name progressive parallelism. It is graphically portrayed in the chart on p. 443.

Brief Outline:

Revelation

THE VICTORY OF CHRIST AND HIS CHURCH OVER SATAN AND HIS HELPERS

1–11	I. The struggle on earth: the church persecuted by the world. The church is avenged, protected, and victorious.
12–22	II. The Deeper Spiritual Background: the Christ (and the Church) persecuted by the dragon (Satan) and his helpers. Christ and the church are victorious.

Expanded outline:

Revelation

THE VICTORY OF CHRIST AND HIS CHURCH OVER SATAN AND HIS HELPERS

1–11	I. The struggle on earth: the church persecuted by the world. The church is avenged, protected, and victorious.
1–3	A. Christ in the midst of the seven golden lampstands.
4–7	B. The book with the seven seals.
8–11	C. The seven trumpets of judgment.
12–22	II. The deeper spiritual background: Christ (and the church) persecuted by the dragon (Satan) and his helpers. Christ and the church are victorious.
12–14	A. The woman and the man child persecuted by the dragon and his helpers (the beasts and the harlot).
15, 16	B. The seven bowls of wrath.
17–19	C. The fall of the great harlot and of the beasts.

20–22 | D. The judgment upon the dragon (Satan), fo lowed by the new heaven and earth, Jer salem the Golden.

With this outline we have finished the discussion of the last boc of the Bible. There is a beautiful connection between the first boc and the last. Scripture resembles a flower. We find the seed Genesis, the growing plant in the books which follow, the ful developed and beautiful flower in the Apocalypse. Observe tl following parallels:

Genesis tells us that God created heaven and earth. Revelatic describes the *new* heaven and earth (21:1).

In Genesis the luminaries are called into being: sun, moon, star In Revelation we read: "And the city has no need of the sun, n of the moon, to shine in it; for the glory of God illumined it, ar its lamp is the Lamb."

Genesis describes a Paradise which was lost. Revelation pictures Paradise restored (Rev. 2:7; 22:2).

Genesis describes the cunning and power of the devil. The Apoc lypse tells us that the devil was hurled into the lake of fire ar brimstone.

Genesis pictures that awful scene: man fleeing from God ar hiding himself from the presence of the Almighty. Revelatic shows us the most wonderful and intimate communion betwe God and redeemed man: "Behold, the tabernacle of God is wi men, and he shall dwell among them, etc."

Finally, whereas Genesis shows us the tree of life, with an angel bar the way to it, "lest man put forth his hand and take of i fruit," the Apocalypse restores to man his right to have access it: "that they may have the right to come to the tree of life" (Re 22:14).

How do we explain the fact that the Paradise Lost of Genes becomes the Paradise Regained of Revelation? This glorious transfo mation was achieved through the power of the Cross of Christ, i. the Gospels supply the key to Genesis and Revelation. The Bible is glorious unity!

PROGRESSIVE PARALLELISM

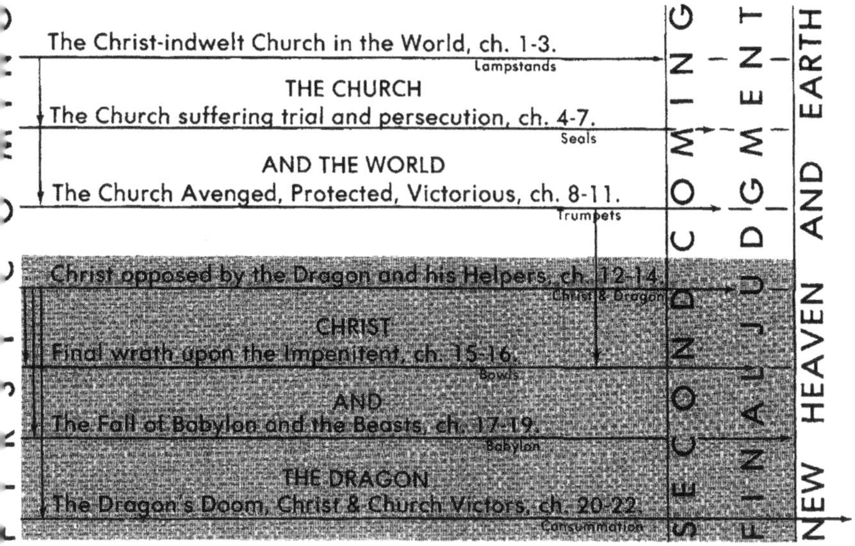

The Christ-indwelt Church in the World, ch. 1-3.
Lampstands

THE CHURCH

The Church suffering trial and persecution, ch. 4-7.
Seals

AND THE WORLD

The Church Avenged, Protected, Victorious, ch. 8-11.
Trumpets

Christ opposed by the Dragon and his Helpers, ch. 12-14.
Christ & Dragon

CHRIST

Final wrath upon the Impenitent, ch. 15-16.
Bowls

AND

The Fall of Babylon and the Beasts, ch. 17-19.
Babylon

THE DRAGON

The Dragon's Doom, Christ & Church Victors, ch. 20-22.
Consummation

SECOND COMING

FINAL JUDGMENT

NEW HEAVEN AND EARTH

Explanation

References are to *More than Conquerors, An Interpretation of the Book of Revelation* by William Hendriksen, copyright 1939 and 1967 by the author and published by Baker Book House.

1. **Parallelism.** The parallel lines indicate the seven parallel sections. See Proposition I, chapter II.

2. **Progress in intensity of spiritual conflict.** Notice light and shaded portions. See Proposition II, chapter II.

3. **Progress in the revelation of the principles of human conduct and of divine, moral government; inner, organic unity.** Seals of persecution bring about (↓) trumpets of judgment, etc. See Proposition III, chapter III.

4. **Progress in eschatological emphasis.** Notice horizontal arrows (→). See Proposition IV, chapter IV.

Part Four

Bible Chapters and Passages

Structure from Roman times that contains a flour mill, on the shore of Galilee near Magdala (Mejdel).
Levant Photo Service

Bible Chapters 34

ll the chapters of Scripture are equally inspired. They are all food r the soul. Nevertheless, in view of the fact that the Bible has so ry many chapters, it is impossible for most students to become quainted with them all. Whether rightly or wrongly, the following apters are among the most familiar. We quote a few well known ords from each chapter as a general hint concerning its content. For better understanding of the place of the chapter in the organism of oly Writ the outline of the book in which the chapter occurs should consulted. *All children should be acquainted with the first list.* each them this list in your Bible class. They will enjoy it. We know ecause we have used it. *Next, get them to become thoroughly miliar with the Gospel of John. For this purpose use the second t.* The key words given in connection with each chapter are not emes but merely cues. Get them to commit to memory the passage r each chapter. *The third list is for yourself!*

List for Beginners

Old Testament

1. Genesis 1: *In the beginning . . .* (the Creation account).
2. Genesis 3: *"And I will put enmity . . ."* (the Fall).
3. Genesis 17: *"And I will establish my covenant. . . ."*
4. Genesis 22: *"Take your son, your only son. . . ."*
5. Exodus 20: *And God spoke all these words, saying, "I am Jehovah your God, who brought you out of the land of Egypt, out of the house of bondage. You shall have no other gods before me"* (the Ten Commandments; cf. Deut. 5).

6. Numbers 21: "*Make a fiery serpent. . . .*"
7. Joshua 24: "*Choose this day whom you will serve. . . .*"
8. Ruth 1: "*Your people shall be my people, and your God m God. . . .*"
9. Job 19: . . . *I know that my Redeemer lives. . . .*
10. Psalm 19: *The heavens declare the glory of God. . . .*
11. Psalm 23: *Jehovah is my shepherd* . . . (the Shepherd Psalm).
12. Psalm 42: *As the hart pants after the water brooks. . . .*
13. Psalm 84: *How amiable are thy tabernacles. . . .*
14. Psalm 90: *Lord, thou hast been our dwelling place. . . .*
15. Psalm 91: *For he will give his angels charge over you. . . .*
16. Psalm 100: . . . *come before his presence with singing.*
17. Psalm 103: *As far as the east is from the west. . . .*
18. Psalm 105: *He has remembered his covenant for ever. . . .*
19. Psalm 139: *O Jehovah, thou hast searched me and known me.*
20. Ecclesiastes 12: *Remember also your Creator in the days of you youth. . . .*
21. Isaiah 7: "*Therefore, the Lord himself will give you a sign behold, a virgin shall conceive. . . .*"
22. Isaiah 9: *For unto us a child is born. . . .*
23. Isaiah 11: *And there shall come forth a shoot out of the stock o Jesse. . . .*
24. Isaiah 35: *Then the eyes of the blind shall be opened. . . .*
25. Isaiah 40: *Comfort, comfort my people. . . .*
26. Isaiah 53: *Surely, he has borne our griefs, and carried ou sorrows. . . .*
27. Isaiah 55: *Pause, every one who is thirsty. . . .*
28. Micah 5: *But you, Bethlehem Ephrathah. . . .*
29. Malachi 3: "*Behold, I send my messenger. . . .*"

New Testament

1. Matthew 2: . . . *behold, wise men from the east. . . .*
2. Matthew 5: "*Blessed are the poor in spirit. . . .*"
3. Matthew 27: *And when they had crucified him, they divided hi garments among them* . . . (the Crucifixion).
4. Luke 2: *In those days, there went out a decree from Caesa Augustus* . . . (the Birth of Christ).

5. Luke 15: "*. . . Father, I have sinned, against heaven, and in thy sight. . . .*"
6. Luke 24: "*Why do you seek the living among the dead?*" (the Resurrection of our Lord).
7. Acts 2: *And when the day of Pentecost was now come. . . .*"
8. Romans 5: *Being therefore justified by faith, we have peace with God. . . .*
9. Romans 8: *There is therefore now no condemnation. . . .*"
0. I Corinthians 13: *If I speak with the tongues of men and of angels, but have not love . . .* (the Hymn of Love).
1. Ephesians 6: *Stand, therefore, having girded your loins with truth. . . .*
2. Philippians 4: *Whatever things are true, whatever things are honorable. . . .*
3. Hebrews 11: *Now faith is the assurance of things hoped for . . .* (the Heroes of Faith).
4. Revelation 7: "*Therefore are they before the throne of God. . . .*"

. List from the Gospel of John

The general idea of making a list of chapter names and passages om John was derived from W. W. White, *Studies in the Gospel of hn,* pp. 14, 122. However, the list which we give is different in any respects from the one found in that excellent booklet. We have ften used our list in classes for children, ages 12-16. Drill them so at they acquire the ability to recite the chapter name and the assage whenever you mention a chapter. Explain the passage to em. For the purpose of a thorough drill, let the teacher mention a apter; for example, 3. The class or pupil then answers: "Chapter ree, Nicodemus—verse sixteen: 'For God so loved the world, that e gave his only begotten Son, that whoever believes in him should ot perish, but have everlasting life.' "

Do this for every chapter, first taking them in their regular order; en at random. Ask them to read a chapter of John each week, and come with questions, to be answered in class. Gradually they will arn to know this Gospel in such a manner as never to forget. Notice at our list contains the seven "I Am's."

1. John the Baptist, 1:29: . . . *"Behold the Lamb of God who take away the sin of the world."*
2. First Signs, 2:19: . . . *"Destroy this temple, and in three days will raise it up."*
3. Nicodemus, 3:16: *For God so loved the world, that he gave hi only begotten Son, that whoever believes in him should no perish but have everlasting life.*
4. Samaritan woman, 4:24: *"God is a Spirit; and those who wor ship him must worship in spirit and truth."*
5. Bethesda, 5:24: . . . *"He who hears my word, and believes hin who sent me, has everlasting life, and does not come int condemnation, but has passed out of death into life."*
6. Bread, 6:35: . . . *"I am the bread of life. . . ."*
7. Water, 7:37: . . . *"If any one is thirsty let him come to me an drink."*
8. Light, 8:12: . . . *"I am the light of the world."*
9. Darkness, 9:4: *"We must work the works of him who sent m while it is day: the night is coming when no one can work."*
10. Good Shepherd, 10:9, 11: *"I am the door. . . . I am the goo shepherd: the good shepherd lays down his life for the sheep.*
11. Lazarus, 11:25: . . . *"I am the resurrection and the life."*
12. Greeks, 12:32: *"And I, if I be lifted up from the earth, will dra all men to myself."*
13. Supper, 13:8: . . . *"If I do not wash you, you have no part wit me."*
14. Comfort, 14:6: . . . *"I am the way, and the truth, and the lif no one comes to the Father but by me."*
15. Admonition, 15:5: *"I am the vine; you are the branches. . . ."*
16. Prediction, 16:33: . . . *"In the world you have tribulation; bu be of good cheer; I have overcome the world."*
17. Prayer, 17:9: *"I pray for them. I pray not for the world, but fo those whom thou hast given me; for they are thine."*
18. Trial and Denial, 18:37: . . . *"Every one that is of the trut listens to my voice."*
19. Crucifixion, 19:30: . . . *"It is finished. . . ."*
20. Resurrection, 20:31: *These are written, that you may believ that Jesus is the Christ, the Son of God; and that believing yo may have life in his name.*

21. Simon, 21:17: ... *"Lord, thou knowest all things. Thou knowest that I love thee."*

II. Additional List for Advanced Bible Students

Old Testament

1. Genesis 49: *"The scepter shall not depart from Judah. . . ."*
2. Genesis 50: *"And as for you, you meant evil against me; but God meant it for good. . . ."*
3. Exodus 15: *Then Moses sang this song . . . , "I will sing to Jehovah. . . ."*
4. Exodus 32: *"Yet now, if thou wilt forgive their sins—and if not, blot me, I pray thee, out of thy book, which thou hast written."*
5. Deuteronomy 32: *"Give ear, O heavens, and I will speak. . . ."*
6. Deuteronomy 33: *"The eternal God is thy dwelling place. And underneath are the everlasting arms."*
7. Ruth 4: *"And he shall be to you a restorer of life, and a nourisher of your old age. . . ."*
8. II Samuel 7: *". . . I will establish the throne of his kingdom forever."*
9. Job 1: *". . . Jehovah gave, and Jehovah has taken away; blessed be the name of Jehovah."*
10. Job 42: *"I had heard of thee by the hearing of the ear; But now my eye sees thee. Wherefore I abhor myself; and repent in dust and ashes."*
11. Psalm 1: *Blessed is the man who does not walk in the counsel of the wicked. . . .*
12. Psalm 2: *Why do the nations rage . . . ?*
13. Psalm 8: *O Jehovah our Lord. How excellent is thy name in all the earth!*
14. Psalm 11: *In Jehovah do I take refuge. . . .*
15. Psalm 14: *The fool has said in his heart, "There is no God."*
16. Psalm 16: *For thou wilt not leave my soul to Sheol. Neither wilt thou suffer thy holy one to see corruption.*
17. Psalm 24: *The earth is Jehovah's, and the fulness thereof. . . .*

18. Psalm 25: *All the paths of Jehovah are lovingkindness an truth, to such as keep his covenant. . . .*"
19. Psalm 27: *Jehovah is my light and my salvation. . . .*
20. Psalm 29: *Ascribe to Jehovah, O sons of the mighty. . . .*
21. Psalm 31: *Into thy hand I commend my spirit; for thou has redeemed me.*
22. Psalm 32: *Blessed is he whose transgression is forgiven. . . .*
23. Psalm 40: *Then said I, "Lo, I am come. . . ."*
24. Psalm 46: *God is our refuge and strength. . . .*
25. Psalm 47: *God is gone up with a shout. . . .*
26. Psalm 48: *Great is Jehovah and greatly to be praised. . . .*
27. Psalm 51: *Against thee, thee only have I sinned. . . .*
28. Psalm 63: *O God, thou art my God. . . .*
29. Psalm 65: *Praise waits for thee, O God, in Zion. . . .*
30. Psalm 66: *Come and hear, all you who fear God, And I wi declare what he has done for my soul.*
31. Psalm 68: *Thou hast ascended on high. . . .*
32. Psalm 69: *Reproach has broken my heart, and I am full o heaviness. . . .*"
33. Psalm 72: *He shall have dominion from sea to sea. . . .*
34. Psalm 73: *Surely, God is good to Israel. . . .*
35. Psalm 74: *Have respect to the covenant. . . .*
36. Psalm 79: *O God, the nations are come into thine inher tance. . . .*
37. Psalm 81: *"Open your mouth wide, and I will fill it."*
38. Psalm 87: *. . . Jehovah loves the gates of Zion. . . .*
39. Psalm 89: *"I have made a covenant with my chosen. . . ."*
40. Psalm 95: *Let us come before his presence with thanksgiv ing. . . .*
41. Psalm 108: *My heart is fixed, O God. . . .*
42. Psalm 110: *Jehovah says to my Lord, "Sit at my righ hand. . . ."*
43. Psalm 115: *Not to us, O Jehovah, not to us. . . .*
44. Psalm 116: *I love Jehovah. . . .*
45. Psalm 118: *. . . his lovingkindness endures forever.*
46. Psalm 119: *Wherewith shall a young man cleanse his way?*

47. Psalm 121: *I will lift up my eyes unto the mountains. . . .*
48. Psalm 122: *I was glad when they said to me, "Let us go into the house of Jehovah!"*
49. Psalm 123: *Behold, as the eyes of servants look to the hand of their master. . . .*
50. Psalm 125: *They that trust in Jehovah are as Mount Zion. . . .*
51. Psalm 127: *Except Jehovah build the house. . . .*
52. Psalm 130: *Out of the depths. . . .*
53. Psalm 133: *Behold, how good and how pleasant. . . .*
54. Psalm 145: *Jehovah is good to all. . . .*
55. Psalm 147: *He counts the number of the stars. . . .*
56. Psalm 148: *Praise Jehovah from the heavens. . . .*
57. Psalm 150: *Praise God in his sanctuary. . . .*
58. Proverbs 8: *Jehovah possessed me in the beginning of his way. . . .*
59. Proverbs 22: *Train up a child in the way he should go. . . .*
60. Proverbs 31: *a . . . woman that fears Jehovah, she shall be praised.*
61. Ecclesiastes 11: *Cast your bread upon the waters. . . .*
62. Isaiah 6: . . . *I saw the Lord sitting upon a throne. . . .*
63. Isaiah 12: *Therefore with joy you shall draw water out of the wells of salvation.*
64. Isaiah 14: *"How are you fallen from heaven, O day Star . . . ?"*
65. Isaiah 42: *Behold, my servant, whom I uphold. . . .*
66. Isaiah 46: *Bel bows down, Nebo stoops. . . .*
67. Isaiah 54: *"Sing, O barren, who did not bear. . . ."*
68. Isaiah 59: *Behold, Jehovah's hand is not shortened, that it cannot save. . . .*
69. Isaiah 60: *Arise, shine, for your light is come. . . .*
70. Isaiah 61: *The Spirit of Jehovah is upon me. . . .*
71. Isaiah 64: *O that thou wouldest rend the heavens. . . .*
72. Jeremiah 18: *"And if at any time I declare concerning a nation. . . ."*
73. Jeremiah 23: *". . . I will raise to David a righteous Branch. . . ."*
74. Jeremiah 31: *". . . I will make a new covenant. . . ."*
75. Ezekiel 1 and 10: . . . *a wheel within a wheel. . . .*

76. Ezekiel 2: "*. . . be not afraid of them. . . .*"
77. Ezekiel 3 and 33: "*Son of man, I have made you a watchma for the house of Israel. . . .*"
78. Ezekiel 18: "*Have I any pleasure in the death of th wicked . . . ?*"
79. Ezekiel 38 and 39: "*. . . I am against you, O Gog. . . .*"
81. Daniel 2: "*And in the days of those kings shall the God c heaven set up a kingdom that shall never be destroyed. . . .*"
82. Daniel 7: *I saw in the night visions . . . one like a son c man. . . .*
83. Daniel 9: "*Seventy weeks are decreed upon your people. . . .*
84. Hosea 11: *How shall I give you up, Ephraim?*
85. Hosea 14: *I will heal their backsliding. I will love the freely. . . .*
86. Joel 2: "*. . . I will pour out my Spirit upon all flesh. . . .*"
87. Amos 5: "*Seek me, and you shall live. . . .*"
88. Amos 9: "*In that day will I raise up the tabernacle of Dav that is fallen. . . .*"
89. Jonah 4: "*And should not I have regard for Nineveh . . . wher in are more than a hundred and twenty thousand persons . . and also much cattle?*"
90. Micah 7: *Who is a God like thee, who pardons iniquity . . . ?*
91. Nahum 1: *Behold, upon the mountains the feet of him wh brings good tidings. . . .*
92. Habakkuk 2: *. . . but the righteous shall live by his faith.*
93. Habakkuk 3: *For, though the fig tree shall not flourish. . . .*
94. Zephaniah 3: "*. . . he will rejoice over you with singing. . . .*"
95. Haggai 2: *The latter glory of this house shall be greater tha the former. . . .*
96. Zechariah 3: "*. . . I will bring forth my servant, the Branch.*"
97. Zechariah 9: "*Rejoice greatly, O daughter of Zion!*"
98. Zechariah 11: *So they weighed for my hire thirty pieces c silver.*
99. Zechariah 12: "*. . . they shall look upon me, whom they ha pierced. . . .*"
100. Malachi 4: "*But for you that fear my name shall the sun c righteousness arise. . . .*"

New Testament

1. Matthew 6: *"Lay not up for yourselves treasures upon the earth. . . ."*
2. Matthew 7: *"Do not pass judgment. . . ."*
3. Matthew 10: *"Behold, I send you out as sheep in the midst of wolves. . . ."*
4. Matthew 11: *"Come to me, all who are weary and burdened. . . ."*
5. Matthew 13: *"Behold, the sower went out to sow."*
6. Matthew 18: *"If your brother sins against you. . . ."*
7. Matthew 24: *"You shall hear of wars and rumors of wars. . . ."*
8. Mark 10: *"Let the little children come to me. . . ."*
9. Luke 10: *"A certain man was going down from Jerusalem to Jericho. . . ."*
0. Acts 9: *"Saul, Saul, why do you persecute me?"*
1. Acts 15: *"Wherefore my judgment is that we should not trouble those who turn unto God from the Gentiles."*
2. Acts 20: *"And now I commend you to God and to the word of his grace. . . ."*
3. Acts 27: *And when it was determined that we should sail for Italy. . . .*
4. Romans 7: *Wretched man that I am!*
5. Romans 12: *Be tenderly affectionate. . . .*
6. I Corinthians 1: . . . *Christ, the power of God and the wisdom of God.*
7. I Corinthians 2: *Now the natural man does not accept the things that come from the Spirit of God. . . .*
8. I Corinthians 3: . . . *all are yours; and you are Christ's; and Christ is God's.*
9. I Corinthians 7: . . . *only in the Lord.*
0. I Corinthians 8: *But take care lest somehow their liberty become a stumblingblock to the weak.*
1. I Corinthians 11: *For I received of the Lord that which I also delivered to you, that the Lord Jesus in the night in which he was betrayed took bread. . . .*
2. I Corinthians 12: *Now there are diversities of gifts, but the same Spirit. . . .*

23. I Corinthians 15: "*O death, where is your victory?*"
24. II Corinthians 4: *But we have this treasure in earthen vessels. . .*
25. II Corinthians 5: *For we know that if the earthly tent we li in. . . .*
26. II Corinthians 6: *Be not unequally yoked with unbelievers.*
27. Galatians 2: *I have been crucified with Christ. . . .*
28. Galatians 3: *And if you are Christ's, then you are Abraham seed, heirs according to promise.*
29. Philippians 2: "*Have this mind in you which was also Christ. . . .*
30. Philippians 3: *Nevertheless, such things as once were gains t me, these I have counted loss for Christ.*
31. Colossians 3: *If then you were raised together with Christ. . . .*
32. I Thessalonians 4: *But we would not have you ignorant, brot ers, concerning those that fall asleep. . . .*
33. II Thessalonians 2: . . . *it will not be except* . . . *the man of s be revealed. . . .*
34. I Timothy 1: . . . *Christ Jesus came into the world to sa sinners.*
35. II Timothy 4: *I have fought the good fight. . . .*
36. Hebrews 9: . . . *apart from shedding of blood there is no remi sion.*
37. Hebrews 13: *Jesus Christ, the same yesterday, today, yes, an forever.*
38. James 1: *Blessed is the man that endures temptation. . . .*
39. James 5: *Be patient, therefore, brothers, until the coming of th Lord.*
40. I Peter 1: *Blessed be the God and Father of our Lord Jes Christ, who* . . . *begot us again unto a living hope. . . .*
41. I Peter 2: "*But you are an elect race, a royal priesthood. . . .*"
42. II Peter 1: . . . *men spoke from God, being moved by the Ho Spirit.*
43. I John 3: *Behold, what manner of love the Father has bestowe on us. . . .*
44. Revelation 5: "*Worthy is the Lamb who has been slain. . . .*"
45. Revelation 12: . . . *and she was delivered of a son, a ma child. . . .*

6. Revelation 21: *And I saw a new heaven and a new earth. . . .*
7. Revelation 22: *And he showed me a river of water of life. . . .*

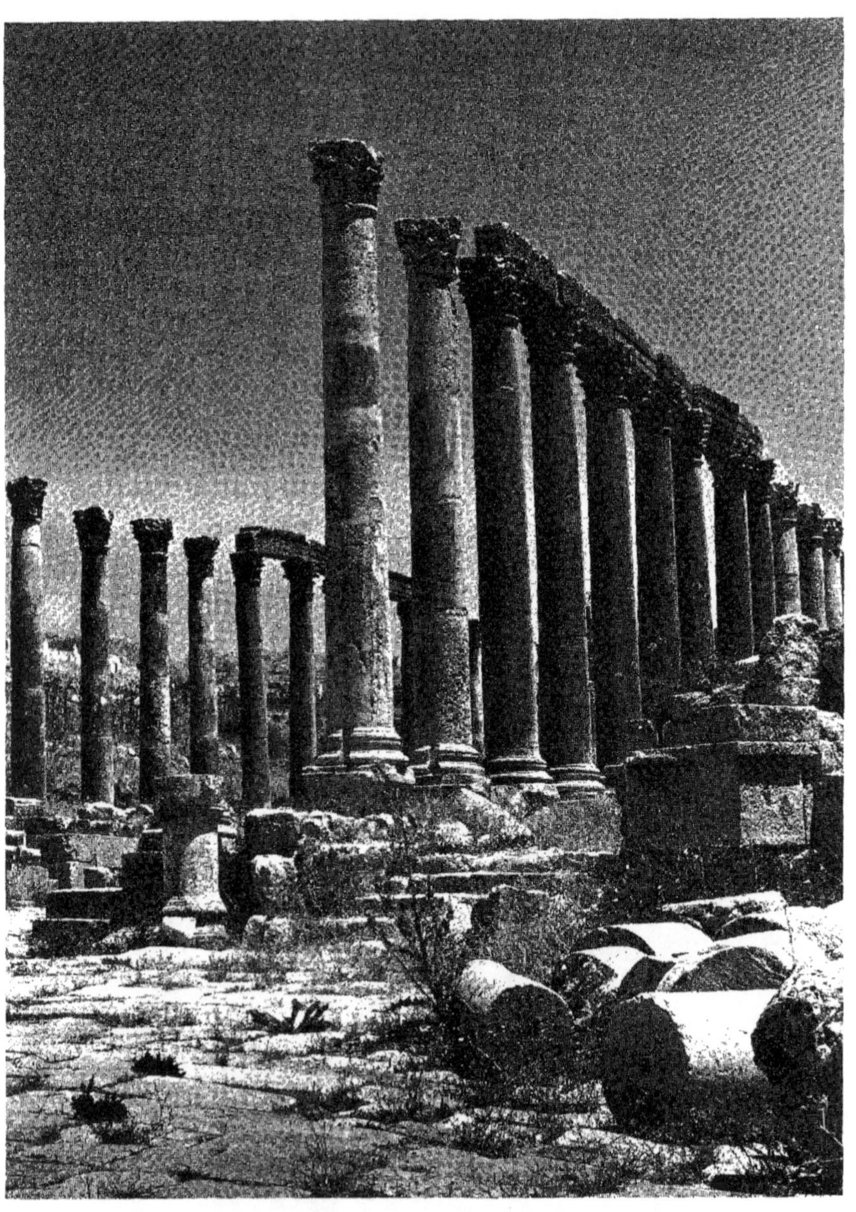

Entrance to the Street of the Columns, at Jerash, one of the cities of the Decapolis region.
Levant Photo Service

Bibles Passages 35

ssages for Personal Meditation

flicted

Rom. 8:31-39; Phil. 4:4-7; Heb. 4:16; *see also* Chastened; Fearful; Homesick or lonely; Misjudged; Neglected; Overwhelmed with sudden grief; Rebuffed; Sick or dying; Visited with grief.

reaved

Job 1:20-22; Ps. 27:10; John 11:1-27.

astened

Ps. 23, 27, 42; *see also* Afflicted; Fearful; Overwhelmed with sudden grief; Sick or dying; Visited with grief.

ubting

Matt. 11:1-6; John 20:19-29; I Cor. 2:14; *see also* Fearful; Worried.

tering upon a new task; beginning a new year; etc.

Exod. 33:14, 15; Ps. 127:1, 2; Rom. 8:31, 32; *see also* Leaving home.

arful

Josh. 1:1-9; Matt. 14:22-33; John 14:1; *see also* Doubting; Worried.

ateful

A believer should always be grateful; but there are times when gratitude abounds—Ps. 40:1-8; Ps. 103; Ps. 116.

omesick or lonely

Gen. 28:10-17; Ps. 23; I Cor. 10:13; *see also* Leaving home.

capable

Seized with the consciousness of your own incapability to perform a task assigned to you (particularly, in God's kingdom; e.g., newly elected elders, deacons)—II Cor. 12:7-10; Phil. 4:13, 19; I Tir 4:12; *see also* Entering upon a new task.

Jubilant

Ps. 145, 146, 147; *see also* Grateful.

Kindly disposed to this present world, its pleasures and treasures

II Cor. 6:14-18; Phil. 4:8, 9; I John 2:15-17.

Leaving home

Ps. 91, 121; Prov. 3:1-12; *see also* Entering upon a new task.

Misjudged; slandered

Matt. 18:15-20; Rom. 12:14-21; I Peter 2:21-25; *see also* N glected; Persecuted; Reproached.

Neglected; ignored; shunned "for righteousness' sake"

I Kings 19:1-18; John 16:32, 33; Phil. 3:7, 8; *see also* Misjudge Persecuted; Reproached.

Overwhelmed with sudden grief

Ps. 30:4, 5; 61:1, 2; Ps. 142; *see also* Bereaved; Chastened; Visit with grief.

Persecuted

Matt. 5:10; I Peter 4:12-19; Rev. 7:13-17; *see also* Misjudge Neglected; Persecuted.

Questioned concerning the hope that is in you

Josh. 24:15; Matt. 10:32; I Peter 3:15.

Reproached by the world "for righteousness sake"

Neh. 6:13, 14; Isa. 53:7; Luke 6:22, 23; *see also* Misjudge Neglected; Persecuted.

Sick or dying

John 14:1-3; James 5:13-18; II Tim. 4:6-8; *see also* Afflicte Chastened; Overwhelmed; Visited with grief.

Tempted

Gen. 22:1-18; Luke 4:1-13; James 1:12-18.

Unforgiving

When it is hard to forgive a suffered wrong, read: Ps. 103:1-1 Matt. 6:14, 15; 18:21-35.

Visited with grief

Ps. 22, 73; Matt. 10:29-31; *see also* Afflicted; Chastened; Ov whelmed; Sick or dying.

Worried

Isa. 43:2; Matt. 6:24-34; Luke 11:4-7; Phil. 4:6-7; *see also* Dou ing; Fearful.

Passages for Special Occasions Observed by Public Worship

New Year's Day

Gen. 1:1; Exod. 14:15; 33:14, 15; Deut. 11:12; 31:6; Josh. 1:5; 24:15; Ruth 1:15-18; II Kings 2:12; 6:16; Esther 4:14; Ps. 4:6; 11:1; 20:7; 23; 30:4, 5; 37:5; 40:3; 81:10; 91; 121:1, 8; 123:2; 127:1, 2; Prov. 3:8; Eccles. 11:1; Isa. 26:3, 4; 41:10; 43:1-3; Jer. 6:16; Zech. 4:7; Matt. 6:19-21, 31-33; 9:2; 14:27; 25:14-30; Luke 13:8; John 16:33; Rom. 8:28, 31, 32; I Cor. 3:21-23; II Cor. 5:17; 12:9; Eph. 4:3; 5:16; Phil. 3:13, 14; 4:6, 7, 8, 9, 19; II Peter 3:18; Heb. 12:1; James 4:13-17; Rev. 1:13; 3:8, 18, 25; 21:1, 5. *See also* New Year's Eve.

Day of Prayer

Gen. 5:28, 29; 26:12; Deut. 8:3; 33:28, 29; Ruth 2:4; I Sam. 7:5; I Kings 8:37-40; II Kings 7:3; I Chron. 4:9, 10; II Chron. 7:13, 14; Ps. 37:25; 65:9-13; 81:10; 90:17; 102:17; 111:5; 121:1; 123:1, 2; 145:15, 16; 147:7-11; Prov. 30:8, 9; Isa. 41:17; Joel 2:21-27; Hab. 3:17-19; Hag. 2:19; Matt. 5:43-45; 6:11, 25, 33; 14:13-21; 15:32-39; Mark 3:1-6; John 2:1-11; Acts 4:31; Rom. 8:18-25, 31, 32; Phil. 4:6, 7, 19; I Thess. 5:17; I Tim. 4:4, 5; Heb. 4:14-16; James 1:17; 4:3; 5:17, 18; Rev. 8:3-5. *See also* Thanksgiving Day.

Good Friday

Gen. 3:15; 22:1-19; Exod. 2:1-14; Num. 21:8; Ps. 22:1, 7, 16, 18; 31:5; 40:7, 8; 69:20, 21; Isa. 53; Zech. 11:12; 12:10; the Passion account found in Matthew 26 and 27, in Mark 14 and 15, in Luke 22 and 23, and in John 18 and 19; Mark 10:45; John 10:11, 27, 28; 13:8; Acts 2:36; Rom. 4:25; 5:6-11; 8:1-3, 31-39; I Cor. 11:23-25; II Cor. 5:21; 8:9; Gal. 2:20; 3:13; 6:14; Eph. 2:13-18; Phil. 2:13-18; I Tim. 1:15; Heb. 9:22, 28; 13:12, 13; I Peter 1:17, 18; 2:21-24; Rev. 5.

Easter

Gen. 3:15; Job 19:25; Ps. 2:7; 16:10; 118:22-24; Isa. 25:8; 53:11; the last chapter of Matthew, of Mark, and of Luke; John 20; 21; Mark 8:31; 9:30-32; 10:34; John 11:25, 26; 14:19; Acts 2:22-36; 4:10-12; 5:30; 10:40; 13:32-39; 17:30-32; 26:8; Rom. 1:4; 4:24, 25; 6:5-11; 8:11, 34; 10:9; I Cor. 6:14, 15; II Cor. 4:14; Gal. 1:1; 2:20; Eph. 1:20–2:6; Phil. 3:20, 21; Col. 2:12; 3:1-4; I Thess. 1:10; II Tim. 1:10; 2:11, 18; Heb. 7:25; I Peter 1:3, 21; Rev. 1:4, 5, 18.

Ascension Day

Lev. 16 (especially vss. 15, 16); Ps. 24:7-10; 68:18; 110:1; Luk 24:50, 51; John 14:1-4; 16:7; 17:5; Acts 1:9-11; 2:33-36; 3:2 5:31; 7:56; Eph. 1:20, 21; 4:7-10; Phil. 2:9-11; 3:20; Col. 3:1, I Tim. 3:16; Heb. 4:14-16; 9:12, 24; 10:12; Rev. 12:5, 7-1 20:4-6.

Pentecost

Lev. 23:15-21; Deut. 16:9-12; Ps. 2:7, 8; 72:8, 9; Isa. 32:15; 44: Ezek. 36:27; Dan. 2; Joel 2:28-32; Zech. 4; John 3:5; 7:37-3 14:16, 17, 25, 26; 15:26; 16:7-14; Acts 2; 6:5; 10:44-48; 19:1- Rom. 8:8-16, 26; I Cor. 2:12; 12:3; II Cor. 3:17, 18; Gal. 4: 5:22; Eph. 2:8.

Thanksgiving Day

Num. 7:1, 2; 13:27; Deut. 6:10-12; 16:13; I Kings 17:16; Ps. 2 30:14; 33:5; 97:1, 2; 100:4; 103:17, 22; 107:8; 111:4, 5; 115:1 116:1, 12, 13; 119:68; 126:3; 136:1; 144:15; 145:9; 147:2 Prov. 20:4; Eccles. 11:4; Isa. 9:3; 12:1, 2, 5; 28:26; 61:11; Je 5:21-24; Ezek. 20:6; Hos. 2:21, 22; 14:5; Jonah 2:9; Mark 4:2 John 6:48; 21:12; Acts 12:24; 14:17; 21:39; I Cor. 3:6, 9; Re 4:11; 5:13; 19:6. *See also* Day of Prayer

Christmas

Gen. 3:15; 49:10; Deut. 18:15-18; II Sam. 7:12-17; Ps. 40:7; Is 7:1-17 (especially vs. 14); 9:1-7 (especially vs. 6); 11:1-5; 40: Jer. 23:5, 6; Mic. 5:2; Hag. 2:6, 7; Zech. 9:9; Mal. 3:1, 2; 4: Matt. 1; 2; Luke 1; 2; John 1:1-14; 3:16; 10:10; II Cor. 8:9; G 4:4, 5; I Tim. 1:15; 3:16; Heb. 10:8, 9; Rev. 12:5.

New Year's Eve (the evening before New Year's Day)

Gen. 32:10; Deut. 4:9; 33:27; I Sam. 7:5-12; II Sam. 7:18, 1 Esther 6:1-3; Job 1:21; 2:10; Ps. 39:1-5; 48:9, 10; 66:16; 9 102:18; 103:2, 15-18; 130:3, 4; Isa. 21:11, 12; 38:1-8; 63: Lam. 3:22; Dan. 5; Hab. 3:2; Matt. 25:13; Mark 6:31; John 1:3 II Cor. 5:10; Heb. 4:7; 13:8; I Peter 4:7; I John 2:17, 18; Re 7:13-17; 14:14-20; 22:17, 20. *See also* New Year's Day.

Passages to prove the various doctrines.

See L. Berkhof, *Systematic Theology*.

Index

Index

Question Manual

HOW TO USE THIS MANUAL

This Question Manual can be used with profit by both beginners and more ...vanced students.

All Students

1. The references printed above each lesson (such as, Chapter 1, pp. 13-30, ...inted above Lesson 1) refer to chapters and pages in this *Survey of the Bible.* ...e numerals folowing certain questions in both sections A and B refer to pages ... this *Survey of the Bible* on which one can find the answer to the question. ...e stipulated material should be read in its entirety before any attempt is made ... answer specific questions. First read and study all the material; then turn back ... the beginning of the lesson and see whether you can answer the questions.

2. Try to make your answers as brief as possible without sacrificing com-...eteness. Often one sentence or a short paragraph will be all that is needed. ...nswer in the language of the book or, even better, in your own words.

3. Always have your Bible lying open next to *Survey of the Bible.* Consult ...our Bible constantly. Not this survey, but the Bible itself is your textbook. This ...*rvey of the Bible* is merely a help. Therefore, before you try to commit to ...emory any outline of a Bible book, first see whether you can trace the outline ... the Bible book itself. Before studying any Bible story read that story in your ...ble. Before studying any Bible book read at least part of the book.

4. The opinion of some educators notwithstanding, *memory work occupies a ...ry important place in Bible study.* You cannot *think* about Bible facts unless ...u first *know* the facts. Therefore a high percentage of the questions requires ...emorization. However, the ultimate aim—calm reflection about the material ...at has been committed to memory—has not been entirely lost sight of even in ...is survey. Hence, in certain cases you are asked to make your own outline of a ...ible book to show how, in your own opinion, Paul's missionary principles can ... applied today, to indicate, as you see it, the present-day value of the ...storals, etc. Here you will have to do your own thinking; the answers will not ... found in the book.

Advanced Students

1. Try to answer *all* the questions.
2. Commit to memory the summary outlines. Diligently study the expande outlines.
3. If a *lesson* at a time is to much, take a *section* at a time.

Beginners

1. Read what is stated above under the heading *All Students.*
2. Answer *only* the questions that are printed in boldface. Thus, in Lesson beginners should answer questions 1, 2, 3, 4, 9, and 10; *not* questions 5, 6, and 8. The numbers which follow these simple or easy questions show on wh pages in this Bible survey the answers to the questions are to be found. Thus, th answer to the first question of the first Lesson is found on pp. 14 and 15. Mak your answer as brief as possible. A few sentences—sometimes *one*—or a bri paragraph will suffice.
3. When an outline of a Bible book is called for, the summary (i.e., shorte outline is meant. Do not just copy it. First, study it, trying to trace it in yo Bible. Then commit it to memory. Then reproduce it from memory.
4. For beginners we suggest that *Survey of the Bible* be divided into tw courses: the first covering Parts I and II, *The Bible* and *The Bible Story,* p 13-199; the second course covering Part III and Part IV, *Bible Books* and *Bib Chapters and Passages,* pp. 201-462.

PART ONE: THE BIBLE

Lesson 1
Chapter 1, pp. 13-30

Section 1

1. **What is the real difference between the conservative and the liberal view Scripture? 14-15**
2. **What is meant by the inspiration of Scripture? 15**
3. **How did the sacred writings look originally? 16-17**
4. **How did the MANY books grow into ONE Book? 17**
5. What is an autograph and why is it a blessing that all the autographs ha vanished?

Section 2

6. What is an uncial? Name a few of the most famous uncials.
7. Describe the work of the Masorites.
8. Describe the work of textual criticism.
9. **Why do we not include the Apocryphal Books in our Bible? 20-22**
10. **Why do you believe that these sixty-six books (no more, no less) co stitute the Bible? 22-24. Do recent discoveries support your answe 24-30**

Lesson 2
Chapter 2, pp. 33-40

ection 3

1. **How are the books of the Bible arranged in our English versions, and what do you think of that division? 33, 203**
2. **What is the arrangement which one finds in the Hebrew Old Testament, as to the three main groups? 33-34**
3. Enumerate the books of the Old Testament as arranged in the Hebrew.
4. Give the list of the Old Testament books in their probable chronological order.
5. Do the same for the New Testament. (This material is found on p. 315.)

ection 4

6. Tell the story of the Septuagint translation.
7. What do you know about the early Syriac and Latin translations?
8. **Discuss English Bible versions from 736 to the present. 37-39**
9. **What qualifications should a Bible translator possess? 39**
0. Give a summary of important dates and facts in Bible translation.

Lesson 3
Chapter 3, pp. 43-47

ection 5

1. **What is the first thing one should do in order to gain a rather thorough knowledge of the Bible? 43**
2. **Mention some valuable helps for the study of the Bible. 43-44**
3. How can you discover whether the theme which is assigned to a Bible book is a good one?
4. **Give the themes of the following books: Ruth, Nehemiah, Habakkuk, Acts, Colossians, Hebrews, and Revelation. 45**
5. Does every Bible book have a theme? Discuss.

ection 6

6. Mention (without discussing) the characteristics of a good outline.
7. Why should an outline be indicative of the material contents of a book?
8. **Show the unity of thought in the Book of Daniel. 46-47**
9. **Do the same for Deuteronomy and Esther. 47, 217-218, 304**
0. Thoroughly discuss: Should an outline be memorizable, and if so, why?

Lesson 4
Chapter 4, pp. 49-53
(first set of questions)

ection 7

1. Mention (merely STATE without discussing) the sixteen essential steps in the interpretation of the Bible.

2. Discuss Steps 1 and 2.
3. Discuss Steps 3 and 4.
4. Why do you regard the context as being important?
5. Discuss Step 6.

Section 8

6. Are the marginal renderings found in the American Standard Version some significance? Why? Give an illustration.
7. Discuss the importance of word order and of word study in the work interpretation.
8. Why is a thorough knowledge of grammar (Greek, Hebrew, Aramaic) nece sary?
9. Discuss the various figures of speech, and give an example of each. (Th presupposes that you have looked up all the references given in the text.)
10. Should everything that is found in Scripture be interpreted literally? Gi New Testament illustrations in support of your answer.

Lesson 5
Chapter 4, pp. 53-56
(second set of questions)

Section 9

1. What is meant by parallelism and how does it help us to interpret certa passages?
2. Of what value is a good concordance?
3. Illustrate the use of parallel passages in Bible interpretation.
4. What is the fundamental rule which should be observed in explaining passage in the light of its parallel?
5. Fully discuss three principles of prophetic interpretation.
6. How many main lessons does a parable contain?
7. What furnishes the key to the interpretation of a parable?
8. What place does Christ occupy in the organism of Holy Writ?
9. Is the believer who has not enjoyed a theological training able to interpr the Bible? Fully discuss this question.
10. Discuss the value of Bible commentaries and of Bible reading.

PART II: THE BIBLE STORY

Lesson 6
Chapter 5, pp. 59-81

Section 11

1. Discuss date memorization, its importance, and the three characteristics dates to be memorized. (See also p. 43.)
2. State the four main periods (see headings of Charts I, IV, V, and VI) in which Bible history can be divided. 72, 73, 74

3. Reproduce from memory the chronological chart for the period extending FROM THE DAWN OF HISTORY TO THE DIVISION OF THE KINGDOM. DISCUSS the dates. (The chart itself is found on p. 69. The material upon which the discussion is based is found on pp. 60-62; and so for each chart.)
4. Similarly reproduce (recite and discuss) Chart II, FROM INTERTRIBAL WARFARE TO THE RETURN FROM THE BABYLONIAN CAPTIVITY.
5. Similarly, Chart III, FROM THE RETURN TO IMMANUEL'S BIRTH.

Section 12

6. Reproduce Chart IV, FROM INTERTRIBAL WARFARE TO IMMANUEL'S BIRTH.
7. Similarly, Chart V, FROM THE MANGER TO THE MOUNT (OF OLIVES).
8. Similarly, Chart VI, FROM PENTECOST TO PATMOS.
9. Similarly, Chart VII, IMPERIAL REIGNS.
0. Does the study of Bible chronology present any difficulties? (This question is based on the material found on pp. 76-78.) Illustrate your answer and discuss.

Lesson 7

Chapter 6, pp. 83-102

Section 13

1. **Discuss the one, central theme of Old Testament history. 83**
2. **Relate the main events that occurred between THE DAWN OF HISTORY and THE FLOOD; and between THE FLOOD and THE CALL OF ABRAHAM. 84-89**
3. **Trace the history from THE CALL OF ABRAHAM to THE DESCENT INTO EGYPT. 89-91**
4. **Trace the history from THE DESCENT INTO EGYPT to THE EXODUS. 91-93**
5. **Trace the history from THE EXODUS to JOSHUA'S DEATH. 93-95**

Section 14

6. **Trace the history from JOSHUA'S DEATH to SAUL'S ACCESSION. 95-97**
7. **Discuss the LIFE OF SAUL, as recorded in Scripture, giving the main events and describing Saul's character. 97-99**
8. **Do the same for the LIFE OF DAVID. 99-101**
9. **Do the same for the LIFE OF SOLOMON. 100-102**
0. **Where in Scripture do you find the record of the lives of these three kings? 225-226; also heading, p. 97**

Lesson 8

Chapter 7, pp. 105-124
(first set of questions)

Section 15

1. Properly divide the period 932-722 B.C., giving the five subdivisions (a, b, c, d, e).

2. Discuss INTERTRIBAL WARFARE. 105-107
3. Discuss the HOUSE OF OMRI period and HAZAEL'S OPPRESSIO 107-111
4. Describe the GLAMOR AGE. 111-112
5. Enumerate and discuss the main events which occurred in the peri 736-722. 112-114

Section 16

6. Properly divide the period 722-586 B.C., giving the three subdivisions (a, c).
7. Discuss the entire period 722-586, giving the main events in their ord 114-117
8. Fully discuss the BABYLONIAN EXILE, its three divisions and its threef purpose. 117-119
9. Illustrate the typological, prophetical, historical, and psychological prepa tion for Christ during the period of MEDO-PERSIAN RULE. 119-123
10. How do you divide the period 333-200 (a and b), and what are the m happenings? 123-124

Lesson 9

Chapter 7, pp. 124-129
(second set of questions)

Note: *As the average student is probably less familiar with this material onl few pages of text are covered in the assignment.*

Section 17

1. How do you divide the period 200-63?
2. Discuss the period of Syrian Rule. 124-125
3. Relate the story of Mattathias and his sons Judas, Jonathan, and Sim 125-126
4. How do the later Maccabean rulers compare with the earlier leaders (th discussed under question 3)? 126
5. Discuss: Scribes and Pharisees. 126-127

Section 18

6. Give the main happenings in the history of Israel under John Hyrcanus a Alexander Janneus. 126-127
7. Who was Antipater and what was his significance for later Bible histo 127-128
8. Trace the history of the Maccabean rulers who followed Alexander Janne 127
9. What events led to the appointment of Antipater as procurator of Judea a of Herod as governor of Galilee; later, king of the Jews? 127-129

. Describe Herod and show how God triumphs in the conflict between "the woman" and "the dragon." 129

Lesson 10
Chapter 8, pp. 131-145
(first set of questions)

ction 19

. What four periods (1, 2, 3, 4) are discussed in this chapter? 131, 141, 145, 148, 151

. Briefly summarize and discuss Gospel criticism, and state your own reaction.

. Do the Gospel writers offer a Life of Jesus? What is their purpose?

. Discuss Messianic expectation. 132-134

. In what threefold sense can we speak of "the fulness of the time" in connection with the coming of Christ? 133-134

ction 20

. Show that the Christmas story begins before the "manger." (This is based on the material found on p. 134: The Word Becomes Flesh.)

. Discuss the two genealogies.

. Discuss the Annunciations. 137-139

. Discuss the birth of Jesus and his life in Nazareth. 139-141

. Trace the history of the INAUGURATION period. 141-145

Lesson 11
Chapter 8, pp. 145-155
(second set of questions)

ction 21

. What four events occurred during THE EARLY JUDEAN MINISTRY? Discuss them briefly. 145-148

. Describe the political background of Gospel history.

. Summarize the GALILEAN MINISTRY and characterize it. 148-150

. Discuss demon possession.

. What were some of the reasons for Christ's self-concealment?

ction 22

. Relate the story of the antagonism of the leaders. 152-153

. What is the historical background of the SERMON ON THE MOUNT? 153

. Give the theme and the division of this great discourse.

. Give the contents of the next paragraph: INCREASING ANTAGONISM versus INCREASING ENTHUSIASM. 154-155

. Fully discuss the close of the GALILEAN MINISTRY: LARGE-SCALE DESERTION. 155

Lesson 12
Chapter 9, pp. 157-173

Section 23

1. Is the church a democracy? Give reasons for your answer. 158
2. Tell the story of the RETIREMENT MINISTRY. 157-159
3. Tell the story of the LATER JUDEAN MINISTRY. 159-160
4. Show that during the PEREAN MINISTRY the Lord definitely interpret the meaning of his approaching suffering. Also, trace the main events of th period. 160-162
5. Fully discuss in their historical order the events which occurred on Sund of the PASSION WEEK. Do the same for Monday. 162-163

Section 24

6. Discuss Christ's ESCHATOLOGICAL ADDRESS, indicating how it shou be interpreted. 164-166
7. Give an account of the events which occurred on Tuesday and Wednesd 163-166
8. Discuss the happenings which took place on Thursday. 166-168
9. Relate the story of that most important day in the history of the worl Friday of the PASSION WEEK. 168-171
10. Relate what happened on Saturday, Sunday, and afterward; i.e., trace t events which ended with Christ's ascension to heaven. 171-173

Lesson 13
Chapter 10, pp. 175-189
(first set of questions)

Section 25

1. Did the disciples expect that Jesus would arise from the grave? Prove yo answer. How do you explain the fact that they became witnesses of t Resurrection? 175-176
2. Discuss the manner in which the disciples filled a vacancy in their ranks. 1
3. What happened at Pentecost and what is the significance of that great eve 176-177
4. Enumerate in proper order the events which occurred between Pentec and the year 33. 177-179
5. Show how the Gospel spread from Jerusalem into all Judea, Samaria, a the surrounding regions during the period 33-44. 179-180

Section 26

6. Describe the man Paul: his character, suffering, origin, and early traini 181-183
7. Discuss: Paul the Persecutor. Tell the story of his conversion and of t events which followed during the years 34-37. 183-184
8. What events occurred in Paul's life during the years 37-44? 185

9. Tell the story of Paul's FIRST MISSIONARY JOURNEY. (In studying Paul's journeys, use a map.) 185-187
0. Discuss the JERUSALEM CONFERENCE and its significance. 188-189

Lesson 14
Chapter 10, pp. 189-199
(second set of questions)

Section 27
1. How do you explain the triumph of the Gospel during the period of Paul's three missionary journeys? 189-190
2. Mention the first three elements in PAUL'S MISSIONARY STRATEGY. Are they applicable today to any extent? 190-191
3. Mention the last three elements in PAUL'S MISSIONARY STRATEGY. Are they applicable today to any extent? 192-197
4. Trace and tell the story of Paul's SECOND MISSIONARY JOURNEY. 189-194
5. Trace and tell the story of Paul's THIRD MISSIONARY JOURNEY. 194-197

Section 28
6. What happened to Paul in Jerusalem and Caesarea? 197-198
7. Relate the events that occurred during the period 60-63. 198-199
8. Discuss the closing chapter of Paul's life (the period 63-67). (The answer to this question should be based on g., p. 199, and on the material found on pp. 405-407.)
9. Discuss THE CLOSE OF THE APOSTOLIC AGE. (The answer should be based not only on the material found under 3, on p. 199, but also on the material found on the pages to which reference is made in that paragraph.) 67, 75, 415, 421-422
10. Compare GENESIS and REVELATION. The answer should be based on p. 442.

PART III: BIBLE BOOKS
Division 1: The Old Testament

Lesson 15
Chapter 11, pp. 203-207

Section 29
1. What objections are there to studying the books of the Bible in accordance with the order found in our English Bibles?
2. Discuss the arrangement of the Bible books to which liberal scholars give preference.

3. Arrange the books of the New Testament according to the order followed i *Survey of the Bible.*
4. How are the Old Testament books arranged in *Survey of the Bible?*
5. When were the New Testament books written? (This is a review questio You have answered it before. The answer is found on p. 315).

Section 30

6. Why are II Peter and Jude discussed in the same chapter?
7. What change in the order of discussing the New Testament books may b considered preferable for certain purposes?
8. What difficulty is encountered when this change is made?
9. Do we arrange the Old Testament books strictly according to date c composition? Discuss. When were the Old Testament books written? (a other review question). The answer is found on pp. 35-36
10. How does our arrangement of the Old Testament books compare with tha found in the Hebrew Bibles?

Lesson 16
Chapter 12, pp. 209-218

Section 31

1. Discuss the Mosaic authorship of the Pentateuch.
2. **What is the significance of the Book of Genesis? 211**
3. **Give the theme and outline of Genesis. (These themes and outlines shou be thoroughly mastered. No effort has been spared to make them easy t memorize.) 211-212**
4. **Point out the significance of the Book of Exodus. 212**
5. **Give the theme and outline of Exodus. 213**

Section 32

6. **What is the significance of Leviticus? Discuss the contents of chapters 1-7 8-10; 11-15; and 16. 213-215**
7. **Discuss the contents of chapters 17-22; 23-25; and 26-27. 215, 216**
8. **Give the theme and outline of Leviticus. 216**
9. **State its significance and give the theme and outline of Numbers. 216-21**
10. **Do the same for Deuteronomy. 217-218**

Lesson 17
Chapter 13, pp. 221-227

Section 33

1. **Give a brief introduction to the Book of Joshua. (The answer should b based on the material found on pp. 221-222.)**
2. **Give the theme and outline of Joshua. 222-223**
3. **Introduce the Book of Judges. 223**

. Give the theme and outline of Judges. 223-224

. Introduce I and II Samuel. 224

ction 34

. Give the theme and outline of I and II Samuel. 224

. Discuss what was said in the introductory material on I and II Kings. 225-226

. Give the theme and outline of I and II Kings. 226

. Review Questions: Give the themes and outlines of Genesis, Exodus, Leviticus, Numbers, and Deuteronomy. (In questions of this nature the SUMMARY outlines are meant.)

. Review question: Give the themes and outlines of Joshua, Judges, I and II Samuel, and I and II Kings.

Lesson 18
Chapter 14, pp. 229-238

ction 35

. Arrange the prophets chronologically. The answer can be gathered from the material found on pp. 35-36

. Tell all you know about Amos the man. 229-230

. What is the main thrust of the Book of Amos, its style, and message? 230-231

. Discuss and make a diagram of THE SPIRAL OF JUDGMENTS in Amos. 231

. Give the theme and outline of Amos. 231-232

ction 36

. Reproduce what you know about the prophet Jonah. 233-234

. Discuss the date and significance of the Book of Jonah. 234

. Give the theme and outline of Jonah. 234-235

. Tell the story of Hosea and Gomer and show how the facts in the story have a symbolic significance. Comment on the cyclical or parallelistic arrangement of the book. 235-236

. Give the theme and outline of Hosea. 236

Lesson 19
Chapter 15, pp. 241-246

ction 37

. Compare Isaiah's emphasis with that of Amos, Jonah, and Hosea, i.e., state what divine attribute each respectively stresses. 241

. What is Isaiah's central theme? What do you know about Isaiah the man? 241

. Show that the Book of Isaiah is characterized by remarkable literary variety. 241

4. Discuss the historical background of the prophecies of Isaiah and Micah. questions of this nature be sure to study not only what is found in P Three of *Survey of the Bible* but also the material in Part Two, i.e., in t particular case, not only pp. 241-242 but also pp. 112-115 to wh reference is made in the text.
5. Fully discuss the authorship of Isaiah 40-66.

Section 38

6. Give the theme and outline of Isaiah. 243
7. What sins does Micah denounce and how does this book compare w Hosea and Amos? 245
8. Comment on the artistic structure and division of the book and its impr sive beginning. 245
9. Discuss the Messianic content and style of Micah. 245
10. Give the theme and outline of Micah. 246

Lesson 20

Chapter 16, 249-254

Section 39

1. Discuss the historical background of the prophecies of Nahum. 249
2. Comment on the style and purpose of the Book of Nahum. 250
3. Give the theme and outline of Nahum. 250
4. Reproduce the important facts concerning the historical background Zephaniah. 251
5. What is the thrust of Zephaniah's book? 251
6. Give the theme and outline of Zephaniah. 252

Section 40

7. Discuss Habakkuk's time and his questions. 252-253
8. Give the theme and outline of Habakkuk. 253-254
9. Review question: Give the themes of all the books studied so far, beginni with Genesis.
10. Review question: Give the summary outlines of all the prophets studied far. (Elementary classes should at least give the main divisions if the ent outline should prove to be too difficult).

Lesson 21

Chapter 17, pp. 257-268

Section 41

1. Divide the prophetic activity of Jeremiah into six periods and discuss t first three. 257-260
2. Discuss the last three periods similarly. 260-263
3. Give the theme and outline of Jeremiah. 263-264

4. Discuss historical background, date, and purpose of Obadiah. 264-265
5. Give the theme of Obadiah and make your own outline. 265

Section 42

6. Who was Ezekiel and what is the character of his book? 265-266
7. Give the theme and summary outline of Ezekiel. 266
8. Make a thorough study of the longer outline and see whether you can reproduce its first main division together with the subdivisions that fall under it.
9. Do the same with the second main division.
10. Now reproduce from memory the entire outline of Ezekiel, if you are able to do so.

Lesson 22
Chapter 18, pp. 271-278

Section 43

1. Discuss the historical background of the prophecies of Haggai and Zechariah. 271
2. Describe, in some detail, the prophecy of Haggai. 272
3. Give the theme and outline of Haggai. 272-273
4. Mention in proper order the visions of Zechariah and give the thrust of each vision. 273-274
5. Summarize the contents of the second and third division of the book.

Section 44

6. Fully discuss the problem relative to chapters 9-14 and the predictions contained in these chapters.
7. Which Messianic prophecies are found in Zechariah? (Be sure to look up the references in the Bible.) 274
8. Give the theme and outline of Zechariah. 275-276
9. What reasons are advanced by those who assign a post-exilic date to the prophecies of Joel? What is the purpose of that book? What is its theme and outline? 276-277
10. Describe, in some detail, the prophecy of Malachi. Give the theme and outline. 277-278

Lesson 23
Chapter 19, pp. 281-292

Section 45

1. Discuss the grouping of the Psalms, ancient and modern.
2. Discuss the Psalter from the point of view of its leading ideas: misery, deliverance, and gratitude. 281-283
3. Give the caption and divisions of the Book of Psalms. 283

4. Characterize the Book of Proverbs. 283-284
5. Give its theme and divisions. 284-285

Section 46

6. Can you give an example of each of the literary types (contrasts, observ tions, etc.) found in the Book of Psalms?
7. What is the purpose of the Book of Job? 285
8. Give the theme and outline of the MATERIAL CONTENTS of the boo 287-288
9. Have you carefully read the quotations from the book given on p 289-292?
10. Review question: Give the themes of all the books studied so far.

Lesson 24

Chapter 20, pp. 295-304

Section 47

1. Mention the five smaller rolls in the order in which they were READ, a show why each was read at the given time.
2. Comment on the date and authorship of each of these five rolls.
3. Discuss the literal and the allegorical interpretation of the Song of Song Which interpretation do you accept? 297-298
4. Give the theme and outline of Canticles. 299
5. Discuss the historical background and the purpose of the Book of Rut 299-300

Section 48

6. Give the theme and outline of Ruth. 300
7. Describe the Book of Lamentations. State the caption and division 300-301
8. Distinguish between dirges and plaints. 301
9. What is meant by "goads" and "nails" in Ecclesiastes? Give the them 301-303
10. Give, in summary, the story of Esther. What is the purpose of the Book Esther? Give the theme and outline. 304

Lesson 25

Chapter 21, pp. 307-312

Section 49

1. Summarize the conservative position with respect to the Book of Danie reproducing the seven "propositions." 307-308
2. Give the theme and outline of Daniel. 309
3. What is the purpose of Chronicles-Ezra-Nehemiah? 310
4. What can you say regarding the authorship and time of composition Chronicles-Ezra-Nehemiah?
5. How does Chronicles-Ezra-Nehemiah compare with Kings?

Section 50

6. Give the theme and outline of I and II Chronicles. 311
7. Give the theme and outline of Ezra. 311
8. Give the theme and outline of Nehemiah. 311-312
9. Review question: Give the themes of all the Old Testament books.
10. Review question: See how many summary outlines of Old Testament books you are able to recall.

Division 2: The New Testament
Lesson 26
Chapter 22, pp. 315-320

Section 51

1. Give a list of the New Testament books arranged in probable chronological order. (This question has been asked before.)
2. Show that there is a striking similarity between the Epistle of James and the Sermon on the Mount.
3. What "James" wrote this epistle? Does he emphasize the physical relationship? 316
4. Is there any resemblance between the phraseology of this epistle and the words of James recorded in Acts 15? The references will have to be looked up and studied.
5. Tell what you know about James the man. 316-317

Section 52

6. Was James the opponent of Paul? Prove your answer. 317
7. Discuss the historical background of this epistle. 317-318
8. What is the central thought of the epistle? Prove your answer. 318-319
9. What is meant by duodiplosis?
10. Give the theme and outline of James. 319

Lesson 27
Chapter 23, pp. 323-331

Section 53

1. What is the relation between James and Galatians? 323
2. Give the historical background of Galatians. 323-324
3. Do you endorse the Northern or the Southern Galatian theory? Give reasons for your answer.
4. Give the theme and outline of Galatians. 326
5. What is the relation between Galatians and I Thessalonians? 328

Section 54

6. Give the historical background of I Thessalonians. 328
7. State the purpose of this epistle. 329
8. Give the theme and outline of I Thessalonians. 329

9. Give the historical background and purpose of II Thessalonians. 330
10. Give the theme and outline of II Thessalonians. 331

Lesson 28
Chapter 24, pp. 333-344

Section 55

1. Show the connection between the historical background of the epistl studied in the last chapter and I Corinthians. 333
2. Why did Paul write this epistle? 333-334
3. Give the theme and outline of I Corinthians. 334
4. What is the connection between I and II Corinthians? 338
5. Why did Paul write II Corinthians? 339

Section 56

6. Give the caption and divisions of II Corinthians. 339-340
7. Show the connection between the writing of II Corinthians and of Roman 341-342
8. What was Paul's purpose in writing Romans? 342
9. Were the readers, for the most part, Jews or Gentiles? Prove your answe 342
10. Give the theme and outline of Romans. 342-343

Lesson 29
Chapter 25, pp. 347-358

Section 57

1. What happened to Paul between the writing of Romans and of Colossian (The answer should be based not only on what is found on p. 347 but als on the material found on pp. 196-199. Thus, in every similar case.)
2. What occasioned the writing of Colossians? 347-348
3. Describe the Colossian heresy. 348
4. What is the thrust and purpose of Colossians? 348-349
5. Give the theme and outline of Colossians. 349

Section 58

6. Fully discuss Philemon: historical background, purpose, and character the epistle. Give the theme and, after having read the epistle several time make and commit to memory your own outline. 351-352
7. Was Ephesians written to the church at Ephesus or was it a circular lette Give reasons for your answer.
8. Characterize the epistle. Give its theme and outline. 355
9. Give the historical background of Philippians. Indicate its purpose and gi the caption and divisions. 357-358
10. Tell all you know about the following: Chloe, Phoebe, Tertius, Epaphra Onesimus, Philemon, Apphia, Archippus, and Epaphroditus. (For pages, s the index.)

Lesson 30
Chapter 26, pp. 361-368

ction 59

1. What is the relation between Paul's imprisonment epistles and I Peter? 361
2. What is the historical background and purpose of I Peter? 361
3. Give the theme and outline of I Peter. 362
4. Show the connection between I and II Peter. 363-364
5. Compare I and II Peter as to contents and style.

ction 60

6. What can be said in favor of the position that the apostle Peter wrote II Peter?
7. What was the purpose of II Peter? 365
8. Give the theme and outline of II Peter. 365-366
9. In your opinion, did Jude precede II Peter or vice versa? Give reasons for your answer.
10. Give the theme of Jude and your own outline. Why did Jude write his epistle? 366-368

Lesson 31
Chapter 27, pp. 371-380

ction 61

1. What connection is there between Peter and the Gospels? 371, 374
2. What steps led to the formation of the Gospels? 31, 372
3. What is meant by Q?
4. What is the purpose of the Gospel of Matthew? Of Mark? Of Luke? 372-375
5. Is it incorrect to speak of four Gospels?

ction 62

6. Tell the story of the formation of Mark's Gospel. Who was Mark? 373-374
7. Who was Luke? Why do you regard it as being probable that he made use of Mark's Gospel? 374-375
8. Give a full account of the Synoptic Problem.
9. Why are Matthew, Mark, and Luke so similar? Why are they so different?
10. Illustrate the three theories of literary dependence by drawing diagrams. In which respect are the three diagrams alike? How do they differ?

Lesson 32
Chapter 28, pp. 383-396

ction 63

1. What theme do the Synoptics have in common, and how is that theme differentiated for each Gospel? 383
2. Give the outline which all three seem to follow. 383-384

3. Why do you favor ONE summary outline for all three (Matthew, Mar Luke)?
4. Fully discuss Luke 9:18–19:27.
5. Carefully study the detailed outline of the Gospel according to Matthe Notice how very easily it is committed to memory. Thus, under II we hav A. To the MULTITUDES, and B. To the DISCIPLES. Moreover, under A kingdom gospel, kingdom miracles, kingdom ambassadors, kingdom heral kingdom enemies, and kingdom blessings. Under B 2, the lesson of the cros we have: its necessity, glory, blessings, self-sacrificing motive, and substit tionary character. Have you tried to commit the detailed outline memory? It will be a great help in finding your way through the Gospel.

Section 64

6. How does the detailed outline of Matthew compare with that of Mark?
7. How do the outlines of Matthew and Mark compare with that of Luke?
8. In what section of Luke's Gospel do you find several parables? Name the and tell where (in what chapter) each is found.
9. Review question: Mention the themes of all the New Testament boo studied thus far.
10. Review question: Reproduce from memory the summary outlines of t New Testament books which have been studied.

Lesson 33
Chapter 29, pp. 399-403

Section 65

1. Produce the evidence which links Luke with Acts.
2. Was Luke an accurate historian? Give reasons for your answer.
3. Mention some of Luke's sources.
4. **Who was Theophilus? 401**
5. **What is the purpose of the Book of Acts? 401**

Section 66

6. **What is the relation between Luke's Gospel and the Book of Acts? 401**
7. **Give the theme and summary outline of the Book of Acts. 402-403**
8. The more detailed outline should also be mastered: it is brief and easy memorize. Moreover, a student of the Bible should know his way throu the Book of Acts.
9. Now turn to p. 74, and (re)commit to memory the chronological chart f the PERIOD FROM PENTECOST TO PATMOS. Compare this chart wi the outline of the Book of Acts.
10. What emperors reigned during the period covered by the Book of Act Four of those are mentioned on the chart, p. 75. Which four?

Lesson 34
Chapter 30, pp. 405-412

ection 67

1. With the aid of a map point out the journey of Paul during the period between the First and Second Roman Imprisonment. Is there any certainty with respect to the order in which you have arranged the places which Paul visited on this tour?
2. **Discuss the historical background and purpose of I Timothy. Who was Timothy? 407**
3. **Discuss the historical background and purpose of Titus. 407**
4. **Discuss the historical background and purpose of II Timothy. 408**
5. In what respect do I Timothy, Titus, and II Timothy resemble each other?

ection 68

6. **How do I Timothy, Titus, and II Timothy differ? 408**
7. **Give the theme and outline of I Timothy. 408**
8. **Give the theme and outline of Titus. 410**
9. **Give theme and outline of II Timothy. 411**
10. **Of what practical use are these Pastoral Epistles today? Carefully study the detailed outlines and read the books themselves, and the answer will become clear.**

Lesson 35
Chapter 31, pp. 415-419

ection 69

1. **Discuss the historical background and purpose of Hebrews. 415-416**
2. **Prove, by looking up the references, that apostasy was, indeed, the paramount danger. 415**
3. Prove that Paul did not write Hebrews.
4. Mention two theories with respect to the authorship of Hebrews. What is the best answer?
5. Who were the readers of this epistle? Prove your answer.

ection 70

6. **Does the author warn against the danger of returning to INFIDELITY or against the danger of returning to JUDAISM? Supply evidence for your answer. 418**
7. In outlining this book what fact must be borne in mind?
8. **Give the theme and outline of Hebrews. 419**
9. Now turn to the Book of Leviticus, discussed on pp. 214-216. Do you see any resemblance between Leviticus and Hebrews?
10. In your opinion, should Leviticus be studied before Hebrews or vice versa?

Lesson 36
Chapter 32, pp. 421-432

Section 71

1. **Tell all you know about the apostle John. 421-422**
2. Prove that it was he who wrote the fourth Gospel.
3. **What was John's purpose in writing his Gospel? 423**
4. Compare the Synoptics with John's Gospel.
5. Discuss the plan and arrangement of John's Gospel. (In this connection, n only the material found on pp. 423 and 424 but also the longer outline pp. 424-427 should be carefully studied.)

Section 72

6. **Give the theme and summary outline of John's Gospel. 424**
7. **Give the historical background of John's epistles, with emphasis on t heresy which the apostles had to combat. 428-439**
8. Compare the parallelism in I John and Revelation.
9. **Give the theme and outline of I John. 430-431**
10. **What occasioned the writing of II John? Of III John? Give the theme of John; of III John. How would you expand these brief summarizing sta ments into an outline? 431-432**

Lesson 37
Chapter 33, pp. 435-443

Section 73

1. **What is the purpose of the Book of Revelation and what is its them 435-436**
2. Who wrote this book? When?
3. How is the book arranged?
4. Show the beautiful thought progression which characterizes this book.
5. Supply scriptural evidence to indicate that the teaching of this book agre with the rest of the Bible.

Section 74

6. Learn to draw from memory the diagram of Progressive Parallelism.
7. Can you fully explain this diagram? Consult the author's book *More Th Conquerors* for a fuller explanation.
8. **Give the theme and outline (summary outline AND ALSO the more co plete outline) of Revelation. 441**
9. Indicate the relation between the contents of Genesis and Revelation.
10. **Are you able to recite the themes (captions) of every Bible book?**

PART IV: BIBLE CHAPTERS AND PASSAGES

Lesson 38

Chapter 34, pp. 447-451
(first set of questions)

ection 75

1. In the following list, connect THE REFERENCE with the proper CHAPTER TITLE or CHAPTER PASSAGE; e.g., 1. GEN. 1 should be connected with 10. THE CREATION ACCOUNT. 447-451

1. Gen. 1	1. As far as the east is from the west.
2. Isa. 35	2. Therefore are they before the throne of God.
3. Eph. 6	3. I know that my Redeemer lives.
4. Rev. 7	4. For unto us a child is born.
5. Gen. 3	5. Pause, every one who thirsts.
6. Ps. 103	6. Behold, I send my messenger.
7. Ps. 139	7. The Fall.
8. Phil. 4	8. Make a fiery serpent.
9. Luke 15	9. Whatever things are true . . . honorable.
10. Job 19	10. The Creation Account.
11. Rom. 5	11. O Jehovah, thou hast searched me and known me.
12. Ps. 90	12. For he will give his angels charge over you.
13. Mal. 3	13. Lord, thou hast been our dwelling place.
14. Matt. 5	14. The Shepherd Psalm.
15. Ps. 23	15. Being therefore justified by faith.
16. Luke 24	16. Father, I have sinned against heaven.
17. Isa. 55	17. Blessed are the poor in spirit.
18. Num. 21	18. The Birth of Christ.
19. Isa. 9	19. Then the eyes of the blind shall be opened.
20. Luke 2	20. Pentecost.
21. Ps. 91	21. Stand, therefore, having girded your loins.
22. Acts 2	22. The Resurrection of our Lord.

2. Do the same with the following list. 447-451

1. Gen. 17	1. Come before his presence with singing.
2. Heb. 11	2. The Heroes of Faith.
3. Ps. 100	3. As the hart pants after water brooks.
4. Isa. 7	4. There is therefore now no condemnation.
5. Isa. 11	5. The Hymn of Love.
6. Rom. 8	6. How amiable are thy tabernacles.
7. I Cor. 13	7. Remember also thy Creator.
8. Gen. 22	8. Therefore, the Lord himself will give you a sign.
9. Exod. 20	9. But you, Bethlehem, Aphrathah.
10. Matt. 27	10. Behold, wise men from the east.
11. Josh. 24	11. And I will establish my covenant.
12. Isa. 40	12. Take now your son, your only son.
13. Isa. 53	13. The Ten Commandments.
14. Mic. 5	14. The Crucifixion.
15. Ruth 1	15. Choose this day whom you will serve.
16. Ps. 19	16. And there shall come forth a shoot.
17. Eccles. 12	17. Comfort, comfort my people.
18. Ps. 84	18. Your people shall be my people.

19. Ps. 42	19. The heavens declare the glory of God.
20. Ps. 105	20. He has remembered his covenant forever.
21. Matt. 2	21. Surely, he has borne our griefs.

3. The method of conducting a drill on the list from the Gospel of John suggested on p. 441 of *Survey of the Bible.* Master that list thoroughly s that you will be ready for the drill.

Section 76

4. Where (i.e., in what book and chapter) do you find the following: 447-45
   a. The Heroes of Faith.
   b. Samaritan Woman.
   c. Bethesda.
   d. The Shepherd Psalm.
   e. Pause, every one who is thirsty.
5. What chapter title or chapter passage do the following references sugges 447-451
   a. John 21.
   b. Isa. 7.
   c. Matt. 27.
   d. Gen. 1.
   e. Rom. 5.
6. Also the following? 447-451
   a. John 5.
   b. John 9.
   c. John 13.
   d. Mal. 3.
   e. Ps. 90.
7. And the following? 447-451
   a. John 8.
   b. Isa. 53.
   c. Mic. 5.
   d. I Cor. 13.
   e. Ps. 100.

Lesson 39
Chapter 34, pp. 451-454
(second set of questions)

Section 77

1. What chapter title or chapter passage do the following references sugge Gen. 49, Deut. 32, Job 42, Ps. 1, Ps. 11, Ps. 24, Ps. 31, Ps. 63, Ps. 66, 79?
2. And the following: Ps. 110, Ps. 123, Ps. 130, Ps. 145, Ps. 48, Ps. 69, Ps. 8 Ps. 121, Ps. 150, and Isa. 61?
3. Also the following: Exod. 15, Ruth 4, Ps. 32, Isa. 64, Ezek. 47, Amos Zeph. 3, Zech. 11, Mal. 4, and Ps. 16?

Section 78

4. Where (book and chapter) do you find the following?
   a. Surely, God is good to Israel.

b. Except Jehovah build the house.
c. I saw the Lord sitting upon a throne.
d. Sing, O barren, you who did not bear.
e. Be not afraid of them.
f. And in the days of those kings shall the God of heaven set up a kingdom.
g. Who is a God like thee, that pardons iniquity?
h. But the righteous shall live by his faith.
i. They shall look on me, whom they have pierced.

Also the following?

a. Then said I; Lo, I am come.
b. God is our refuge and strength.
c. Behold, Jehovah's hand is not shortened, that it cannot save.
d. Arise, shine, for your light is come.
e. And should not I have regard for Nineveh?
f. I will raise for David a righteous Branch.
g. I saw in the night visions . . . one like a son of man.
h. For, though the fig tree should not flourish.
i. The latter glory of this house shall be greater than the former.
j. I will bring forth my servant, the Branch.

And the following?

a. Yet now, if thou wilt forgive their sins.
b. His lovingkindness endures forever.
c. They that trust in Jehovah are as Mount Zion.
d. If at any time I declare concerning a nation.
e. Seventy weeks are decreed upon your people.
f. In that day will I raise up the tabernacle of David that is fallen.
g. Rejoice greatly, O daughter of Zion.
h. I am against you, O Gog.
i. I will pour out my Spirit upon all flesh.
j. The eternal God is your dwelling-place.

In the following list link the reference and the chapter passage to which it belongs:

1. Deut. 33	*A wheel within a wheel.*
2. II Sam. 7	*Bel bows down, Nebo stoops.*
3. Job 1	*Not to us, O Jehovah, not to us.*
4. Ps. 2	*Behold, my servant, whom I uphold.*
5. Ps. 8	*How are you fallen from heaven, O day star?*
6. Ps. 14	*The eternal God is your dwelling place.*
7. Ps. 25	*I will establish the throne of his kingdom forever.*
8. Ps. 29	*Behold, how good and how pleasant.*
9. Ps. 47	*Jehovah gave, and Jehovah has taken away.*
10. Ps. 51	*Open your mouth wide, and I will fill it.*
11. Ps. 65	*Why do the nations rage?*
12. Ps. 68	*God is gone up with a shout.*
13. Ps. 72	*Praise waits for thee, O God, in Zion.*
14. Ps. 74	*Against thee, thee only have I sinned.*
15. Ps. 81	*Thou hast ascended on high.*
16. Ezek. 1 and 10	*Train up a child in the way he should go.*
17. Isa. 46	*A woman who fear Jehovah, she shall be praised.*
18. Isa. 42	*Wherewith shall a young man cleanse his way?*

19.	Isa. 14	*I was glad when they said to me, Let us go.*
20.	Ps. 147	*He counts the number of the stars.*
21.	Isa. 12	*He shall have dominion from sea to sea.*
22.	Eccles. 11	*All the paths of Jehovah are lovingkindness.*
23.	Prov. 31	*The fool has said in his heart, There is no God.*
24.	Prov. 22	*O Jehovah, our Lord, How excellent is thy name.*
25.	Prov. 8	*Ascribe to Jehovah, O sons of the mighty.*
26.	Ps. 133	*Have respect to the covenant.*
27.	Ps. 122	*Jehovah possessed me in the beginning of his way.*
28.	Ps. 119	*Cast your bread upon the waters.*
29.	Ps. 115	*Therefore with joy you shall draw water.*
30.	Ps. 116	*I have made a covenant with my chosen.*
31.	Ps. 89	*My heart is fixed, O God.*
32.	Ps. 95	*I love Jehovah.*
33.	Ps. 108	*Let us come before his presence with thanksgiving.*

Lesson 40

Chapter 34, pp. 455-457

Section 79

1. Mention ten familiar chapters in Matthew's Gospel, giving reference a chapter title or chapter passage. (Only seven are given in List III B, p. 45 but three more are given in List I B, p. 448. Bear this in mind also connection with the following questions.) Which chapter contains t Lord's Prayer?
2. Mention the familiar chapters in Mark, Luke, and Acts, giving reference a gem passage as above. Use both Lists (I and III).
3. Do the same for Romans and I Corinthians.

Section 80

4. Do the same for II Corinthians, Galatians, Ephesians, Philippians, a Colossians.
5. Do the same for I Timothy, II Timothy, Hebrews, and James.
6. Do the same for I Peter, II Peter, and I John.
7. Do the same for Revelation.

Lesson 41

Chapter 35, pp. 459-460
(first set of questions)

Section 81

You should be ever ready to find the right passage at the right time. Hence, t following exercise is very valuable:

1. **Give the Scripture references to at least two passages which can imp comfort to those who are afflicted. 459**
2. **Give three references that would be fitting in case of bereavement. 459**
3. **To what Scripture passages would you refer in order to combat doubt? 4**

ection 82

4. It often happens that one is asked to suggest proper passages in connection with the difficulties connected with entering upon a new task. Which passages can you suggest? 459
5. There are also seasons of gratitude and praise. Suggest passages. 459
6. Those who are overwhelmed with sudden grief should be comforted. Give the helpful Scripture passages. 460
7. You will find some people for whom it is hard to forgive a wrong which they have received. What would you read to them? 460

Lesson 42

Chapter 35, pp. 461-462
(second set of questions)

ection 83

uggest five passages that are appropriate for:

1. New Year's Day or for New Year's Eve.
2. The Day of Prayer or for Thanksgiving Day.
3. Good Friday.

ection 84

uggest five passages that are appropriate for:

4. Easter.
5. Ascension Day.
6. Pentecost.
7. Christmas.

CPSIA information can be obtained
at www.ICGtesting.com
Printed in the USA
LVHW081543250822
726785LV00005B/345

9 780801 05415

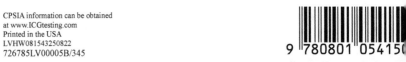